Collectible Toys

Built To Last
THE TOYS OF KINGSBURY

The New Hampshire Historical Society

 30

Park Street, Concord

ON SUNDAY, NOVEMBER 23RD, 1986 • FROM 3:00–5PM

Photo: Kingsbury workers demonstrate the strength of the Kingsbury toys in this case, a pressed steel fire engine with rubber tires. (Photo courtesy of Kingsbury Machine Tool Corporation)

T his exhibition is on loan from the Kingsbury Machine Tool Corporation of Keene, N.H. and is co-sponsored by the Historical Society of Cheshire County. It continues through January 3, 1987.

GALLERY HOURS: MON–SAT 9AM–4:30PM & WED 9AM–8PM

The Official® Price Guide To Collectible Toys

Richard Friz

Fourth Edition

The House of Collectibles
New York, New York 10022

Cover art courtesy of Garry Darrow—Fund Antiques N.Y.

This book is dedicated to my son Josh—may his enthusiasm for collecting never diminish.

TABLE OF CONTENTS

ACKNOWLEDGMENTS

For their invaluable assistance, I would like to extend a sincere acknowledgment of appreciation to the following: Carl Burnett, San Diego, California; Noel Barrett Auctions, Carversville, Pennsylvania; Bernard Barenholtz, Marlboro, New Hampshire; Bill and Nan Bopp, Walpole, New Hampshire; Dave Bauer, Allentown, Pennsylvania; Lee and Rally Dennis, Peterborough, New Hampshire (The Game Preserve); William G. Holland, Gladwyne, Pennsylvania; Stephen Leonard, Albertson, Long Island, New York; Mrs. Ralph Merkle, Allentown, Pennsylvania; Dana Hawkes, Collectibles Department, Sotheby's, New York City, New York; Eric Alberta, Phillips Auctioning & Appraising, New York City, New York; Ginger Sawyer, Skinner Auctions, Bolton, Massachusetts.

An extra special thanks is due the following people who took extended time and effort to help make this guide possible: Mark and Lynn Souzzi of M & L Antiques, Ashfield, Massachusetts; Linda Mullins of Carlsbad, California; Richard Opfer Auctioneering, Timonium, Maryland.

My appreciation also goes to the Kingsbury Machine Tool Corp. and the New Hampshire Historical Society for providing the frontispiece, which portrays Kingsbury workers demonstrating the strength of Kingsbury toys, in this case a pressed-steel fire engine with rubber tires. (Photo courtesy of Kingsbury Machine Tool Corp. of Keene, NH; poster courtesy of the New Hampshire Historical Society, announcing their exhibition of Kingsbury/Wilkins toys from November 23, 1986 to January 3, 1987.)

"The beauty of a good toy . . . ," © American Heritage, a division of Forbes Inc., was reprinted with permission from *American Heritage*, Dec. 1959.

The beauty of a good toy is that
it picks out the really important things.
Oarsmen who actually row, for instance,
or the steamer's great walking beam,
or a good loud bell on a train.
Imagination does the rest. Any boy knows that.
A toy is very like a primitive painting,
a crude imitation of life;
yet for all that a very shrewd glimpse at it too,
for the collection we exhibit here
is kind of a push-pull
pageant of American history.

—Dec. 1959, *American Heritage*

HOW TO USE
THIS GUIDE

The toys in this book are grouped alphabetically by category, and within these groupings we have again broken them down into ABC order. The exceptions are in "Political," where we have listed items sequentially as each president entered office. In the "Trains" section, we have restricted this vast collecting universe to the four major U.S. manufacturers, American Flyer, Ives, Lionel, and Marx, in that order. The trains and rolling stock are then listed numerically as they appeared in the makers' catalogs. We have tried to glean as much descriptive matter about each entry as possible. Many guides have proven so sketchy as to remind one of the old Wally Ballou, ace sports reporter, skits from Bob and Ray days, when Wally would rattle off football scores without giving the names of the teams. You'll know the score and a lot more in this guide, which helps you decide what to buy and how much to pay.

THE PRICES
IN THIS BOOK

No doubt you've heard all about the pitfalls of consulting a price guide. That it is outdated by the time it hits the bookstands. That it fails to compensate for geographical and market variables. That it doesn't stress *strongly* enough that these prices reflect toys in like-new condition, with each flaw exacting its toll from the final asking price. Further, that dealers and auction houses will take *their* pound of flesh, thereby further shrinking profits by a third to half the guided price. Then too, there is the old bromide frequently cited as a caveat in many price guides, that the only true barometer of price is that established between a willing buyer and willing seller.

But . . . that age old question, "How much is it worth?" still remains to be answered. While we have factored in all kinds of raw data—from auction records to toy trade magazine ads, from roaming the aisles of endless toys shows to good old word of mouth from the movers and shakers in this zany hobby—we fully realize that we've gone out on a limb and may be accused of sawing it off in the process. We have tried to pack this guide with helpful information on identifying and dating toys, as well as background as to why certain toys are much more coveted than others. If, in the final analysis, we can deter a would-be seller from practically *giving* away a true rarity—or prevent an overeager buyer from paying an outrageous price for a toy, on the premise that he has never seen another like it—then all this effort to arm you with the facts will have been well worth it.

TOY MARKET
OVERVIEW

There was a time, not too many years back, when the old pyramid theory prevailed in the toy and train hobby. The top, representing a few affluent freespenders seemingly willing to pay any price for classic, uncommon specimens, was a mighty thin, rarefied area, indeed. What's more, the hobby obviously lacked a broad base needed to keep the pyramid from sagging in the middle.

Times have changed. One could see it building and 1986 provided the kicker. Record-breaking crowds attended the San Francisco International Antique Toy Convention in San Francisco; the Kennedy International Antique Toy Convention in Chicago; the Antique Toy and Doll World Show in Chicago; Christie's East; the Atlanta Toy Museum Auction; the Galerie Andre Auction in Brussels, Belgium; Sotheby's Tinplate Toys, Dolls and Teddy Bears September Auction in London; and a toy and train extravaganza in Chatham, Ontario. All attest to the steamrolling growth and intensity of the hobby.

With toys of all types—tin, slush cast, composition, lithographed wood, hard rubber, celluloid, and even plastic—the question is not what's hot, but what's not. [Offhand, we would be pressed to cite only a few stragglers (i.e., steam-driven toys and post-World War II American-made tin toys.)] Any toy of quality, age (particularly pre-1900s), worthy of its name, in working order, and with good original paint, commands top dollar.

The big news is that cast iron, recently spurned, has rebounded with a vengeance, despite persistent encroachment by some very clever reproductions.

Cast-iron toys are indigenous to America and the Industrial Revolution of the late 19th century. While examples of English and German cast-iron toys, banks, and trains do exist, it remains Messrs. Ives, Harris, Carpenter, Hubley, Arcade, Stevens, Kenton, and Wilkins—all home-grown artisans—who have combined to make cast-iron creations, most notably horse-drawn rigs and later motor-toys, truly an American art form. Cast iron, as an enduring, rugged metal admired for its heft and feel, clearly ranks right up there with enameled tinplate in the "precious metals" category among toys.

3

At the recent 8th Annual Allentown, Pennsylvania, Toy Show and Fair, regarded by many observers as the premier toy event of the year, over 2,000 toy enthusiasts flooded the Exposition Hall gates to vie for the well-stocked wares of over 300 dealers—clear evidence of growth and vitality in the hobby. While the current rage may still be German and Occupied Japan tin, we noted a phenomenal demand for everything from penny toys and toy candy containers to the superb lithograph paper-on-wood creations of W.S. Reed, R. Bliss, and M. Converse, especially the oversized sidewheelers and fire engines. Nineteenth-century board games and target games, reflecting the finest of the golden age of chromolithography, have belatedly gained a new aura of respectability. Wood and composition platform pull and riding toys from the 19th century are sought by hordes of converts as a form of folk art.

While there's no denying the intensity and tenacity of robot- and space-related toy collectors, their numbers are still small, the market is considered "thin," and the category appears due for a "shakedown" cruise if Allentown and other recent toy conclaves are any barometer. Prices of space toys have reached interplanetary proportions in recent years, but we noted vast discrepancies in pricing, with $500 to $600 variances on the floor for like examples in comparable condition, clearly underscoring the volatility of this mini-market. Frankly, we find it incomprehensible that a contemporary upstart, such as the tin and plastic robot Mr. Atomic, unproven by the test of time, can command prices of $2,000 and up.

A few years ago, the market for comic and character toys, along with that for motortoys (one of the most universally appealing of categories), suddenly behaved as erratically as one of its crazy-car windups and then went into a prolonged slump. It may have been a case of embarrassment of riches, spurred on by the bankruptcy sale of the entire warehouse stock of Louis Marx & Company. Judging by recent toy auctions and shows, however, it is apparent that collectors are once again paying dearly for the more elusive comic pieces.

In mid-1985, at the Raymond E. Holland Toy Auction conducted by Sotheby's in New York City, a number of outstanding rarities came on the block. Holland, one of the nation's leading motortoy enthusiasts, had amassed in a brief span a stunning assortment of Gebruder Bing and Maerklin tinplate boats and trains, rarely seen and much less offered early tin classics by Ives and Fallows, a Carpenter cast-iron Tally-Ho, and perhaps the rarest toy in the hobby, the Hubley Royal Circus cast-iron monkey cage wagon. Of the 165 lots offered at the Holland sale, an alarming number failed to make reserves. While some nay-sayers declared that the Holland collection sale presaged a moratorium on big spending, they were soon silenced by what happened to the toy market in 1986. During that year—at Christie's East, Sotheby's, Lloyd Ralston Auctions in Darien, Connecticut, Christmas Toy Auctions by Skinner's in Bolton, Massachusetts, Richard Opfer's in Timonium, Maryland, and most spectacularly, the Atlanta Toy Museum Auction in Philadelphia—gaveled prices often soared as high as double, and even triple, pre-sale estimates.

Indisputable 19th-century toy classics clearly exemplify the three U's, Unique, Unusual and well-nigh Unattainable. As prices ascend into orbit, venerable toy collectors can only shake their heads in disbelief. While they can well afford to be pleased by the obviously enhanced value of their own vast toy holdings, they also must be resigned to intense competition from vast hordes of newcomers to the hobby. The opportunity to upgrade, or to fill in one's collection with a rare elusive find, is rapidly diminishing.

A favorite quote of ours is by the eminent dealer in antique furniture, Albert Sack: "With masterpieces, there is no limit." This can be said for the toy collecting hobby as well.

Who ever said this fascinating field of toy collection was child's play?

TOY CATEGORY TRENDSETTERS TO KEEP AN EYE ON IN THE '80s

The following toy categories reflect intensified activity and sustained interest on the part of dealers and collectors at recent auctions, shows, and exhibitions.

Militariana—Britains Ltd.

Henry Kurtz, Director of Collectibles at Phillips in New York City, reports that a rapidly ascending category at their most recent toy auctions has been that of Militariana—lead soldiers and Britains, in particular. "Whereas one of the smaller Britains Ltd. sets might have gone for a $150 to $200 a year or so ago," Kurtz indicates, "They now bring $250 to $300—a significant jump in so brief a time span." Kurtz believes that the stimulus for collecting Britains stems from their being well crafted, with impeccable attention to detail. The larger sets, prior to World War II, were always attractively boxed. A Scotch Regiment, for example, featured a full-color clan symbol on the numbered box set. At Phillips' recent Christmas

Collectibles sale, a marvelous Regimental grouping by Britains (Boer War Army Service Supply Column) sold at $12,100, while a Britains Royal Horse Artillery Unit fetched $9,350. The fact that Malcolm Forbes, Jr., and artist Andrew Wyeth are lead soldier enthusiasts (Winston Churchill was also an inveterate collector) further adds to the mystique of collecting Militariana. Surprisingly enough, in the world of cast-iron toys, very few examples appear on the market that are military related. When they do appear, however, sparks fly, as was the case in 1978 when a miniature artillery caisson with horses and riders, by Pratt and Letchworth of Buffalo, New York, brought $9,500 at auction, with Lloyd Ralston of Fairfield, Connecticut, presiding.

Pedal Cars

In the past several years, we have covered several sizeable estate auctions of pedal-powered or battery-powered child-size automobiles. Like many an endangered species, the comparatively large size of these fascinating vehicles may well have hastened their demise. Julie Collier, Director of Collectibles at Christie's East, New York City, was quoted recently in *Antiques & Collecting* as saying "They are the kind of object you leave behind when you move. Most . . . were three feet long, often longer, with an average size of approximately 45 inches." Despite their relative scarcity, or perhaps because of it, child-size autos, construction rigs, farm tractors, train engines, and even airplanes are cooking on all cylinders with a growing coterie of collectors, many of whom have an affinity for the adult-size vintage models as well. The most desireable are those in pristine condition, superbly crafted, and authentically detailed to replicate specific adult-size models. A 40-inch pedal car, modeled after a late 1920s Hudson, for example, produced by American National Co., Toledo, Ohio, recently sold at $2,200 at a Christie's East auction. A baby blue, pedal-powered Austin two-seater, with battery-powered headlights and lift-up hood, circa 1920s, sold for $750 at Sotheby's in New York City recently, while what outwardly appeared to be a more desireable toy—a restored Packard two-seater touring car with canvas top—at the same auction failed to meet reserves. The operative word here is "restored."

Summary: Here is a case where a select number of "rabid" private collectors are vying for a dwindling number of motortoys that were produced in limited quantities from their very *inception*.

Toy and Bank Related Ephemera

Riding on the crest of the unprecedented wave of toy collecting popularity is an intriguing spinoff, toy and bank related ephemera—the catalogs, flyers, billheads, and advertising trade cards with which leading manufacturers enticed youngsters and parents to purchase their wares. According to Brian Riba, of Riba-Mobley Auctions in South Glastonbury, Connecticut, toy catalogs and trade cards have made shambles of pre-sale estimates over the past two years. At Riba-Mobley's October 25, 1986, auction, a delightful "Bad Accident" mechanical bank trade card in full color more than tripled the guided catalog price and topped off at $1,540. The new owner just happened to own one of the banks and was seeking the elusive card to display it side by side with the real thing. Many mechanical bank trade card collectors are crossover collectors of ephemera, thus sparking some fiercely contested bidding duels. A number of other mechanical bank trade cards at R & M, performed respectably in the $500 to $600 range, despite less than perfect condition. Toy catalogs have also moved up in rarefied company. A battered Selchow and Righter Gameboard Catalog, for example, brought over $200 at a recent ephemera auction. At the November Allentown Toy Show we noted several circa 1915 full-color Schoenhut Humpty Dumpty Circus Catalogs hovering in the $300 to $350 range. "I think I'll just wait around for the reprint," was the comment of one disappointed toy catalog collector we encountered at a recent Yankee Doodle Drummer Show. Toy related ephemera has made so many converts that *Antique Toy World* now features a monthly column on the subject by a leading collector, Anthony Annese.

Soft Toys

Echoing through the toy auction halls from Los Angeles to London is the chant, "There's nothing 'soft' about the market for soft toys." Noel Barrett and Bill Bertoia, who managed the Atlanta Toy Museum sale in Philadelphia last October, could point to their offering of early Steiff swivel neck with center seam character dolls, for example. A Steiff French legionnaire doll brought $1,500; a chef, $1,100; a black-shirted cadet, $1,200! (A Sunny Jim doll, meanwhile, which could not be positively identified as Steiff, managed only $325. Ah, the magic of a name.) Even a pair of Steiff rabbits multiplied to $700. A very uncommon Lenci Aviatrix doll at the Atlanta Toy Museum sale soared to $1,200. Meanwhile, some time ago, at Skinner's Auctions in Bolton, Massachusetts, a Steiff

German foot soldier, circa 1915, in full uniform more than doubled pre-sale estimates at $2,090; this is not to mention a grouping of Steiff teddy bears who ranged in price (depending on wear and tear) from $550 to $1,000. Even some of the small Steiff animal toys from the 1960s averaged over $30 apiece at the Skinner sale.

HISTORY OF TOYS

Those delightful artifacts we call toys have existed in many subtle guises in almost every culture and period since the dawn of civilization. Single-movement string-worked toys have survived from over 5,000 years ago in the Indus Valley. Articulated toys, dolls, board games, and rattles have been discovered in Egyptian tombs dating back 2,000 years; limestone pull toys from Persia pre-date the birth of Christ. The British museum has in its vast holdings a wooden tiger from Thebes circa 1,000 B.C. Toy horses and chariots mounted on wheeled platforms and pulled by strings date from the 4th or 5th century B.C.; Roman youngsters played with baked clay marbles and rag dolls. Toy Roman banks were discovered in the ruins of Pompeii. Unaccountably, toys were simple and few, particularly following the decline of the Roman Empire to the 13th century. It was not until the 16th century that Germany, with Nuremberg and Sonnenberg as major toy centers, developed lever-manipulated wooden and tin toys as an offshoot of local craft guilds. The word "toy" itself dates to this era. Daniel Defoe, in *History of the Life and Adventures of Mr. Duncan Campbell,* refers to toys being bought in a toy shop in Edinburgh in 1720.

From the fascinating Hieronymus Bestelmeier illustrated catalogs dating from the 1790s to 1807, we have a rare glimpse of the toys of the period: dolls, games, wooden villages, and zoos, as well as tiny armies of lead soldiers and painted tinplate warships. With the decline of the forests in Germany, mass-production techniques and "mother necessity" led to the innovation of the casting of iron and stamping of tinplate toys. Metal toys were produced in substantial quantities, beginning in 1840. By the 1870s Germany was exporting toys to France, Great Britain, and America. From 1890 to 1914, Nuremberg boasted as many as 300 toy factories, over two-thirds of which were engaged in the metal toy trade.

Germany produced the first clockwork train sets from 1865 to 1867, with zinc and lead decorations and painted tinplate engines and stock. In France, two leading firms, Rossignol and Martin, turned to manufacturing automata. Salvaging old tin soon became a minor Paris industry. In France, quality toy production reached its zenith from 1903 to 1914, their La Belle Epoque.

Germany and France were not alone in invading the field of

child's play. Some of the most marvelous, highly collectible wood toys were fashioned by itinerant carvers in America, particularly in Pennsylvania Dutch country. The folk art toys of Wilhelm Schimmel (1817–1890), Aaron Mountz during the second half of the 19th century, and George Huguenin in the late 19th century, reflect whimsical barnyard scenes, Noah's arks, crude animals, eagles, and churches.

Although less prolific than the German manufacturers, their U.S. counterparts, the Pattersons of Berlin and New Britain, Connecticut, for example, made toys from scrap as early as the late 18th century. The earliest known clockwork toys patented in America are the Walking Zouve, a Stevens & Brown, Forestville, Connecticut, walking doll and Autoperipatetikos by Enoch Morrison and manufactured by Martin & Runyan, New York City. July 15, 1862, is the patent date. By 1848, the Philadelphia Tin Toy Mfg. Co. was producing brightly colored horses, cows, locomotives, and boats. In 1856, George Brown featured a veritable menagerie on wheels, all handsomely stencil decorated. Hot air toys emerged in the late 1860s by Ives & Blakeslee, Plymouth, Connecticut. Moving figures were fitted with pulleys and with paper wheels and placed over a lamp, register or gas burner to ingeniously set the toy in motion.

J. & E. Stevens, Cromwell, Connecticut, was probably the first American manufacturer to produce cast-iron toys, introducing their firecracker pistols beginning in 1859. By the late 1860s, Stevens, along with James Fallows, J. Hall, and J. Serrell, began to turn out hundreds of variations of still and mechanical banks in tin and cast iron.

The first American cast-iron toys appeared as miniature trains, horse-drawn drays, brakes, landaus, hansoms, tally-hos, and wagons. They were rather crude and stiff imitations of earlier tin incarnations. Soon, however, manufacturers began paying closer attention to authenticity and detail. In the golden era of cast-iron toys, the 1880s and '90s, the premier makers were F.W. Carpenter of Harrisville, New York; John Hubley, Lancaster, Pennsylvania; Henry Dent, Fullerton, Pennsylvania; Pratt & Letchworth, Buffalo, New York; E.R. Ives, Plymouth, Connecticut; and James Wilkins, Keene, New Hampshire.

In 1850, the U.S. Census Bureau listed 47 toy makers; by 1880, the number had quadrupled to 173 toy and game manufacturers, with annual sales figures equivalent to such successful industries as sporting goods, telephone and telegraph, cleaning and dyeing.

In the 1850s, the dean of wooden toy manufacturers was William Tower of South Hingham, Massachusetts. With Joseph Jacobs, Crocker Wilder, and several other members, Tower created a cooperative workshop known as the Tower Guild. Other wood toy innovators included three generations of the Charles Crandall family from Pennsylvania and New York (1867 through the 1890s); Joel Ellis, Springfield, Vermont; Brown & Eggleston and A. Christian & Son, New York City (1856); R. Bliss, Pawtucket, Rhode Island (1870s); Morton Converse, Winchendon, Massachusetts (1884); and W.S. Reed, Leominster, Massachusetts (1875). These firms produced handsomely lithographed paper-on-wood Noah's arks, churches, transportation toys, doll houses, and doll furniture, as well as hobby horses.

Fanciful cast-iron bell toys were led by Gong Bell Mfg., East Hampton, Connecticut. Gong Bell may well have produced the first example, the Revolving Chimes Bell, in 1873. Another East Hampton maker, Watrous Mfg. (1880s–1930s), which later merged with N.N. Hill (circa 1890), produced bell toys.

The major collecting focus today is on toys that have been mass produced from mid-19th century on—American toys with obvious European exceptions. Many leading collectors establish the turn of the century as a cut-off point. Cast-iron toy specialists, however, are more inclined to extend their parameters to include later examples by Hubley, Kenton, and Arcade, and a handful of other U.S. firms who continued to produce superb toys up to World War II. The scarcity and expense of adding vintage examples to one's collection has prompted a whole new cult of enthusiasts to seek solace in space and robot toys and transportation toys of the postwar period.

HISTORY OF TOY COLLECTING

Toy collecting is a relatively recent phenomenon. Only in the last twenty or so years has the hobby lured significant numbers of collectors, as well as scholars and antiquarians. John Brewer, in his essay *Childhood Revisited: The Genesis of the Modern Toy,* explained that in 17th-century Colonial America the play of both adults and children was condemned as a sinful and idle pursuit. In England as well, there was a noticeable lack of toys in the household. Dr. Johnson's *Dictionary* defined "toy" as "a petty commodity; a trifle; a thing of no value; a plaything or bauble."

Somehow, the philosopher John Locke and another free-thinker, Frederick Froebel, were instrumental in helping to break the moralist hold of the Calvinists and Puritans, leading to a more advanced approach of encouraging the development of a child's intelligence through the liberalization of play. "Even so," added Brewer, "it was an affluent audience in America and in England who had the time, the money and the social predisposition to lavish attention on their children." Patrick Murray, in his book *Toys,* points out that in Victorian England toys were referred to as "rich boy's pretties."

Murray adds that one single event helped to swing the tide of public sentiment: the manufacturer Gebruder Maerklin, of Göppingen, a name synonymous with originality and quality, staged an exhibition at the Leipzig Spring Fair in 1891 that clearly foretold the imaginative potential of the hobby. As early as the 1870s the Bavarian Museum in Nuremberg displayed collections of old and new toys. The designs and mechanisms of these toys were closely scrutinized and widely copied by manufacturers of that period.

Ernest King, an eminent English toy collector at the turn of this century, specialized in the ha'penny tuppeny (now simply known and coveted as "penny toys") in Lilliputian-sized tin toys from the late Victorian and Edwardian era (1890–1914). In 1917, he endowed the British Toy Museum with his fabulous collection of over 1,650 penny toys. In 1957, the King Collection went on display in the Children's Room at Kensington Palace in London. In covering the event, toy author Leslie Daikin wrote in *The Illus-*

trated London News, "Thanks to the late Ernest King, we may re-capture in microcosm something of a social pattern that is forgotten."

On these shores, toys may well have been "discovered" on the coattails of folk art. The Whitney Studio club of New York City mounted the first folk art exhibition in 1924. By the early 1930s, major exhibitions including folk art and toys were staged by the Museum of Modern Art and by the Newark Museum. In the late 1920s, the Ives Co. recalled their glory days of the 1880s in their advertisements and catalogs. They also promoted themselves in their New York showrooms, with a special display of vintage Ives clock-work toys. After the crash of 1929, business failed, but Lionel, which absorbed Ives a few years later, assembled the earlier display with their own vast collection of early train sets. Toys were well on their way—"on track," so to speak—in striving for respectability.

Numerous collecting societies materialized in the United States in the 1960s, including The Antique Toy Collectors of America, Mechanical Bank Collectors of America, and the American Train Collectors Association. In 1985, The American Game Collector's Association was founded. (See additional organizations listed under "Collecting Organizations" in the back of this book.)

John Brewer writes, "Toys are cultural messages—sometimes simple, occasionally complex and ambiguous, but invariably reveal-ing." An endless multitude of enthusiasts are discovering the infi-nite variety and fascination of toys.

HOW TO GAIN GREATER SATISFACTION FROM TOY COLLECTING

The following guidelines, distilled from the teachings of some of the most prominent collectors in the hobby, may prove helpful to beginning, as well as seasoned, toy enthusiasts.

1. Most toy people tend to gravitate toward a category that they can pinpoint in time which is from their own realm of experience. In many cases, specialization is an extension of one's profession or trade. While it may sound simplistic, it is essential to collect what *you* like. Resist if you will the follow-the-leader syndrome that occurs in toy collecting and other hobbies. A few years back, the big crunch was for Lehmann toys among one of the toy societies. Suddenly, even the more uncommon Lehmanns were almost impossible to find, except at ridiculous prices. Leading collector author Bernard Barenholtz counsels: "Make sure that the toys you are interested in are within your financial grasp. Buy the best toys you can afford. One fine toy is worth five ordinary ones."

2. Familiarization breeds contentment. Visit as many museums and private collections as possible. Just recently we were privileged to visit the exhibition, "Built To Last: The Toys of Kingsbury," at the New Hampshire Historical Society in Concord, New Hampshire. We came away with a far deeper appreciation for Kingsbury toys and their predecessor, Wilkins. In addition to a variety of pressed steel examples, it was obvious that Wilkins' Brownie Fire Department, twin cyclists, side-wheelers, and other cast-iron toys compared favorably with the best of Ives and Carpenter.

3. Research, research and more research. Surround yourself with

as many toy books, reference guides, trade catalogs, advertising trade cards, billheads from various toy makers, newspaper clippings, and photographs as possible and don't let this material gather dust in your files and library shelves. Consult your sources frequently.

4. Get to know your fellow collectors. There are any number of clubs and organizations that will open their doors to you. Many groups conduct seminars, museum tours, reprint toy catalogs, and serve as a conduit of information on everything relating to the hobby. Other groups are merely social, but the importance of interfacing with others who have the same infectious enthusiasm for toy collecting cannot be underestimated. Through seminars at conventions, club auctions, and simple conversation with fellow club members, you'll be exposed to more quality toys than you are likely to come across in a lifetime. To quote Barney Barenholtz again (from his book *American Antique Toys*), "The most important reason (to collect) may not be intrinsic to the toys themselves, but to the wonderful people we have met all over the world, whose paths never would have crossed ours but for the sharing of this special interest in antique toys." Many leading collectors we know, for example, are simply not "joiners." They still find ample opportunities to make contact with fellow collectors at major toy auctions. There is also today such a proliferation of toy extravaganzas and exhibitions, enough to fill out one's social calendar for an entire year, that there is every opportunity to make contact with collectors with areas of specialization akin to your own.

5. Noted collector/author Lillian Gottschalk, in a recent interview in *Antique Toy World*, had this to say about learning the toy field backwards and forwards: "I feel (the toy) with my hands, with my eyes. Then experience and knowledge take over." Learn to observe fellow collectors, particularly at major shows and toy auctions where it is often crowded and there are many distractions. Note the thoroughness with which they examine any toy they might be intent on purchasing. One collector of our acquaintance always carries the following in her handbag: a loupe or magnifying glass, a black light, a magnet, and (seriously) a dose of smelling salts. The latter pulls her through those rather feverish bidding duels at auctions.

6. Seek out only the more knowledgeable, experienced dealers whose integrity and judgment are respected within the hobby. Toy collecting has grown by leaps and bounds in recent years, and there are scores of new faces among us. The field is, never-

theless, a tightly knit universe and the word is soon out as to who is reputable and who is not.

A surprising number of prominent collectors rely on their "pet" dealers to locate rarities for them, even going so far as to keep them on retainer. To maintain a low profile (*why*, we have never been able to ascertain), some collectors even have their dealers execute bids in their behalf at auction. (One wonders whatever happened to the thrill of the chase?) Implicit in any transaction with toy dealers or auction houses is that your money be fully refundable if, for any reason, the specific toy fails to match up to its advertised or "as stated" condition.

7. Despite all the articles and books that talk about "collecting for fun and profit," approaching toys from an investment standpoint can be an expensive lesson. Someone once said that mutual funds, government bonds, and real estate would be safer investments. We feel rather strongly that a toy collection was meant to be lived with, not stored in safety deposit boxes or otherwise "squirreled away" under lock and key. There is no denying, however, that collectors should have a thorough understanding of the value of the toy they own.

8. This leads up to an essential point; too many of us fail to sit back and determine which direction our collection is to take and which limits need to be set. To quote Yogi Berra: "If you don't know where you're going, you'll wind up somewhere else." Running off in all directions at once and acquiring toys willy-nilly inevitably results in a squandering of time and money. Avoid also those so-called real "buys"—toys missing a wheel, an arm, a driver—those toys bereft or paint, rusted out, which appear to have been run over by a steamroller. Unless you are a professional restorer, the cost of returning this toy to its original condition will be prohibitive.

9. Resign yourself to the prospect that somewhere along the line you will make errors of judgment. Take heart; mistakes can often pay for themselves if they are factored in as part of the total experience. They will only heighten your perception in future transactions.

10. Dave Bausch, a venerable collector of over 30 years from Allentown, Pennsylvania, offered this conclusion in an interview in *Collectors' Showcase*: "The best piece of advice I can give . . . is to be patient. All too often someone wants to build a collection overnight. It can be a very expensive lesson. Learn as much as you can and have *fun*. That's what it's all about."

HOW TO
DOCUMENT A TOY
BY MAKER AND
DATE OF
MANUFACTURE

There are those compulsive accumulators of toys who could care less about a toy's history—whether it be fashioned in a large city factory, somebody's backyard, or at the North Pole by elves. Others are less concerned with age or pedigree than with its visceral impact—its patina, form, and condition. To these enthusiasts, the *toy* is the thing.

We like to think that historical elements connected with a toy not only add to its value but to the enjoyment of the toy as well.

DATING TOYS

A neat bit of detective work can uncover the actual or approximate date of a toy even when there are few clues to go by. Only a few U.S. toys were patented in the mid-1850s. After 1870, most examples were patented or trademarked, indicating a copyright. Should any stenciled, embossed, or printed patent numbers appear on the toy itself or on its original box, the year of issue can be traced by using the chart found under "Toy Patents." For a nominal fee, a number can be verified by the U.S. Patent Office as to original patent application and names of both inventor and manufacturer. Major libraries and historical societies are additional sources for various patent data. German patents date back to 1878, and two recent books, *German Patent Books Vol. I: 1878–1915* and *Vol. II: 1916–1940*, should prove indispensable for the serious collector. Patent dates, of course, can sometimes be misleading. Earnest Paul Lehmann, for example, bought the patent rights to the original Tom the Climbing Monkey on string (from an American, William Pitt Shattuck) in 1881. Over the past 75 years Lehmann produced five European variations, including a 1953 version of Tom with his little red fez.

MAKERS' MARKS

Represented on the following pages are makers' marks covering over 50 of the giants in the U.S. and European toy industry, many of which have existed since toys were first mass produced.

In compliance with the McKinley Tariff Act of 1891, imported toys made from that time forth were marked with the country of origin. Unfortunately, many of these toys either bore no maker's marks or, if they had paper labels, they may have long since disappeared. Some of the best sources for identifying unmarked toys are manufacturer's and jobber's wholesale and retail catalogs, flyers, broadsides, and order forms. A number of toy organizations and museums have reprinted much of this valuable material. You'll also find examples advertised in various toy trade journals, such as *Antique Toy World, Collectors' Showcase,* and *The Antique Trader.* For more recent vintage toys, back issues of jobber trade publications, such as *Toys and Novelties,* provide new-product announcements, trade gossip, and a myriad of advertisements which help unscramble the puzzle of which toys were made to whose specifications (as with broker George Borgfeldt, who marketed many toys under a "no name" line). Borgfeldt was also the American representative for Steiff and Nifty toys, and the New York broker for Gibbs Mfg. of Canton, Ohio.

Harris Toy Co. of Cleveland, to further complicate matters, acted as jobbers for their competition, Dent, Hubley and Wilkins, in addition to producing their own premier cast-iron horse-drawn rigs. In the early years of Hubley Mfg., the firm produced all manner of spare parts for other companies. Now you can begin to see why identifying toys by manufacturer is far from child's play!

An excellent sourcebook for identifying Walt Disney franchised merchandise by manufacturer was produced by Herman "Kay" Kamen from 1934 to 1950 (there were seven 48-page United Artists Corp. catalogs in all). Actually, the catalogs have become collector's items in themselves. Sears & Roebuck's catalogs from the '30s and '40s also provide excellent reference material for Mickey Mouse and various other comic collectibles enthusiasts.

Bliss, U.S.

Carette, German

Chein, U.S.

Gunthermann, German

Ideal, U.S.

Lehmann, German

Bing

CHARRETTES PEUGEOT

Peugeot, French

Lionel, U.S.

Charles Rosignol,
French

Manoil, U.S.

Jouet de Paris (JEP),
French

Cuberly, Blondell, Gerbeau,
French

Oro Werke Neill,
German

Muller–Kadeder, German

Righter, German

Brimtoy, G.B.

French Toy Seal of Quality

Greppert, Kelch, German

Arcade, U.S.

Strauss, U.S.

Metalgraf, Italian

Wilhelm, Kraus, German

Ives, U.S.

D.S

Dessein, German

Hess, German

Marx, U.S.

Maerklin, German

Kenton, U.S.

Gray Iron, U.S.

Walter Stock, German

J.P.
FRANCE

Edmond Faire, French

Meccano, G.B.

Rossignol, French

TOYS

Althof Bergmann, U.S.

Britains, G.B.

Burnett Ltd., G.B.

Fischer, German

IDENTIFYING GERMAN TOYS BY TRADEMARK INITIALS

Figures or combinations of letters often appear as follows:

George Carette	G.C. & Co.
Greppert Kelch	G.&K.
Kellerman	C.K.O.
Karl Bub	K.B.N.
Wilhelm Kraus	J.K. & Co.
Hathius Hess	H.J.L.
Muller & Kadeder	M.K.
Walter Stock	Marke Stocke
Siegfried Gunthermann & Adolph Weige	SG.AW
Tipp & Co.	T.C.O.
Johann Distler	J.D.N.
Theodor Frederich	
Wilhelm Marklin	G.M.; G.M. & Co.
Oro Muller	OROBR
Richter & Company	J.S.
Johann Philipp Meier	No letters used but a small image of dog pulling cart. Usually appears on underside of toy. Meier registered the logo in 1894.

TOY PATENTS—1860–1942

Toys may be dated and identified by maker by listings in the annual *U.S. Patent Gazette*, but in many cases the data is very sketchy. The best solution is to write the U.S. Patent Office in Washington, D.C., with a list of patent numbers required, and for a nominal fee they will send you copies of the patent drawings with copy description in printed form.

The only drawback with patent papers is that there is no way of determining if the toy was ever manufactured. Here is where cross-referencing with manufacturer's catalogs, business record books, and toy trade magazines will assist you in making a positive identification.

Year	*Patent Number*
1860	26,642
1861	31,005

Autoperipatatikos, first patented clockwork toy in America, by E.R. Morrison, July 15, 1862.

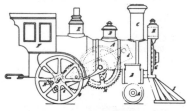

E.R. Ives cast iron locomotive, patented August 19, 1884.

H.T. Kingsbury motor for toy automobile, patented October 14, 1902 (711,323).

J.E. Hubley elevated railroad, patented April 11, 1893 (495,184). Regarded as Hubley's finest toy.

Arcade cast-iron Packard sedan, 1920s.

Gong Bell ringer pull toy, c. 1915.

Mickey Mouse wood-jointed toy, 1929.

C. W. F. DARE, Manufacturer,
47 Cortlandt St., New York.

THE TALLY HO SULKY.

SMALL SIZE.

THE TALLY HO SULKY.
(PATENTED.)

The Tally Ho Sulky is suitable for either boy or girl. The small size from 4 to 10 years, and the large size from 8 to 18 years of age.

The Tally Ho Sulky is the most pleasing, healthful and practicable toy of the motor kind. It has the rowing motion, being driven by the arms and steered by the feet. Moves easily and is capable of great speed. It can be used in the house in an ordinary sized room. It is strongly made and durable.

Small Size **$8.00**

Large " **10.00**

Dare catalog page from the 1890s. Tally-Ho Sulky was manufactured by Bookhut Bros. C.W.F. Dare was a leading 19th-century jobber as well as a manufacturer. $1400–$1600.

Year	Patent Number
1862	34,045
1863	37,266
1864	41,047
1865	45,685
1866	51,784
1867	60,658
1868	72,959
1869	85,503
1870	98,460
1871	110,617
1872	122,304
1873	134,504
1874	146,120
1875	158,350
1876	171,641
1877	185,813
1878	198,733
1879	211,078
1880	223,211
1881	236,137
1882	251,685
1883	269,820
1884	291,016

Year	Patent Number
1885	310,163
1886	333,494
1887	355,291
1888	375,720
1889	395,305
1890	418,665
1891	443,987
1892	466,315
1893	488,976
1894	511,744
1895	531,619
1896	552,502
1897	574,369
1898	596,467
1899	616,871
1900	640,167
1901	664,827
1902	690,385
1903	717,521
1904	748,567
1905	778,834
1906	808,618
1907	839,799
1908	875,679
1909	908,436
1910	945,010
1911	980,178
1912	1,013,095
1913	1,049,326
1914	1,083,267
1915	1,123,212
1916	1,166,419
1917	1,210,389
1918	1,251,458
1919	1,290,027
1920	1,326,899
1921	1,364,063
1922	1,401,948
1923	1,440,362
1924	1,478,996
1925	1,521,590
1926	1,568,040

Year	Patent Number
1927	1,612,790
1928	1,654,521
1929	1,696,897
1930	1,742,181
1931	1,787,424
1932	1,839,190
1933	1,892,663
1934	1,944,449
1935	1,985,878
1936	2,026,510
1937	2,066,309
1938	2,101,004
1939	2,142,080
1940	2,185,170
1941	2,227,418
1942	2,268,540

MANUFACTURERS

Acme Toy Works, Chicago, Illinois
1903-1907
Founder: Jacob Lauth
Specialty: Clockwork toy autos.

All Metal Products Co.

American National Co., Toledo, Ohio
Early 1900s
Founders: Walter, Harry, and William Diemer
Slogan: "Raise the Kids on Wheels"
Trade Name: "Giant"
Specialty: Produced sidewalk toys (scooters, bicycles) and pressed steel trucks, competing briefly with Keystone and Buddy "L" in the late 1920s.

Andes Foundry Co., Lancaster, Pennsylvania
1919-1930s
Founder: Eugene Andes
Specialty: First made paper caps and cast-iron components for Kilgore cap guns and cannons. Merged with Kilgore and Federal Mfg. in 1927, and became American Toys until the company dissolved a few years later. Specialized in Arctic ice cream wagon, airplanes, stake and dump trucks.

Arcade Mfg. Co. Freeport, Illinois
1868-1946
(Originally under name Novelty Iron Works)
Slogan: "They Look Real" (adopted in 1920)
Founder: E.H. and Charles Morgan
Specialty: First made toys and coffee mills in 1884.
As late as 1939, Arcade's toy line included over 300 toy items. Yellow Cab was first successful toy. Andy Gump in 348 and Chester Gump in His Pony Cart (all three pictured) were other popular toys with collectors. Arcade also made toy banks, doll house furniture, and cast-iron penny toys.

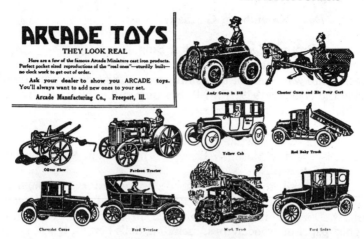

Few cast-iron toy makers could match the quality and attention to detail of Arcade Toy Manufacturing of Canton, OH. This late 1920s advertising gives samplings of a vast, diversified range of toys.

Auburn, Auburn, Indiana (Double Fabric Tire Corp.)
1913–1968 (Made first toys in 1935)
Specialty: English Palace Guard toy soldiers, as well as military miniatures for European and American branches of service. Made number of animal and wheeled vehicle toys. Toy division moved to Deming, New Mexico, in 1960.

Barclay Mfg. Co., Hoboken, New Jersey
1923–1971
Founders: Leon Donze, a Frenchman, and Michael Levy
Specialty: Introduced line of toy soldiers in 1932; became the largest U.S. producer of toy soldiers up to World War II.

Bassett-Lowke, Northampton, England
1899 to date
Founder: Wenman J. Bassett-Lowke
Specialty: The first to recognize the quality workmanship of German toy train manufacturers (i.e., Maerklin, Bing, Carette, and Ismayer) and to commission specific British designs. Bassett-Locke also innovated the mail-order catalog of toys concept, mailing its first edition, with tipped-in photographs, in 1899.

Gebruder Bing, Nuremberg, Germany
1866–1933
Founders: Brothers Ignaz and Adolf Bing
Specialty: Wide-range spring-driven cars, buses, boats. Perhaps its biggest coup was a line of trains initiated in 1882. Bing went under during the crash of 1929; Karl Bub acquired the toy trains division and Fleischmann the toy boats.

R. Bliss Mfg. Co., Pawtucket, Rhode Island
1832–1914 (Sold to Mason & Parker, Winchendon, Massachusetts)
Founder: Rufus Bliss
Specialty: Bliss had over a one-hundred-year history, although the earliest known advertisement for toys appeared in *New England Business Directory* in 1871. Pioneered in development of lithographed paper on wooden toys, including dolls houses, boats, trains, and building blocks.

George Borgfeldt & Co., New York City, New York
1881–1962
Founders: George Borgfeldt, and Marcell and Joseph Kahle
Specialty: Importer and wholesaler of toys, including comic novelty tin wind-ups under name "Nifty." Trademark was "Nifty" smiling moon face. Also distributed "Oh Boy" pressed steel trucks and cars.

Milton Bradley & Co., Springfield, Massachusetts
1861 to date
Founder: Milton Bradley
Slogan: "Maker of the World's Best Games"
Specialty: Variously identified as Milton Bradley Company, Milton Bradley & Co., and Milton Bradley Co. Launched his business with "The Checkered Game of Life," a board game with high moral overtones. Milton Bradley also became well known for educational games, books, kindergarten teaching aids, and school supplies, as well as a small range of toys.

William Britains Ltd., London England
1893 to date
Founder: William Britain
Specialty: Introduced a three-dimensional hollow toy soldier line, faithfully replicating over 100 British Army regiments in their first decade of doing business. Britains expanded to become the world's

largest producer of lead toy soldiers. (Since 1966, alas, the figures have been produced in plastic.)

George W. Brown & Co., Forestville, Connecticut
1856–1880
Founders: George W. Brown and Chauncey Goodrich
Specialty: The first manufacturer to produce toys with clockwork mechanisms, beginning perhaps as early as 1850. Known for classic boats, vehicles, animal platform toys, dancing figures, and hoop bell toys fashioned in painted tin. Merged with J. & E. Stevens in 1868.

Karl Bub, Nuremberg Germany
1851–1966
Founder: Karl Bub
Specialty: A superbly enameled (and later lithographed) line of clockwork tin transportation toys, including trains. Many Bub toys reached the American market via exclusive distributor F.A.O. Schwartz, New York City, during the 1920s–1930s.

Buddy "L," Salem, Massachusetts
1910 to date
Founder: Fred Lundahl
Specialty: Known under the following corporate names through the years, Moline Press Steel (1910–1913); Buddy "L" Wood Products (1944); Buddy "L" Manufacturing (1930); Buddy "L" Corp. (to date). Buddy "L" toys were named after the founder's son. Lundahl introduced the line in 1921. Starting with a small pressed steel pickup truck, Buddy "L" had expanded to a veritable fleet of almost 30 cranes, steam rollers, trucks, and other construction toys some five years later.

Buffalo Toy & Tool Works, Buffalo, New York
1924–1968
Specialty: Lightweight pressed steel aeronautical, automotive, and carousel toys, many of which were activated by a special spiral rod connected to a spring.

Butler Brothers, New York City, New York
1876–1950s
Specialty: One of the largest wholesale distributors of toys in the United States during first quarter of 20th century, carrying the most elite lines. Sold by catalog exclusively to merchants, with sample houses in most major U.S. cities.

Georges Carette, Nuremberg, Germany
1886–1917
Founder: Georges Carette (with Gebruder Bing's backing)
Specialty: Tin mechanical cars, boats, trains, mostly lithographed. Best known for electric streetcars and model trains. Carette, as a French citizen, was deported from Germany in 1917, thus closing the firm.

Carlisle & French Co., Cincinnati, Ohio
1895–1915 (For toy line, firm continues to date as marine lighting manufacturer.)
Founders: Robert Finch and Morton Carlisle
Specialty: Produced first successful electrically run toy train in the United States in 1897. Later expanded line to include steam outline locomotives and rolling stock. Also functioned as distributor, handling the first toy automobile (made by Knapp Electric in 1900).

Francis W. Carpenter, Port Chester, New York
1880–1890 (Sold patent rights and inventory to Pratt & Letchworth, but produced several outstanding toys on his own through the first decade of the 20th century.)
Specialty: Cast-iron horse-drawn vehicles, including what many collectors regard as *creme de la creme,* the tally-ho.

N.D. Cass, Athol, Massachusetts
1890s to date
Specialty: Wooden toys, some with clockwork mechanisms, including autos, trucks, doll houses, and barns.

Champion Hardware Co., Geneva, Ohio
1883–1954 (Toys from 1930–36)
Founders: John and Ezra Hasenpflug
Specialty: Cast-iron transportation toys; cast-iron parts for other leading toy makers.

J. Chein & Co., New York City, Harrison, New Jersey
1903–1979 (Toy producing years)
Founder: Julius Chein
Specialty: Lithographed tin mechanical toys, banks, drums, tea sets. Chein's line of comic and circus tin toys received wide acceptance in the 1930s and leading up to World War II. Became known as Chein Industries, Inc., in 1970s.

Andre Citroen, Paris, France
1919 to date (Toys first produced in 1923)
Founder: Andre Citroen
Specialty: Exact replicas of the automotive manufacturer's real thing, the full-size models (as an advertising gimmick); later, other brands of autos were replicated. A stencil on the underside usually identifies Citroen.

D.P. Clark, Dayton, Ohio
1898–1909 (Renamed Schieble Toy & Novelty in 1909)
Founder: David P. Clark
Specialty: Sheet-steel novelty and automotive toys with friction and flywheel mechanisms.

Morton E. Converse Co., Winchenden, Massachusetts
1878–1934 (Mason & Converse until 1883)
Founder: Morton Converse
Specialty: "Toytown Complex" was once recognized as largest wood toy factory in the world. Known for Noah's arks, ABC blocks and doll furniture, many of which were lithograph on wood. Made steel toys in the 1890s, comprised mainly of transportation vehicles with clockwork mechanisms.

Corcoran Mfg. Co., Washington, Indiana
1920s–1940s
Specialty: Large, pressed-steel riding toy autos and trains under trademark "Cor-Cor."

Corgi Toys, Mettoy Playcraft Ltd., Swansea, South Wales
Since 1956. (Mettoy Playcraft Ltd. originated in 1934).
Specialty: Miniature toy vehicles in metal and plastic.

Charles M. Crandall, Covington, Pennsylvania
1867–1905 (Relocated to Montrose, Pennsylvania, in 1875; to Waverly, New York, 1888)
Founder: Charles Crandall
Specialty: Interlocking tongue-and-groove lithograph paper-on-wood joints that children used to create multiple figure forms. Some of the most popular sets: "District School House," "Acrobats," and "Treasure Box." Charles' son Jesse started his own toy business soon after the Civil War, relocating in Brooklyn. Jesse Crandall was issued a number of patents for rocking toys, alphabet blocks, and construction toys.

Jesse Crandall, Brooklyn, New York
1840s–1880s
Specialty: Hobby horses, rocking horses, velocipedes, and board games.

A.A. Davis, Nashua, New Hampshire
1860s–?
Specialty: Novelty toys featuring small lithographed figures of celebrities, animals, butterflies with movable parts set in wooden cups, covered by glass (i.e., "Magic Major General Grant," see "political" listing.)

Dayton Friction Toy Works, Dayton, Ohio
1909–1935
Founder: D.P. Clark (see D.P. Clark)
Specialty: Pressed-steel friction toys with patented horizontal flywheel (1926) under trade name "Gyro."

Dayton Toy & Specialty Co., Dayton, Ohio
1920s–early 1930s
Specialty: Large, heavy-gauge pressed-steel transportation toys.

Dent Hardware Co., Fullerton, Pennsylvania
1895–1937 (Continued to manufacture cold storage hardware until 1973)
Founders: Henry H. Dent, with four additional partners
Specialty: Cast iron and aluminum transportation toys and banks. "Pioneer" fire truck, Ford Tri-Motor, and large hook-and-ladder toys were popular items.

Charles William Doepke Manufacturing Co., Rossmoyne, Ohio
1920s and 1930s
Specialty: Faithful replicas of transportation, fire fighting, farm, and construction vehicles under name "Model Toys." Known for rugged, heavy-gauge steel construction and ease of operation.

Dowst (Tootsietoy), Chicago, Illinois
Late 1890s
Founders: Charles O. and Samuel Dowst
Specialties: Miniature cast-metal cars, trains, and planes. Tootsietoy name introduced in 1922 when Dowst introduced a line of doll furniture (named after a Dowst granddaughter, Toots). Merged with

Cosmo Mfg. in 1926; acquired Strombeck-Becker toy line in 1961 and made name change as Strombecker Corp.

Ellis, Britton & Eaton, Springfield, Vermont
1859–early 1900s
Founder: Joel Ellis
Specialty: Wooden dolls, sleds, pianos, rolling hoops, toy carriages. In 1873, Ellis patented his most popular toy, the Jointed Wood Doll, made of maple with cast-iron hands and feet. Two nearby firms, Cooperative Mfg. Co. and Vermont Novelty Works, continued the patent.

Gibbs Mfg. Co., Canton, Ohio
1884–to date
Founder: Lewis E. Gibbs
Specialty: Originally manufactured plows. Added toys in 1886. Mechanical spinning tops, wagons and lithographed paper-on-wood, metal, and advertising toys.

A.C. Gilbert Co., New Haven, Connecticut
1908–1966
Founder: Albert C. Gilbert
Specialty: Began as manufacturer of boxed magic sets. Introduced Erector Sets in 1913, an instant success (30 million would be sold over next 40 years). Bought out Richter Anchor Block and American affiliate of Meccano at beginning of World War I. Pressed-steel autos and trucks were added to line in 1914, plus a variety of scientific toys. Purchased American Flyer in 1938 and retained only the name for a line of trains. Gilbert subsequently had its own financial woes and the toy train line was sold to Lionel in 1966.

Girard Mfg. Co., Girard, Pennsylvania
1935–1975

Girard Model Works, Inc.
1922–1935

The Toy Works
1919–1922 (spinning tops, skates, banks and walking porter)
Founder: Frank E. Wood
Specialty: In the late 1920s, Girard made Louis Marx a commission agent and for several years produced toys under the Marx label, along with its own line of steel autos, trucks, and trains,

Advertisement from *Playthings*, c. 1915, featuring Gibbs, a toy maker famed for its lithograph on wood and metal pull and push toys, as well as mechanical humming tops. Note that Gibbs had four New York agents, a factor that often adds to the confusion when identifying toys from jobbers catalogs. Toys pictured are in the $75–$125 range with "Jumbo the Wonderful Performer" (middle left) and "Pony Circus" (lower right) $200–$400. Tops are rated at $35–$50 each.

which were produced at Girard Model Works. Marx and Girard toys are for all intents indistinguishable (a few of the Girard toys bore the slogan "Making Childhood's Hour Happier"). Girard declared bankruptcy in 1934, although toy production continued until 1975. Quaker Oats had bought out Marx's interest in Girard when they bought Marx's American and English toy division in 1972.

Gong Bell Mfg. Co., East Hampton, Connecticut
1886–late 1930s
Specialty: Hardware bells and cast-metal bell pull and push toys.

Grey Iron Co., Mount Joy, Pennsylvania
1900 (under name Brady Machine Shop) to date. (First produced toys in 1903)
Specialty: Grey Klip Army toy soldiers (1917–1941) in cast iron, nickel plated. "Iron Men" series, 1936; "Uncle Sam's Defender," 1938. Still operating today as John Wright division of Cons Co.

Hafner Mfg. Co., Chicago, Illinois
1900–1950
Founder: W. F. Hafner
Specialty: Joined with Edmunds–Metzel Co. in 1907 to manufacture trains and mechanical toys. Became American Flyer Manufacturing in 1910 and was sold to Wyandotte in 1950. When Wyandotte closed its doors, Marx acquired Hafner dies.

Hardware and Woodenware Mfg. Co., New York City
1907–1912
Founder: Consortium
Specialty: Consortium purchased Grey Iron Casting, Jones and Bixler, Stevens, Kenton, and eleven other toy companies, but went into bankruptcy two years later.

Harris Toy Co., Toledo, Ohio
Circa 1887–1913
Specialty: Produced cast iron toys in the 1880s. Harris also acted as jobber for Dent, Hubley, and Wilkins. Financial difficulties forced them out of toy production by 1913.

N. N. Hill Brass Co., New Jersey
Circa 1889–1960
Specialty: Branch of National Novelty for four years ending in 1907. In 1905, merged with Watrous Mfg. Co., another bell toy maker. Specialized in cast-iron and pressed-steel bell push and pull toys, toy telephones and target games.

Hoge Mfg. Co., New York City
1920s–mid 1930s
Specialty: Pressed-steel cars and trucks closely resemble Marx and Girard toys (reported manufactured by Girard and distributed by Henry Katz). Best known for Popeye Tru-To-Life Mechanical Rowboat, produced in 1935.

Hubley Mfg. Co., Lancaster, Pennsylvania
1894 to date

Founder: John E. Hubley
Specialty: Originally manufactured electric toy train equipment and parts. Purchased Safety Buggy Co. factory and moved to site in 1909. First manufactured cast-iron toys, horse-drawn wagons and fire engines, circus trains, and cap guns. Toy autos became the headliners in the 1930s. By quickly converting to cheaper small toys during the Depression, they avoided financial woes experienced by many other toy companies. Iron shortages in World War II and commitments to fill war contracts did spell the demise of Hubley's toy division in 1942. The name was later changed to Gabriel Industries and still existed as a division of CBS as of 1978.

Ideal, Brooklyn, New York
1903 to date
Founders: Rose and Morris Michtom
Specialty: Stuffed toys and dolls, anchored by the original Teddy Bear. Ideal still ranks as one of the top producers of stuffed toys and dolls.

Ives Corp., Bridgeport, Connecticut
1868–1932

E. R. Ives & Co., Plymouth, Connecticut
1868–1870
Founder: Edward R. Ives
Specialty: Originally made baskets and hot air toys.

Ives and Blakeslee & Co., Bridgeport, Connecticut
1872–1931
Specialty: Ives joined partner Cornelius Blakeslee, a brother-in-law. Ives moved to Bridgeport in 1870; by the 1880s, they were leaders in superb clockwork toys designed by Jerome Secor, Nathan Warner, and Arthur Hotchkiss. Ives also acted as jobber for other manufacturers' toys. The firm filed for bankruptcy in 1929, another victim of the Depression. Lionel took over the company at that time, and the name Ives and Blakeslee remained until 1931.

Jeanette Toy & Novelty Co., Jeanette, Pennsylvania
1898–?
Specialty: Lithographed tin toys, including trays, tea sets, and figural glass candy containers.

Jones & Bixler Co., Freemansburg, Pennsylvania
1899–1914
Founders: Charles A. Jones and Louis S. Bixler
Specialty: "Red Devil Line" of cast-iron auto toys (introduced in 1903, when J & B became part of National Novelty Corp.). From 1909–1913, J & B and Kenton Hardware (which also became part of National Novelty toy trust) produced toys that were indistinguishable from each other.

Kelmet Corp., New York City
1923–late 1920s
Specialty: Large pressed-steel trucks under name "Kelmet" and "Trumodel." Parts were frequently subcontracted and A. C. Gilbert assembled the finished product. A further designation was "Big Boy," modeled after the White Truck.

Kenton Hardware Co., Kenton, Ohio
1890–1952
Founder: F. M. Perkins (Patented line of refrigerator hardware)
Specialty: Toy production began in 1894 with line of horse-drawn fire equipment, banks, and toy stoves. Renamed Kenton Hardware in 1900. Became part of mammoth National Novelty Corp. merger in 1903, it continued its toy line under the name Wing Mfg. Co. Involved in several unsuccessful takeovers, it eventually emerged as a separate unit, the Kenton Hardware Co., and again produced toys successfully from 1920-1935. Kenton ceased production in 1952 and assets were sold in 1953. The Littlestown Hardware & Foundry acquired many Kenton toy designs and marketed them under the brand "Utexiqual." Littlestown folded in 1982.

Keystone Mfg. Co., Boston, Massachusetts
Circa 1920
Specialty: Originally produced toy motion picture machines and children's comedy films (Keystone Moviegraph). Gained permission from Packard Motor Co. in mid-1920s to market pressed-steel riding trucks copied from full-size Packard models, including famous radiator design and logo. Keystone, in competing with Buddy L, added such refinements as nickeled hub caps and radiator caps, transparent celluloid windshield, and engine crank. For 50 cents extra you could get rubber tires and headlamps. Keystone trucks also featured steering and signal arms for "stop" and "go." Keystone introduced line of "Siren Riding Toys" in 1934 with saddle riding seat and handlebars for steering. In 1936, one of its big sellers

was a "Ride-Em" mail plane. In the post–World War II years, most of Keystone's toy output was based on tools and dies purchased from the defunct Kingsbury toy division.

Kilgore Mfg.Co., Westerville, Ohio
1920s–possibly late 1940s
Specialty: Slogan was "Toys That Last." Originated in 1925 with purchase of George D. Wanner Co., makers of "E-Z-Fly" kites. In 1928, Kilgore introduced cast-iron trucks, cars, and fire engines, along with cast-iron cap guns, cannons, and toy paper caps (after its merger with Andes Foundry and the Federal Toy Co. under the aegis of American Toy Co.). Butler Brothers became its biggest distributor. Later Kilgore would fall back on its cap pistol and toy paper cap line, and the company remained in business until 1944.

Kingsbury Mfg. Co., Keene, New Hampshire
1919–1942 (See also Wilkins Toy Co.)
Specialty: Harry T. Kingsbury bought Wilkins in 1895 and combined with the Clipper Machine Works, which specialized in farm equipment. In the early 1900s, toy automobiles were introduced to the company line. The Wilkins name was dropped following World War I in favor of Kingsbury, by now an established name in the field. Kingsbury specialized in copying famous models of aircraft and assembly-line roadsters, trucks, and busses. World War II saw Kingsbury shifting to war contracts and never returning again to toy production. All production equipment was sold to Keystone in Boston. The company still exists, but as Kingsbury Machine Tool Division, a subcontractor for such giants as IBM, General Motors, and GE.

Kingston Products Corp., Kokomo, Indiana
1890s
Founders: Charles T. Byrne and James F. Ryan
Specialty: Byrne and Ryan started the Kokomo Brass Works to produce brass castings for the plumbing industry. Kingston soon became an alliance of many kindred companies. Their line of toys, under the name Kokomo Toys, came into prominence in the 1920s and 1930s with racers, trucks, fire engines, and transportation toys a specialty. Electrically run racers were an ingenious addition, though so expensive for Depression times that Kingston dropped them in 1931. Kingston today is part of Scott & Fetzer Co., and makes components for auto manufacturers.

Kirchoff Patent Co., Newark, New Jersey
1852 to date
Founder: Charles Kirchoff, a German builder of weaving looms and other weaving machinery
Specialty: Small metal toys, noisemakers, Christmas ornaments and novelties. Kirchoff essentially was a developer of patents and in addition to toys produced Braille printers and ticker-tape machines. (Although no longer in business under the Kirchoff name, the company did undergo a number of changes in ownership over the years and was still recorded as being active up to the 1950s.)

Knapp Electric Novelty Co., New York City, New York
1899 to date
Specialty: One of our earliest manufacturers of transportation toys powered by wet cell batteries. Carlisle & Finch, noted for its toy trains and other novelty toys that were electrically run, served as Knapp's distributor.

Kyser & Rex, Philadelphia, Pennsylvania
1880–1884
Founders: L. Kyser and Alfred Rex
Specialty: Cast-iron toys and mechanical banks. Among their highly desirable banks are: Hindu with Turban, Uncle Tom, Chimpanzee, The Organ Bank, Lion and Monkeys.

Earnest Lehman Co., Brandenberg, Germany
1881 (Re-established in 1951 in Nuremberg and still producing toys)
Founder: Earnest P. Lehman
Specialty: Lehman exported vast quantities of toys to the United States from 1895 to 1929 (excluding years of World War I). Specialized in lithographed tinplate, mechanical transportation toys and figures known for their colorful patina. Some of the most desirable Lehmans include: Mr. and Mrs. Lehman, Dancing Sailor, Icarus and Autobus.

Gebruder Maerklin, Göppingen, Germany
1859 to date
Founders: Theodor and his wife, Caroline Maerklin
Specialty: Originated as maker of doll-size tinplate kitchenware. When sons took over in 1888, firm name was changed to Gebruder Maerklin. Branched out to variety of enameled tinplate boats, carousels, aeronautical toys. Unsurpassed in production of clockwork, steam and electric trains. Introduced first standardized tinplate

tracks in 1891. Maerklin switched to plastic train sets in the late 1950s.

Manoil Mfg. Co., New York City, New York and Waverly, New York
1937–1941
Specialty: Hollow-cast toy soldiers (sometimes called dimestore soldiers).

Fernand Martin, Paris, France
1887–1919
Specialty: Widely copied maker of amusing double-action tin mechanicals, including Le Clochard (Tramp) and Ivorogne (Toper or Drunk).

Mason & Parker, Winchendon, Massachusetts
1899–1966
Founders: H.N. Parker and Orlando Mason
Specialty: Pressed-steel transportation toys. Later (1907), Mason & Parker switched to wood products, including the proven standard, Boy's Tool Chest.

McLoughlin Brothers, New York City, New York
1850s–1920 (Milton Bradley acquired McLoughlin in 1920)
Specialty: Known early on for "revamping" popular European juvenile games, McLoughlin created as well, including such staples as Pilgrims Progress, Fish Pond, Peter Coddle, and Jack Straws. Lithograph paper-on-wood construction toys included the Palmer Cox Brownie series; also alphabet blocks and numerous educational toys.

Meccano (Dinky Toys), Liverpool, England
1901–1964 (Taken over by Lines Bros. in 1964)
Founder: Frank Hornby
Specialty: Metal construction sets (a la Erector). First produced miniatures called Dinky Toys in 1933

Johann Philipp Meier, Nuremberg, Germany
1879–1917
Specialty: One of the more prolific penny toy manufacturers at the turn of the century. Meier also produced painted tin mechanical toys. Trademark: Dog pulling cart.

Metalcraft Corp., St. Louis, Missouri
1920–1937
Specialty: Playground equipment such as teeter-totters. Produced pressed-steel trucks in 1928 and acquired rights to pressed-steel airplane in kit of Lindbergh's "Spirit of St. Louis." Produced millions of toy truck premiums known as "Business Leaders."

Moline (See Buddy "L")

Parker Brothers, Salem, Massachusetts
1883 to date
Founder: George S. Parker
Specialty: Created first card game, Banking, in 1883. World renowned for producing board game Monopoly beginning in 1934. Another game, Chivalry, later updated under the name Camelot, has been regarded by many board game experts as a more challenging game. Acquired the rights of a number of smaller makers, including W. & S. B. Ives and the U. S. Playing Card Co.

National Novelty Corp., New Jersey (See N. N. Hill Brass Co.)
1903–1907
Specialty: A trust or consortium of over 30 leading manufacturers of cast-iron and wood toys, formed to cut costs and stifle competition. Poorly managed, the "Toy Trust" soon failed. A number of participating toy makers reorganized under the aegis, Hardware & Woodenware Manufacturing Co., but it, too, soon faded.

Neff-Moon Toy Co., Sandusky, Ohio
1920–1925
Specialty: Pressed-steel automotive toys with interchangeable bodies packaged with single chassis.

Nonpareil Toy & Novelty Co., Newark, New Jersey
Post–World War I–late 1940s
Specialty: Lithographed tin toy trucks and wagons, mostly of the penny toy or tiny prize package toy variety.

Parker Brothers, Inc., Salem, Massachusetts
1883 to date
Founder: George S. Parker
Specialty: Board games, puzzles, children's books.

Philadelphia Tin Toy Co., Philadelphia, Pennsylvania
Toy firm of Francis Field and Francis carried this name in Philadelphia area in late 1840s.

Pratt & Letchworth, Buffalo, New York
1880–1900
Founders: Pascal P. Pratt and William P. Letchworth
Specialty: Cast-iron toy trains, horse-drawn hansom cabs, pumpers, artillery wagons. Originally known (1870s) as Buffalo Malleable Iron Works. Francis Carpenter's stock and patent rights were acquired by Pratt & Letchworth in 1890.

W.S. Reed Toy Co., Leominster, Massachusetts
1875–1897
Founder: Whitney S. Reed
Specialty: Lithographed paper-on-wood toys and construction sets. Patented one mechanical bank, "The Old Lady In the Shoe."

Richter (Anchor Blocks), Rudolstadt, Germany
1508–1920s (Reputedly the oldest toy company, with a 16th-century founding date.)
Specialty: Anchor Toy Building Bricks, alphabet and puzzle blocks. A.C. Gilbert, the Erector Set people, bought the American interest of Anchor Blocks in 1913.

Riemann, Seabrey Co., Inc., New York City, New York
1920s–1944
Specialty: Manufacturers' representatives acting as sole sales agents for Kenton, Grey Iron, N.N. Hill Brass, J. & E. Stevens, and other leading cast-iron toy makers.

Schieble Toy & Novelty Co., Dayton, Ohio
1909–1931
Specialty: Carried on line of "Hill Climber" friction toys, initiated by D.P. Clark & Co.

Selchow and Righter, New York City, New York
1860s–?
Founder: Elish G. Selchow (John H. Righter later became partner
Specialty: Board games and puzzles.

C.G. Shepard and Co., Buffalo, New York
1866–1892
Founders: Walter J. and Charles G. Shepard

Specialty: Tin horns; still and mechanical banks (beginning in 1882). Sold mechanical bank business in 1892; three Shepard banks were later reissued by J. & E. Stevens.

J. &. E. Stevens, Cromwell, Connecticut
1843–1930s
Founders: John and Elisha Stevens
Specialty: Cast-iron mechanical banks from 1870 to the turn of the century. Elisha Stevens later joined George Brown to establish the Stevens & Brown toy firm. J. & E. Stevens supplied Gong Bell and Watrous with castings for their bell toys.

Stevens & Brown, New York City, New York
1869–1880
Founders: Elisha Stevens and George Brown (who pooled their tin and cast-iron lines and also distributed for other toy makers)

Walter Stock, Solingen, Germany
1905–1930s
Founder: Walter Stock
Specialty: Lithographed tin mechanical toys much similar to Lehmann line; also penny toys exported to America.

Ferdinand Strauss Corporation, New York City, New York
Circa 1900s–mid-1940s
Founder: Ferdinand Strauss
Specialty: Major producer of tin mechanical toys from 1914 to 1927.

Structo Manufacturing Co., Freeport, Illinois
1908–1975
Founders: Louis and Edward Strohacker
Specialty: Construction kits and pressed-steel toy automobiles based on the Stutz Bearcat. Later teamed up with American.

Tipp & Co., Nuremberg, Germany
1912–1971
Founders: Tipp and Carstans
Specialty: Military line of tin toys

Tower (Guild), South Hingham, Massachusetts
1830s–1850s
Founder: William S. Tower
Specialty: Founded Tower Guild, a marketing cooperative for

woodworkers and carpenters, who fashioned much prized wooden toys.

John C. Turner Co., Wapakoneta, Ohio
1915–1948
Founder: John Turner
Specialty: Known for a line of "Victory Is Won" flywheel toys sold by direct mail.

Union Manufacturing Co., Clinton, Connecticut
1853–1869
Hull & Stratford acquired this small tin toy-producing firm in 1869.

Weeden Mfg. Co., New Bedford, Massachusetts
1883–1939
Founder: William N. Weeden
Specialty: Produced working toy steam engine in 1884; also live steamboats, fire engine, and automobile with steam as motive power. Sold to Pairpont Company in the 1930s.

Wilkins Toy Co., Keene, New Hampshire
1890–1919 (See also Kingsbury)
Founder: James S. Wilkins
Specialty: One of the earliest manufacturers to produce toy automobiles, circa 1895. Another Keene, New Hampshire, firm headed by Henry T. Kingsbury bought out Wilkins that same year, but the toy line carried the Wilkins name and trademark until 1919.

A.C. Williams Co., Ravenna, Ohio
1886 to date
Founder: John W. Williams
Specialty: Produced cast-iron, horse-drawn rigs, autos, airplane, and tractor toys from 1893 to 1923; line included mostly miniatures distributed through Woolworth, Kresge's, and other five-and-dime emporiums.

WILKINS
Rubber Tired Mechanical Autos
THE STANDARD OF EXCELLENCE

All Equipped with Long Distance Motors and Rubber Tires.

A catalog page from the 1910 era for five top-of-the-line pressed-steel toys. Wilkins was acquired by another Keene, NH, maker, Henry Thayer Kingsbury, in 1895, but the Wilkins name appeared on their motor toys until 1919. The toys illustrated would rate in the $600-$800 range, with the lady in the Phaeton somewhat higher.

THE IMPORTANCE
OF CONDITION

Of all the factors that help determine the value of a given toy, Condition with a capital C *has* to rate right at the top of the list. Toys in mint condition ("mint" is a term borrowed from our philatelist friends, connoting "fresh, superb, as new") can often command prices double that of toys in average condition. Most major toy auction houses make it a point to grade all cataloged examples as to condition, based on a scale of 1–10. In reviewing auction catalogs from a number of galleries over the past five years, it was amazing how consistently the prices realized reflected the condition ratings.

Toys in their original boxes also exact a premium price. The lithography on such popular 1930s Marx toys as the Fresh Air Taxicab of "Amos n' Andy" or Walking Sandy from the comic strip "Orphan Annie," for example, is as graphically appealing as the toys themselves. In the case of the Sandy toy, the original box is assembled to form a dog house that serves as a colorful display for Sandy. In a recent toy auction, two Li'l Abner Dogpatch Bands by Unique Art went on the block; both were graded in excellent condition. The version with a rather shop-worn box sold for $325, while the boxless toy realized $200. The Dogpatch Band with box commanded a 62.5% higher bid! Even when only one panel or two of an original box is still intact collectors are eager to salvage remnants, and some will frame these portions. In addition to their strong graphic appeal, an original box invariably reveals additional information regarding the toy contained therein (i.e., full name of manufacturer, patent date, year of copyright). Robert Lesser of New York City, a leading collector of comic art and memorabilia writes in *A Celebration of Comic Art and Memorabilia* (Hawthorn Books, Inc., New York, 1975): "Try to collect (toys) in mint condition in the original boxes. Yes, it is an impossible dream today, but by establishing this internal discipline you will be amazed that dealers recognize you as a mint collector and will therefore offer you their finest pieces, and you will be paying more, but getting the best of their wares."

THE UNDESIRABLE THREE "R's"— REPRODUCTIONS, REPAINTS (RETOUCHES), REPAIRS (REPLACED PARTS)

GRADING SCALE

The following is a grading scale that might prove helpful in future communications regarding toys, banks, and trains.

About Mint: No chips, scratches, fading; no rust; fully operable. (10 points on grading system)

Pristine: May have minor paint or litho wear, but 98% plus is still perfect. (8–9 points)

Fine: Still excellent, with 90% considered perfect. (6–8 points)

Good: Average condition with 70% litho or paint intact. (4–6) points)

Fair: Below average with only 50% coverage. (2–4 points)

Poor: Example has less than 30% and is barely salvageable. (0–2 points)

HOW TO COPE WITH REPRODUCTIONS

One of the first toys to enter our possession some 20 years ago was a cast-iron pull toy on wheels of a lady in a large sunbonnet riding sidesaddle on a donkey. The only problem with "Sunbonnet Sue," as she came to be affectionally known, was that she was an out-and-out fake. (Sue has even managed to fool certain toy book people; we've seen it pictured as an original and guided in the $100 range. Actually, purists would argue that she qualifies as a "fantasy," created from scratch and not intended to replicate an earlier, original toy.)

While it came as a severe blow to our egos as well as our pocketbooks, we kept "Sue" on display with our collection for a number of years as a reminder to keep our acquisitive emotions under control, while remaining ever alert and cautious.

Unfortunately, "Sunbonnet Sue" runs in fast company with an untold number of cast-iron reproductions that plague the hobby today. Some questionable banks and toys are merely an attempt by certain manufacturers to provide promotional or commemorative items to our nostalgia-conscious society. A good example are the World Book Encyclopedia replications of early mechanical banks. World Book made no pretense of the fact that the banks were re-pros; they cast their logotype on the underside of the base of each bank. This did not deter unscrupulous tricksters from grinding off the World Book mark and passing a bank off as a 19th-century original. A few years ago, a number of horse-drawn and automotive Kenton molds were purchased and marketed clearly as reproductions by Sears and Roebuck. These toys appear frequently at flea markets and auctions, priced right up there with the originals. Many reproductions appear on the market today that are so crudely cast and poorly finished that few people are fooled by the deception. The trouble lies with reproductions that are fiendishly clever.

The following story was related to us recently by a very reliable source in the hobby: a gentleman approached a toy auctioneer and one of the leading cast-iron toy and bank collectors with two seemingly identical examples. "One of these is the real McCoy and the other is a copy; which is which?" Both auctioneer and collector picked the bogus piece over the original! Apocryphal or not, this poses a real dilemma facing not only fledgling collectors but real pros. Fortunately, of the tens of thousands of cast-iron circus wagons, fire rigs, carriages, and walking horses manufactured from 1870 until World War II, only a minuscule percentage have been reproduced. There are certain dead giveaways and here are some ways to avoid getting stung:

1. One of the most common categories to be reproduced is that of still banks. Learn which ones have been faked. (Our listing of still banks and mechanical banks reveals many of the more commonly copied examples.) Actually, there are very few scarce

still banks that are being passed off as old (i.e., Bear Stealing Pig, Polish Rooster, Baby in the Cradle, Nesting Hen, and Two-Faced Devil. By learning as much as you can about each specimen you will know, for example, that the repro pig in Bear Stealing Pig is cast in brass, while the original is in iron (a magnet will quickly detect the deception). We know many collectors who wouldn't be without a magnet, loupe or magnifying glass, and a black light whenever they're out "prospecting." Some repro banks are heavier than the originals, as is the case with the Polish Rooster. In the case of the North Pole Bank fake, the pole itself is not nickel-plated like the original.

2. Other telltale repro signs are bright shiny paint, dead black or shiny gold finish, and no signs of wear except in suspicious places where a repro identification may have been obliterated.

3. Most figural toys and banks were cast in two parts, mated and assembled with bolts or screws. Watch for mismating, where parts do not fit together snugly; new screws are also easily detected.

4. Following the sand-casting process, cast-iron repros usually aren't tumbled smoothly; the finish has a rough, pebbly feel, a bit like cement; in the modern product, most makers have yet to duplicate the smooth, almost soapstone like feel of the old-timers.

5. Normally, re-cast toys and banks tend to be heavier, thicker, and slightly smaller than the original. The latter occurs due to the iron shrinking in the mold as it cools. In the case of mechanical banks, a number of helpful books are available that contain base tracings of originals for comparison purposes.

6. Watch the price. A lowball price, while it may appeal to your baser instincts to close a deal on a toy that is far below market value, more often is the first indication that its pedigree is spurious.

7. Don't be shy about questioning the seller about *his* knowledge of the toy; and don't hesitate about seeking a second opinion.

8. Deal with only reputable people—dealers, auctioneers, and fellow collectors who, without hesitation, back up everything they sell.

9. Train yourself to become almost instinctive in the selection process. Meyric Rogers, a leading authority on antiques, would first walk through the American wing of the Metropolitan Museum of Art to get his eye attuned to quality authentic pieces before going shopping so that he would possess a higher degree of perception. While there may not always be access to great

collections of toys, there is certainly a treasure-trove of reference books, early toy catalogs, flyers, and clipping files to consult.

10. Above all, know your specialty. In a recent *Antique Toy World*, noted motortoy collector Lillian Gottschalk offered this advice: "If you're a diamond collector, you better know your diamonds or find someone who does—at least until you gain the knowledge and experience to work alone. This comes with time and handling toys. There should be no fears."

Note: Within the last several years, a number of leading toy show promoters have taken positive steps by policing their exhibitors' wares to make doubly certain that reproductions are not being offered for sale. As a result, the situation has vastly improved, although there is still evidence of toys being offered that exemplify the other two dreaded "Rs," Repairs and Repaints.

A number of leading antique and collectible trade publications keep tabs on the latest reproductions as they come on the market, as a service to their subscribers. In Joel Sater's *Antiques News*, for example, Harry Llewellyn writes a "Reproduction Hotline." One of the most recent repros cited was a 1933 Arcade Plymouth. Made of linotype lead vs. cast iron with tires and hubs of old stock, there apparently is no intent to deceive. Available in several body styles, the price is $25 per unit.

There *is* a law on the books that requires that imitations of various kinds of Americana be marked "Reproduction," or with a similar term, in a prominent place and in a nonremovable manner. Signed into law by Congress as the Hobby Protection Act (Public Law 93-167), it was ironically the last action by President Richard M. Nixon just prior to his resignation. Unfortunately, some manufacturers and entrepreneurs are unaware of the law or choose to ignore it. More collectors, dealers, show promoters, and auctioneers should be alerted to the fact that this law can be enforced. There is, of course, no substitute for sound knowledge.

REPAINTS (RETOUCHES)

Lithographed or decaled toys are less likely to fall victim to the retouch artists since their finish is so difficult to duplicate. Even if possible, it would be prohibitively expensive. It is with the classic early enameled tin mechanicals and cast-iron toys and banks where we see the most evidence of cosmetic trickery. Look for old paint characteristics as follows:

1. Generally shows evidence of crazing (tiny hairline cracks).
2. Shows wear and chipping in normal wear areas (i.e., next to key wind) and around moving parts (i.e., where legs and arms connect to torso on animal and human figures).
3. Has a harder finish than new paint; will not scratch easily.
4. Will appear a different color than new paint under black-light test (i.e., original red will appear olive green under ultraviolet light; newer red may come out as bright orange).

New paint may be detected as follows:

1. Often betrays its presence by odor.
2. Easily scratches because of softness of paint.
3. Parts of same color match up and change color uniformly under black-light test.
4. By using cotton swab tip on obscure part of toy. Applied with xylene or acetone agents, new paint quickly dissolves while old paint remains unaffected.

Any one or a combination of the above tests may be employed to expose new paint-altered examples.

In addition, seeking the advice of an authority on paint can lead to a quick, precise resolution to the mystery of new paint vs. old paint. I am fortunate to have as a father-in-law a chemical engineer who worked with the Pigments Department of E.I. Du Pont. A few years ago, I showed my father-in-law a cast-iron Toonerville Trolley that had been resurrected from the old Dent Toy works in Fullerton, Pennsylvania. An enterprising collector/dealer had assembled parts from remaining stock and ostensibly used original paint that was found on-site still good in the cans. In effect, the toy then appeared to be as original as those that came off the assembly line when the toy was actually in production in the late 1920s. Taking a tiny sliver of paint from under the trolley, my father-in-law subjected it to a battery of tests. He was able to determine that the paint purported to be germane to the toy had not been introduced until some 30 years later.

Someone might well ask, "What difference does this make?" Obviously, from an aesthetic point of view, very little. There are many collectors who have no intent to deceive, but simply want to present or exhibit their toys in the best possible light. It is when a repainted toy is *resold* that the ethical question arises. It is a general rule-of-thumb that a repainted specimen is worth about 50% that of an all-original. When confronted with such a dilemma, it is well worth considering this fact and revising the amount you are willing to pay for a reprint, since it is obviously in a devalued state. Obviously, if it is an extremely rare or unique toy and the quality of the restoration is A-one, one should have fewer qualms about the matter.

REPAIRS (REPLACED PARTS)

On a recent visit to the Allentown Toy Show & Sale, we spotted a familiar dealer transacting business in one of the back rows of Agricultural Hall. Arranged on his table were boxes and boxes of wheels, axles, headlamps, drivers—literally thousands of spare parts. "These are all original spare parts from my own collection," we overheard him tell a prospective customer. We remember this dealer well; years ago, in a transaction with this writer, he tried to pass off an Arcade cast-iron Andy Gump roadster as an original unadulturated toy. The retouch job was the worst I'd ever encountered and he'd even painted white polka dots on Andy's driving gloves! Chances were that the license plate, the front grille, and even the Andy figure itself were repros. There are all manner of sources for repro parts cast in zinc, lead, brass, and cast iron. The quality ranges from excellent to fairly crude, but collectors eagerly grab them up. There is a whole universe of miniature junkyards with toy vehicles missing spare wheels, steering columns, headlights, etc., that are ripe for restoration. Here again, the majority of purchases are made to transform the toy whole again, to make it presentable in the collection. Only a small percentage are added with intent to pass off as originals. Replacing parts leads to retouching and repainting. To quote Sir Walter Scott, "Oh, what a tangled web we weave who only practice to deceive."

The best advice on combating these pesky "doctored" toys with replaced parts and repaints is to know your craft or rely on someone who does. Use your second sense or "third eye" to determine if the toy is "right." Again, it pays to deal with only those whom you can trust and will guarantee the originality of the toy—the sum of its parts and the whole.

INOPERABLE TOYS

The survival rate of toys with wind-up mechanisms capable of activating a toy is suspect, often as erratic as the crazy erratic motions they intend to convey. Rust and overwinding of spring mechanisms are major culprits, as well as the flimsiness or built-in obsolescence inherent with certain manufacturers.

A surprisingly sizeable group of collectors is caring less about a toy's ability to operate and more about its facility for showing well in one's collection. Even if operable, certain purists would not think of turning the key, as if winding would endanger the toy's mortality.

In selling a toy that is inoperable, however, there is no doubt that your bargaining position as seller is substantially weakened. We pass along this advice from a leading tin toy practitioner: If the toy is pre–20th century and is of the type where mated halves have been soldered or braised together, to obtain access to the mechanism by softening the closures would char the finish. It would be best to leave well enough alone. On toys made after 1900, however, with the familiar tab closures, it is relatively easy to take the toy apart and have the spring mechanism rewound or shortened. (We've had this done by jewelers and watch repairmen for a nominal fee.) In instances where cams, cogs, and other movable parts are missing or have been damaged, we suggest the services of a toy restoration specialist. The best advice is to avoid attempting any of these delicate operations yourself.

BUYING AND SELLING AT AUCTION

In recent years, many leading toy collectors or their heirs have chosen to liquidate large collections at auction. In the past year alone, for example, such noted collections as those of Charles W. Gasque, Dr. Clinton B. Seeley (a noted toy authority who wrote under the pen name, C.B.C. Lee), and Dr. Ralph Merkle (one of the founders of the Antique Toy Collectors of America), as well as the train collection of Paul Bidonde and, of course, Part I of the Atlanta Toy Museum collection, all went on the block.

Toy auctions, particularly such spectaculars as the Atlanta Toy Museum sale in Philadelphia in October of 1986, are the next closest thing to the Circus Maximus of the Holy Roman Empire. Over 650 avid collectors were in attendance and the bidding marathons were not for the faint of heart. We've talked to many toy enthusiasts who swear (at least until the next one comes along) they'll never again attend another auction. In the case of the ATM sale, where there were any number of uncommon quality entries, the prices often doubled, even tripled, pre-sale estimates. This does not mean that there are no longer buys to be had at auction. At the recent Dr. Ralph Merkle Auction in Allentown, Pennsylvania, for example, we noted that any number of fine examples of early cast-iron motortoys were sold quite reasonably. One dealer remarked, rather ruefully a few days later, that he'd bypassed the sale because he felt sure all the "high rollers" would be there, since the Allentown Toy Show and Sale was scheduled the following day.

In a December 1985 article in *Collectors' Showcase*, toy enthusiast Dave Bausch tells of picking up a Maerklin gooseneck sleigh from the turn of the century for only $90. Granted, the auctioneer was not known for specializing in toys, and, by a stroke of luck, Bausch's competitors happened to be out of town at the time, but here was a find that was worth about $8,000! So take heart and keep your eyes peeled for auction listings—no matter how obscure the gallery's reputation or how remote the site, treasures are still to be found at auction.

In buying at auction, the following suggestions may prove helpful:

Always get to the preview as early as possible so that you can give any entries of interest a thorough inspection, without being rushed or distracted by the crowd. If you have any questions regarding condition or provenance, or wish to have the item put up at a certain time (providing it is not a cataloged sale), you will have time to discuss it with the auction manager.

Be sure to find a seat or a place to stand where you can be readily spotted by the auctioneer. Make positive bidding motions. Some bidders we know go through all manner of method-acting machinations, such as eye twitchings, shoulder tics, and head scratchings, to indicate a bid (as if to disguise their identity from others while bidding). What generally happens is that the auctioneer is the one who misses your bid and you may be "out" a very desirable toy.

Try to contain your excitement by taking a few deep breaths between bids and don't raise your own bid. Most auctioneers are charitable about this, but we do know of a few who will have you up there well beyond what you should be paying. If you are not certain who has the high bid, don't be shy about asking the auctioneer.

This advice is easier to give than to follow, but decide *beforehand* the very maximum you'd be willing to pay, and hold to it.

Above all, don't be intimidated by any bidding "pool" that may be working in the audience. Remember, those involved in the pool are usually dealers who still have to hold their little "side auction" and be able to resell the item at a profit. As long as they are in there bidding with you, in all probability the toy remains within the realm of reason.

The consignor's role in an auction is often clouded in mystique and most auction goers find it more complex to comprehend than the buyer's role. Usually this is because the seller is the silent partner in the auction process. Once the would-be seller has consigned his property to the auction house, his participation ends. Unless a single item is of significant value, an auction house usually elects not to accept one item, preferring, of course, sizeable lots of items. The latter balances things out; an item might go disappointingly low, but the law of averages dictates that other items will correspondingly top off beyond expectations.

Auction houses charge varying rates to consignors and for different services, including transportation, insurance, photography, advertising, and repairs. There is also a seller's commission to be exacted. Rates vary from house to house, according to how the contract is negotiated. You pay the house a 10-21% fee, depending upon whether there is a buyer's premium. There have been, of course, auction houses who have accepted extremely coveted properties without charging a seller's fee.

Before choosing an auction house, it pays to check out their commission arrangement thoroughly. Also, most houses assume complete responsibility as to how the consignments are described in the catalog or advertisements. Be certain to touch bases with your auction house to make sure that the item will accurately be described. Resolve any differences before committing yourself to anything.

To protect your investment, you may also want to discuss selling your consignment subject to reserve. This price is usually determined by the seller and ranges from 50-80% of the low estimate. On items of higher value, the reserve is usually mid-range between the low and high estimate. If, perchance your consignment fails to meet reserves, you still may be money-out-of-pocket. At many big auction houses, the contract stipulates that the consignor authorize the house to act as exclusive agent for 60 days following the auction to sell the property privately for the previously agreed reserve price.

Consignors can expect to be paid, minus seller's commission and set fees, as soon as the buyers have paid *them*. Usually this is 35 days after the gavel falls.

This may sound like an awful headache, considering the negotiating that is required, but there are those who swear by selling at auction as the best way to get their maximum return on investment.

HOUSING YOUR COLLECTION

When one talks about a toy "finding a home," there is more truth there than figure of speech, as these little remembrances from the past assume a very intensely personal meaning. There is nothing atypical about toy collectors, and how their collections should be housed and displayed depends entirely on each individual and the limits of his or her taste, personality, and imagination or creative flair.

We know of individuals who, as compulsive accumulators, stash away toys willy-nilly, as if they were preparing for the great flood or some revolution and hope that the toys may be used as some sort of barter. On the opposite end of the spectrum is the enthusiast who transforms his home into a museum or shrine. To further carry this to extremes, there are individuals who become so obsessed with toys that they have long since lost touch with the real world and have become veritable recluses.

Our middle-of-the-road credo is that toys, trains, dolls, and games were all created not only for the obvious purpose of being played with, but to excite the eye and stir the soul. They were meant to be studied and admired as prized remnants, not to be hidden away in some safety deposit box, bank vault, or secluded niche.

This does not infer that there shouldn't be certain restraints. There are inherent dangers in toys and other artifacts being exposed on a continuing basis to excessive handling, dust, humidity, and direct sunlight. To avoid extended exposure to these elements, many collectors wisely rotate their collection, thus keeping the balance of their toys carefully packed away and protected. A preference among many collectors is for glass-enclosed cases, and a special effort is made to find display cases from old country stores or dry goods emporiums that are in keeping with the period of their toys. Other types of display cases are available through museum supply houses and hobby stores. You'll find them in the *Yellow Pages* as well as in many leading toy trade publications.

Comparative deterioration is particularly high with 19th-century toys, with ultraviolet rays posing a major menace. Fluorescent

57

lights afford less possibility of fading favorite objects, but purists argue that this type of lighting distorts colors and tones, making it difficult to distinguish variations. Low wattage, incandescent mini-shelf lights, arranged in tandem, are a suitable compromise and show off the artifacts to great advantage.

Lithographed paper-on-wood toys and games, in particular, are highly susceptible to moisture and other elements, including silver-fish and other pests who seem addicted to the glue or paste used as binding agents. They can quickly reduce a prized possession to confetti. Although quite expensive, special custom-made shadow boxes and frames are currently available in which air is forced out, creating a vacuum in which to encapsulate the toy or game—assurance that it will be preserved for posterity.

TOY GLOSSARY

Animated toys: Any plaything that simulates lifelike movements, whether powered or activated by spring, string, flywheel, rubber-band, gravity, controlled movement of sand, gyroscopic mechanism, steam, electricity or batteries.

Automata: Plural of automat; refers to figures that are relatively self-operating and capable of performing multiple complex movements. Early examples featured doll-like bodies with composition or bisque heads. Modern day robot toys are the latest rage in automata.

Balance toys: Earliest European example was 16th-century Grench, although most widely known in the Orient. Swinging weight is usually above or below toy. Many popular papier-mache roly-poly toys circa 1900 were counterweighted with pebbles or buckshot.

Balance wheel: Most often seen on horse-drawn vehicles, it is a small rotating or stationary wheel that is normally attached to a front hoof or a shaft suspended between two horses, which cascs passage across the floor.

Carpet runners: Transport or other moving toys used out of their proper medium (i.e., tin or cast-iron trains with smooth rims, rather than grooved wheels, that did not run on tracks but were usually hand-propelled).

Cast-iron toys: Made of molten gray high-carbon iron, hand-poured into sandcasting molds; usually cast in halves, then mated and bolted or riveted as one. More elaborate versions incorporated interlocking, nickel-plated grills, chassis, bumpers, people, and other accessories.

Clockwork mechanism: Made of machined brass and steel; used to animate toys for as long as 30 minutes as interlocking gears move as spring uncoils. Produced as drive system for toys by clockmakers beginning in 1862 and ending about 30 years later in the Northeastern United States, Connecticut in particular.

Composition toys: Material may be wood or paper pulp, sawdust and glue, molded into various shapes and painted.

Die-casting: Method of mass-producing under great pressure molten zinc and white-metal alloys into permanent molds. Sharp clean detail can be achieved. Die-cast toys were very inexpensive and generally found in the five-and-dime emporiums.

D.R.G.M.: Often mistaken for a manufacturer's mark, the initials stand for Deutsches Reichs Gebrauchmuster (translation: in-use model).

Dribbler: Nickname for British solid brass steam-powered toy locomotives made from the 1840s to the turn of the century; so called because they were known to leave trail of water deposited from steam cylinder.

Drive wheel: Attached to piston rod that transmits energy from power source, as on toy locomotives.

Elastolin: A type of composition material from Germany, molded around wire supports, which has questionable survival rate.

Flats: Two-dimensional lead soldiers with engraved decorations.

Floor runner: See Carpet-runners.

Friction wheel: A central inertia wheel, also known as a flywheel, that is activated by spring in rear wheels to set toy in motion. American toys utilized a cast-iron friction wheel; Europeans used cast lead. Friction toys were popular from 1900 to the early 1930s.

Grazing: Aging lines that run through paint on vintage toys, akin to the "crows-feet" their owners get in advanced years.

Hollow cast: Also known as a slush cast, whereby molten lead alloy is poured into mold, which is then inverted, leaving a thin layer of cooling metal adhering to its surface. Pot metal toys, as they are commonly called, tend to have less definition and are more fragile than die-cast toys.

Japanning: A decorative technique that includes several layers of paint finished with a coat of lacquer; commonly applied on early American and European tin. In France, a cheaper "dyeing" method was used; a varnish paint mix was burned on in alcohol, then baked, achieving a thin hard translucence.

Lithographed tin: The process was introduced to toys in the 1880s whereby various colors and detail were printed on flat sheets of metal by a lithographic press; the toys were subsequently formed by tools and dies.

Married parts: Mating of two parts of a toy that did not originally belong together, down-scaling it in desirability.

Patent date: If the patent number appears on the toy or on the box it came in, one can get a good approximation of the year any U.S. toy from 1860 to date was manufactured. German toys produced after 1890 usually bear patent dates.

Sheet metal: A toy material that is rolled into a thin plate made of brass, copper, and, in the case of most toys, steel; first toy usage in the United States dates back to 1895.

Solids: Three-dimensional figures, usually refers to lead soldiers.

Spring-driven: Stamped tinplate gears activate by a spring uncoiling on what are popularly known as toy wind-ups. Actually, they wind down after two to three minutes. Usually a key does the rewinding; in the case of Kingsbury, a flanged cover on a patented, sealed round housing must be turned; a lever activates certain spring-driven toy banks. Tin wind-ups date back to the 1890s.

Still bank: Not a bank that's quiet; the term merely differentiates between mechanical banks and banks with no moving parts.

Tab-and-slot: Applied to tin toys wherein two parts are mated and small flaps on one half are inserted into corresponding narrow slots of the other half, then bent to secure the connection.

AIRCRAFT

Any number of toy makers capitalized on the inaugural flight of the Wright brothers in 1903 by introducing very fanciful replications of the primitive kitelike flying machine. Unfortunately, there were prolonged lapses extending through World War I and the late 1920s when the marvelous early flyers were never immortalized in tin, wood or cast iron. (Obvious exceptions were the dirigibles or zeppelins, including the famed Los Angeles and the Graf Zeppelin.) The reasons for this lack of imagination or marketing acumen are obscure. Perhaps it was due to the early incursion of scale model aircraft kits, an entity in itself whereby the great aircraft of the world were recreated to a "T." Lindbergh's solo trans-Atlantic flight finally awakened U.S. toy makers, as did the pioneering flights of Rear Admiral Richard Byrd, Amelia Earhart, Wiley Post, Billy Mitchell, and others. Lindbergh's "Spirit of St. Louis" was copied to a fare-thee-well. What is generally available from U.S. makers are cast-iron or tin mutations that appear to be so clumsy as to be incapable of actual flight. By far, the most imaginative and whimsical aircraft toys emanate from continental Europe, where Maerklin, Bing, Carette, and Jepp, and others produced truly representative, handsomely enameled, clockwork-powered flying machines.

FIXED WING

	Price Range	
☐ **Air Devil,** F. Strauss, 1927, blunt-nosed lithographed tin mechanical, stands on nose, spins, then rights self, 8¼" length	150.00	200.00
☐ **Airplane and Hangar,** Cardini, 1915, lithographed tin bi-plane mounted on support rods flying atop hangar with lead-weight world globe as counterbalance, bi-wing, 8½" length	1000.00	1100.00
☐ **Amphibian Plane,** Chein, 1930s, lithographed tin mechanical, 7¾" length	50.00	100.00
☐ **Army Bomber,** Boycraft, 1929, bi-wing, pressed steel, 24½" length	400.00	500.00

62

Few captured the glory of the early days of aviation than did the German firm of Gebruder Maerklin. These superbly enameled clockwork toys, c. 1915–20, all rank in the rare echelons of toy collecting.

	Price Range	
☐ **Army Bomber Tri-Motor,** Marx, 1935, lithographed tin with rachet noise maker, 25½″ length	200.00	250.00
☐ **Bi–plane,** Kingsbury, 1920s, sheet-steel mechanical, rubber tires, yellow fuselage with red wings, pilot is cast iron, called "The Taxiplane", 16″ length.	300.00	400.00
☐ **Bi-plane,** maker unknown, patented 1921, sheet steel, handpainted friction toy, 16″ length	250.00	300.00
☐ **Bi-wing,** Girard Mfg., 1920s, lithographed tin mechanical, Air Force insignia on wings, 9½″ length	250.00	300.00
☐ **Bleiriot Monoplane,** Gunthermann, 1910, lithographed tin clockwork, 10″ length, 9″ wingspan	900.00	1000.00
☐ **Boeing Strato Cruiser,** Japan, 1960s, lithographed tin, friction, 16″ length	150.00	200.00
☐ **Cabin Plane,** maker unknown, 1920s, lithographed tin, 18″ length	300.00	350.00
☐ **China Clipper,** Wyandotte, 1940s, painted pressed steel	75.00	100.00

Price Range

☐ **C-R-S Monoplane,** maker unknown, 1920s, has French tri-color on tail section, 15½″ length 250.00   300.00

☐ **Dare-Devil Flyer,** Marx, 1930, lithographed tin monoplane and dirigible at opposite ends of rod spins atop Empire State Building 450.00   500.00

☐ **Empire Express Monoplane,** maker unknown, pressed-steel friction, 19″ length .. 125.00   150.00

☐ **Fighter Plane,** Marx, 1940s, lithographed tin mechanical, pair of machine guns shoot sparks from each wing, 7″ length 50.00   60.00

☐ **Four-Engine Bomber,** Marx, 1940s, lithographed tin mechanical, 13″ length 50.00   75.00

☐ **French Monoplane #250,** Jepp, France, 1920s, lithographed tin mechanical, two passengers in open cockpit, 7⅝″ length 250.00   300.00

☐ **High-Wing Monoplane,** Boycraft, 1929, pressed steel, motor noise rachet, 21½″ and 23½″ lengths 250.00   300.00

☐ **International Airline Tri-Motor,** Marx, 1931, lithographed tin, 17½″ wingspan 200.00   250.00

☐ **Loopover Monoplane,** Marx, 1947, lithographed tin, 6″ wingspan 75.00   100.00

☐ **Monoplane,** French, 1910, lithographed tin mechanical, pilot in open cockpit, high landing gear, 6″ length 200.00   250.00

☐ **Monoplane,** Kingsbury, 1925, lithographed mechanical, 12″ length 250.00   300.00

☐ **Parachute Plane,** maker unknown, 1929, lithographed mechanical, 15¾″ length 150.00   200.00

☐ **Rollover Monoplane,** Air Force, Marx, 1930s, 6″ wingspan 50.00   75.00

☐ **Single-Engine Monoplane,** Tipp and Co., circa 1936, Bears No. 1416, dark blue, purple and yellow with black stripes and red prop, 12½″ wingspan 150.00   200.00

Price Range

☐ **Sky Bird Flyer,** Marx, 1930s, lithographed tin, variation of Dare-Devil Flyer except that it spins atop lighthouse, 8½" height .. 150.00 200.00

☐ **"Spirit of America,"** American Flyer, 1928, lithographed tin pull toy, friction, 20" length 450.00 500.00

☐ **"Spirit of Columbia,"** American Flyer, 1928, lithographed tin, friction, 18½" length 200.00 300.00

☐ **Transport,** Boycraft, 1932, tri-Motor, all three props spin, rubber tires, 23½" length 350.00 400.00

☐ **Tri-Motor,** Boycraft, 1931, nickel-plated steel, three props, one stable, two spinning, cabin door opens, 21" and 23" lengths 350.00 400.00

☐ **Tri-Motor,** Steelcraft, 1930s, painted pressed steel, 18" length 250.00 300.00

☐ **Tri-Motor Monoplane,** Kingsbury, circa 1920s, 15" length 350.00 400.00

☐ **TWA, Twin Engine Transport,** Marx, 1940s, lithographed tin mechanical double tail, 13" length 50.00 75.00

☐ **TWA 727,** Japanese, 1960s, lithographed tin friction, 17½" length 50.00 75.00

☐ **U.S. Air Force Voodoo,** Japanese, 1970s, lithographed tin friction 75.00 100.00

☐ **U.S. Mail Plane,** Steelcraft, 1930s, painted pressed steel, battery-operated lights, 21" length 75.00 100.00

☐ **U.S. Marines Monoplane,** #59, Marx, 1935, rachet noise maker, lithographed tin, 25½" length 200.00 250.00

☐ **Wright Bros. Aircraft,** Muller & Kadeder, 1909, painted tin with three props, string toy, flies in circles
  6" length 600.00 700.00
  8¾" length 700.00 800.00

CAST IRON

Price Range

☐ **Air Express,** Dent, 1920s tri-Motor, bright colors with red and gilt trim, nickel-plated props and gear, this model also available in cast aluminum 250.00   300.00

☐ **"Air Force,"** maker unknown, 1930, red, blue and aluminum colors, 6¼″ length 75.00   100.00

☐ **Air Force UX166,** maker unknown, 1930, red, blue and aluminum, 6¼″ length 75.00   100.00

☐ **Air Ford,** maker unknown, 1929, green with gilt trim, nickeled prop and wheels, 4″ length 75.00   100.00

☐ **"Air Line,"** Dent, circa 1920, cast iron, also in bright colors with nickeled trim, two sizes: 10¾″ and 12½″ wingspan 150.00   200.00

☐ **"America,"** maker unknown, 1930, cast iron, triple engines, balloon rubber tires, two passengers, rachet attachment, wire spring drive, pull cord, "America" appears on wing, 14″ length 250.00   300.00

☐ **Army Plane,** Champion, circa 1930, nickel-plated fuselage, red, blue or silver wings, air-cushion rubber tires 50.00   75.00

☐ **"Bremen,"** Hubley, 1933, floor runner, prop moves when wheels move, imitation exhaust, 10⅛″ length 200.00   250.00

☐ **"Bremen,"** maker unknown, 1929, green with gilt trim, nickel assessories, three aluminum-finish passengers, "Bremen" appears on fuselage, 7¼″ length 150.00   200.00

☐ **Cabin Monoplane,** Arcade, 1932, black body with orange wheels, nickel wheels, prop and running gear, 7½″ length 150.00   200.00

☐ **Ciro-Plane,** Hubley, 1936, assorted colors, 4½″ length 125.00   150.00

Ford Tri-Motor, Dent, 1920s. Corrugated cast iron, rubber wheels, $250–$350.

	Price Range	
☐ **"Dornier" or DOX Plane,** Hubley, 1936, painted aluminum with red wings, four sizes: 3¾", 4¾", 6", and 7¾" length	125.00	150.00
☐ **Ford Cabin Plane,** Dent, 1920s, corrugated wing and body, triple nickel-plated engines and polished steel props, two sizes: 9⅝" and 12" length	200.00	350.00
☐ **Ford Tri-motor,** Dent, 1920s, corrugated cast-iron finish, silver painted, "Ford" embossed on tail section rudder, approx. 9½" length	300.00	350.00
☐ **"Friendship,"** maker unknown, 1930, amphibian, triple engines, rachets, spring steel drive, "Friendship" on wings, 11¼" length	200.00	250.00
☐ **"Lindy,"** Hubley, 1928, 11¼" length, also with slight variations in 9½" size	200.00	300.00
☐ **"Lindy,"** maker unknown, 1929, cast aluminum, red trim, nickel accessories, 4½" length	75.00	100.00
☐ **"Lindy" Glider,** Hubley, 1933, pull toy, rider detaches, rachet motor, 10" length ..	200.00	300.00

Price Range

☐ **Lockheed Sirius,** Hubley, 1933, two passengers in open cockpit, rubber tires, 8½" length 250.00   300.00

☐ **"Lone Eagle,"** American Flyer, lithographed tin mechanical, brass fittings, adjustable rudder, 21½" length 250.00   300.00

☐ **"Lucky Boy,"** Dent, 1920s, high-wing monoplane, bright colors, available in five sizes, also in cast aluminum as well as cast iron 50.00   150.00

☐ **Mail Plane,** Keystone, 1929, pressed steel, green and red fuselage, rubber tires, cabin door opens, leather mail bags, pull toy 250.00   300.00

☐ **Monocoupe,** Arcade, 1928, cast iron, four sizes: 4", 5", 6", and 7" lengths 100.00   150.00

☐ **Single-Engine Closed Cockpit,** Hubley, 1938, assorted colors with nickel-plated wings, 3½" and 4½" lengths 75.00   100.00

☐ **Single-Engine Monoplane,** Kilgore, 1930, 4¼" length 75.00   100.00

☐ **Tri-Motor,** Arcade, 1932, cast iron with nickeled wheels and props, assorted colors, 3¾" length 75.00   125.00

☐ **Tri-Motor T.A.T.,** maker unknown, two-tone red, blue, ivory, orange, and lavender, 11" length 100.00   150.00

☐ **Twin-Engine Cabin Model,** Hubley, 1938, assorted colors, 4½" length 75.00   100.00

☐ **United Boeing,** Arcade, 1937, green finish, 3⅝" length 100.00   125.00

PRESSED STEEL

☐ **Hi-Wing Monoplane,** Keystone, 1929, 8-cylinder motor rachet attachment, red and olive drab finish, rubber tires, 25" length, 24" wingspan 250.00   300.00

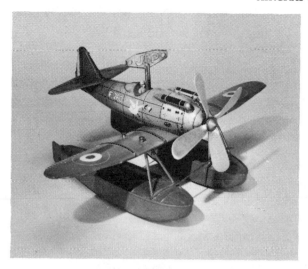

Tin clockwork seaplane "F-260," by Jep, French, c. 1935; with pilot, twin engines, propeller and two pontoons, 19" wingspan, $2000 plus. (Photo courtesy of Sotheby's, New York.)

	Price Range	
☐ **Tri-Motor,** Keystone, 1933, pistons in engines move up and down making clicking noise, leather mail bags, swinging doors on each side, 25" length	250.00	300.00

TIN

☐ **Airship,** maker unknown, 1922, tin mechanical covered with light canvas, bi-wing, pilot in open cockpit	75.00	100.00
☐ **R.A.F. Monoplane,** Britains, 1940s, lithographed tin, 8" length	1000.00	1200.00

ZEPPELINS AND HOT AIR BALLOONS

☐ **Airship,** German, 1910, painted tin, double-blade celluloid propellors, two passenger baskets, string wind-up, 10½" length	250.00	300.00

Price Range

☐ **"Akron,"** maker unknown, lithographed tin, all white 250.00   300.00

☐ **"Akron" Zeppelin,** Champion, circa 1930, balloon rubber tires, lithographed tin 150.00   200.00

☐ **Dirigible With Umbrella Parachute,** maker unknown, 1910, painted tin, side propellors, openwork basket, string toy, when balloon rises to top of string parachute is released by automatic lever, 10″ length 350.00   400.00

☐ **Floor Zeppelin,** Marx, 1930, lithographed tin mechanical, aluminum finish, flies in circles when suspended in air, 9½″ length   100.00   150.00

☐ **Flying Zeppelin,** F. Strauss, 1929, aluminum and brass 250.00   300.00

☐ **Glass Zeppelin,** maker unknown, 1920s, crocheted stocking over glass tube, hanging basket, 24″ length 300.00   350.00

☐ **"Graf Zeppelin,"** maker unknown, 1920, lithographed tin, 8″ length 100.00   150.00

☐ **"Graf Zeppelin,"** maker unknown, 1932, lithographed tin mechanical 150.00   200.00

☐ **"Graf Zeppelin,"** maker unknown, 1935, lithographed tin mechanical, dull silver finish, double-disc wheels, 30½″ length 100.00   150.00

☐ **Hot Air Balloon,** German, early 1900s, handpainted tin string toy, 8″ height 350.00   400.00

☐ **Lehmann Zeppelin** (see Lehmann listing)

☐ **"Los Angeles" Zeppelin,** Dent Hardware, 1920s, cast iron with nickel-plated wheels, 12⅝″, 10¾″, and 8¾″ lengths in various colors, Dent also produced these sizes in cast aluminum 150.00   350.00

☐ **Metalcraft Zeppelin Construction Kit,** Metalcraft, 1920s, sheet steel 200.00   250.00

☐ **Monoplane,** Girard Mfg., 1920s, painted tin mechanical, 12½″ length 150.00   200.00

Price Range

☐ **"New York" Zeppelin,** F. Strauss, 1920s, lithographed tin with celluloid propellors, 9″ length 200.00   250.00

☐ **"Trans Atlantic,"** F. Strauss, 1920s, lithographed tin, 9″ length 200.00   250.00

☐ **Zeppelin,** Muller & Kadeder, 1909, painted tin with two gondolas, side and front props, replica of first zeppelin, 9¼″ length, also available in 12½″ and 5½″ lengths 350.00   450.00

☐ **Zeppelin,** Boycraft, 1929, lithographed steel with spinning propellors, 28″ length 300.00   350.00

☐ **Zeppelin,** Boycraft, 1931, "Graf Zeppelin," pressed steel, aluminum finish, 27¼″ length, also available in 30″ length 250.00   300.00

☐ **Zeppelin Kit,** A.C. Gilbert, 1929, erector set builds zeppelin and other models, 53″ length assembled (Erector Set #8) 400.00   500.00

☐ **Zeppelin Roundabout,** Muller & Kadeder, 1910, four models on carousel, painted tin mechanical, 13″ height 2000.00   2500.00

☐ **Zeppelin-Tipp,** German, 1920s, "Graf Zeppelin," lithographed mechanical, 24″ length 600.00   650.00

BANKS

Jerome B. Secor, of Bridgeport, CT, a sewing machine manufacturer, produced but one mechanical bank, and it proved to be the most coveted mechanical of all time, the Freedman bank, 1878–1883. One of the hobby's foremost collectors, the late Andrew Emerine, is said to have acquired his Freedman bank from a Mexico City librarian who had read his advertisement in quest of mechanicals. The asking price (read it and weep) at the time was $11.

BANKS—MECHANICAL

Mechanical banks date back as early as 1793 in the United States, but full-scale production of banks with intricate, highly complex coin-activated mechanisms had their inception in the 1870s and extended to the end of World War I. Actually, mechanical banks are still being produced today in limited editions. Leading makers include J. & E. Stevens, W.J. Shepard, Kyser & Rex, and J. Hall. Oddly enough, Ives produced only a few mechanicals, The Boy and Bulldog bank being an obvious exception. John Harper

Three popular favorites among mechanical banks: Darktown Battery, J.H. Bowen, 1888, $400–$600; Bad Accident, J. & E. Stevens, 1890s, $500–$700; Girl Skipping Rope, J. & E. Stevens, 1890, $2000 plus.

Ltd. was the leading toy bank maker from Great Britain. German and French toy makers stuck to their tin and never entered the cast-iron mechanical bank arena. Mechanical banks are coveted by an ever-widening circle of enthusiasts, attributable to cleverness of animation as well as being almost exclusively American phenomena.

Mechanical Banks Inner Circle

The following is a list of the 10 most elite banks as nominated by a consensus of collectors:

Bowling Alley, Kyser & Rex, 1879
Breadwinners, J. & E. Stevens, circa 1880s
Bureau, J. Serrell, 1869
Darky Fisherman, Shephard Hardware, 1891

Fowler, J. & E. Stevens, 1892
Freedman's, Jerome Secor, 1880
Frog in Den (Toy Toad), Jas. Fallows, 1871
Girl Skipping Rope, J. & E. Stevens, 1890
Jonah and Whale on Pedestal, J. & E. Stevens, 1890
Red Riding Hood, origin unknown, 1880s

Honorable Mention: Bulldog Savings, Race Course, Leapfrog, Girl in Victorian Chair, Calamity, Bismark, Shoot-the-Chute, Weeden's Plantation, J. Hall's Yankee Notion, The Camera, Turtle, Lion Hunter, Frog on Arched Track, Moonface.

Note: Numbers in parentheses indicate reference to catalog number in *Handbook of Old Mechanical Banks* by John D. Meyer.

	Price Range	
☐ **Acrobats,** E. L. Morris and J. & E. Stevens, 1883, 5″ height × 7¼″ length (1) ...	1500.00	2000.00
☐ **Always Did Spise a Mule,** J. H. Bowen, 1897, 6½″ height (4)	400.00	450.00★
☐ **Artillery (Cannon Bank),** C. A. Bailey, 1898 (37)	350.00	550.00
☐ **Atlas,** world on top of Atlas spins when penny is inserted	300.00	400.00
☐ **Bad Accident,** J. & E. Stevens, circa 1890, black man on two-wheeled cart pulled by donkey, 6″ height	200.00	300.00
☐ **Bill-E-Grin (Clown),** J. W. Schmitt, 1915, 4¾″ height (15)	200.00	300.00
☐ **Bird on Roof,** E. Stevens, 1878 (16)	750.00	800.00
☐ **Bismark,** J. & E. Stevens, 1880s, count's head pops out of pig, 5″ height	2000.00 plus	
☐ **Blacksmith at Anvil,** John Deere, 1950	50.00	75.00
☐ **Bowling Alley,** Kyser & Rex, 1879, 5¾″ height (17)	2000.00 plus	
☐ **Boy and Bulldog,** Ives, Blakeslee & Co., patented by Enoch Morrison, 1878, clockwork mechanism, one of few banks by Ives, 7½″ height	2000.00	2500.00

★Sold for $1,100.00 at Atlanta Museum Toy Auction, October 1986.

Price Range

☐ **Boy Robbing Bird's Nest,** Charles Bailey (Stevens), circa 1906, 8″ height 1400.00 1600.00

☐ **Boy Scout Camp,** Charles Bailey, patented by J. & E. Stevens, 1917, scout raises flag when coin drops, 4¾″ height 800.00 1000.00

☐ **Boy Stealing Watermelon** 650.00 850.00

☐ **Boy on Trapeze,** J. Barton Smith, Philadelphia, 1880s 550.00 750.00

☐ **Breadwinners,** J. & E. Stevens, circa 1880s, political propaganda, labor vs. capitalism .. 2000.00 plus

☐ **Bucking Goat** 300.00 400.00

☐ **Bull and Bear,** maker unknown, 1890s 1000.00 1200.00

☐ **Bulldog,** E. R. Morrison, 1878, 5⅝″ height 400.00 500.00

☐ **Bulldog** (seated), J. & E. Stevens, 1880 .... 450.00 550.00

☐ **Bureau,** picture pops up 3000.00 4000.00

☐ **Bureau,** J. Serrell, 1869 .... 1500.00 2000.00

☐ **Butting Buffalo,** A.C. Rex, 1888 .... 900.00 1100.00

☐ **Cabin,** J. & E. Stevens, 1890, 4″ length .. 200.00 300.00

☐ **Calamity,** J. H. Bowen, 1905, original sold as Football bank .... 2000.00 plus

☐ **Camera,** Wrightsville Hardware, Mt. Joy, Pennsylvania, circa 1890 .... 1400.00 1600.00

☐ **Cat and Dog (Organ),** Kyser & Rex, 1882 (177) 400.00 500.00

☐ **Chimpanzee,** Kyser & Rex, 1880 (43) 450.00 500.00

☐ **Circus Ticket Collector,** William C. Bull, circa 1892, semimechanical 1000.00 1200.00

☐ **Clock,** Kingsbury, circa 1900, 7″ height .. 350.00 450.00

☐ **Clown on Bar,** G. H. Bush & Co., Providence, Rhode Island .... 2000.00 plus

☐ **Clown on Globe,** J. & E. Stevens, 1890, patented by Jas. Bowen, two distinct sets of movements, identical mechanism to Girl Skipping Rope 1000.00 1200.00

Price Range

☐ **Clown Harlequin and Columbine,** J. & E. Stevens, 1877, patented by J. Blanc, Columbine is twirled around by clown (119) ..   2000.00 plus

☐ **Confectionary Store,** R. M. Hunter, 1881 (51) ....   2000.00 plus

☐ **Creedmore,** J. H. Bowen, 1877, J. Secor (54) 300.00   400.00

☐ **Cupola,** J. & E. Stevens, 1874, patented by D. Dieckman, New York City, cupola raises, man moves back and forth exposing coin slot (27) 1500.00   2000.00

☐ **Darktown Battery,** J. H. Bowen, J. & E. Stevens, 1888, black pitcher, catcher, batsman, 7¼″ height 500.00   600.00

☐ **Darktown Battery,** J. H. Bowen, J. & E. Stevens, 1888, white pitcher, catcher, batsman, 7¼″ height 700.00   750.00

☐ **Dentist,** J. & E. Stevens, black's tooth is pulled by dentist, coin in dentist's pocket falls into gasbag receptacle, both figures lunge forward 1100.00   1300.00

☐ **Dinah,** English, John Harper Ltd., 1911, bust of black woman, cast metal 100.00   200.00

☐ **Dog Tray,** Kyser & Rex, 1880, weight of coin in dog's mouth tips him forward to deposit coin, crank on side, 5″ height (70) ...   300.00   400.00

☐ **Doll's Head,** semimechanical, doll appears to have hatched from egg, all white bank, bellows makes a baby sound when bank is opened 300.00   400.00

☐ **Eagle and Eaglets,** J. & E. Stevens, 1883, patented by C. M. Henn, 6″ height, 8″ length (75) 300.00   500.00

☐ **Elephant Baby,** D. Cooke patented, 1892 (77) ....   2000.00 plus

☐ **Elephant With Howdah,** C. F. Olm and J. Thalheim, 1901 (83) 350.00   400.00

Price Range

☐ **Elephant Three Stars,** C. A. Bailey, 1880 (78) 350.00   450.00

☐ **Fowler,** E. I. Pyle, J. & E. Stevens, 1892, (The Sportsman), hunter brings gun around and fires at bird (97) ....   2000.00 plus

☐ **Frog on Arched Track,** Jas. Fallows, 1871 ....   2000.00 plus

☐ **Frog in Den,** Jas. Fallows, 1871 ....   2000.00 plus

☐ **Frog on Lattice,** patented by R. Frisbie, 1872 ....   200.00   300.00

☐ **Frog on Rock** 150.00   250.00

☐ **Frogs,** J. & E. Stevens, 1882, patented by J. H. Bowen, 4¼″ height, 8¾″ length 500.00   600.00

☐ **Giant in Tower,** English, John Harper and Co., 1892 ....   2000.00 plus

☐ **Girl Skipping Rope,** patented by J. H. Bowen, J. & E. Stevens, 1890 ....   2000.00 plus

☐ **Girl in Victorian Chair,** maker unknown, 1880s, 4″ semimechanical, 4″ height ....   2000.00 plus

☐ **Goat, Frog and Old Man,** patented by Geo. Eddy, 1880 ....   1500.00 plus

☐ **Grenadier,** English, circa 1890 ....   250.00   300.00

☐ **Guessing,** patented by E. M. McLoughlin, 1877, man sits atop round mechanism with dial (117) 2000.00   2500.00

☐ **Hall's Excelsior,** J. Hall, 1869 (118) 150.00   250.00

☐ **Hall's Yankee Notion,** J. Hall, 1875 ....   1200.00   1500.00

☐ **Hindu,** Kyser & Rex, 1882, Hindu with turban, swallows coin and rolls eyes (122)   450.00   500.00

☐ **Hoop-La,** John Harper, English, 1897, clown holds hoop and dog prepares to leap through 300.00   400.00

☐ **Horse Race,** J. & E. Stevens, patented by John Hall, 1871, 4¾″ height 1500.00   2000.00

Price Range

☐ **Humpty Dumpty (Clown),** patented by P. Adams, Chas. Shephard, name inspired by G. W. Fox, 19th-century pantomimist, not nursery rhyme character, 7″ height 500.00 600.00

☐ **Indian Shooting Bear** 200.00 300.00

☐ **Initiation—First Degree,** Mechanical Novelty Works, patented by Geo. Eddy, 1880, goat butts black in backside, depositing coin in frog's mouth (130) 2000.00 3000.00

☐ **Jonah and Whale,** Shephard, 1890, patented by P. Adams, Jonah is in boat ready to be swallowed, coin placed on Jonah's tray, whale opens mouth to receive it, 10½″ length, 4¾″ height (138) 400.00 500.00

☐ **Jonah and Whale,** Shephard, a rarer version with pedestal, Jonah emerges from whale's mouth, 3″ height .... 2000.00 plus

☐ **Jumbo the Elephant** 350.00 400.00

☐ **Kiltie,** John Harper Ltd., English, 1931 ... 700.00 800.00

☐ **Leap Frog** 550.00 650.00

☐ **Lion Hunter,** C. A. Bailey, 1911 (148) 1500.00 2000.00

☐ **Little Jocko,** Strauss Mfg., New York, 1912, tin musical bank 900.00 1100.00

☐ **Little Joe High-Hat** 100.00 200.00

☐ **Magician,** patented by W. C. Bull, Philadelphia, J. & E. Stevens, 1901, coin disappears when hat is placed over it (154) 400.00 500.00

☐ **Mama Katzenjammer** (see listing under "Comic and Character Toys") Kenton Hardware, circa 1900 .... 1400.00 1600.00

☐ **Mammy Feeding Baby,** A. C. Rex, 1884 (155) 300.00 400.00

☐ **Mason and Hod Carrier,** C. G. Shephard, 1887, bricklayer with hod-carrying helper (156) 1200.00 1500.00

	Price Range	
☐ **Merry-Go-Round,** Kyser & Rex, 1880s, semimechanical, 5¾" height, ...	250.00	350.00
☐ **Mikado-Moonface,** 1886	2000.00 plus	
☐ **Milking Cow,** J. & E. Stevens, 1880, cow kicks boy milker	1200.00	1400.00
☐ **Monkey and Coconut,** J. & E. Stevens, 1886, Jas. Bowen patented, monkey's left hand lifts top of coconut to receive coin (163)	700.00	900.00
☐ **Monkey With Organ Grinder,** Hubley, 1920–1940, 8⅞" height	200.00	250.00*
☐ **Motor Bank,** Alfred Rex, Philadelphia, 1889, Trolley Motor Car (228)	2000.00 plus	
☐ **Mule Entering Barn,** J. & E. Stevens, 1880, patented by Edw. Morris, 8½" length (169)	400.00	500.00
☐ **North Pole,** patented by Charles Bailey, J. & E. Stevens, 1910 (177)	1500.00	2000.00
☐ **Old Woman Who Lives in Shoe,** W. S. Reed, 1883	2000.00 plus	
☐ **Organ Bank,** Kyser & Rex, 1881, 6" height	200.00	250.00
☐ **Organ Grinder and Dancing Bear**	1500.00	2000.00
☐ **Owl,** turns head, J. H. Bowen, 1880, 7½" height (182)	100.00	200.00*
☐ **Paddy and the Pig**	500.00	700.00
☐ **Panorama**	1200.00	1500.00
☐ **Patronize the Blind Man,** H. H. Loetz, Chicago, 1878	1500.00	2000.00
☐ **Peg-Leg Begger**	1000.00	1200.00
☐ **Picture Gallery,** C. G. Shephard, circa 1885	2000.00 plus	
☐ **Pig in High Chair,** P. Adams, 1897 (194)	400.00	500.00

*Sold for $475.00 at Atlanta Toy Museum Auction, October 1986.
*Sold for $350.00 at Atlanta Toy Museum Auction, October 1986.

	Price Range	
☐ **Pineapple,** patented by Thomas Enswiley, 1960, limited edition of 500 commemorating Hawaii statehood	150.00	200.00
☐ **Professor Pug Frog's Great Bicycle Feat,** J. & E. Stevens, 7½" height	1450.00	1650.00
☐ **Punch and Judy,** C. G. Shephard, circa 1884, 6¾" height (203)	500.00	600.00
☐ **Reclining Chinaman,** Jas. Bowen, 1882 ...	1500.00	2000.00
☐ **Red Riding Hood,** manufacturer unknown, 1880s		2000.00 plus
☐ **Rooster,** Kilgore, circa 1900s, 6" height ..	250.00	300.00
☐ **Santa Claus at Chimney,** J. & E. Stevens, 1889, 6" height, 4" width (214)	700.00	800.00
☐ **Schley Bottle Up Cervera,** glass bottle bank, black with gold, red trim, 4¾" height		2000.00 plus
☐ **Shoot-the-Chute Bank,** Buster Brown and Tige, C. A. Bailey, 1906, J. & E. Stevens manufacturer (218)		2000.00 plus
☐ **Speaking Dog,** C. G. Shephard, 1885, 7¼" height (69)	500.00	600.00*
☐ **Tammany (Fat Man),** J. Hall, 1873, J. & E. Stevens	200.00	300.00
☐ **Teddy and the Bear**	550.00	650.00
☐ **Teddy Shooting Lion**	850.00	1000.00
☐ **Toad in Den,** Jas. Fallows, 1871 (100)		2000.00 plus
☐ **Toad on Rock**	200.00	300.00
☐ **Trick Dog,** Hubley, 1888, 9⅝" height	150.00	200.00
☐ **Trick Pony,** C. G. Shephard, 1885 (196) ..	350.00	450.00
☐ **Tricky Pig**	300.00	400.00
☐ **Turtle,** Kilgore, Waterville, Ohio, semi-mechanical	1500.00	1700.00
☐ **Uncle Remus**	1200.00	1500.00

*Sold for $1500.00 at Atlanta Toy Museum Auction, October 1986.

Price Range

☐ **United States and Spain, Cannon,** U.S., 1898, Spanish-American War bank, cannon fires coin at mast, Jas. Bailery, J. & E. Stevens (37) 1100.00   1300.00

☐ **Weeden's Plantation,** Weeden, 1888, Negro dances while another plays banjo in front of shack 350.00   450.00

☐ **Woodpecker,** Germany, 1890s, musical bank with crank, bird sticks head out of hole and retrieves coin from perch 1150.00   1350.00

☐ **World's Fair,** C. A. Bailey, 1893 (244) 400.00   600.00

☐ **Yankee Notion,** J. Hall, 1875 .... 1800.00   2000.00

BANKS—STILL

Outsiders often consider the term "still" in still banks misleading, feeling that it connotes something to do with Prohibition. The term merely distinguishes banks with no mechanical motion involved when a penny is inserted. Tinplate banks predominated from the end of the Civil War to the 1890s, with Schlesingers, George Brown, William Fallows, and Althof Bergmann as the principal makers. Mass-produced cast-iron stills, using highly detailed molds, delighted youngsters and taught them the virtue of saving. From the late 19th century to the 1930s, A.C. Williams, J. & E. Stevens, Hubley, and Kenton were the leaders in their field.

Still Banks Inner Circle

Here is a consensus selection of the 10 most elite "stills" in the hobby:

Note: Figures appearing in parentheses indicate original listing numbers from the Whiting catalog.

1. Globe Savings Building (299)
2. Bear Stealing Pig (246)
3. Noah's Ark (290)
4. Steamboat on Tin Base, circa 1890s
   (See *Perelman Antique Toy Museum*, by Leon J. Perelman)
5. Seashell
6. Main St. Trolley With Passengers (164)

A pyramid of nice, early still banks, mechanicals, and pull toys. The safe banks (bottom left) are priced in the $50-$75 range; Independence Hall bank at very top, $350-$400. Columbian cast-iron pull toy in cast iron (third shelf down) rates a $450-$550 price tag.

7. Little Red Riding Hood (34)
8. Basset Hound (261)
9. "Oriental" Camel on Rockers (263)
10. Cannon (165)

Honorable Mention: Tugboat (147); Professor Pug Frog (230); Board of Trade (Bull and Bear) (264); Hen on Nest (253); American Eagle (255); Santa With Pack (33); Rabbit on Base (97); General Butler (294); Old South Church (448); Tom Turkey (Large) (194), Apple Bank With Bumblebee (299).

Animal Still Banks

Bears

Price Range

☐ **Bear (Teddy)**, 1900s, has word "Teddy" on side, 4" wide (331) (see "Political and Patriotic Toys" listing) ....

Price Range

☐ **Bear Stealing Pig,** classic pose in finite detail makes this the most desirable of still banks, 5½″ height (246) 500.00   600.00

☐ **Board of Trade,** bear and bull vie for sack of grain, black figures, silver sack, green base, 4¾″ height (264) 900.00   1100.00

☐ **Small Bear Eating Honey,** 2½″ height 200.00   300.00

Camels

☐ **Camel With Pack** is on all fours with pack on back, 2½″ height (256) 300.00   400.00

☐ **Camel With Saddle,** light brown with red, yellow trim, 7¼″ height, 6¼″ width (201)   350.00   450.00

☐ **Camel With Saddle,** light brown with red, yellow trim, 4¾″ height, 4″ width (202) ..   100.00   200.00

☐ **Oriental Camel With Young Camel on Rockers,** "Oriental" appears on rockers, one of the most uncommon animal banks, 4″ height (263) 350.00   450.00

Cats

☐ **Cat With Ball,** green cat is sprawled out to pounce on gold ball, 2½″ height (247) 150.00   200.00

☐ **Cat With Bow Tie,** sits primly with nicely curled tail, gold finish (244) 100.00   200.00

☐ **Cat Standing,** believed to be a Tom, bronze finish, 4½″ height (245) 100.00   150.00

Deer

☐ **Elk,** A. C. Williams, 1934, 6¼″ height (195), large version is 9″ height (196) 100.00   150.00

Dogs

☐ **Basset Hound,** long-eared little fellow with oversized head, a tough bank to find, 3″ height (261) 450.00   550.00

☐ **Bulldog,** seated, 4⅜″ height (102), Hubley, 1920–1930 (105) 50.00   60.00

☐ **Dog With Pack,** St. Bernard, A. C. Williams, 1905, black finish, 5½" height, 8" width (113) 75.00   150.00

☐ **Dog With Pack,** St. Bernard, A. C. Williams, 1905, black finish, 3¾" height, 5½" width (106) 50.00   100.00

☐ **Lost Dog,** undetermined breed, sits on haunches with mouth open and appears to be baying, 5½" height 350.00   450.00

☐ **Pup on Cushion,** one of numerous wide-eyed puppy versions from the 1920s, has "Fido" on collar, sits on flowered cushion, 5" height (337) 35.00   50.00

☐ **Spitz,** Hubley, 1920–1930, 4¼" height (103) 100.00   150.00

Ducks

☐ **Duck,** white with orange bill, preening, 5" height (332) 50.00   100.00

☐ **Duck on Tub,** wears red top hat with umbrella tucked under wing, "Save For A Rainy Day" embossed on gold tub, 5¼" height (323) 35.00   50.00

Elephants

☐ **Elephant,** the largest of a vast herd of elephant still banks, also probably the best detailed, live gray finish, 4¾" height, 7" width (62) 100.00   150.00

☐ **Elephant With Chariot,** bright red and yellow chariot, 3½" height, 5½" width (62) 300.00   400.00

☐ **Elephant With Howdah,** gold finish, 4" height, 6½" width 75.00   150.00

☐ **Elephant on Tub,** gilded elephant with elaborate blanket stands erect on circus platform, 5¼" height (60) 75.00   150.00

Price Range

☐ **Seated Elephant,** nice stylized features, looks like Babar, 4½" height (66) 75.00   150.00

Horses

☐ **Horse,** prancing, on oblong base, black horse on gold platform rears on hind legs, 7½" height (78) 75.00   150.00

☐ **Horse,** small, black with red harness, 2¾" height 50.00   100.00

☐ **Horse With Fly Net,** gilded horse looks like it is wearing medieval armor, 4" height (80) 200.00   300.00

Lions

☐ **Green Lion,** A.C. Williams, circa 1935, offered in blue, red, green or gold in two sizes, 2½" height (94) 35.00   50.00

☐ **Lion,** gilded king of beasts with wide stance as if confronting an enemy, 3" height (92) 50.00   100.00

☐ **Lion,** standing, Dent Hardware, 1935, gilded, 5½" height 35.00   50.00

☐ **Lion on Wheels,** made by Dent or Hubley, 1920s, the common standing version on wheeled platform, becomes pull toy, gilded with nickeled wheels, 5" height (95) 75.00   150.00

Pigs

☐ **Bismark Pig,** believed to be identical pig to one used in mechanical bank by same name, 3½" height 150.00   250.00

☐ **Decker's Iowana Pig,** advertising slogan (probably for hog mash) appears on both sides of gilded porker, 2½" height 75.00   150.00

☐ **Pig,** very uncommon miniature black piglet, 1¾" height 250.00   350.00

☐ **Pig,** bears words "I Made Chicago Famous," black finish, has nice primitive look about it, 2¼" height (177) 100.00   150.00

	Price Range	
☐ **Pig,** nickeled finish, "A Christmas Roast," 7″ width	100.00	200.00
☐ **Seated Pig,** the most colorful of all porkers is also one of the more common still banks, black pig wears yellow outfit trimmed at collar in red, 3″ height (178)	100.00	150.00
☐ **Thrifty Pig,** gilded with verse on silver box hanging from pig's neck, "Thrifty" appears at base, 6½″ height (175)	50.00	100.00

Rabbits

☐ **Rabbit Standing,** upright gilded figure, 5¼″ height (98)	50.00	100.00
☐ **White Rabbit,** nicely detailed rabbit on green base, word "bank" appears on one side, "1884" on the other (97)	350.00	450.00

Roosters

☐ **Rooster,** black Polish breed with red, silver, and gold trim, 5½″ height	100.00	150.00
☐ **Rooster,** gilt with red trim, 4¾″ height (187)	50.00	100.00

Miscellaneous

☐ **Bird on Stump,** excellent detail, 4¾″ height (209)	150.00	250.00
☐ **Buffalo,** "Amherst Stoves," 5″ height (207)	75.00	150.00
☐ **Bull,** aluminum alloy, embossing on inside bank reads "There is Money in Aberdeen Angus," 4½″ height, 7½″ length (190)	100.00	150.00
☐ **Cow,** underfed little dogie is hard to find, 2½″ height (188)	100.00	200.00
☐ **Cow,** bright red finish, 3½ (200)	75.00	150.00
☐ **Donkey,** gilt with red saddle, 6¼″ height (198)	75.00	125.00
☐ **Hen,** black layer has soapstonelike feel, 6″ height	50.00	100.00

Price Range

☐ **Hen on Nest,** gilt, 3″ height (253) .... | 350.00 | 450.00

☐ **Hippopotamus,** gilt with incredible detail, 2½″ height (251) .... | 300.00 | 400.00

☐ **Lamb,** same lamb accompanied nursery rhyme Mary bank, 3″ height (192) .... | 75.00 | 100.00

☐ **Opossum,** gilt, 2½″ height (205) .... | 100.00 | 200.00

☐ **Pecking Duck,** short little waddler, gilt, 4″ height (213) .... | 100.00 | 200.00

☐ **Red Goose,** "Red Goose Shoes" slogan, 4½″ height .... | 75.00 | 150.00

☐ **Rhino,** 2″ height (252) .... | 150.00 | 250.00

☐ **Seal,** black sea lion sits on gray rock, 3½″ height (199) .... | 150.00 | 250.00

☐ **Squirrel,** holds pecan, gilt, 4″ height ...... | 250.00 | 350.00

☐ **Steer,** long horns, white, 4″ height (189) | 75.00 | 125.00

☐ **Three Monkeys,** traditional "See No Evil" trio, brown, 3¼″ height (236) .... | 100.00 | 200.00

☐ **Turkey,** magnificent Tom, black with red wattles, 4½″ height (194) .... | 150.00 | 250.00

☐ **Two Kids,** pair of goats butting each other over tree stump, black goats, silver stump, gold "Two Kids" embossed on green base, 4¼″ height (262) .... | 250.00 | 350.00

Building Still Banks, Cast Iron

☐ **Old South Church,** famous old Boston landmark, features roof with multiple slots for coins, gray with green roof, one of largest and rarest of building banks, 13″ height .... | 400.00 | 500.00

☐ **Victorian House,** George Brown design, 1870s, tin, ornate gingerbread with four gables and three chimneys, white with blue chimneys, red roof, gold stenciling, 6¼″ height .... | 500.00 | 600.00

	Price Range	
☐ **Woolworth Building,** rendering of New York City skyscraper, gold finish, 8″ height, also a 5¾″ height version	75.00	100.00
☐ **World's Fair Administration Building,** a white with gold and red trim replica of building from Colombian Exposition in 1893, Chicago, small red safe in main entrance	100.00	125.00

Fictional Figures Still Banks

☐ **Andy Gump,** Arcade, 4½″ height (see "Comic and Character Toys," listing)	500.00	600.00
☐ **Billiken,** A. C. Williams, 1902, 4½″ height	50.00	100.00
☐ **Billy Can,** A. C. Williams, 5″ height	300.00	400.00
☐ **Black Beauty Horse,** 4″ height	50.00	100.00
☐ **Buster Brown and Tige,** A. C. Williams, 1900s, (see "Comic and Character Toys" listing)	100.00	200.00
☐ **Campbell Kids,** 3¼″ height, 4″ width	150.00	250.00
☐ **Captain Kidd,** 5½″ height, 4″ width	250.00	350.00
☐ **Devil, Two-Faced,** 4¼″ height	350.00	450.00
☐ **Foxy Grandpa,** 5¾″ height (see "Comic and Character Toys" listing)	300.00	400.00
☐ **Gollywog** (English doll character), 6¼″ height	200.00	300.00
☐ **King Midas,** 5½″ height	200.00	300.00
☐ **Little Red Riding Hood,** Harper, English	850.00	950.00
☐ **Mary Had a Little Lamb,** 4½″ height	350.00	450.00
☐ **Mermaid in Boat,** 4½″ height	300.00	400.00
☐ **Mutt and Jeff,** A. C. Williams, 5¼″ height (see "Comic and Character Toys" listing)	150.00	250.00
☐ **Porky Pig,** 5¾″ height (see "Comic and Character Toys" listing)	100.00	200.00

Price Range

☐ **Professor Pug Frog,** 3¾" height 250.00 350.00

☐ **Rumplestiltskin,** "Do You Know Me?" on base, 6½" height 250.00 350.00

☐ **Santa Claus With Pack,** 5" height (see "Holiday Toys" listing) 300.00 400.00

☐ **Santa Claus With Tree** 350.00 450.00

☐ **Sunbonnet Girl,** 1940s, 4" height 75.00 150.00

Historic Figures and Landmarks Still Banks

☐ **American Eagle,** nice detail with shield of stars and stripes, 4" height 300.00 400.00

☐ **Benjamin Franklin,** bronze finish, cast metal, 5" height 50.00 100.00

☐ **Boss Tweed Bank,** based on cartoon representation of Tammany Hall figure by Thomas Nast, "Savings Bank" embossed on lapels of Tweed's coat, 3¾" height (see "Political and Patriotic Toys" listing) 750.00 850.00

☐ **Bunker Hill Monument,** 7½" height 75.00 150.00

☐ **Charles Lindbergh,** bust figure 150.00 250.00

☐ **Coronation Bank,** heads of King George V and Queen Mary in relief, English, 6¾" height, 7¼" width 175.00 250.00

☐ **Dreadnought Bank,** two clasped hands and two British flags, English, 6¾" height, 7¼" width 350.00 450.00

☐ **General Pershing,** 1918, 8" height 100.00 200.00

☐ **General Sheridan,** Arcade, 5½" height 200.00 300.00

☐ **George Washington,** magnificent bust on gold pedestal, in colorful colonial mufti, 8" height 550.00 650.00

☐ **Independence Hall,** 10¼" height, 8" width 300.00 400.00

Price Range

☐ **Liberty Bell,** musical bank, eagle embossed on front, "Centennial 1776–1886," the rarest of any number of Liberty Bell still banks, 5¾" height 400.00   500.00

☐ **Moody and Sanky,** oval photographs of Civil War Revivalists, 4½" height, 4½" width (see "Political and Patriotic Toys" listing) 750.00   850.00

☐ **Old South Church,** 9¾" height 550.00   650.00

☐ **Smiling Jim and Peaceful Bill,** Taft-Sherman campaign bank, 1908, bronze finish, caricature face back-to-back, 4" height 450.00   550.00

☐ **Statue of Liberty,** 6" height 50.00   75.00

☐ **Statue of Liberty,** 9½" height 200.00   300.00

☐ **Teddy Roosevelt,** bust of T. Roosevelt in Rough Rider uniform (see "Political and Patriotic Toys" listing) 100.00   200.00

☐ **Transvaal (Paul Kruger),** John Harper Ltd., 1885–1900, 6" height 400.00   500.00

☐ **Washington Monument,** 6" height 100.00   200.00

Household and Personal Effects Still Banks

☐ **Clothes Basket,** two doves on top of cover, gilt, 2½" height (339) 75.00   125.00

☐ **Cook Stove,** advertises "Oak" kitchen stove, 2½" height (134) 75.00   125.00

☐ **Cradle,** baby sleeps in rocker-type cradle with small dove perched on headboard, 3½" height (231) 150.00   250.00

☐ **Furnace,** "Gem" advertising on front, black, cast by A. Bendroth Bros., New York, 4½" height (131) 50.00   100.00

☐ **Gas Stove,** white enamel range advertising "Roper," 3¾" height 50.00   100.00

☐ **Grandfather's Clock,** "Grandfather's Clock" embossed, dark finish, 5½" height (222) 150.00   250.00

☐ **Ice Cream Freezer,** "North Pole" slogan embossed on bucket with "Save Your Money and Freeze It," 4" height (156) 75.00   125.00

☐ **Kodak Bank,** one of Kodak's early Brownies in nickel finish with handsome scrollwork, 4½" height 150.00   250.00

☐ **Mail Box,** green, eagle with "U.S. Mail" embossed on face, 3½" height (123) 75.00   125.00

☐ **Mail Box,** one of the largest of many mail box banks, wide-based pedestal, eagle perched atop, padlock closure, red with gilt patina, 9½" height (119) 150.00   250.00

☐ **Pump and Bucket,** painted cast metal, 4½" height (235) 35.00   50.00

☐ **Purse,** black coin purse with "Put Money in Thy Purse" on side, as plain as it is rare, 2¾" height 300.00   400.00

☐ **Radio,** floor model GE from the late 1920s, 4" height 35.00   50.00

☐ **Radio,** a No. 70 Crosley in green, 4½" height 35.00   50.00

☐ **Refrigerator,** top has honeycomb unit popularized by GE, 3¾" height (237) 50.00   75.00

☐ **Rocking Chair,** dark finish, seat is bank, patented 1898, comprises six separately cast pieces, an intricate rarity, 7" height 550.00   650.00

☐ **Sun Dial,** nice example on gilt column, 4¼" height (153) 250.00   350.00

☐ **Wood Parlor Stove,** decorative black column stove with silver finial, 7" height 75.00   125.00

"Little People" Figure Still Banks

	Price Range	
☐ **Barrel With Arms,** caricature figure of barrel with arms, legs, and man in the moon's face, key slot is in stomach of barrel, 3½″ height (151)	150.00	200.00
☐ **Baseball Player,** A. C. Williams, 1909, 5¾″ height (10)	150.00	250.00
☐ **Billy,** 4¾″ height (22)	200.00	300.00
☐ **Boy Scout,** A.C. Williams, 6″ height (14)	100.00	200.00
☐ **Butler,** A. C. Williams, 5¾″ height (4)	300.00	400.00
☐ **Capitalist,** 4¾″ height (21)	450.00	550.00
☐ **Clown,** 6½″ height (29)	75.00	150.00
☐ **Clown,** with crooked hat, 6¾″ height (28)	400.00	500.00
☐ **Cop (Mulligan the Cop),** 5¾″ height (8)	100.00	200.00
☐ **Doughboy (World War I),** 6⅞″ height (15)	250.00	350.00
☐ **Dutch Boy,** 6½″ height (25)	350.00	450.00
☐ **Dutch Girl,** 6½″ height (24)	400.00	500.00
☐ **Fireman,** 5½″ height (9)	200.00	300.00
☐ **Football Player,** with large football aloft, 5″ height	500.00	600.00
☐ **Football Player,** gold finish, 5¾″ height (11)	200.00	300.00
☐ **Indian,** Hubley, 1920s, 6″ height (39)	100.00	200.00
☐ **Indian Family,** chief, squaw, papoose, 3¾″ height	400.00	500.00
☐ **Mammy,** holds spoon, 5¾″ height (17)	75.00	150.00
☐ **Mammy,** 5″ height	75.00	150.00
☐ **Man on Bale of Cotton** (37)	400.00	500.00
☐ **Middy,** 5¼″ height (26)	100.00	200.00
☐ **Share Cropper** (18)	100.00	200.00
☐ **Sailor With Oar,** Hubley, circa 1925, 5¾″ height (16)	250.00	350.00
☐ **Save and Smile,** moonfaced girl with sunbonnet, 4″ height (46)	450.00	500.00
☐ **Two-Faced Indian,** chief in full headdress, 4½″ height (291)	450.00	550.00

	Price Range	
☐ **Two-Faced Woman,** 4″ height (43)	150.00	250.00
☐ **Woman With Bustle,** English pottery bank, 1890s, 18″ height	2000.00 plus	

Military Still Banks

☐ **Armored Car,** red, World War I vehicle, 3½″ height, 6½″ length (160)	300.00	400.00
☐ **Battleship Maine,** "Maine" embossed midships, gold and black, 4½″ height, 4½″ length (142)	100.00	200.00
☐ **Battleship Massachusetts,** battleship gray, rides green waves, 6″ height, 10″ length (143)	250.00	350.00
☐ **Battleship Oregon,** green, 5″ height, 6″ width (146)	100.00	200.00
☐ **Battleship Oregon,** green, 4″ height, 6″ width (144)	75.00	100.00
☐ **Cannon,** black cannon with red wheels, 3″ height, 7″ length (165)	400.00	500.00
☐ **Doughboy,** World War I soldier, khaki uniform, one knee flexed, 8½″ height	200.00	300.00
☐ **Doughboy Hat,** brim, American shield on crown, 3¾″ diameter	100.00	150.00
☐ **Shell,** deactivated World War I bullet shell, brass finish, 8″ height (385)	50.00	75.00
☐ **Soldier,** sometimes called "Minuteman" but uniform looks more like Spanish-American War era, 6″ height (15)	150.00	200.00
☐ **Tank,** "U.S. Tank Bank," turretless, dark finish, 1¾″ height, 4″ length	50.00	100.00
☐ **Tank,** "Tank Bank U.S.A. 1918," red with turret, 3¼″ height, 6″ length (161)	100.00	200.00

Transportation Still Banks

☐ **Auto,** red coupe with passengers, 3″ height, 5½″ length (157)	200.00	300.00
☐ **Auto,** four-door Model A, dark green, 3½″ height, 7″ length (159)	200.00	300.00

	Price Range	
☐ **Dirigible,** "Graf Zeppelin" on side, silver, 6¾" length (171)	100.00	150.00
☐ **Ferry Boat,** sidewheeler, believed to be by Dent, 2½" height, 7¾" length (148)	100.00	200.00
☐ **Ferry Boat,** sidewheeler, silver, believed to be by Dent, 2½" height, 8" length (150)	100.00	200.00
☐ **Monoplane,** tin, 8" length	50.00	100.00
☐ **Small Sailboat,** dark red, "When My Fortune Ship Comes In," 4" height (249)	300.00	400.00
☐ **Steamship Bank,** tin twin-stack vessel on wheeled base, circa 1900s	1000.00	1100.00
☐ **Street Car,** gilt trolley with passengers, 3" height, 6½" length (164)	200.00	300.00
☐ **Trolley Car,** yellow and red with black wheels, 2½" height, 4½" length (265)	200.00	300.00
☐ **Tug Boat,** has wheels, red and black, 3½" height, 5½" length	1200.00	1300.00
☐ **Yellow Cab,** yellow and black, "Yellow Cab Co." on door, 4" height (158)	250.00	350.00

Miscellaneous Still Banks

☐ **Alphabet,** 26-sided gilt bank with letter of alphabet embossed on each facet, 3¹/₂" height	300.00	400.00
☐ **Apple With Bumblebee,** juicy red apple with green twig and leaf, bumble rests on top, another candidate for "Number One" among stills (299)	400.00	500.00
☐ **Chimney Sweep,** figure on roof ready to clean chimney, cast metal, thought to be English, 4" height	100.00	200.00
☐ **Money Bag,** sack tied with cord, "100,000" on sack, 3½" height (295)	300.00	400.00
☐ **Noah's Ark,** red and black with five separated flat-cast animals (elephant, lion, cow, hippo, and camel), 4½" height, 7½" length (290)	700.00	800.00

	Price Range	
☐ **Old Volunteer Fire Department,** octangular-shaped hydrant with gold raised letters, 1890s, 6″ height	400.00	500.00
☐ **"Pingree" Potato,** World War I victory garden promotion by Mayor Pingree of Detroit, 5½″ length (301)	200.00	300.00
☐ **Seashell,** white conch shell on round base, "Shell Out" appears on outer lip, 2½″ height, 5″ length (293)	200.00	300.00
☐ **Street Clock,** red with gold face, "Bank Clock" on face, 6″ height	150.00	250.00

Dime Register Banks, Tin

Intriguing offshoots for still bank enthusiasts are the tin daily dime register banks produced in the United States in the 1930s and 1940s, with some versions as recent as the late 1960s. Generally, these banks are 2½″ square, with rounded corners, and feature a small window where the total amount appears as each dime is inserted. Usually, the appealing little banks held 50 dimes ($5.00) and provided a real incentive to save, as the bank opened automatically when the $5.00 goal was reached.

Comic characters dominate this group of Dime Register banks.

Top row (left to right):   "Dopey" from Snow White and The Seven Dwarfs, 1938, $35–$50

"Superman," King Features Synd., 1940, $45–$55

"Popeye," 1950s, silver version, King Features Synd., $15–$25

"Popeye," 1950s, full color, King Features Synd., $15–$25

"Popeye," 1929–1930s, silver, King Features Synd., $25–$35

"Clown," 1950s (with monkey playing saxophone), $15–$25

Middle row (left to right):   "Snow White and The Seven Dwarfs" 1938–1940, $35–$50

"Captain Marvel," Fawcett Pub., 1944–1946, $50–$60

"Astronaut," early 1960s, $35–$45

"P-40 Fighter Plane," 1940s, $35–$45

"Little Orphan Annie," Famous Artists Synd., 1936, $45–$55

"New York World's Fair," 1964–1965, $15–$25

Third row (left to right):   "Jackie Robinson," early 1940s, $45–$55

"Elf" 1950s, $10–$15

"Mickey Mouse," Walt Disney Prod., 1939 (Mickey teaches nephews to save), $50–$75

"Piggy," 1960s (smiling head of pig), $15–$20

"Little Girl," with pet rabbit and duck, titled "Vacation" bank, 1960s, $15–$20

"Young Cowboy" (little boy in cowboy suit with two bags of money), $15–$20

BATTERY-OPERATED TOYS

Often considered an offspring of contemporary electronics wizardry, battery-operated toys originated as early as the mid-1920s, following the inception of the self-contained dry cell battery. These fledgling attempts, however, were readily susceptible to corrosion and not really affordable in the face of competition from wind-up versions, particularly during the Depression. Battery-operated toys made their greatest inroads in the post–World War II years, as the occupied zones of Germany and Japan began to flood the market. Today, highly sophisticated remote control robots and space toys are already being trumpeted as collectible "futures." Whether justified or not, only time will determine if they merit the attention as the hottest collectible category in the hobby today.

CARTOON, MOVIE, AND TELEVISION PERSONALITIES

	Price Range	
☐ **Barney Rubble and Dino,** Marx, 1963, litho tin mech, plastic, 8⅛" length	75.00	100.00
☐ **Blushing Frankenstein,** Rosko, Japan, 1960s, litho tin, plastic, sways, makes roaring sound, arms move, pants drop, face reddens	50.00	75.00
☐ **Charlie Weaver Bartender,** Rosko, 1960s, litho tin, plastic, Jack Parr's "Tonight Show" celebrity, smoke emits from ears ...	35.00	50.00
☐ **Dennis the Menace Xylophone Player,** Marx, litho tin, plastic musical, plays "London Bridge"	100.00	125.00
☐ **Frankenstein Monster,** T-N., Japan, 1960s, six actions, 14" height	50.00	75.00
☐ **Fred Astaire,** Tap Dancer, Alps, Occupied Japan, 1950s celluloid, tin	150.00	200.00

Price Range

☐ **Fred Flintstone and Dino,** Marx, 1960s, plush-dressed tin, vinyl, Fred rides dinosaur, 22″ length 75.00   100.00

☐ **Howdy Doody Electric Doodler,** 1950–1955, litho question-and-answer game, 9″ × 13″ 50.00   60.00

☐ **James Bond 007 Car,** M101, Daiwa, Japan, 1960s, seven actions, ejectable driver, 11″ length 75.00   100.00

☐ **Louis Armstrong,** Rosko, Japan, 1960s, litho tin, vinyl, cloth mechanical 9½″ height 125.00   150.00

☐ **Mighty Kong,** Marx, 1950s, five actions, litho tin, plastic, 12″ height 100.00   125.00

☐ **Mother Goose,** Japan, late 1940s, plush-covered tin, celluloid beak, big red tin shoes, waddles, tail vibrates 35.00   50.00

☐ **Mr. Magoo Car,** Hubley, circa 1961, litho tin, cloth roof, vinyl head, bump-and-go action 50.00   75.00

☐ **Pinocchio Playing "London Bridge,"** Marx, 1960s, litho tin, plastic, three actions, 10″ length 75.00   100.00

☐ **Tarzan,** San Co., Japan, 1960s, litho tin, vinyl head, cloth dressed (loin cloth), Tarzan walks, 13″ height 100.00   125.00

SPACE AND ROBOT BATTERY-OPERATED TOYS, POST–WORLD WAR II

☐ **Apollo, U.S.A., N.A.S.A.,** K. K. Masutoku Toy Factory, Japan, 1960s litho tin, rubber wheels, 9⅝″ length 100.00   150.00

☐ **Apollo Spacecraft,** Alps Shop Ltd., Japan, 1960s, litho tin, plastic, 9½″ length 100.00   125.00

☐ **Apollo-X Moon Challenger,** Nomura Toys Ltd., Japan, 1960s, litho tin, plastic, 15¾″ length 100.00   150.00

One of the earliest, and more primitive, robots produced in Occupied Japan in the 1950s, $150-$250.

	Price Range	
☐ **Atomic Robot Man,** Japan, late 1940s, litho tin, 5″ height	350.00	450.00
☐ **Big Loo,** Marx, 1961, litho tin, plastic, 3″ height	250.00	300.00
☐ **C3PO,** GM FGI, Hong Kong, plastic, late 1970s, 12⅗″ height	100.00	125.00

Price Range

☐ **Cape Canaveral Series 2000 Kit,** Marx, 1960s, contains four-stage rocket, flying saucer, missile, and NASA personnel figures 125.00   150.00

☐ **Chief Robotman,** K.O. Co., Japan, 1950s, four actions, 12″ height 125.00   150.00

☐ **Dino Robot,** S.H. Co., Japan, 1960s, five actions, 11″ height 75.00   100.00

☐ **Fighting Robot,** Horikawa Toys, 1966, litho tin, plastic, 9⅝″ height 75.00   125.00

☐ **Flying Saucer,** Cragston, Japan, 1960s, hatch opens and closes as astronaut enters, siren, 10″ diameter 125.00   150.00

☐ **Friendship 7,** Modern Toys, Japan, 1960s, astronaut's space capsule, 6½″ height 25.00   35.00

☐ **Great Garloo,** Marx, 1961; litho tin, plastic 150.00   200.00

☐ **King Flying Saucer,** Japan, circa 1950, litho tin, plastic, tilt-and-roll motion, 7¼″ diameter 125.00   150.00

☐ **Laser 008,** Japan, 1960s, plastic, 7″ height 100.00   125.00

☐ **Man in Space Astronaut,** Alps, circa 1960, litho tin, plastic, 6″ height 75.00   100.00

☐ **Mars Explorer Car,** EXECO, Japan, 1950s, light and dark green tin litho, astronauts are in twin plastic bubbles, simulated exhaust flame in red plastic 150.00   200.00

☐ **Mars Explorer Robot,** S.H. Co., Japan, circa 1950s, litho tin, plastic, seven actions; 9½″ height 50.00   75.00

☐ **Martian Robot,** S.J.M. Co., 1970s, litho tin, plastic, four actions; 12″ height 50.00   75.00

☐ **Mechanical Jumping Rocket,** S.Y. Co., Japan, litho tin, plastic, robot astride rocket, rocks and rolls when activated, 6″ height ... 100.00   150.00

	Price Range	
☐ **Mechanized Robot,** F.N. Co., Japan, circa 1950s, four actions, 13½″ height	100.00	150.00
☐ **Mr. Atomic,** Cragston, Japan, 1960s, litho tin	1500.00	2000.00
☐ **Mystery Universe Car,** Taiwan, ME #089, 1960s, litho tin with plastic fins, oval dome, makes noise, 4″ height × 10″ length	75.00	100.00
☐ **N.A.S.A. Space Saucer,** Hong Kong, 1960s, plastic and rubber, bumps and turns	50.00	75.00
☐ **Office Rex Mars Planet Patrol,** Marx, 1930s, 10″ length	150.00	200.00
☐ **Omni Robot,** Hong Kong, 1970, litho tin, plastic, 10⅛″ height	50.00	75.00
☐ **Piston Robot,** Linemar, 1950s, 5½″ height	75.00	100.00
☐ **Robot,** K.O. Co., Japan, 1950s, tin and plastic, lights, bumps and turns	100.00	150.00
☐ **Robot Cosmic Raider Force,** Taiwan, 1970s, plastic, blinking lights, 14½″ length	50.00	60.00
☐ **Robot 2500,** Hong Kong (for Durham Industries, New York) plastic, 9¾″ height ..	50.00	60.00
☐ **Rocket Launcher T-12,** Daiya, Japan, 1960s, 10″ length	100.00	150.00
☐ **Roto Robot,** maker unknown, 1960s, litho tin, plastic, 8½″ height	35.00	50.00
☐ **Saturn Robot,** Taiwan, 1970s, plastic, lighted eyes, TV screen, 11⅝″ height	50.00	75.00
☐ **Silver Robot,** maker unknown, 1960s, red circle lights up in robot's "heart" area, 9½″ height	30.00	50.00

Price Range

☐ **Son of Garloo,** Marx, 1960s, litho tin, off-spring of Great Garloo (two versions: one has Son of Garloo medallion as part of design; other wears medallion on chain around neck) 100.00   150.00

☐ **Space Capsule,** Horikawa, Japan, 1960s, tin, plastic and rubber, 9⁵⁄₁₆″ length 50.00   75.00

☐ **Space Explorer,** Horikawa, Japan, 1960s, litho tin, plastic, TV monitor 75.00   100.00

☐ **Space Patrol Car,** VW-Rosko, litho tin silver body with red and silver trim, coiled wire bumpers, clear plastic panel with light, 12″ length 150.00   200.00

☐ **Space Rocket Solar X,** T-N Co., Japan, 1960s, litho tin, plastic wings retract 50.00   75.00

☐ **Space Saucer,** maker unknown, 1960s, plastic, rubber, 4″ length 25.00   50.00

☐ **Space Scooter,** M-T Co., Japan, circa 1960s, plastic, litho tin, three actions, 8″ length 50.00   75.00

☐ **Space Tank,** K.O. Co., Japan, 1960s, litho tin, plastic, tilt-and-roll motion, 8″ length 50.00   75.00

☐ **Sparky Robot,** K.O. Co., Japan, 1960s, tin, lights beam from eyes, 9½″ height 75.00   100.00

☐ **Strange Explorer,** Horikawa, 1950, litho tin, plastic, 8″ length 75.00   100.00

☐ **Super Space Capsule,** maker unknown, 1960s, litho tin, blinking lights, body revolves, door opens and astronaut pops out, 9½″ length 35.00   50.00

☐ **Super Space Commander,** Horikawa, 1960s, litho tin, plastic, 9⅝″ length 75.00   100.00

☐ **Talking Robot,** Cragston, Japan, 1960s, litho tin, plastic, 12″ height 125.00   150.00

☐ **Television Space Man,** maker unknown, 1950s, litho tin, revolving antenna, TV monitor 35.00   50.00

Price Range

☐ **UFO-XO5,** M-T Co., Japan, circa 1960s, plastic, litho tin, three actions, 7½" diameter 15.00   25.00

☐ **Universe Televibot,** Taiwan, circa 1960s, litho tin, plastic, rubber wheels, 13½" length 50.00   75.00

CAP PISTOLS AND CAP BOMBS

Toy cap pistols and cap bombs are making big noise at the cash register in recent years, particularly the animated figural versions from the late 19th century. We can recall a time when the Yellow Kid cap bombs, for example, were so common that Baltimore dealer Frank Whitson used them as window shade pulls! This highly specialized collecting category is still a relatively uncrowded field, but amusing and ingenious animated examples are eagerly snapped up on those rare occasions when they come on the market.

	Price Range	
☐ **Brat Cap Pistol,** 4¼″ length	50.00	75.00
☐ **Butting Match,** two boys, cast iron, 5″ length	200.00	250.00
☐ **Butting Monkeys Cap Pistol,** 4″ length ...	100.00	150.00
☐ **Chinese Must Go,** Ives, 1880s, cap pistol, 4¾″ length	450.00	550.00
☐ **Dewey Cap Bomb,** 1¾″ height	100.00	150.00
☐ **Doc Cap Pistol,** patented 1929, single cap shooter, 4″ length	75.00	100.00
☐ **Eagle Cap Pistol,** 7½″ length	75.00	100.00
☐ **Echo Cap Pistol,** single cap, 4¼″ length ..	35.00	50.00
☐ **Federal Cap Pistol,** Kilgore No. 1, 1890s, 5¼″ length	35.00	50.00
☐ **George Washington Cap Bomb,** 1¾″ height	150.00	200.00
☐ **Ibex Cap Pistol,** 4½″ length	100.00	125.00
☐ **Invincible Cap Pistol,** fired rolls, 4¾″ length	50.00	75.00
☐ **Lighting Express Cap Pistol,** 4⅝″ length	100.00	125.00
☐ **No. 25 Jr.,** 4″ length	50.00	75.00
☐ **Pluck Cap Pistol,** 3⅛″ length	50.00	75.00

Selection of early cap pistols, cap bombs, and a toy cannon. Kid Cap Pistol, Kilgore, 1925, $35–$50; Negro Cap Bomb, Ideal, 1910, $150–$200; Yellow Kid Cap Bomb, maker unknown, $150–$200; Cupid Cap Pistol, Ideal, 1910, $35–$45; Swamp Angel Cannon, Ideal, 1910, $250–$350.

	Price Range	
☐ **Powder Keg Cap Bomb,** 2¼″ height	200.00	250.00
☐ **Punch and Judy,** 5¾″ length	300.00	350.00
☐ **Shoot the Hat,** 4¾″ length	400.00	500.00
☐ **Single-Face Chinaman Cap Bomb,** 1¾″ height	100.00	150.00
☐ **Spitfire Cap Pistol,** 4½″ length	35.00	50.00
☐ **Squirrel With Nut,** brass master casting, tail is pulled back to cock pistol, one of six originals, 5″ length	1000.00	2000.00
☐ **Two Dogs on Bench Cap Shooter,** maker unknown, 1890s, 5⅞″ length		2000.00 plus
☐ **William McKinley Cap Bomb,** 1¾″ height	150.00	200.00
☐ **Wizard Stick Shooter Cap Pistol,** 4⅞″ length	50.00	75.00
☐ **Yellow Kid Cap Bomb,** 1¾″ height	100.00	125.00
☐ **Zip Cap Pistol**	100.00	150.00

CIRCUS

Few collecting categories evoke more nostalgia or amusement than circus and fairground toys. Any number of toy makers have outdone themselves in terms of creativity to produce their finest work. Prime examples include Schoenhut with their Humpty Dumpty Circus; Hubley and the Royal Circus cast-iron menagerie (owning the entire entourage has been likened to holding a royal flush in poker); Kenton's more recent Overland Circus wagons, and, not to be overlooked, the ingenious animated bell ringer pull toys featuring cavorting clowns and tumbling acrobats by Gong Bell and Watrous from the turn of the century.

CIRCUS AND FAIRGROUNDS AMUSEMENT RIDES

	Price Range	
☐ **Aerial Carousel,** Chein, 1930s, lithographed tin mechanical, four rocket-shaped rides with propellors, two passengers in each, 18″ height	150.00	200.00
☐ **Carousel,** German, circa 1910, handpainted tin mechanical and musical, with five swings, 13″ height	700.00	800.00
☐ **Carousel,** German, circa 1915, lithographed tin mechanical, three swings with three blown figures, 13″ height	400.00	500.00
☐ **Carousel,** German, early 1930s, imported by Gibbs, painted tin clockwork, 8″ height	300.00	400.00
☐ **Double-Action Revolving Observation Swing,** French, 1910, tower with twin American flags atop, six cars suspended from three double swings, each with two passengers, 13″ height	500.00	600.00
☐ **Double Ferris Swing,** French, 1910, double-revolving swings on twin columns, passengers ride in tiny gondolas, bright painted colors on tin, mechanical, 13½″ length	350.00	400.00

Three classic circus toys. *Top left:* maker unknown, late 1890s, painted tin mechanical, canvas tent, $650–$750. *Bottom left:* Crandall's Lively Horseman wooden pull toy, 1880s, $550–$650. *Right:* "Jumbo" gravity string toy, maker unknown, early 1900s, $350–$450.

Price Range

☐ **Ferris Wheel,** German, circa 1915, hand-painted tin mechanical with blown figures, 16″ height 300.00   350.00

☐ **Ferris Wheel,** German, circa 1915, hand-painted tin with crank, composition figures, two-color flat atop small roof over wheel, very ornate, 15½″ height 400.00   500.00

☐ **Ferris Wheel,** German, 1915, lithographed tin, steam attachment, four seats with passengers, 13″ height 350.00   400.00

☐ **Ferris Wheel,** Chein, 1930s, lithographed tin mechanical, 12″ height 100.00   150.00

☐ **Midget Roller Coaster,** maker unknown, 1930s, tiny car runs down incline and raised by chute to starting point 75.00   100.00

☐ **Musical Carousel,** French, 1910, painted tin mechanical, three children on goats on revolving platform, six children in swings suspend from revolving canopy as music plays, 11½″ height 350.00   450.00

☐ **Musical Russian Carousel,** German, circa 1900, painted tin, hand-crank mechanical, three horses and riders revolve around single hub while music plays 450.00   500.00

CIRCUS WAGONS, CAGES, AND OTHER ASSEMBLAGES

☐ **Cage Wagon,** Schoenhut (from Humpty Dumpty Circus), 1920s, paper lithographed on wood, tops lift off to reveal cages, on wooden wheels, minus animals 1400.00   1600.00

☐ **Circus Platform Pull Toy,** from Oscar Strausburger Catalog, circa 1890, painted tin with cast-iron wheels, features musicians, two horses with feet on drum, smaller figure with pony jumping through hoop, painted tin, 13½″ length 1400.00   1500.00

Price Range

☐ **Circus Train,** Cole Bros. and Wardie Jay, 1930s, for 0 gauge railroads, a kit featuring Britains cast-metal figures, includes over a dozen cars, including cage cars and a calliope 600.00 700.00

☐ **Circus and Two Poodles,** Muller & Kadeder, circa 1900, painted tin mechanical, revolving carousel on small stand with jutting rod that has poodles jumping over each other on one end, spinning prop on other 450.00 550.00

☐ **Circus Wagon,** Wyandotte, 1920s, pressed steel and tin, truck with attached trailer cage, cardboard lithographed animals, 20″ length 150.00 200.00

☐ **Polar Bear Cage Wagon,** Bliss 1915, lithographed paper-on-wood, pair horses pull wagon with mechanical bear 350.00 400.00

☐ **Pony Circus Wagon,** Gibbs, 1920s, paper lithographed on wood and tin, cast-iron wheels 200.00 250.00

☐ **"Ring-A-Ling" Circus,** L. Marx 1927, ringmaster snaps whip, clown turns somersault, elephant, lion, and monkey do stunts, lithographed tin mechanical, 9½″ diameter 200.00 250.00

☐ **Trained Circus Horses,** German, 1904, painted tin clockwork, ringmaster on barrel, clown holds hoop on edge of platform, horses dance around ring on hind feet, 11½″ height 1200.00 1400.00

☐ **Turning Circus,** German, 1904, double-tiered spinning round platform, flagstaff and large bannerette in center, four circus horseback riders move in one direction, two riders in another when clockwork mechanism is activated, while music plays, 9″ diameter 1200.00 1400.00

AMUSEMENT RIDES

Price Range

☐ **Acrobat Wheel,** Wilkins, circa 1900s, five acrobats perform on Ferris wheel-type rig on four-wheeled platform pull toy, painted cast iron, 9½″ length 600.00   700.00

☐ **Aerial Merry-Go-Round,** maker unknown, 1910, painted tin, battery operated or electrical, flies American flag atop canopy, six suspended cars, 18″ height 1200.00   1400.00

☐ **Bath House,** maker unknown, 1929, lithographed tin mechanical, green celluloid swimming tank, painted swimming suits on steel bar, 5¼″ height, 5½″ width 100.00   150.00

☐ **Carousel, Four Horses,** German, circa 1910, painted tin mechanical, nice filagreed canopy topped by bannerette, 13″ height ... 650.00   750.00

☐ **Coney Island Carousel,** maker unknown, circa 1910, three horses with riders circle as music plays, high platform, painted tin mechanical, 9½″ height 250.00   300.00

☐ **The Giant Dip, Coney Island,** maker unknown, 1929, lithographed tin mechanical, with four passengers, double-action spring, airplane revolves above, amusement booths and other attractions lithographed on base, 18″ length, tower, 13″ height, car, 1¾″ length 200.00   250.00

☐ **Hy and Lo,** maker unknown, 1924, lithographed tin mechanical, cars run on double-incline runway, drop to lower track and glide back to starting point where spring mechanism sets it on its way again, 9¾″ length 50.00   70.00

☐ **Musical Carousel,** Converse, 1915, lithographed paper on wood, five seats (five pair of horses), music box in base, 36″ diameter   1200.00   1400.00

Price Range

☐ **Reindeer Circus Train,** Milton Bradley, circa 1890, lithographed on wood, engine tender and four cage cars, animals include rhino, bear, bison, tiger, 45″ length 500.00   600.00

☐ **Roundabout,** German, 1910, painted tin mechanical zeppelin and early bi-wing revolve around pylon, 15″ height 400.00   500.00

CIRCUS RIGS, CAST IRON

Hubley Royal Circus Series: 1919–1926

☐ **Animal Cage,** 1920, drawn by four horses, includes driver, two caged animals, painted cast iron, 23″ length 1200.00   1400.00

☐ **Band Wagon,** 1920, painted cast iron, four horses, driver, six or eight musicians, 30″ length 1800.00   2000.00

☐ **Bear Cage,** 1920, two horses with balance wheels, driver, pair caged bears, painted cast iron, 15¾″ length 800.00   1000.00

☐ **Bear (Tiger, Rhino or Lion) Circus Wagon,** 1924, painted cast iron, Hubley produced a less elaborate Royal Circus Series, only 12¼″ long, minus the ornate embossing with an option of four wild animals 650.00   700.00

☐ **Buffalo Van,** 1920, has buffalo embossed in oval on cage, painted cast iron, two horses with driver, 13¼″ length 800.00   900.00

☐ **Calliope,** 1920, two horses, painted cast iron, some models featured chimes, boiler, sizes 9¼″, 12¾″, 16″ length 1800.00   2000.00

☐ **Chariot,** 1920, painted cast iron, less elaborate standing clown driver, only 5½″ length 350.00   400.00

☐ **Chariot With Clown,** 1920, painted cast iron, standing clown holds reins of three black horses, 9½″ or 12½″ length 1200.00   1400.00

Price Range

☐ **Clown Van,** 1920, painted blue cast iron, similar to Monkey Van, with clown's head and trapeze projecting from top of van, also with oval mirror, sliding doors, embossed angels trumpets in gold, 16½" length 900.00   1000.00

☐ **Eagle Van,** 1920, painted cast iron, eagle embossed in gold in oval on enclosed cage wagon, sizes: 6", 7", 8½" length (also featured lion variation) 500.00   600.00

☐ **Farmer Van,** 1920, pair draft horses, hauling wagon with pressed-steel floor and roof, painted cast iron, cast aluminum, bearded farmer with straw hat and spectacles projects from top of cage, embossed rhino appears in gold on cage against deep green background, wheels are bright red with gold starburst centers, farmer's head revolves as toy is pulled, 16¼" ....   2000.00 plus

☐ **Giraffe Cage,** 1920, caged mother giraffe (whose head projects out of top of cage) and baby, horses wear plumes on harness, painted cast iron and sheet metal, cast lead, sizes available of two horses 16½" length or four horses 24½" length ....   2000.00 plus

☐ **Lion Circus Wagon,** 1924, two horses, driver, two caged lions, painted cast iron, 15¾" length, Hubley produced a slightly longer (16¼" length) version of the same wagon in 1924 .... 700.00   800.00

☐ **Monkey Van,** 1920, painted cast-iron van, pair horses and driver, monkey's head projects from top of van, with trapeze, large oval mirror on each side of van, 13" length 800.00   900.00

☐ **Rhino Cage,** 1920, two horses, two caged rhinos (in open cage), plus driver, painted cast iron and pressed steel, 16" length 700.00   800.00

The distinction of ranking as the rarest of cast-iron toys invariably goes to the Hubley painted cast-iron Revolving Monkey Cage Wagon, c. 1919–1926. One of the two known is in the Perelman Museum of Philadelphia. This toy was estimated at between $15,000 and $20,000 at the Bill Holland Toy Collection Auction at Sotheby's in April, 1985. (Photo courtesy of Sotheby's, New York.)

	Price Range	
☐ **Tiger Van,** 1920, has tiger embossed in oval on side of fully enclosed cage, painted cast iron, two horses with driver, 12¼″ length	700.00	800.00

Other Manufacturers

☐ **Band Wagon,** Ives, 1900s, painted cast iron (similar to Hubley example except for more ornate wheels), 31″ length		2000.00 plus

Price Range

☐ **Band Wagon,** Kenton, 1950, painted cast iron and sheet metal, features driver, six musicians, two men riding white horses, rubber balance wheel, 15½" length 250.00   350.00

☐ **"Big Six" Circus Wagon,** Arcade, 1920s, painted and stenciled wood and cast iron, head of cowboy and words "Big Six Circus—Wild West" on side of wagon, 14½" length 250.00   300.00

☐ **Circus Band Wagon,** Schoenhut Humpty Dumpty Circus, 1910, embossed and painted wood, four dappled horses, eight bandsmen, one driver in felt outfits, leather harnesses on horses, 40" length .... 2000.00 plus

☐ **Circus Band Wagon Wind-up Phonograph,** Charles Belknap Manufacturing, circa 1910, painted red wood with gold trim, plays miniature 78-RPM record as wagon is pulled, plywood musicians atop wagon, 15" length 500.00   600.00

☐ **Circus Calliope,** Kenton, 1940s, cast iron and sheet metal, two horses, driver, musician playing calliope, unlike Hubley calliope, there is no boiler, 14" length 550.00   650.00

☐ **Circus Set,** Schoenhut Humpty Dumpty Circus, 1924, seven pieces, 3 clowns, two ladders, barrel and chair, columns 8" height (also available in 4, 5, 8, and 10-piece sets) 300.00   400.00

☐ **Circus With Tent,** Schoenhut Humpty Dumpty Circus, 1910, painted wood figures, cloth tent, 18 pieces include ringmaster, lady bareback rider, clown, each 6½" height, animals: elephant 6¼" height, donkey and horse 8" height, trapeze, two ladders 8½" height, two chairs, barrel, hoop, two whips, tent and flags 1500.00   1700.00

Price Range

☐ **Circus Wagon,** Arcade, 1928, painted cast iron, two horses, driver is a large lion in elaborate cage, partially of pressed steel, approximately 14″ length 1600.00   1800.00

☐ **Elephant With Clown in Cart,** Harris, 1903, painted cast iron, seated clown holds reins of elephant, 7½″ length 600.00   800.00

Horse-Drawn Cage Wagon, Schoenhut Humpty Dumpty Circus, 1910, painted wood, tin and embossed cardboard, two dappled horses, driver and caged leopard, 29″ length .... 2000.00 plus

☐ **Polar Bear Cage,** Kenton, 1940, painted cast iron and sheet metal, small, nonfunctional wheel on left leg of pair of white horses (later Kenton models feature movable balance wheel), 14″ length 200.00   250.00

☐ **Show Wagon,** Schoenhut Humpty Dumpty Circus, circa 1910, painted and embossed cardboard and wood, decorated panels depict bareback rider, tiger, and elephant, canopy top 1200.00   1400.00

☐ **Teddy's Adventures in Africa,** Schoenhut, 1910, painted wood animals and Safari figures, 12 figures include Teddy Roosevelt, photographer, two native bearers, rhino, giraffe, elephant, alligator, hippo, zebra, and gorilla, box marked "T. R. Mombasa" (the gorilla is probably the most difficult Schoenhut animal figure to find) .... 2000.00 plus

CIRCUS CLOWNS

☐ **Balancing Clown,** German, 1910, hand-painted tin cloth-dressed clown on wood platform with balancing bar 600.00   650.00

Price Range

☐ **Balancing Toy Clown,** German, 1915, handpainted composition wood, iron-weighted balancing bar, 11″ height 550.00 650.00

☐ **Carnival Strong Man,** German, 1920s, clown hits gong on strength machine with large hammer, 4½″ length 100.00 150.00

☐ **Cirko Clown Cyclist,** maker unknown, 1924, lithographed circus figure appears on large wheel of high-wheeler, clown wears high peaked cap, 8½″ height 250.00 300.00

☐ **Clown Balancing Bears,** German, 1900s, painted and stenciled tin, clown is on back, resting on platform with feet in air balancing a spinning ball with bar, at each end of bar is a bear suspended in a swing, small bells at each end of bar ring as toy is activated, 11½″ height 1400.00 1600.00

☐ **Clown Barrel Walker,** Chein, 1940s, lithographed tin mechanical (variation of Chein's Popeye and Barnacle Bill toys), 7¾″ height 150.00 200.00

☐ **Clown Bell Toy,** gong bell, 1910, clown rides in cart pulled by pig 350.00 450.00

☐ **Clown and Black on See-Saw,** Watrous Mfg. Co., 1905, tin and cast-iron bell pull toy, 5¾″ length 300.00 500.00

☐ **Clown Cello Player,** maker unknown, 1920s, clown saws away at cello, music comes from seven-note disc under chair, 8″ height 400.00 450.00

☐ **Clown Circling Flag,** maker unknown, circa 1900, double-motion painted tin mechanical, clowns on three-wheeler circle flag as toy runs erratically across floor 300.00 350.00

☐ **Clown Dog Trainer,** French, circa 1914, clown has switch, small dog rides in swing, poodle dog dances on hind feet, 8″ height 300.00 350.00

☐ **Clown Doing Handstand,** German, circa 1915, painted tin, cloth costume, mechanical, 9″ height 350.00 400.00

☐ **Clown Drummer,** German, 1900s, hand-painted tin mechanical of dressed clown beating on large drum (with actual drum skin), hand-crank mechanical, 6″ height .. 200.00   250.00

☐ **Clown Four-Piece Set,** Schoenhut, 1924, painted wood jointed, 8″ height, clown with chair, 5″ height, ladder, 12″ height, barrel, 2¾″ height, full-size figures 75.00   125.00

☐ **Clown and Goat,** German, 1920s, lithographed tin mechanical with cloth clown outfit, clown has whip, goat butts cart from behind 200.00   250.00

☐ **Clown Hand Car ("Hoky Poky"),** Wyandotte, 1920s, two clowns pump handle, keywind mechanical, lithographed tin, 5¾″ length 100.00   150.00

☐ **Clown Hoop Toy,** German, circa 1910, tin mechanical, figure revolves inside hoop, 6½″ height 550.00   600.00

☐ **Clown on Horse Rocker,** German, 1900s, clockwork mechanical, papier-mache, cloth dressed, wood rockers, 8″ height 250.00   300.00

☐ **Clown on Ladder,** German, 1900s, composition tin, wood and cloth, crank activated, beats cymbals together, 11½″ height 300.00   350.00

☐ **Clown on Ladder,** maker unknown, circa 1915, composition wood with cloth costume, hand crank brings cymbals together as clown tumbles on ladder, 11½″ height ... 250.00   300.00

☐ **Clowns on Mechanical See-Saw,** maker unknown, 1910, painted tin, cloth outfits .. 200.00   250.00

☐ **Clown With Merry-Go-Round,** German, 1920s, lithographed tin mechanical, pull toy, clown rings gong and small carousel revolves 150.00   200.00

☐ **Clown With Monkey on Railroad Baggage Truck,** maker unknown, 1904, painted tin mechanical, clown pushes truck and monkey bangs cymbals 450.00   500.00

Price Range

☐ **Clown with Pig,** German, circa 1910, painted tin mechanical, 8″ length 350.00   400.00

☐ **Clown on Pig Rocker,** German, late 1890s, painted tin clockwork mechanical, activates clown to wave arms, pig to wiggle ears, has swinging pendulum weight, 6″ length 650.00   750.00

☐ **Clown Playing Harp,** German, 1910, painted tin, cloth outfit, head and arms move as if strumming harp, 8″ height 450.00   500.00

☐ **Clown and Poodle,** Gong Bell, 1903, clown swings dog who rings bell attached to muzzle, cast metal, painted, 8¼″ length 350.00   450.00

☐ **Clown Push Chime Toy,** Watrous Mfg. Co., 1905, tin and nickeled wheels and bells, on wooden stick, 5″ length 250.00   300.00

☐ **Clown Pushing Another Clown in Wheelbarrow,** German, 1920s, lithographed tin mechanical, 4½″ length 450.00   550.00

☐ **Clown Quartette,** German (possibly Guntermann), circa 1915, painted clockwork mechanical, musicians wear red, green, yellow, blue on yellow base, 11¾″ length 1200.00   1400.00

☐ **Clown Riding Bareback,** Ives, 1893, tin painted clown with cloth outfit stands up in saddle of horse, clockwork mechanical ..... 2000.00 plus

☐ **Clown Riding Hog,** Muller & Kadeder, circa 1900, painted tin mechanical, figures ride on small three-wheel platform, clown holds on for dear life by grabbing pig's ears 450.00   500.00

☐ **Clown Roly-Poly,** Schoenhut, 1920s, papier-mache, handpainted, 15″ height 350.00   400.00

☐ **Clown With Stubborn Pig,** German, circa 1914, painted tin mechanical, clown attempts to lead pig (on pair of wheels) by ears, other versions of toy appeared in 1920s, 7½″ length 250.00   300.00

☐ **Clowns Throwing Ball,** German, 1920s, two clowns seated on platform toss ball back and forth (may be penny toy), 3½″ length 150.00   200.00

Price Range

☐ **Clown With Trained Poodle,** German, circa 1900, painted tin, clockwork mechanical, clown rides poodle which is on heavy cast-iron wheels 400.00   450.00

☐ **Clown With Trick Dogs,** German, 1904, painted tin mechanical on platform, clown and poodle turn rope as smaller terrier type jumps rope 300.00   350.00

☐ **Clown Trick Mule Target Game,** W. S. Reed, 1915, lithographed paper-on-wood, rolling balls at target activated mule to unseat clown, 22″ length 1000.00   1200.00

☐ **Clown With Trick Poodle,** maker unknown (possibly Guntermann), 1904, figures on platform, painted tin mechanical, clown in cloth outfit, seated in tilted chair, is pushed back and forth by poodle wearing peaked clown's cap, clown tosses celluloid ball, 8½″ length 350.00   400.00

☐ **Clown Violinist,** Schuco, 1920s, cloth covered tin mechanical, 4½″ height 150.00   200.00

☐ **Clown on Wheels With Monkey,** maker unknown, 1910, painted tin mechanical, clown on small cart pursued by monkey ... 250.00   300.00

☐ **Comical Clowns in Roadster,** maker unknown, 1920s, lithographed tin mechanical, three clowns, one drives, the other pair beat each other on head with umbrellas 250.00   300.00

☐ **Dandy Jim Clown,** Strauss, 1920s, 10″ height, clown dances on roof and plays cymbals 250.00   300.00

☐ **Donkey-Drawn Clown Chariot,** Schoenhut, 1920s, wood, 16″ length 1400.00   1600.00

☐ **Forepaugh's Trained Elephants,** maker unknown, 1904, clown on unicycle moves whip as elephants, also on wheels, move along floor on hind legs, approximately 8″ height 450.00   500.00

Price Range

☐ **Hanging Dancing Clown,** Ives, 1900s, cloth costume, lead tin, wood figure (Ives box is marked No. 22-11, "Mechanical Hanging Dancer") 10½" length ....   2000.00 plus

☐ **Le Clown Orchestra,** Fernand Martin (French), circa 1900, clown wears bells on hands, feet, and head 400.00   450.00

☐ **Mule Clowns,** possibly Ives, tin clockwork figures on wooden base, clowns riding mules on opposite ends of wire shaft, lots of bucking and rearing ....   2000.00 plus

☐ **Pair Clowns With Instruments,** Guntermann, circa 1915, handpainted tin, larger clown plays trombone, smaller figure in barrel toots trumpet, 9½" height 550.00   600.00

☐ **Poodle and Clown Hoop Jumper Bell Toy,** Gong Bell, 1903, clown holds hoop and dog leaps through in both directions ringing bell at each end of wheeled platform, cast metal, cast iron, 12" length 350.00   450.00

☐ **Tom Twist,** F. Strauss, 1920s, lithographed tin mechanical, painted clown with bells for earrings, flat cap (variation of Boob McNut comic toy by Strauss) so toy can be turned upside down and Tom dances on head 150.00   200.00

☐ **Tumbling Clowns,** German, circa 1910, painted tin mechanical, front clown grabs barbell, back clown holds his partner's feet in the air and pushes along, 5⅞" height ...   800.00   1000.00

☐ **Unique Artie,** Unique Art, 1920s, lithographed tin mechanical, clown rides crazy car, small dog sits on hood, 9½" height ...   150.00   200.00

☐ **"What's It?,"** F. Strauss, 1927, lithographed tin, clown with high peaked hat pilots speedboat on wheels (two large center wheels, two small pivoting wheels at each end), 9½" length 150.00   200.00

COMIC AND
CHARACTER TOYS

Four visionaries are credited with launching the comic art form that inspired a legion of lovable, laughable toys and games in their images. James Swinnerton created a jolly menagerie of animal characters in "Little Bears and Tigers." Richard Outcault made the first real comic strip breakthrough in America with "The Yellow Kid" in *The New York Sunday World* in 1896. Rudolph Dirks originated "The Katzenjammer Kids" for the Hearst Syndicate a year later. Fred B. Opper introduced the eternal scapegoat, "Happy Hooligan," via the color comics section of the *New York Journal* in 1896. Outcault's artistry with the pen was soon matched by his marketing acumen. At the 1904 St. Louis World's Fair, Outcault set up shop with the express purpose of merchandising the services of his latest creation, "Buster Brown," and succeeded in signing up hundreds of licensees. Fontaine Fox, also a marketing innovator, laid the foundation for numerous franchises when he created "Toonerville Folks" in 1915. The transformation from the comic pages to exceptional, colorful lithographed and painted tin and cast iron has continued uninterrupted to this day. The advent of the Golden Age of Radio in the 1920s and 1930s inspired another toy parade recreating actual real-life personalities in their various roles, including Joe "Wanna Buy a Duck?" Penner, Ed "Fire Chief" Wynn, and the irrepressible "Amos 'n' Andy," created by Freeman Gosden and Charles Correll. From the movie lots of Hollywood would emerge Charlie Chaplin, W. C. Fields, Felix the Movie Cat, Betty Boop, and Shirley Temple. The 1940s and 1950s were dominated by Edgar Bergen (and his sidekicks, Charlie McCarthy and Mortimer Snerd), "The Lone Ranger," "Tom Corbett, Space Cadet," "Radio Orphan Annie," and "Sky King." TV in the 1950s spawned its "Captain Video," "Uncle Miltie," "The Honeymooners," and "Howdy Doody"—all making the transition from the tube to tin, composition, and plastic playthings. The super heroes, "Buck Rogers," "Flash Gordon," "Superman," and "Captain Marvel," may be upstaged today by Han Solo, Luke Skywalker, Captain Kirk, and He-Man, but the early movie serial characters and comic heroes were the prototypes of what we have today. Comic

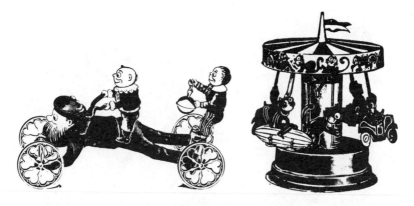

Two "Inner Circle" comic toys: "Captain and the Kids" bell toy, Gong Bell Manufacturing Co., $2000 plus; Felix musical carousel, German (probably Nifty), 1927, $1200–$1500.

toys are assured some form of immortality as nearly three generations of toy collectors keep steadfastly on their trail.

AGGIE

A comic strip moppet from "Reg'lar Fellers" by Gene Byrnes in 1923.

	Price Range	
☐ **Aggie,** lithograph tin, Nifty, 1925–1926 ...	400.00	500.00
☐ **Reg'lar Fellers Bowling Game,** Selchow & Righter, 1920s, figures of heavy cardboard with wood base, 10″ height	125.00	150.00

ALPHONSE AND GASTON

Comic strip characters created by Fred B. Opper in 1896, whose names became synonymous with exaggerated politeness. ("After you, my dear Gaston. No, after *you*, my dear Alphonse.")

☐ **Alphonse and Gaston Auto,** Kenton, 1910, cast iron, yellow and orange with gold trim, 8″ length 1000.00   1200.00

Amos 'n' Andy Walkers, $400–$500 each; Amos 'n' Andy Fresh Air Taxicab, $450–$550.

Price Range

☐ **Alphonse Nodder in Circus Cart,** cast iron, bright colors, figure is interchangeable with Happy Hooligan, another Opper character. *Note:* Both the figures and cart have been recast in recent years, the repro version has the name "Nodders" cast on the donkey pulling cart, original version has "The Nodders" 500.00   700.00

AMOS 'N' ANDY

Two radio characters created by Freeman Gosden and Charles Correll in 1928. Amos 'n' Andy also appeared in a comic strip, movies, and TV (1950–1955).

☐ **Andrew H. Brown Wood-Jointed Figure,** 1930s, manufacturer unknown, Andy wears orange derby and smokes a cigar 40.00   50.00

☐ **Fresh Air Taxicab,** Dent Hardware, cast iron, 1930, 6″ length, this toy has sparked considerable controversy among collectors, as it probably never advanced past prototype stage; samples of the toy were assembled from married parts a few years ago after a "find" in Dent's factory 500.00   600.00

Price Range

☐ **Fresh Air Taxicab,** Marx, 1930, litho tin, wind-up, cab runs with erratic, jerky motion, 8″ length (two versions: one with headlights, one without headlights but with inscription, "Andy Brown Prez, Amos Jones Driver" on door); make certain that hand crank, meter flag, and horseshoe radiator cap are intact and all three are there for toy to be complete 450.00 550.00

☐ **Sparklers,** German, early 1930s, litho tin with glass eyes that light up when squeezing plunger, each 700.00 800.00

☐ **Walking Toys,** Marx, 1930, litho tin windups, 12″ height (deluxe models featured rolling eyes and command 10–20% higher prices), each 400.00 500.00

BARNACLE BILL

A comic figure inspired by the 1920s song hit, "I'm Barnacle Bill the Sailor."

☐ **Barnacle Bill in the Barrel,** Chein, 1930s, litho, 6″ height (both this toy and the Barnacle Bill Walking Figure, by Chein, incorporated the same dies for Popeye versions, which are more highly prized by comic collectors) 75.00 125.00

☐ **Barnacle Bill in a Rowboat,** manufacturer unknown, 1930s, tin litho wind-up 500.00 600.00

☐ **Barnacle Bill Walking Figure,** Chein, 1930s, litho tin wind-up, 6″ height 75.00 100.00

BARNEY GOOGLE

A cartoon character that first appeared in syndication in 1919 and was created by Billy DeBeck. Also inspired the Billy Rose song hit in the 1920s, "Barney Google With the Goo-Goo-Googly Eyes."

☐ **Barney Google Riding Sparkplug,** Nifty, 1924, litho tin wind-up, 7½″ height 1000.00 1200.00

Boob McNutt, F. Strauss, 1925, $400–$500; Barney Google Riding
Sparkplug, Nifty, 1920s, $1000–$1200; Charlie Chaplin standing figure,
German, 1920s, $650–$750.

	Price Range	
☐ **Barney Google Scooter Race,** German, 1924, litho tin wind-up, Barney on scooter, Sunshine is jockey aboard Sparkplug	1500.00	2000.00
☐ **Barney Google and Sparkplug,** Schoenhut, late 1920s, wood-jointed figures with cloth outfit and horse blanket, each	300.00	400.00
☐ **Barney Google and Sparkplug Platform Toy,** Nifty, 1924, litho tin wind-up, variation of racing toy, Barney rides up front on scooter, Sparkplug's barn in rear shows Snowflake drawing water, Rudy eating oats and Sparkplug trying to jump over Dutch doors, only one known example, 9¼″ length	2000.00	2500.00

Price Range

☐ **Rudy the Ostrich,** Nifty, 1924, tin wind-up, litho body with handpainted tail, neck and body, Rudy was Barney's pesky little friend, 9″ height 1000.00   1200.00

☐ **Sparkplug Platform Pull Toy,** manufacturer unknown, 1930s, wood toy hinged in two places to create greater animation, 9″ length 35.00   50.00

BETTY BOOP

In the early 1930s this pixy-like character starred in animated movie cartoons created by Max Fleischer. Later she appeared in a comic strip as a movie queen. A contemporary wooden and plexiglass Betty Boop, 5 feet high, sold for $1100 at the Atlanta Toy Museum Auction in October 1986.

☐ **Betty Boop and Bimbo Racer,** Keeneye Inc., 1932 .... 500.00   600.00

☐ **Betty Boop Standing Figure,** CK, Japan, 1930, celluloid figure on tin base, 7″ height 250.00   300.00

☐ **Betty Boop Wood-Jointed Figure,** manufacturer unknown, 1930s 150.00   200.00

BLONDIE

In the early 1930s Chic Young created this long running family comic strip; later "Blondie" was adapted to radio, a movie series in the 1940s, and a TV series in the 1950s.

☐ **Blondie's Jalopy,** Marx, late 1930s, litho tin wind-up, open sedan with Dagwood and Baby Dumpling in front seat (variation of Marx's Mortimer Snerd Private Car) 15″ length 650.00   750.00

☐ **Dagwood Musical Sandwich,** Midwest Corp., Milwaukee, 1947, 5″ length 50.00   75.00

Price Range

☐ **Dagwood the Driver,** Marx, 1935, tin litho wind-up, pictures of Blondie, Daisy the dog, and Cookie are litho'd on side panels of auto, 8″ length (copyright dates appear on the car as 1930, 1934, 1935, but since new baby Cookie didn't arrive in the Bumstead household until 1935, we assume the latter date to be the manufacture date) 450.00   550.00

☐ **Dagwood the Pilot,** Marx, late 1930s, tin litho wind-up, 7″ length (variation of Marx's Popeye the Pilot, but Dagwood is not as easy to come by) 650.00   750.00

BOOB MCNUTT

Rube Goldberg, who is best remembered for his wacky, complicated cartoon inventions, created Boob McNutt in a syndicated strip in 1918.

☐ **Boob McNutt,** Schoenhut, mid-1920s, wood-jointed, cloth outfit, 9″ height 400.00   500.00

☐ **Boob McNutt Walker,** Strauss, 1925, litho tin wind-up, 9½″ height, there are two variations of this toy: one shows him with tiny hat atop his head, another has hat upside down so that Boob could perform on his head 350.00   450.00

BONZO

A clever little spotted Boston Bulldog appearing in a Hearst syndicated comic strip created by an English cartoonist, G.E. Studdy.

☐ **Bonzo on Scooter,** S.G. (a German manufacturer), circa 1930s, litho tin wind-up 250.00   350.00

BRINGING UP FATHER

Maggie and Jiggs, the stars of this comic strip created by George McManus in 1913.

Price Range

☐ **Jiggs and His Jazz Car,** Nifty, 1924, litho
tin wind-up, King Features Service, Inc.
copyright on side of auto, 6½ ″ length 800.00   1000.00

☐ **Maggie and Jiggs Family Squabble,** Gebruder Einfalt (Nifty), 1924, litho tin wind-
up, figures joined by 2 ″ connecting strip
which undulates when toy is activated to
give illusion of Maggie and Jiggs attacking
each other, 7 ″ length 1500.00   2100.00

☐ **Maggie and Jiggs Squeeze Toy,** German,
late 1920s, tin with steel handles, squeeze
handles and couple seems to be fighting ...   350.00   450.00

☐ **Maggie and Jiggs Standing Figures,**
Schoenhut, mid-1920s, wood-jointed with
cloth outfits, Maggie has a rolling pin and
Jiggs a bucket of his favorite corned beef
and cabbage, each 350.00   400.00

BUCK ROGERS

The first of the great science fiction cartoon characters stepped
into the 25th century in 1929. Buck was created by John Dille,
drawn by Lt. Dick Calkins, and written by Phil Nowlan. Buck,
Wilma, and their fellow astronauts also provided their share of thrills
in movie serials and in the 1970s on TV.

☐ **Buck Rogers Rocket Police Patrol Ship,**
Marx, 1939, litho tin wind-up, shoots sparks
....   125.00   150.00

☐ **Rocket Ship,** Marx, 1934, litho tin wind-
up, shoots sparks, 12 ″ length 150.00   175.00

☐ **Rocket Ships,** Tootsietoys, 1930s, Series of
three pot metal models: Venus Duo De-
stroyer, Battlecruiser, and Flash Blast At-
tack Ship with names embossed on painted
metal, 5 ″ length, each 100.00   125.00

BUSTER BROWN

One of the earliest comic characters, Buster Brown was created
by Richard Outcault in 1902; his faithful companion was a somewhat mean-looking talking bulldog named Tige. Although they've

been funny page dropouts since just after World War I, they continue to be popular advertising spokesmen for a variety of products.

Price Range

☐ **Bob and Bruno** (a knockoff version), Gong Bell, pull toy, cast iron 800.00   1200.00

☐ **Buster Brown in Cart** (variation), manufacturer unknown, believed 1920s, cast-iron figures and sheet metal cart, handpainted in bright colors 500.00   600.00

☐ **Buster Brown in Cart Pulled by Tige,** manufacturer unknown, 1910, cast-iron two-piece casting, painted all silver, 7″ length 600.00   800.00

☐ **Buster Brown With Dog,** Muller & Kadeder, 1906, tin litho wind-up, figures pull one another up on string-pulley mechanism, 13″ height 1000.00   1200.00

☐ **Buster Brown and Monkey on Seesaw,** German, handpainted tin rocking toy, 1909, figures roll celluloid ball to each other, 9¼″ height 1200.00   1500.00

☐ **Buster With Poodle,** Muller & Kadeder, 1900s, litho tin wind-up, figures ring bell attached to lantern post, 7½″ height 1700.00   2000.00

☐ **Buster Brown Roly-Poly,** Schoenhut, 1910, papier-mache, turning head, 17″ height ... 450.00   550.00

☐ **Buster Brown and Tige,** A.C. Williams, early 1900s, cast-iron still bank, gold finish, 5″ height 125.00   150.00

☐ **Buster Brown and Tige,** Watrous, 1905, cast-iron bell toy, nickeled wheels, 7¼″ length 1200.00   1400.00

☐ **Buster Brown and Tige Cashier,** Buster appears as cashier at one window, Tige appears at the other three windows, words "Security," "Paying Teller," and "Fidelity" appear under Tige, green, gold with white dial for registering coin input, 5″ height 200.00   250.00

Price Range

☐ **Horseshoe,** black horse framed by gold
horseshoe, bust of Buster Brown appears
above arch in horse's neck, Tige sits at base
of horseshoe, 4″ height 200.00   250.00

BUTTERCUP

This cartoon character was the pride and joy of the comic strip
couple "Toots and Casper," created by Jimmy Murphy in 1918.

☐ **Buttercup and Spare Ribs Platform Toy,**
Nifty, mid-1920s, litho tin wind-up, a
kneeling Buttercup seems to be grooming,
with a whisk broom, her pet dog Spare Ribs,
8″ length 600.00   700.00

☐ **Crawling Buttercup,** German (no manufacturer name), painted tin wind-up, has
Jimmy Murphy copyright, 8″ length 700.00   800.00

CAPTAIN MARVEL

Billy Batson, who was transformed into crime fighter Captain
Marvel upon uttering the magic word "Shazam" and invoking a
lightning bolt, first appeared with Fawcett Publications comic books
in 1941 and continued until 1953, when National Comics brought
legal action, claiming that the Captain infringed on their Superman
copyrights. Charles C. Beck created Captain Marvel and Otto Binder
authored the feature.

☐ **Captain Marvel Lightning Racing Cars,**
copyright Fawcett Publications, 1948, set of
four racing cars with the Captain in flight
litho'd on cars, for the complete set 100.00   125.00

CHARLIE CHAPLIN

The Little Tramp achieved his greatest fame in the movies,
beginning with the Keystone Studio in 1913 and spanning over 50
years. Charlie also inspired a comic strip which first appeared in
1915 and was drawn by several cartoonists, including Elzie Segar
of "Popeye" fame, Ed Carey, and Gus Mager.

	Price Range	
☐ **Charlie Chaplin,** litho paper-on-wood figure, on wood stand, German, 1917, swings with outstretched arms on post	450.00	550.00
☐ **Charlie Chaplin Bell Ringer,** believed Gong Bell, 1917, cast-iron figure with sheet metal three-wheel vehicle	650.00	750.00
☐ **Charlie Chaplin, Boxer Champion,** 1915, tin with felt covering on face, inspired by movie "The Champion" made with Essanay in 1915	1000.00	1200.00
☐ **Charlie Chaplin Dancing Toy,** German, 1920s, 5½ × 7 paper over tin box with jointed figure of Charlie simulating dancing	300.00	400.00
☐ **Charlie Chaplin Squeak Toy,** German, 1917, composition head with cloth body, squeaks when bellows is pressed	450.00	550.00
☐ **Charlie Chaplin Squeeze Toy,** German, early 1920s, litho tin, when plunger is pushed, arm raises and cymbals strike, Charlie holds a cat in left hand	300.00	400.00
☐ **Charlie Chaplin Standing Figure,** German, 1920s, celluloid, Chaplin assumes famous stance with one hand on hip, the other holding a cane	350.00	400.00
☐ **Charlie Chaplin Standing Figure,** German, 1920s, litho tin with cast-iron feet wind-up, rocks back and forth at waist, carries little wire cane, 8¾″ height	650.00	750.00
☐ **Charlie Chaplin Wooden Figure,** French, 1920s	300.00	350.00
☐ **Standing Charlie Chaplin Spinning Cane,** Schuco, 1920s, tin with felt covering on face, cloth outfit, 6½″ height	750.00	850.00
☐ **Whistling Charlie Chaplin Carved Wooden Figure,** German, 1920s, Charlie whistles "How Dry I Am"	500.00	600.00

CHARLIE McCARTHY

An unlikely duo of a ventriloquist named Edgar Bergen and his wooden sidekick, Charlie McCarthy, dominated the airwaves beginning in 1936 to 1948 on the "Chase and Sanborn Hour" on NBC (they switched to CBS with Coca Cola as sponsor for another eight years before calling it quits in 1956). In 1939, Bergen added a companion for Charlie, the country bumpkin Mortimer Snerd. The pair starred in numerous movies, a syndicated comic strip drawn by Ben Batsford, and Whitman Big Little Books.

Many comic toy collections include a variety of Charlie and Mortimer marionettes, with composition heads and cloth bodies (in various sizes from 17″ to 20″) at $200–$250. The best of these, by Effenbee Doll Co., featured Charlie as Sherlock Holmes, a Cowboy, or a French legionnaire.

Effenbee also produced a W.C. Fields doll, inspired by his frequent guest appearances on the show ($450–$500). Ideal Co. produced a Mortimer Doll that featured flexible hands and feet ($250–$300). A McCarthy endorsed hand-puppet with composition head sells in the $35–$50 range.

	Price Range	
☐ **Charlie McCarthy Benzine Buggy,** Marx, 1940s	200.00	250.00
☐ **Charlie McCarthy Drummer,** Marx, 1940s, litho tin wind-up, pushes bass drum on three-wheel car, 8″ height	350.00	450.00
☐ **Charlie McCarthy and Mortimer Snerd Private Car,** Marx, 1939, striped roadster with big bumpers (see also Blondie Jalopie, a Marx variant), Charlie's favorite saying, "We'll mow you down," appears on driver's door, 15″ length, in 1983, this toy with original box sold for $1400 at a Lloyd Ralston Auction, then a record for any toy of 1940s vintage	850.00	1000.00

Price Range

☐ **Charlie McCarthy Still Bank,** manufacturer unknown, 1940s, slush-cast painted, this is a knockoff version, as there is no indication on the bank that this was one of Edgar Bergen's Charlie McCarthy Inc. endorsed toys 100.00   125.00

☐ **"Charlie Strut,"** Marx, 1940s, litho tin wind-up, mouth goes up and down as he waddles, 8″ height 100.00   150.00

☐ **Mortimer Snerd Benzine Buggy,** Marx, 1940s, litho tin wind-up 250.00   300.00

☐ **Mortimer Snerd Drummer,** Marx, 1940s, litho tin wind-up, pushes bass drum on three-wheel cart, 8″ height 350.00   450.00

☐ **"Mortimer Strut,"** Marx, 1940s, litho tin wind-up, hat moves up and down when activated, 8″ height 100.00   150.00

DICK TRACY

Created by Chester Gould in 1931, "Dick Tracy" has the distinction of being the first comic strip to introduce blood and gore to its legions of readers.

☐ **B.O. Plenty Standing Figure,** Marx, 1940s, litho tin wind-up, shuffles along and cap tilts—a variation of Mortimer Snerd Strut windup, another weird character from the strip, B.O. holds his baby Sparkle Plenty in one arm, 8½″ height 75.00   100.00

☐ **Dick Tracy Automatic Police Station,** Marx, 1940s, tin litho with swinging doors, 8½″ length, includes 7½″ length friction squad car which shoots sparks 75.00   100.00

☐ **Dick Tracy Bonnie Braids Game,** Charmore Co., Paterson, N.J., "Watch the Nursemaid Take Bonnie Braids for a Ride," United Artists Synd., 1951, after two decades of courtship, Tracy finally married Tess Trueheart and Bonnie Braids was their progeny. 50.00   60.00

Price Range

☐ **Dick Tracy Riot Car,** Marx, 1939, tin litho
wind-up with battery-operated probe light
and siren, 11″ length, also a 7″ length size.
.... 100.00   150.00

Note: A 16″ length Riot Car was manufactured by Marx in the
1950s which featured plastic figures of Tracy and his partner, Sam
Ketchum ($50-$75 range).

ED WYNN

Wynn was an old time vaudevillian, billed as The Perfect Fool,
who made a successful transition to radio in 1932 as The Texaco
Fire Chief.

☐ **Ed Wynn Firehouse,** Schoenhut, 1933–34,
litho cardboard and wood, rubber-band-
powered horse-drawn toy driven by Chief
Wynn, shoots vehicle out of firehouse when
lever is pressed, 9½″ length (this toy, in
pristine condition, sold for $375 at the At-
lanta Toy Museum Auction in October
1986) 250.00   300.00

FELIX THE CAT

Originated as Felix the Movie Cat, a star in animated movie
cartoons in 1920, his creator was Pat Sullivan. Three years later,
Felix had his own comic strip syndicated by King Features. Often
mistaken for the more cerebral Krazy Kat. Nifty made several toys
for both Felix and Krazy using identical dies, further adding to the
confusion.

☐ **Felix the Bowler,** Nifty, 1931, tin litho,
miniature alley with pins 450.00   550.00

☐ **Felix Hood Ornament on Roadster,** Carl
Bubb, 1930s, litho tin wind-up, 6″ length   1000.00   1200.00

☐ **Felix and Mice Platform on Wheel Toy,**
Nifty, 1931, pull toy, 7½″ length 300.00   350.00

☐ **Felix the Movie Cat Sparkler,** Nifty, 1931,
5″ height 250.00   275.00

Felix on the Scooter, Nifty, 1931, $250–$350; Happy Hooligan Police Patrol, Kenton, 1911, cast iron, $2000 plus.

	Price Range	
☐ **Felix Musical Carousel,** German, manufacturer unknown, 1927, litho tin, little Felixes ride in miniature autos, zeppelins, 7½″ height, 5½″ diameter	1200.00	1500.00
☐ **Felix on the Scooter,** Nifty, 1931, tin litho wind-up	250.00	300.00
☐ **Felix With Umbrella,** manufacturer unknown, cast-iron, painted figure with nodder head attached with spring steel	250.00	300.00
☐ **Felix Wagon,** Nifty, 1931 tin litho, Felix pulls two-wheeler	300.00	350.00
☐ **Jointed Felix,** Nifty, 1931, wood two-dimensional figure	150.00	175.00
☐ **Speedy Felix, Roadster Pull Toy,** Nifty, 1931, litho wood	175.00	225.00
☐ **Walking Felix,** German, 1930s, has name, copyright dates and Sullivan's name on band around waist, painted tin, walks with swaying motion, a rather crude visualization of Felix	250.00	300.00
Note: A knockoff version of this toy was produced by Gama in Germany, 6½″ height, circa 1929, featured arms raised rather than folded. It was marketed as "Comical Cat"	150.00	200.00

Price Range

☐ **Wood-Jointed Felix Three-Dimensional Figures,** Schoenhut, 1932, sizes from 4″ height to 12″ height

smaller versions	75.00	100.00
larger versions	50.00	200.00

☐ **Worried Felix,** German, late 1920s, manufacturer unknown, celluloid figure 250.00 300.00

FLASH GORDON

Along with Prince Valiant, this 1934 strip by Alex Raymond has been acknowledged as one of the best drawn of all comic strips. Raymond also created Secret Agent X-O, Jungle Jim, and Rip Kirby before his untimely death in 1956. Flash Gordon emerged as a TV show in the early 1950s starring Buster Crabbe.

☐ **Flash Gordon Radio Repeater Pistol,** Marx, 1936, tin litho 75.00 100.00

☐ **Flash Gordon Rocket Fighter,** Marx, 1939, 12″ length, tin litho, shoots sparks 150.00 175.00

☐ **Flash Gordon Signal (Space) Pistol,** Marx, 1936, tin litho 75.00 100.00

FOXY GRANDPA

One of the earliest comic strips in the American idiom, along with "Buster Brown," "The Yellow Kid," and the "Katzenjammer Kids." Created by Carl Schultze, he began in the *New York Herald* in 1900 and was finally discontinued in 1927.

☐ **Foxy Grandpa Bell Ringer,** manufacturer unknown, early 1900s, cast iron, Foxy sits sedately at reins of three-wheeled cart featuring two figures of running boys on front wheel 1200.00 1400.00

☐ **Foxy Grandpa Hat Flipper Toy,** manufacturer unknown, early 1900s, cast iron with tin hat, lever is pushed to attempt putting hat on Foxy 1000.00 1500.00

☐ **Foxy Grandpa Still Bank,** Wing, Chicago, Foxy is in black suit and wears derby, cast iron, originally marketed as "Grandpa Bank," 5¾" height 200.00   250.00

☐ **Foxy in Horse-Drawn Cart,** Harris, cast-iron, there are matching versions with figures of Gloomy Gus and Happy Hooligan standing in cart, 7¼" length 1000.00   1200.00

☐ **Foxy Nodder,** Kenton, 1910, cast-iron painted nodder in cart, a companion piece to Kenton's Happy Hooligan and Alphonse Nodders, the words "The Nodders" appears on horse's blanket, 7" length 700.00   800.00

☐ **Foxy Nodder,** Kenton, 1910, circus cart, also features Alphonse and Gloomy Gus, 11½" length 1200.00   1500.00

☐ **Foxy Walker,** German, early 1900s, hand-painted, wheels on feet, tin wind-up action allows Foxy to simultaneously raise and lower arms as hinged legs open and close as toy moves across floor, 8" height 1500.00   2000.00

☐ **Twin Nodder Toy,** Foxy and Happy Hooligan cart, driven by Gloomy Gus, Kenton Mfg. Co., 1900s, drawn by two horses, 16" length .... 2000.00 plus

GASOLINE ALLEY

A strip that mirrors small town life in the U.S.A. was launched on Valentine's Day, 1921, by Frank King. The main characters were Uncle Walt and Auntie Blossom. Skeezix, who later became the main focus of this longrunning strip (it continues to this day), was found abandoned on Walt's doorstep.

☐ **Uncle Walt in Roadster,** Dowst (Tootsie-toy), 1932, one of series of five comic miniatures, cast metal, painted in red 125.00   150.00

GLOOMY GUS

Another Fred Opper creation, Gloomy appeared in a number of "Happy Hooligan" strips opposite his hapless brother.

Price Range

☐ **Gloomy Gus Cart,** Harris, 1903, cast iron, this version with Gloomy standing also featured Happy and Foxy, 7¼" length 1000.00   1200.00

☐ **Gloomy Gus Cast-Iron Cart,** Harris, 1903, Gloomy is standing in horse-drawn cart, 14" length 1200.00   1500.00

☐ **Gloomy and Happy,** Harris, 1903, in cast-iron cart with driver, 18" length ....   2000.00 plus

THE GUMPS

This was the first comic strip to tell a serialized story and the first to deal with real people in real-life situations. Launched in 1917 by Joseph Medill Patterson, one of the owners of the *Chicago Tribune,* it was drawn by a *Tribune* staff artist, Robert Sidney Smith, who later became the first cartoonist to sign a million dollar contract.

A rather crudely drawn strip about a goat named Doc Yak and his son Yutch was the predecessor to the Andy Gump series. Sidney Smith had drawn Doc Yak from 1915–1917, a few years prior to the directive to create The Gumps. The only legacy from the Yak saga was the 348 license plate; Doc Yak had a little roadster that he bought for $3.48 which he considered such a bargain that the price became his plate number and a popular landmark of the strip.

☐ **Andy Gump Still Bank,** Arcade, 1928, cast iron, same figure as used in Arcade's Andy Gump 348 Car, Andy sits on tree stump in two-piece casting, 4¼" height 1000.00   1200.00

☐ **Andy Gump Still Bank,** manufacturer unknown, late 1920s, tin litho 200.00   250.00

Price Range

☐ **Andy Gump in 348 Car,** Arcade, 1924, cast iron, there were three variations of this model: (1) nickle-plated figure, wheels, and 348 grill; (2) painted figure with green wheel covers and red hubs; (3) Andy wears a number of colors (as opposed to dark green in figure 2, including dark blue suit, wheels are white with green center and red hubs, red car chassis is trimmed in green, there is a 348 rear plate, painted like front grill, plus red crank, 6″ height, 7¼″ length 600.00   700.00

☐ **Andy Gump 348 Car,** Dowst (Tootsietoy), 1932, cast metal, one of six toys in Tootsietoy Funnies Series, figures moved up and down with deluxe models, also painted in bright colors, standard models were nonaction with simple color scheme, 2¾″ length .... 100.00   125.00★

☐ **Andy Gump Wood-Jointed Standing Figure,** Sidney Smith copyright 75.00   100.00

☐ **Chester Gump in Pony Cart,** Arcade, 1924, cast iron, 8″ length 550.00   650.00

☐ **Old Doc Yak Still Bank,** believed made by Arcade, 1920s, cast iron, 6½″ height 350.00   400.00

HAPPY HOOLIGAN

Another silly saga by Fred B. Opper (Alphonse and Gaston, Maude the Mule, Happy's brother Gloomy Gus). Happy Hooligan, with the red tin can hat, symbolized the eternal scapegoat. Introduced in new color comics section of the *New York Journal* in 1896.

☐ **Happy Hooligan Automobile Toy,** N.H. Hill Brass, early 1900s, cast-iron, bell-ringing open roadster (the rear end features what looks like a wood stove with stove pipe elbow), perhaps the most uncommon highly prized of all comic toys, car is painted red, Happy wears yellow jacket with blue pants, 6½″ length .... 2500.00 plus

★20% higher for deluxe version

Price Range

☐ **Happy Hooligan Cast-Iron Cart,** Harris, 1903, Happy stands in horse-drawn cart, 14″ length 1200.00   1500.00

☐ **Happy Hooligan on Ladder,** Schoenhut, 1924, wood jointed with cloth outfit 350.00   400.00

☐ **Happy Hooligan Nodder in Cart,** Harris, 1903, cast iron (matching versions included Gloomy Gus and Foxy Grandpa), 7¼″ length 1000.00   1200.00

☐ **Happy Hooligan Police Patrol,** Kenton, 1911, cast iron, wagon is driven by Gloomy Gus, animated cop raps Happy on noggin with nightstick as toy is pulled along, one of the rarest classic comic toys, 17½″ length ....   2000.00 plus

☐ **Happy Hooligan Roly-Poly,** F. Opper copyright, manufacturer unknown, 1920s ... 350.00   400.00

☐ **Happy Hooligan Standing Figure,** Schoenhut, 1924, wood jointed with cloth outfit .. 300.00   350.00

☐ **Happy Hooligan Walker,** Chein, 1932, litho tin wind-up, Happy wears bright green coat with light green trousers and orange oversize shoes, 6″ height 400.00   450.00

HAROLD LLOYD

This star of the silent film era made millions portraying a meek, mild-mannered character with large hornrimmed glasses who overcame obstacles that made strong men quail.

☐ **Harold Lloyd on the Telephone,** German, 1920s, litho tin squeeze toy, by pushing plunger, as with sparkler versions, the same type of facial action is produced as with the Marx walker, 6″ height 225.00   250.00

Price Range

☐ **Harold Lloyd Walker,** Marx, 1925, litho tin wind-up, as toy waddles, top part of face moves up and down, creating smiles or frowns, although the toy does not bear Lloyd's name, the image is unmistakably his, 11″ height 350.00   400.00

☐ **Harold Lloyd Wind-up,** manufacturer unknown, 1920s, celluloid, vibrates when wound, holds straw hat in hand, 5″ height 200.00   250.00

HENRY

This comic strip by Carl Anderson began in the early 1930s, first in the *Saturday Evening Post* with sporadic appearances, then with King Features Syndicate. Violated all the rules by its complete absence of dialogue. (Henry was not only speechless, but expressionless.)

☐ **Henry the Acrobat,** C.K., Japan, 1930s, celluloid, with steel swinging apparatus, wind-up 200.00   250.00

☐ **Henry and Henrietta Travelers,** C.K., Japan, 1934, celluloid, with tin suitcase wind-up, 7¼″ height .... 250.00   300.00★

☐ **Henry and His Brother,** C.K., Japan, celluloid with each figure on tin platform with wheels, wind-up 200.00   250.00

☐ **Henry Riding on Elephant's Trunk,** C.K., Japan, 1930s, celluloid wind-up 250.00   275.00

HI-WAY HENRY

A bearded old gentleman and his rather hefty wife were featured in this comic strip drawn by Oscar Hitt in the early 1920s. Many consider Hi-Way Henry to be the most desirable of all comic toys.

★Sold for 575.00 at the Atlanta Toy Museum Auction

Price Range

☐ **Hi-Way Henry Auto,** German, 1928, litho
tin wind-up, front of car rears up as it trav-
els, whirls about, and re-starts; Henry IV,
a dog appearing in radiator, bobs in and out;
a very delicate toy with many loose-fitting
or removable parts; be sure the following
are intact: stove, stove pipe, wash tub and
board, clothesline; a tiny string runs from
tiny hole in clothesline to headphones Mrs.
Henry is wearing ....   2000.00 plus

☐ **Hi-Way Henry Cross-Country Auto
Game,** late 1920s, litho cardboard 200.00   250.00

HOPALONG CASSIDY

A popular cowboy movie idol played by William Boyd in over
50 feature films in the 1950s. Later, Hopalong inspired a TV series
also starring Boyd.

☐ **Hopalong Cassidy Rocking Horse,** Marx,
early 1950s, litho tin wind-up, toy rocks
when activated and Hoppy swings lariat
astride his white horse, Topper, 11″ length   200.00   250.00

HOWDY DOODY

This show reigned supreme among Saturday morning kiddie's
TV fare from 1947-1960. Emceed by the show's orginator, Buffalo
Bob Smith, "Howdy Doody" featured its namesake as a marionette, along with Phineas T. Bluster, Dilly Dally, Flub-a-Dub,
and other Doodyville denizens. (Clarabelle the Clown was played
by Bob Keeshan, who went on to fame in "Captain Kangaroo.")

To help date Howdy items (over 600 manufacturers received
permission to license and distribute), use following rule-of-thumb:

1948-1951, items marked Bob Smith or Martin Stone Associates
1951-1956, items marked Kagran Corp.
1956-1960, items marked California National Products (an NBC
marketing division)
1960 to date, items marked NBC

Many collections also include the marionettes: Howdy Doody,

Clarabelle, Phineas T. Bluster, Dilly Dally, Flub-a-Dub, Princess Summer-Fall-Winter-Spring, and Heidi Doody, with the latter possibly the rarest of the seven. Price range: $100–150.

Price Range

☐ **Howdy Doody Band,** Unique Art, early 1950s, litho tin wind-up (variation of a host of piano toys by Unique as well as Marx) .. 250.00   300.00

Note: A smaller version of the Howdy Band appeared in the 1950s, manufacturer unknown, $50–$75

☐ **Howdy Doody Clock-a-Doodle,** Japan, 1950s, marketed by Kagran Corp., distributed by Bengor Products, New York City, litho on wood and plastic, features Howdy, Flub-a-Dub, the Princess, and Clarabelle .. 100.00   125.00

☐ **Howdy Doody Phone-a-Doodle,** Japan, 1950s, litho on wood and plastic, features many of Doodyville gang 100.00   125.00

☐ **Howdy Doody Standing Figure,** manufacturer unknown, 1950s, wood jointed, 12½″ height 35.00   50.00

JOE PALOOKA

The heavyweight boxing champion with heart of gold was launched by Ham Fisher for the McNaught Syndicate in 1927. Ironically, to our knowledge there was no toy based on Palooka himself, although there exists a small (4″ height) wood-jointed figure of the Champ ($35–$50).

☐ **Little Max Speshul #1,** Sal Metal Prod., litho tin wind-up, Max rides scooter with shoeshine box, pictures of Palooka and Knobby, his manager, appear on side of box, 7″ length (Max was another admiring pal of Joe) 100.00   125.00

☐ **Humphrey Mobile,** Wyandotte, 1948, litho tin wind-up, Palooka's best pal, Humphrey, pedals an "outhouse-like" version of a mobile home, 9″ length (be sure plastic smokestack is intact on this toy) 125.00   150.00

JOE PENNER

This ex-burlesque comedian emerged as one of the most popular stars in early radio in the 1920s. Although perhaps the most obscure of the comics who inspired toys, Joe Penner was a household name across the United States until his untimely death in the early 1930s.

	Price Range	
☐ **Joe Penner Astride Duck,** manufacturer unknown, early 1930s, heavy die-cut litho'ed cardboard, rocks back and forth	50.00	75.00
☐ **Joe Penner and Goo Goo the Duck,** Marx, early 1930s, litho tin wind-up, a variation of Marx's Popeye and the Parrot Cages wind-up with several ingenious additions, Penner's hat flips up as he waddles and a cigar moves around in his mouth, the famous Penner line, "Wanna buy a duck?" is litho'ed on a cage with three ducks, 8″ height	250.00	300.00

KATZENJAMMER KIDS

Providing perfect counterpoint to the prissy little Buster Brown were two devilish offspring, Hans and Fritz, created by Rudolph Dirks in 1897 for the Hearst syndicate. Dirks left Hearst's *New York Journal* in 1912 and was forced to leave the title to his strip. While another cartoonist, H.H. Knerr, picked up the strip at the *Journal,* Dirks resumed at the *World* with his own version called "The Captain and The Kids." Both strips co-existed for over 80 years. Dirks' characters often made guest appearances in the "Alphonse and Gaston" strip and vice versa.

☐ **Captain and The Kids Bellringer,** Gong Bell, 1912, painted cast iron, Fritz moves back and forth, ringing bell as toy is pulled, the captain is sprawled out and Hans rides his backside	2000.00 plus	
☐ **Katzenjammer Nodders,** German, 1910, papier-mache and wood, Mama and Fritz figures, 9½″ height, each	250.00	300.00

Price Range

☐ **Mama Katzenjammer in Donkey Cart,** believed made by Kenton, early 1900s, painted cast iron, donkey kicks up hind legs 300.00   350.00

☐ **Mama Katzenjammer Standing Figure,** German, 1910, papier-mache with cloth dress and apron, 11½" height 250.00   300.00

KRAZY KAT

In perhaps the most literate of all comic strips, Krazy Kat, Ignatz the mouse, and Offisa B. Pupp acted out one of our culture's most macabre love triangles against a surreal backdrop of Arizona desert country. Created by George Harriman in 1901, the strip continued until the cartoonist's death in 1944.

Many Krazy Kat collections often include the stuffed dolls Krazy and Ignatz, created by Knickerbocker Toy Co., New York City, in 1931. Ignatz bears a striking resemblance to Mickey Mouse. These price between $200–$250 each.

☐ **Ignatz Mouse on Tricycle,** Chein, 1932, litho tin pull toy; Ignatz bangs cymbals as toy is pulled 250.00   300.00

☐ **Ignatz Standing Figure,** manufacturer unknown, 1930s, wood-jointed toy 125.00   150.00

☐ **Krazy Kat on a Scooter,** Nifty, 1927 or 1928, painted tin wind-up (variation of Nifty's Felix the Cat toy), 8" length 250.00   300.00

☐ **Krazy Kat Wheeled Platform Toy,** Nifty, early 1930s, litho tin, toy features noisemaker which emits squeaking sound when pulled, two Ignatz mice appear in front of platform, 7½" length 300.00   350.00

LI'L ABNER

This comic strip dealing with a hillbilly family, the Yokums, was created by Al Capp in 1934. The sharply satirical strip that absorbed Sadie Hawkins Day into our American folklore produced

Little Orphan Annie Skipping Rope, Marx, 1930s, $350–$400; Ignatz Mouse on Tricycle, Chein, 1932, $250–$300; Mutt and Jeff Playing Leapfrog, German, 1920s, $1200–$1500.

a rich gallery of characters—from Moonbeam McSwine to Stupifyin Jones, Jack S. Phogbound, and Joanie Phoanie (a takeoff on Joan Baez). Transferred to the Broadway stage in the early 1950s, it quickly became a hit.

Price Range

☐ **Li'l Abner Band,** Unique Art, Newark, New Jersey, litho tin wind-up, features Daisy Mae at piano, Pappy on drums, Mammy sits atop piano with drumstick and Abner dances a jig 300.00   350.00

☐ **Shmoo Wooden Figure,** manufacturer unknown, 1940s, 6″ height 25.00   35.00

LITTLE KING

Otto Soglow's "Little King" first ran as a series of cartoons in the *New Yorker* in the early 1930s before emerging as a syndicated strip in the daily newspaper.

Price Range

☐ **Little King,** Marx, 1935, painted wooden figure, pulling a string in his crown spun the toy forward, 4″ height 150.00   200.00

LITTLE ORPHAN ANNIE

This wide-eyed moppet with orange hair made a dramatic debut in the *New York Daily News* in 1924 with Harold Gray as her creator. The ageless little orphan girl is still active in the 1980s. In the late 1970s she inspired a broadway hit, "Annie," followed by a full-length movie.

☐ **Andy and Sandy on the Road,** C.K., Japan, 1930s, celluloid and tin wind-up, both figures move on little wheeled platforms as with Henry and Henrietta toys by C.K. ... 250.00   300.00

☐ **Orphan Annie Cart,** Trixy Toys, 1933, litho on wood 75.00   100.00

☐ **Orphan Annie Dime Bank,** 1930s, tin 100.00   125.00

☐ **Orphan Annie Skipping Rope,** Marx, 1930s, litho tin wind-up, Annie skips rope, small gears under her feet allow wire rope to pass around her with this ingenious mechanism, 5″ height 350.00   400.00

☐ **Orphan Annie Standing Figure,** manufacturer unknown, 1930s, wood jointed 75.00   100.00

☐ **Sandy Crawler,** Marx, 1930s, spring-loaded toy activated by lowering tail, litho tin, Sandy's name on collar 100.00   150.00

☐ **Walking Sandy,** Marx, 1930s, litho tin wind-up, Sandy carries valise with Annie's name on it, 4″ height, original box is highly prized as it assembles to become Sandy's doghouse 300.00   350.00

LONE RANGER

The masked rider first appeared on radio in 1933 over station WXYZ, Detroit. First conceived by a motion picture tycoon, George Trendle, who teamed with writer Fran Striker, the show was tested with a premium offer of a free souvenir program and 25,000 letters immediately poured in. Striker also wrote a best-selling series of Lone Ranger novels. "The Lone Ranger" premiered on TV in 1949; a cartoon series was produced by CBS in 1966; in 1981 a full-length feature film, "The Legend of the Lone Ranger," was produced by Universal City, Jack Wrather Productions.

Lone Ranger collections frequently include a pair of dolls of the masked rider with Tonto, 20″ height, circa 1938. The pair pack cast-iron pistols. There is also a hand-puppet of the Lone Ranger from the same era.

	Price Range	
☐ **Hi-Yo Silver Lone Ranger Target Game,** Marx, 1938, tin stand with metal gun and plunger darts (three sizes), nice litho inset illustrative of Lone Ranger and Tonto	35.00	50.00
☐ **Lone Ranger Riding Silver,** Marx, 1938, litho tin wind-up, Silver stands on hind legs and vibrates with winding as Lone Ranger spins lariat, 8″ height	200.00	225.00

MAX AND MORITZ

Wilhelm Busch, one of the best loved creators of illustrated light verse in the German language, created a juvenile history of two malevolent little tykes, Max and Moritz, in the latter part of the 19th century. Undoubtedly, Rudolph later used these mischief-makers as models for his Hans and Fritz characters, The Katzenjammer Kids.

☐ **Max and Moritz Standing Figures,** Schoenhut, 1914–1915, wood jointed with cloth outfits and artificial hair, approximately 9″ height, each	250.00	300.00

MICKEY MOUSE (SEE DISNEYANA)

MILTON BERLE

Milton Berle, a practitioner of broad, brassy buffoonery, earned the title of "Mr. Television" during his 1948–1956 stint. His "Texaco Star Theater" on NBC was the first big production variety show.

Price Range

☐ **Milton Berle Car,** Marx, late 1940s, litho
tin and plastic wind-up, another variation of
Marx's crazy cars, 6½" length 75.00   100.00

MOON MULLINS

Arguably the biggest con artist and lowbrow in all of comic-
dom, Moonshine Mullins (his full name) has been on the scene since
1923, with Frank Willard the creator.

☐ **Kayo on Ice Truck,** Dowst (Tootsietoy),
1932, cast metal, comic series, Kayo sits on
cake of ice, 2¾" length 125.00   150.00

☐ **Moon Mullins and Kayo with Railroad
Handcar,** Marx, early 1930s, two versions:
1st, with Kayo on dynamite box and runs
on simple barrel spring; 2nd, deluxe version
with clockwork spring and bell which rings
as handcar moves around track, body of
heavy gauge steel vs. tin on cheaper version,
6" length 200.00   250.00

☐ **Moon Mullins in Police Patrol Wagon,**
Dowst (Tootsietoy), 1932, cast metal (one
of six in comic series), Policeman drives
Moon (holding hat) off to hoosegow, 2¾"
length 125.00   150.00

☐ **Moon Mullins Standing Figure,** manufacturer unknown, 1930s, wood jointed, Moon
wears his famous derby and smokes cigar 50.00   75.00

☐ **Uncle Willie and Mamie in Motor Boat,**
Dowst (Tootsietoy), 1932, cast metal, comic
series, 2¾" length 100.00   125.00

MUTT AND JEFF

Tall slim Augustus Mutt was a carefree bachelor who loved to
"play the ponies." His friend, Jeff, was an exact opposite—short,
on the plump side, married, and with a son, an eternal victim of
Mutt's pranks. The first strip to run in daily papers, it was created
by ex-sports cartoonist Bud Fisher beginning in 1907 and continu-

ing to this day. Mutt and Jeff were the subject of a Broadway musical in the late 1920s.

Price Range

☐ **Mechanical Mutt and Jeff,** German, 1920s, litho tin wind-up, Jeff appears to be playing leapfrog over his buddy Mutt, except that he faces in the wrong direction, 6″ length ...   1200.00   1500.00

☐ **Mutt and Jeff Standing Figures,** Switzerland, late 1940s, metal-jointed figures with plaster and attired in felt clothing, Mutt 8″ height, Jeff 6½″ height 75.00   100.00

☐ **Mutt and Jeff Still Bank,** A.C. Williams, Ravenna, Ohio, 1915, cast iron, gold finish, also appeared in bright colors, 5¼″ height ...   75.00   100.00*

POPEYE

Elzie Seger, one-time apprentice to Richard Outcault of "Buster Brown" and "The Yellow Kid" fame, sold the idea of his "Thimble Theater" to King Features in 1929. Originally focused on Olive and the rest of the Oyl family, a squint-eyed sailor smoking a corncob pipe soon stole the show and the strip was renamed "Popeye" several years later. The strip later inspired many movie cartoons and a full-length screenplay by Jules Feiffer in 1980. Along with Mickey Mouse, Popeye is the most universally recognized of all cartoon characters. The sailor man may well hold the record for having the most toys created in his image.

☐ **Juggling Popeye and Olive,** Linemar, early 1950s, litho tin wind-up 300.00   400.00

☐ **Popeye in the Barrel,** Chein, 1932, litho tin wind-up, 7″ height 200.00   250.00

☐ **Popeye the Champ,** Marx, 1937, litho tin with celluloid boxers, winding-up produces furious action and bell rings signaling round's end 750.00   850.00

☐ **Popeye Cowboy,** Fisher Price, 1937, wheeled platform pull toy, litho on wood, Popeye rides old plug horse as wheels make clicking sound 125.00   150.00

*As much as 20% higher in bright colors.

Price Range

☐ **Popeye Drummer Boy,** Fisher Price, 1937, platform pull toy, Popeye beats on drum as wheels turn 125.00   150.00

☐ **Popeye Express With Airplane,** Marx, 1937, litho tin wind-up, Popeye soars overhead in tiny plane while Wimpy, Olive, Sappo, and Swee' Pea circle in Union Pacific train below, 9″ diameter 1300.00   1500.00

☐ **Popeye the Flyer,** Marx, 1937, litho tin wind-up, Olive and Popeye circle tower in planes, lithographing varies on a number of versions, 9″ diameter 650.00   750.00

☐ **Popeye the Heavy Hitter,** Chein, 1930s, litho tin wind-up, Popeye wields a mallet to ring the gong on carnival strength tester, 9¾″ height 1000.00   1200.00

☐ **Popeye in Horse Cart,** manufacturer unknown, 1930s, celluloid Popeye figure in steel cart, 7½″ length 150.00   175.00

☐ **Popeye Jigger on Roof,** Marx, 1936, litho tin wind-up 300.00   350.00

☐ **Popeye Knockout Bank,** Marx, late 1940s and early 1950s, litho tin, coin drop produces action 650.00   750.00

☐ **Popeye on Motorcycle,** Hubley, 1938, cast iron, "Spinach Delivery" embossed on sidecar, many are found with reproduced figure which is removable, 5½″ length 350.00   400.00

☐ **Popeye and Olive Ball Toss,** Linemar, early 1950s, tin wind-up, 19″ length 600.00   800.00

☐ **Popeye and Olive Handcar,** Hercules Metal Line (distributed by Marx), 1935, heavy-gauge steel body (similar to Moon Mullins deluxe version handcar), with figures in rubber 1500.00   2000.00

☐ **Popeye and Olive Jiggers on the Roof,** Marx, 1935, litho tin wind-up, Popeye dances and Olive plays the accordion 350.00   450.00

Price Range

☐ **Popeye Paddle Wagon,** Corgi, 1969–1972, cast metal push toy, Swee' Pea, Bluto, Olive, Wimpy and Popeye appear as rubber figures, there are several variations of this toy, 6″ length 25.00   35.00

☐ **Popeye and the Parrot Cages,** Marx, 1930, litho tin wind-up, 8¼″ height 200.00   250.00

☐ **Popeye Patrol,** Hubley, 1938, cast iron, Popeye figure and motorcycle are cast separately, 9″ length 650.00   750.00

☐ **Popeye the Pilot,** Marx, 1937, litho tin wind-up, 7″ length, Marx produced two versions, the earlier model had a wider fuselage and wings 350.00   400.00

☐ **Popeye Pirate Pistol,** Marx, 1950s, litho tin click gun, 10″ length 50.00   75.00

☐ **Popeye and the Punching Bag,** Chein, 1932, litho tin wind-up, punching bag is on spring coming from floor vs. a second overhead Chein version, 7½″ height 300.00   350.00

☐ **Popeye and the Punching Bag,** Chein, 1932, litho tin wind-up with overhead bag (an uncommon version that's tough to come by), 9¾″ height 1000.00   1200.00

☐ **Popeye the Sailor in a Rowboat,** Hoge Mfg., New York City, 1935, litho tin wind-up, the most uncommon of all Popeye toys, 15½″ length 2000.00   2500.00

☐ **Popeye Sparkler,** German, 1932, litho tin, die-cut head of Popeye, sparks appear in hole in one eye and nose 250.00   300.00

☐ **Popeye Sparkler,** Chein, 1959, litho tin, round-shaped, with picture of Popeye's head 50.00   75.00

☐ **Popeye Standing Figure,** manufacturer unknown, 1930s, cast iron, this may have well been cast as a door stop, 8″ height 200.00   250.00

Price Range

☐ **Popeye on a String,** manufacturer unknown, 1930s, variation of any number of toys featuring monkeys and clowns which climb up and down string when figure is in vertical position and cord is pulled taut, 6″ height 50.00   75.00

☐ **Popeye and Swee' Pea,** Fisher Price, 1937, wheeled platform pull toy, litho on wood, Popeye is at helm of ship-shaped platform ...   150.00   175.00

☐ **Popeye and the Wheelbarrow, (a.k.a. "Popeye Express"),** Marx, 1937, litho tin wind-up, 8¼″ height (deluxe model has parrot that pops up out of wheelbarrow) ...   175.00   225.00

☐ **Popeye Wood-Jointed Figure,** Chein, 1932, litho wood 150.00   200.00

☐ **Standing Popeye,** Chein, 1932, litho tin wind-up, they call this toy a "walker," but it mostly just vibrates when wound up, 6″ height 250.00   300.00

☐ **Wood-Jointed and Hard Rubber Figures,** made in various sizes of Popeye, Olive, Wimpy, Swee' Pea, and Jeep 25.00   50.00

PORKY PIG

Leon Schlesinger Productions, which began in 1930 as the producer of Looney Tunes and Merry Melodies, introduced their first important cartoon character, a stuttering, bewildered porker known as Porky Pig. Later, Porky was overshadowed by a nemesis who appeared in his film, "Porky's Hare Hunt," Bugs Bunny, who became the number one animated animal of the 1940s.

☐ **Porky Pig with Umbrella,** Marx, 1935, litho tin wind-up, 6″ height 150.00   175.00

SMITTY

Smitty, a young office "go-fer" created by Walter Berndt in 1922, aspired to be a big tycoon like his boss, Mr. Bailey. (With orange hair and empty circles for eyes, he'd have made a great match for Orphan Annie.)

Price Range

☐ **Smitty and Herby on Motorcycle,** Dowst (Tootsietoy), 1932, cartoon series, cast metal, Smitty drives the motorcycle and brother Herby rides in side car 175.00   200.00

☐ **Smitty on the Scooter,** Marx, 1930, litho tin wind-up, figure is detachable, 5″ length, 8″ height 1000.00   1200.00

SNOWFLAKE AND SWIPES

Oscar Hitt, of Hi-Way Henry fame, created "Snowflake and Swipes" in the mid-1920s. The strip was based on the adventures of a small black boy, Snowflake, and his dog Swipes, a scrappy little fellow who seemed to always get the worst of it.

☐ **Snowflake and Swipes,** Nifty, 1929, platform pull toy, litho tin, Snowflake runs when toy is pulled; Swipes, who has apparently lost a recent dogfight (he is all bandaged), brings up the rear 350.00   450.00

SUPERMAN

The man of steel was the creation of Jerry Siegel and Joe Shuster in 1938. His instant climb to fame quickly earned him his "Superman Comics" by the following year, a radio show in 1940, movies in 1941, and TV by the early 1950s. In the 1980s there have been no less than four full-length Superman movies.

☐ **Superman Fighting Tank,** Linemar, 1960s, litho tin wind-up (several variations), this was a very disappointing toy as Superman was simply lithographed on a small flat piece of tin, when wound, Superman seemed to be dazed by a dose of Kryptonite, as he rarely flipped the tank over 50.00   75.00

☐ **Superman Figure,** manufacturer unknown, 1940s, wood jointed, 12″ height 100.00   150.00

Toonerville Trolley, Nifty, 1922, lithographed tin mechanical, $450–$550; "Katrinka," Jimmy, and wheelbarrow, Nifty, 1924, lithographed tin mechanical, $750–$850.

Price Range

☐ **Superman Racing the Airplane,** Marx, 1940, litho tin wind-up (one of the last quality made toys prior to World War II), Superman spins around airplane on steel wire and turns it over, 5″ length 450.00   500.00

THE TOONERVILLE TROLLEY

Fontaine Fox started the Toonerville Folks in 1908, and the beloved saga that centered around a run-down old trolley entertained readers for over 40 years. A number of small wood-jointed Toonerville folk appeared in the 1930s ($75–$100 range).

☐ **Aunt Eppie Hogg on Flatbed Truck,** Nifty, 1923–1945, litho tin wind-up. Rotund Aunt Eppie slides back and forth on flatbed, when she reaches back end, it sends front of 7″ length truck in the air. Dark green, blue, and orange. Captain is the driver. This ingenious toy is rarely found with all its figures intact. .... $2000.00★

★At the Ray Holland Toy Auction at Sotheby's in spring of 1985, an Eppie Hogg toy *minus* the Captain failed to meet reserves of $6000–$8000.

Price Range

☐ **Mickey McGuire Figure,** manufacturer unknown, wood wind-up with felt clothing, Mickey wears hat and scarf and smokes cigar 300.00   350.00

☐ **Powerful Katrinka with Jimmy,** Nifty, 1924, red and blue litho tin wind-up, Katrinka hoists Jimmy with one hand as she moves across floor, 6¾" height 750.00   850.00

☐ **Powerful Katrinka with Jimmy and Wheelbarrow,** Nifty, copyright by Fontaine Fox, 1924, red and blue litho tin wind-up, Katrinka raises and lowers Jimmy in wheelbarrow as she moves across floor, 6¾" height .. 750.00   850.00

☐ **Tin Miniature Toonerville Trolley,** German, 1922, 1¾" height, 1½" length (crackerjack collectors claim this as one of the surprise giveaways from the popcorn firm; we've also seen it classified as an English penny toy) 450.00   500.00

☐ **Toonerville Trolley,** Dent Hardware, 1929, cast iron, two-color variation green with orange; red with yellow trimmed with gold, 4" length, 6" height 400.00   450.00

☐ **Toonerville Trolley,** copyright by Fontaine Fox, manufacturer unknown, 1923, slush-cast metal, painted, available in yellow, red or green with trim, 4" height 300.00   400.00

☐ **Toonerville Trolley,** Kemtron, 1938; HO gauge electric, brass, unpainted, featured tiny working headlight, 2½" height 500.00   550.00

UNCLE WIGGILY

Howard Garis created this long-eared friend of countless millions of youngsters at the turn of the century. In addition to story books, Uncle Wiggily appeared in a daily comic strip in the 1930s, making his debut in New Jersey's *Newark Evening News.*

Price Range

☐ **Uncle Wiggily Car,** German, early 1920s, litho tin wind-up, auto decorated in bright pastel patches, Uncle Wiggily holds valise in one hand, a red, white and blue cane in the other, Howard R. Garis' name appears across lower edge of radiator panel, 10″ length 750.00   800.00

☐ **Uncle Wiggily Car,** Marx, early 1935, litho tin wind-up, one of earliest Marx crazy cars, rabbit's head spins around, 6½″ length 250.00   300.00

YELLOW KID

There were a number of earlier beginnings, but the first real breakthrough in American comic strips occurred in 1896 with the creation of "The Yellow Kid" by Richard Outcault. An unpleasant little baldheaded street urchin with floppy ears, the Kid wore an oversized yellow night-shirt which was used as a placard upon which dialogue appeared. Format was page-size single panel. When William Randolph Hearst stole Outcault away from bitter rival Joseph Pulitzer (giving birth to the phrase "yellow journalism"), Pulitzer hired George Luks to draw "The Yellow Kid" for *his* paper. Ironically, both versions proved to be short-lived as the violent, foul-mouthed little imp proved not to be the role model that parents had anticipated.

☐ **Yellow Kid,** manufacturer unknown, early 1900s, lever-operated, wood, lead, cloth ...   350.00   400.00

☐ **Yellow Kid Cap Bomb,** cast iron, cap is placed in Kid's mouth 50.00   75.00

☐ **Yellow Kid on Easter Egg,** licensed by Richard Outcault, papier-mache, arms move on metal shaft 500.00   600.00

☐ **Yellow Kid Goat Cart,** Kenton, early 1900s, 7½″ length (cast-iron figure is usually painted all yellow), there is a version in which the Kid is black with a red nightshirt) 150.00   200.00

Price Range

☐ **Yellow Kid Squeeze Toy,** manufacturer unknown, scissor action, papier-mache, wood and cloth 250.00   300.00

MISCELLANEOUS COMIC AND NOVELTY TOYS

☐ **American Newsboy,** Nikko Kogyo, Occupied Japan, 1950s, celluloid; boy rings bell and holds "Extra" newspaper (red, white, and blue outfit) 75.00   100.00

☐ **Archie "Ronson,"** 1920s, litho tin head with sparkling action, 4″ height 50.00   75.00

☐ **Auto, G.&K.** (German), 1920s, litho tin mechanical, 4½″ length 200.00   250.00

☐ **Auto Race,** Jeannette, 1930s, litho tin mechanical, course layout where tiny autos race on track through tunnels, 9″ diameter 150.00   200.00

☐ **Baggage Carrier,** Unique Art, 1950s, litho tin mechanical, figure pulling large cart stacked with baggage, 13″ length 50.00   75.00

☐ **Ballet Dancer,** Marx, 1930s, litho tin mechanical, 5¾″ height 100.00   150.00

☐ **Beetle,** German, 1930s, painted tin mechanical, 7″ length 75.00   100.00

☐ **Bird in Cage,** German, 1920s, litho tin mechanical with bellows, 8″ height 100.00   150.00

☐ **Bird Cage on Stand,** Ges.Gesch (German), 1920s, painted tin and steel, 7½″ height ... 100.00   120.00

☐ **Birds on Swing,** German, 1920s, painted tin mechanical, 14¼″ height 650.00   700.00

☐ **Bird in Tree,** German, circa 1910, painted tin mechanical with bellows, 6½″ height .. 100.00   125.00

☐ **Blue Bird,** German, circa 1910, hand-painted tin mechanical with paper propellers 100.00   150.00

☐ **"Bombo,"** Unique Art, 1950s, litho tin mechanical, 9½″ height 25.00   50.00

Marx Merry Makers, Louis Marx, 1931. Lithographed tin mechanical; some call this stylized band toy "Marx's Revenge." Never able to receive a license to replicate Mickey Mouse from Disney Enterprises, they produced this "crossover" (also clearly a "knockoff" as mice are dead ringers for early Mickeys). Pure art deco, black minstrel, and Mickey combined. This is the most desirable of several Merry Maker versions, as it features a lithograph vaudeville backdrop of two mice dancing to the tune of a tuba-blowing feline. The handsomely lithographed original box enhances its value, $750–$850.

	Price Range	
☐ **Boy and Girl Dancing,** Schuco, 1930s, cloth-dressed tin mechanical, 5″ height	100.00	125.00
☐ **Boy Riding St. Bernard,** Rocker, German, 1910, painted tin, 5″ length	150.00	175.00
☐ **Bus,** Gunthermann, 1920s, litho tin mechanical with man boarding, 8¾″ length ..	100.00	150.00
☐ **Busy Bridge,** Marx, 1940s, litho tin mechanical with battery-operated street lights	75.00	125.00

Price Range

☐ **Busy Lizzie,** German, 1920s, litho tin wind-
up, 7½" height 200.00   250.00

☐ **Busy Lizzie Cleaning Woman,** German,
1920s, litho tin mechanical 75.00   100.00

☐ **Busy Miners,** Marx, 1930s, litho tin mechanical, coal cars on track course, 16½"
length 50.00   75.00

☐ **Butter and Egg Man,** Marx, 1930s, litho tin
mechanical, 7½" height (variation of Joe
Penner comic toy by Marx) 150.00   175.00

☐ **Cat Barber,** Toply, Japan, 1950s, litho tin
mechanical, cat lathers up to shave kitten in
barber chair 75.00   100.00

☐ **Cat With Glasses,** German, 1920s, painted
tin mechanical, 6½" height (similar to
Krazy Kat toy, but without any identifying
mark) 100.00   150.00

☐ **Cat on Scooter,** Chein, 1920s, litho tin
spring action, 7¼" length (very similar to
Felix and Krazy Kat Nifty versions) 100.00   150.00

☐ **Chef on Rollerskates,** Japan, 1960s, litho
tin mechanical, 6½" height 25.00   50.00

☐ **Clarinetist,** German, circa 1910, handpainted tin mechanical, 8" height 200.00   250.00

☐ **Coo-Coo Car,** Marx, 1930s, litho tin me-
chanical, 8" length 100.00   150.00

☐ **Crawling Baby,** German, circa 1910,
painted tin mechanical, 5½" length 125.00   150.00

☐ **Dancing Couple,** F. Martin, circa 1915,
painted tin mechanical, 7½" height .... 350.00   450.00★

☐ **Dancing Couple,** German, 1915, painted tin
mechanical, 6¾" height 250.00   300.00

☐ **Dog Chase,** Stock, German, 1920s, litho tin
mechanical, high-hatted driver on three
wheeler pursued by white dog, 7" length ... 350.00   400.00

★Brought $850 at Atlanta Toy Museum Auction, October 1986.

Price Range

☐ **Dog Chasing Monkey,** Stock, German, 1920s, litho tin mechanical, 6½″ length ...   300.00   350.00

☐ **Dragon With Riders,** maker unknown, Japan, celluloid mechanical 75.00   100.00

☐ **Drinker,** Schuco, 1930s, tin and plastic mechanical, 5″ height 75.00   125.00

☐ **Drinking Man,** F. Martin (French), 1915, painted and cloth-dressed tin mechanical, man in high hat tipples from bottle, 8¼″ height (one of a series of comic toys by Martin from this era) 300.00   350.00

☐ **Drinking Pig,** Schuco, 1930s, cloth-dressed tin mechanical, 5″ height 100.00   150.00

☐ **Drum Major,** Marx, 1930s, litho tin mechanical, with rolling eyes 75.00   100.00

☐ **Drum Major,** Wolverine, 1930s, litho tin mechanical, 13½″ length 50.00   75.00

☐ **Drummer Boy,** Marx, 1930s, litho tin mechanical, 9″ length 75.00   100.00

☐ **Drummer Boy,** Marx, 1950s, litho tin mechanical, eyes roll, 9″ height 35.00   50.00

☐ **Drumming Monkey,** German, 1930s, litho tin mechanical, 8″ height 250.00   300.00

☐ **Drunkard,** manufacturer unknown, Japan, 1930s, celluloid mechanical, 280mm height (clever imitation of F. Martin's version of drinking man toy holding bottle in one hand) 125.00   150.00

☐ **Duck,** German, circa 1910, painted tin mechanical, with paper props, 6″ length 100.00   150.00

☐ **Dude Nodder,** German, 1915, painted tin mechanical, 7¾″ height 100.00   150.00

☐ **Elephant in Evening Attire,** manufacturer unknown, 1930s, tin with felt covering, paper hat, figure has cane and top hat, 8¾″ height 100.00   125.00

Price Range

☐ **Express Boy,** German, 1920s, litho tin mechanical and composition 75.00   100.00

☐ **Fish,** German, 1915, handpainted tin, on three wheels, 10″ length 350.00   450.00

☐ **Fred Astaire at Hollywood and Vine,** Alps, Occupied Japan, 1950s, celluloid and tin mechanical 100.00   125.00

☐ **Funny Harry,** Gama, German, litho tin with composition head, 5¼″ length 100.00   150.00

☐ **Girl and Donkey,** German, circa 1915, handpainted tin mechanical, girl on two wheels holds whip over donkey, 7½″ length 150.00   200.00

☐ **Girl Pulling Cart,** French, circa 1910, stained tin friction, 5″ length 250.00   300.00

☐ **Grinder Steam Toy,** Fleischmann, 1920s, live steam attachment, 3¼″ square 50.00   75.00

☐ **Hee-Haw,** Marx, 1950s, litho tin mechanical, milkman driving donkey cart, 10½″ length 50.00   75.00

☐ **Ho-Bo Train,** Unique Art, 1930s, litho tin wind-up, hobo runs across freight car with dog biting pants, 8″ length 200.00   250.00

☐ **Honeymoon Express,** Marx, 1940s, litho tin mechanical train circles around tracked course 50.00   75.00

☐ **Horse Cart,** Gibbs, 1920s; paper litho and wood, pair of horses pull cart, 16″ length ... 100.00   150.00

☐ **Ice Cream Vendor,** Courtland, 1940s, litho tin mechanical, 6″ length 50.00   75.00

☐ **Jackie the Hornpipe Dancer,** F. Strauss, 1920s, litho tin wind-up, 9″ height 125.00   150.00

☐ **Jenny Balking Mule,** Strauss, 1920s, litho tin mechanical, farmer in cart, mule kicks up heels, 8″ length 150.00   200.00

	Price Range	
☐ **Jolly Pals,** Stock, German, 1920s, litho tin mechanical, monkey in cart pulled by small dog, 8″ length	50.00	75.00
☐ **Joy Rider,** Marx, 1930s, litho tin mechanical (crazy car), 7″ length	75.00	100.00*
☐ **Jumpin' Jeep,** Marx, 1940s, litho tin mechanical, four helmeted passengers in crazy car variant, 6″ length	150.00	200.00
☐ **Kiddie Cyclist,** Unique Art, 1920s, litho tin mechanical, 8½″ height	75.00	100.00
☐ **Lady in Three-Wheel Auto,** Stock, 1920s, litho tin wind-up, 4¾″ length	200.00	250.00
☐ **Leaping Lena,** Strauss, 1920s, litho tin mechanical, 8″ length	100.00	150.00
☐ **Let's Go Happy,** manufacturer unknown, 1920s, litho tin crank toy of character balancing atop cymbals on large drum, 9″ height	100.00	150.00
☐ **Man With Baggage,** Distler, German, 1920s, litho tin mechanical, 7½″ height ...	200.00	250.00
☐ **Monkey,** Schuco, 1930s, cloth on tin mechanical, monkey with steamer trunk, 5″ height	100.00	125.00
☐ **Monkey and Crab,** NPK, Knarit, Japan, 1920s, litho tin, manually activated, monkey climbs up seesaw and drops ball down chute for direct hit on crab, lithographed on base, 225mm height	150.00	200.00
☐ **Mother Duck and Ducklings,** German, 1915, painted tin mechanical, 8″ length ...	100.00	150.00
☐ **Musical Camel,** manufacturer unknown, 1920s, crank-operated musical toy, cloth-covered tin	150.00	200.00

*Reached high of $425 at Atlanta Toy Museum Auction, October, 1986.

Walter Stock Ltd., of Solingen, Germany, produced a variety of novelty toys that were often confused with their rival Ernst Lehmann: Paddy's Pride, $350–$400; Antarctic Mail, $400–$500; Merry Peasant, $350–$400; Joko Driving Tricycle, $450–$550.

	Price Range	
☐ **Native With Hippopotamus,** Toply, Japan, 1950s litho tin mechanical, native rides hippo and leads hippo along by dangling bunch of bananas	100.00	125.00
☐ **Native on Turtle,** Japan, 1950s, litho tin mechanical, 8½" length	50.00	75.00
☐ **Nursemaid with Baby,** German, 1910, painted tin mechanical, 7½" height	350.00	400.00
☐ **Oh Boy,** Fisher, 1920s, litho tin mechanical, boy rides on scooter in this nicely detailed German wind-up, 8" height	200.00	250.00
☐ **Old Jalopy,** Marx, 1950s, litho tin mechanical, another Marx crazy car, 5½" length ..	50.00	75.00
☐ **Oriental Woman,** German, circa 1915, handpainted tin mechanical, figure has fan and parasol, 8½" height	150.00	200.00

Price Range

☐ **Peacock,** EBO, Pao-Pao, German, 1910, painted tin mechanical with bellows squeaker, 9½″ length 200.00   225.00

☐ **Penguin Skier,** Nomura, Japan, 1950s, litho tin mechanical 50.00   75.00

☐ **Pianist,** Yoshiya, Japan, 1930s, litho tin and celluloid mechanical, little girl plays while overhead parasol with little balls spins when activated, 170mm height 75.00   100.00

☐ **Pike,** Bing, German, 1890s, handpainted tin mechanical, fish on wheels, 14½″ length .. 200.00   250.00

☐ **Pinched,** Marx, 1930s, litho tin mechanical, 10″ length [another Marx laid-out course where smaller figures (i.e., police cars and other vehicles) chase each other around a tracked mechanism] 200.00   250.00

☐ **Pony Cart,** Gibbs, 1920s, litho wood and tin, steel wire 100.00   150.00

☐ **Porter,** German, 1920s, litho tin mechanical, porter obviously tries to close stuffed trunk by lying on it, 2″ height 100.00   150.00

☐ **Rabbit Violinist,** Kuramochi, 1930s, celluloid mechanical 75.00   100.00

☐ **Rangerider,** Marx, 1930s, litho tin mechanical, rocker-type with steel lariat (variation of Hop-A-Long Cassidy toy) 50.00   75.00

☐ **Revolving Monkey,** Gesenia, German, 1890s, hand-painted tin mechanical, 6¼″ height 150.00   200.00

☐ **Rocking Horse,** Gibbs, 1920s, litho wood and tin, rider waves hat as horse rocks, 9″ length 100.00   150.00

☐ **Rodeo Joe,** Marx, 1940s, tin litho, plastic mechanical, 6″ length (another Marx variation of the crazy car) 150.00   200.00

☐ **Rookie Pilot,** Marx, 1940s, litho tin mechanical, variation of Popeye and Dagwood Airplane wind-ups by Marx, 6¾″ length .. 175.00   200.00

☐ **Running Pig,** German, 1920s, painted tin mechanical, 6″ length 200.00   250.00

☐ **Sailor,** manufacturer unknown, 1920s, painted tin string climbing toy, 7″ height ... 25.00   50.00

☐ **Sailor Playing Squeezebox,** manufacturer unknown, circa 1915, papier-mache, cloth dressed, 8″ height 50.00   75.00

☐ **School Boy (at Blackboard),** Tippco, circa 1910, painted tin mechanical, 7½″ height ... 400.00   500.00

☐ **Scottie Dog and Shoe,** German, 1940s, tin and celluloid mechanical, 8″ length 25.00   50.00

☐ **Sheriff Sam Patrol Car,** Marx, 1949, litho tin mechanical 50.00   75.00

☐ **Skidoodle,** Nifty, 1920s, litho tin mechanical, family in back of open-bed truck, bright colored cartoon characters, 10½″ length 500.00   550.00

☐ **Sky Bird Flyer,** Marx, 1940s, litho tin mechanical, 9″ height 75.00   100.00

☐ **Snoopy-Gus,** believed made by Marx, 1950s, litho tin mechanical, man with dog are passengers in fire-truck contrivance, another figure is on raised ladder, 8″ length ... 300.00   350.00

☐ **Speedy Boy Deliver,** Marx, 1940s, litho tin mechanical 25.00   50.00

☐ **Steam Locomotive,** manufacturer unknown, Japan, early 1900s, litho tin friction with heavy cast-metal wheels, passengers look out from third-class coach behind steam engine, a classic toy noted for its simplicity and excellent lithography 350.00   400.00

☐ **Teddy Bear and Boy Three-Wheel Cart,** CKO, German, 1920s, litho tin mechanical, 5½″ length 200.00   250.00

☐ **Tidy Tim,** Marx, 1930s, litho tin mechanical, street cleaner with barrel on wheels, 8″ length (variation of Popeye and Wheelbarrow wind-up by Marx) 75.00   100.00

Price Range

☐ **Tom Twist,** Strauss, 1930s, litho tin mechanical, paint-faced character with flat hat, 7″ (variation of Boob McNutt wind-up by Strauss) 75.00   100.00

☐ **Tool Grinder,** Strauss, 1920s, litho tin steam attachment, 4½″ height 50.00   75.00

☐ **Topsy Turvy Tom,** H.E. Nurenburg, 1920s, litho tin mechanical, ingenious car rolls over and rights itself, clown driver, 10¼″ length 600.00   650.00

☐ **Train Station,** Arnold, German, 1920s, litho tin mechanical, tiny train runs from station to roundhouse, 15″ length 50.00   75.00

☐ **Traveler,** German, 1920s, handpainted tin, cloth-dressed mechanical, dapper-looking man in straw hat, checked suit, small valise, 8½″ height 100.00   150.00

☐ **Unique Artie,** Unique Art, 1930s, litho tin mechanical, 7″ length 50.00   75.00

☐ **Violinist,** Martin, 1915, handpainted tin mechanical, cloth, 8″ height 400.00   450.00

☐ **Waltzing Lady,** German circa 1910, painted tin mechanical, 4″ height 200.00   250.00

☐ **Water-Wheel,** Bing, German, 1920s, litho tin steam attachment, 6″ height 75.00   100.00

☐ **What's Wrong Car,** German, 1920s, tin litho and painted mechanical, 7″ length ... 100.00   125.00

☐ **Whoopee Car,** Marx, 1930s, girl with pigtails driver, litho tin and plastic mechanical, 6″ length 50.00   75.00

☐ **Woman With Basket,** German, circa 1915, painted tin mechanical, 7″ height 200.00   250.00

☐ **Woman Pulling Cart,** German, 1920s, litho tin, friction, 6″ length 125.00   150.00

Price Range

☐ **Woman Vendor Pushing Cart,** Martin,
circa 1915, handpainted tin mechanical,
6½″ length 200.00   250.00

☐ **Zylotone,** Wolverine, 1920s, litho tin mechanical, musical toy with discs 350.00   400.00

DISNEYANA

The debut of a little pie-eyed rodent named Mickey Mouse on November 18, 1928, the eve of the Great Depression, took place in "Steamboat Willie," the first sound-animated cartoon, at New York's Colony Theater. The legacy of Mickey, his pals Minnie, Donald, Goofy, Dumbo, Bambi, Snow White and the Seven Dwarfs, and all the beloved cartoon characters are not only enshrined in films, videos, comic strips, books, and world famous tourist attractions, but in the countless products created in their image for well over 50 years—products created by over 400 licensees in the United States, Canada, Great Britain, Japan, Germany, and Taiwan. Walter Ewing Disney's cartoon characters have inspired more toys, in numerous variations, than all other cartoonists combined. Many collectors stick strictly to the vast field of Disneyana.

CLARA CLUCK

This operatic hen was introduced in the Disney short "The Orphan's Benefit" in 1934.

Price Range

☐ **Clara Cluck Pull Toy,** Fisher Price, 1934,
litho and wood platform toy, 8″ length 75.00 125.00

DONALD DUCK

Donald, who in recent years may well have overshadowed his sidekick, Mickey, made his first appearance in a cameo role in "The Wise Little Hen" in 1934. He was his usual, obstreperous self in Mickey's first color cartoon, "The Band Concert," 1935. His first starring role did not come until 1937 in "Donald's Ostrich."

☐ **"Disney Flivver,"** Line Mar, 1940s, litho
tin friction car, Donald at wheel, lithographs of Dopey, Donald's nephews on
chassis, 6″ length 100.00 150.00

☐ **Donald Duck on Bicycle,** Line Mar, 1940s,
litho wind-up, 4″ height 25.00 35.00

Margarete Steiff began producing Mickey, Minnie, and Donald stuffed dolls in the early 1930s. Highly prized, they command $500 and up.

	Price Range	
☐ **Donald Duck Car,** Paperino Politoys, Italy, 1960s, litho tin, Donald drives with nephews in rumble seat	50.00	75.00
☐ **Donald Duck Drummer,** Line Mar, 1950s, litho tin wind-up, 6″ height	75.00	100.00
☐ **Donald Duck Fireman on Ladder,** Line Mar, 1950s	125.00	150.00
☐ **Donald With Nephew,** Line Mar, 1945, litho tin wind-up, 5″ length	50.00	75.00
☐ **Donald Duck in Open Roadster,** Sun Rubber, 1933–1934, hard rubber, painted push toy, 6½″ length	25.00	35.00

Price Range

☐ **Donald Duck and Pluto Rail Car,** Lionel, 1936. Pluto is in doghouse while Donald stands in rear, composition and metal, 10″ length 750.00   850.00

☐ **Donald Duck and Pluto Roadster,** Sun Rubber, 1930s, 7″ length 35.00   50.00

☐ **Donald in the Rowboat,** Sun Rubber, 1940s, hard rubber, 6″ length 50.00   75.00

☐ **Donald Duck Walker,** Shuco, early 1930s, tin, cast iron and felt cloth, 5½″ height ...   700.00   800.00

☐ **Donald Duck Xylophone,** Fisher Price, 1939, lithographed wood, 7½″ length 150.00   200.00

DUMBO THE ELEPHANT

A feature film by RKO Radio Pictures released in 1941.

☐ **Dumbo Walker,** Marx, 1940s, lithograph tin wind-up, Walt Disney's "Dumbo" appears on left ear, 6″ height 75.00   100.00

ELMER ELEPHANT

☐ **Elmer Elephant Pull Toy,** Fisher Price, 1936, litho and wood, 7½″ length 35.00   50.00

FERDINAND THE BULL

Disney adapted the book *The Story of Ferdinand,* by Munro Leaf and Robert Lawson, to a special short feature film in 1938.

☐ **Ferdinand the Bull,** Marx, 1938, litho tin wind-up (tail spins), 7½″ length 100.00   150.00

☐ **Ferdinand Composition-Jointed Figure,** Ideal, 1938, 9″ length 50.00   75.00

GOOFY

☐ **Goofy Gardiner,** Line Mar, 1940s (see also Donald Duck Duet, with Goofy playing bass fiddle) 25.00   35.00

Price Range

☐ **Goofy Walker,** Line Mar, 1940s, tin litho
wind-up, 7" height 25.00   35.00

LUDWIG VON DRAKE

☐ **Ludwig Von Drake,** Line Mar, 1950s, litho
tin wind-up, 6" height 75.00   100.00

MICKEY AND MINNIE MOUSE

☐ **Climbing Mickey,** Dolly Toy Co., Dayton,
Ohio, early 1930s, copyrighted by Walt
Disney Enterprises, die-cut pasteboard, 9"
height 150.00   200.00

☐ **Dancing Mickey and Minnie,** Japan, 1930s,
celluloid wind-up, variations include Minnie and Elmer the Elephant, Donald and El-
mer dancers, 3½" height 250.00   300.00

☐ **Fun-E-Flex Mickey and Minnie on Dog
Sled Pulled by Pluto,** George Borgfeldt,
wood and composition, 10¾" length 250.00   300.00

☐ **Fun-E-Flex Minnie and Mickey,** 1931, distributed by George Borgfeldt, wood-jointed
bodies with composition heads, figures produced separately for Minnie, Mickey, and
Pluto, ears were leatherette or felt, 7"
height, each 100.00   125.00

☐ **Mickey With Banjo,** Japan, 1935–1936,
copyrighted by Walt Disney litho tin base
with celluloid figure of Mickey, rubber band
mechanical (see Betty Boop for similar ver-
sion) 150.00   200.00

☐ **Mickey in Bathing Suit,** Japan, 1930s, celluloid, 5½" height 200.00   300.00

☐ **Mickey on Bicycle,** Japan, 1940s, celluloid
and tin wind-up, with metal bell behind
seat, 5¾" height .... 500.00   600.00★

★Sold for $1125.00 at same Lloyd Ralston Auction as previous Mickey toy.

Price Range

☐ **Mickey and Donald Acrobats,** Line Mar, 1950s, litho tin, steel with celluloid figures (also Minnie and Mickey Acrobats versions), 17″ height 300.00   350.00

☐ **Mickey and Donald in Rowboat,** Japan, 1930s, celluloid, 6″ length 600.00   700.00*

☐ **Mickey and Felix Picnic Basket,** Isla, Spain, circa 1930, litho tin spring action, lid pops up to reveal Felix the Cat, 4½″ height 650.00   750.00

☐ **Mickey and Felix Sparkler,** Isla, Spain, circa 1930s, litho tin spring action, Mickey and Felix light up cigars on sparks ignited by friction of flint on sandpaper, action is seen through die-cut hole in candle's flame, 5½″ height 750.00   850.00

☐ **Mickey Jack-in-the-Box,** Japan, 1930s, celluloid Mickey figure, box is paper-covered wood, 6″ height 350.00   400.00

☐ **Mickey in Life Preserver,** Japan, 1930s, hard rubber, 4½″ height (serves as both toy and baby rattle) 300.00   350.00

☐ **Mickey and Minnie Circus Pull Toy,** Nifty, distributed by George Borgfeldt, 1930s, litho and wood, wood composition figures of pair, paper bellows emits squeaking sound 700.00   800.00

☐ **Mickey and Minnie on Motorcycle,** Tipp, Germany, early 1930s, litho tin wind-up, Tip logo appears on gas tank, "Dunlop Cord" lithographed on wheels, Mickey and Minnie are five fingered, as was typical of early 1930s versions, 10″ length (this toy intended for export to Great Britain) ....   2000.00 plus

☐ **Mickey and Minnie Motoring,** Japan, 1930s, litho tin three-wheel cart, celluloid figures, 5½″ length 250.00   300.00

---

*Sold for $1175.00 at Lloyd Ralston Auction, April 1981.

Price Range

☐ **Mickey and Minnie Mouse Handcar,** Lionel, 1934, litho tin, composition figures of Mickey and Minnie, made in red, green, orange or maroon (the latter is rarest), 8″ length. *Note:* Orders for over $350.00 of the $1.00 handcars saved Lionel from bankruptcy. (Lionel needs another Mickey handcar as they are in financial difficulty again.) 600.00   700.00

☐ **Mickey and Minnie Riding Elephant,** Japan, distributed by George Borgfeldt, 1935, celluloid, wind-up vibrates, head bobs and ears flap when activated, elephants appeared in both red and white variations, 8″ height, 10″ length 350.00   400.00

☐ **Mickey and Minnie Seesaw,** Japan, 1930s, copyrighted by Walt Disney, distributed by George Borgfeldt, celluloid and tin, pendulum and rubber band mechanism, 6″ length
.... 650.00   750.00

☐ **Mickey and Minnie Standing Figures,** Japan, 1930s, celluloid, heads attached by elastic, nonanimated, each 200.00   250.00

☐ **Mickey Mouse Baby Grand Piano,** mail order, Sears, 1935, dark oak with Mickey decal on top 200.00   250.00

☐ **Mickey Mouse Balancer,** Japan, 1940s, celluloid wind-up, Mickey with umbrella balances on ball, 9½″ height .... 500.00   600.00★

☐ **Mickey Mouse Ball Trap Game,** Migra, France, 1934 .... 450.00   500.00

☐ **Mickey Mouse Band,** Fisher Price, 1935, litho wood pull toy, Mickey bangs cymbal on Pluto's backside, 12″ length 100.00   125.00

★Sold for $900.00 at November 1980 Lloyd Ralston auction.

Price Range

☐ **Mickey Mouse Cast-Iron Still Bank,** French, 1930s handpainted, Mickey stands with arms akimbo. Possibly unique; owner is said to have turned down offers for as high as $15,000. .... 2000.00 plus

☐ **Mickey Mouse Cast-Iron Still Bank,** manufacturer unknown, 1970s, Mickey leans against book 50.00   75.00

☐ **Mickey Mouse Circus Tent,** Wells O'London, England, 1935, made to accompany the Circus Train Set, litho tin, magnificent lithography, $5^{1}/_{2}''$ height, 8″ diameter 800.00   1200.00

☐ **Mickey Mouse Circus Train,** Lionel, 1935, lithographed tin and steel with 7″ length Commodore Vanderbilt Engine, Mickey sits in tender, five cars in all, 30″ long, 84″ of track (originally sold for $1.79) 600.00   700.00

☐ **Mickey Mouse Circus Train Set,** Wells O'London, England, Brimtoy Brand, 1935, features Silver Link engine No. 2509, "Mickey the Stoker" composition figure in coal car (swivel action allows him to shovel coal), circus car, Mickey Mouse Band car, circus dining car, engine $7^{1}/_{2}''$ long, tender 4″ long, cars 6″ long, made to run on 0 gauge track 1000.00   1500.00

☐ **Mickey Mouse Crazy Car,** Line Mar, mid 1950s, litho tin wind-up plastic figure, see Donald Duck companion version, $5^{1}/_{2}''$ length 200.00   250.00

☐ **Mickey Mouse Dime Register Bank,** copyrighted by Walt Disney Productions, 1939, Mickey at blackboard with nephews 200.00   250.00

☐ **Mickey Mouse Drummer,** Nifty, distributed by George Borgfeldt, 1931, litho tin, lever activated, 7″ height 350.00   400.00

Price Range

☐ **Mickey Mouse Express,** Marx, 1940s, litho tin, shows Disneyville train depot, small streamliner goes around track as Mickey circles in airplane (on wire) overhead, variation of Popeye Express, 9½" diameter 750.00   800.00

☐ **Mickey Mouse Handcar,** Wells O'London, England, 1935–1936, litho tin with celluloid figures of pair, features bell, 7½" length 250.00   300.00

☐ **Mickey Mouse Locomotive,** Fisher Price (Choo-Choo No. 432), 1938, copyrighted by Walt Disney Enterprises, litho wood with tin bell on locomotive, Mickey doffs engineer's cap, 8½" length 100.00   150.00

☐ **Mickey Mouse Meteor Train Set,** Marx, 1930s, litho tin, five cars, 43" length 500.00   600.00

☐ **Mickey Mouse Paddle Boat,** licensed by Walt Disney Enterprise, distributed under Macy's label, litho tin and wood, 12" length .... 2000.00 plus

☐ **Mickey Mouse Play Piano,** Marks Bros., Boston, 1935, wood, glass and cardboard, as keys are depressed cardboard cutout figures of Mickey and Minnie dance in front of colorful lithographed panel atop piano, 10" height, 9" width (variations featured Big Bad Wolf and Three Pigs). 450.00   500.00

☐ **Mickey Mouse Rocking Horse,** copyrighted by Walt Disney, Japan, 1930s, celluloid Mickey on wooden horse, 7½" height 250.00   300.00

☐ **Mickey Mouse Saxophone Player,** German, early 1930s, litho tin, pressing metal wire activates arms and legs and crashes cymbals attached to Mickey's heels, 6" height 1000.00   1500.00

Price Range

☐ **Mickey Mouse Slate Dancer,** Johann Distler, Nuremberg, 1930–1931, litho tin, handcrank mechanism has Mickey tapping lively tune, 6½" height (has registration number 508041) .... 2000.00 plus

☐ **Mickey Mouse Sparkler,** Nifty, 1931, litho tin, spring activated, 4½" height 450.00   500.00

☐ **Mickey Mouse Tin Still,** Great Britain, "Happynak Series," 1940s 50.00   75.00

☐ **Mickey Mouse Walker,** Japan, 1940s, celluloid wind-up, 7⅜" height .... 600.00   700.00★

☐ **Mickey the Musical Mouse,** Distler, litho tin, distributed by George Borgfeldt with exclusive arrangement with Ideal Films, lower half has three Mickey torsos playing fiddle, dancing, and playing cymbals, top half has Mickey heads that pivot as handle is turned to play tune .... 750.00   850.00★

☐ **Mickey and Pluto in Three-Wheel Cart,** Japan, litho tin and celluloid, 4½" length ... 150.00   200.00

☐ **Mickey in Roadster Pull Toy,** licensed by Walt Disney, Japan, 1934, roadster is tinted celluloid, Mickey figure is string-jointed wooden beads, 12" length 500.00   600.00

☐ **Mickey's Musical Money Box,** still bank, Combex, England, tin, 6" height 50.00   75.00

☐ **Mickey Walker,** Distler, 1930–1931, litho tin with rubber tail, wind-up features big orange pointed feet and decidedly rodent-like countenance, handpainted, 9" height, only a few of this example are known to exist .... 1500.00 plus

---

★Sold for $1350.00 at Lloyd Ralston auction cited earlier.
★A second version shows Minnie pushing carriage at left, while Mickey grinds organ.

Price Range

☐ **Minnie Mouse Pushing Baby Carriage (Pram),** Wells O'London, England, early 1930s, litho tin with Minnie figure in composition, wind-up features dimensional tin figures of Pluto (sitting in front) with two baby mice in pram 1500.00   2000.00

☐ **Minnie Mouse and Seated Felix in Carriage,** Isla, Spain, early 1930's, Minnie pushes carriage while Felix sits under umbrella, 7½" height 500.00   600.00

☐ **Pluto Pulling Mickey on Tricycle,** Japan, 1933, copyrighted by Walt Disney, litho tin and celluloid, approximately 6" long 250.00   300.00

☐ **Rambling Mickey,** Japan (for George Borgfeldt), 1934, celluloid wind-up, steel tail provides balance, 7" height 350.00   400.00

☐ **Running Mickey Bell Toy,** N. N. Hill Brass Co., 1935, litho wood with large pressed-steel back wheels, 13" length, other versions depicted Donald and Pluto 150.00   200.00

☐ **Santa Handcar, No. 1105,** Lionel, 1935, litho tin with composition figures of Santa, a Christmas tree, and a Mickey Mouse in Santa's sack, 11" length, 6½" height (all Lionel handcars were for 0 gauge track; 72" track included in set) 900.00   1100.00

☐ **Standing Mickey,** Rhenische Rubber and Celluloid Fabric Co., Germany, late 1920s or early 1930s, celluloid wind-up, vibrates when activated, 6" height 800.00   900.00

☐ **The Toy Peddler,** German, 1935, litho tin, man rolls eyes and jiggles string of toys, including Mickey Mouse and monkeys, 6½" height 200.00   250.00

PINOCCHIO

This was the second full-length animated technicolor film produced by Disney Studios. It was released in February, 1940, and regarded by many critics as Disney's most brilliant technical extravaganza.

	Price Range	
☐ **Jiminy Cricket Composition-Jointed Figure,** Knickerbocker Toy Co., 1940s	75.00	100.00
☐ **Joe Carioca Walker,** VB and Cie, France, celluloid wind-up	75.00	100.00
☐ **Pinocchio the Acrobat,** Marx, early 40s, litho tin wind-up, puppet swings high up on platform as toy rocks below, 16½" height ...	100.00	150.00
☐ **Pinocchio Walker,** George Borgfeldt, 1940s, litho tin wind-up, 10½" height	200.00	250.00
☐ **Pinocchio Walker,** Marx, early 1940s, litho tin wind-up, 8" height	150.00	200.00
☐ **Pinocchio Walker,** VB and Cie, France, celluloid wind-up	100.00	150.00
☐ **Pinocchio Wood-Jointed Figure,** Ideal, 1940s, 11" height	35.00	50.00

PLUTO

Pluto, after playing second banana in a number of Disney productions, assumed a starring role in "Pluto The Pup" in 1938.

☐ **Pluto,** Marx, 1939, pressed steel with leatherette ears, push tail to activate	50.00	75.00
☐ **Pluto Roll Over,** Marx, 1939, litho tin wind-up, 7" length	125.00	150.00
☐ **Stretchy Pluto,** Line Mar, 1940s, litho tin on wheels, front and back halves of Pluto are joined by large coiled spring	50.00	75.00
☐ **Top Hatted Pluto Blowing Horn,** Line Mar, 1950s, litho tin wind-up, 6½" height	50.00	75.00

Note. See also Pluto toys listed under Donald Duck and Mickey Mouse headings.

SNOW WHITE AND THE SEVEN DWARFS

The first full-length animated technicolor opus by Disney debuted in 1938, a masterful retelling of Grimm's fairy tale.

Price Range

☐ **Doc and Dopey,** Fisher Price, 1940s, litho wood pull toy, 10″ length 75.00   125.00

☐ **Dopey Walker,** Marx, 1940, litho tin wind-up, 7″ height 125.00   150.00

☐ **Snow White and Dwarfs Figures,** Sieberling, 1940s, handcolored hard rubber, 6″ height 35.00   50.00

☐ **Snow White and Dwarfs Marionettes,** Alexander Doll Co., New York City, 1940s 100.00   150.00

☐ **Snow White Piano,** Marks Bros., Boston, 1940s, variation of Mickey Mouse Piano with animated figures of Snow White 100.00   125.00

☐ **Snow White and Dwarfs Wood Pull Toy,** N. N. Hill Brass Co., 1940s, with large pressed-steel back wheels (variation of Mickey Mouse toy) 100.00   150.00

THREE LITTLE PIGS

Another Grimm's fairy tale-based film, "The Three Little Pigs," came to the screen in 1933, the most famous of all Disney's Silly Symphonies.

☐ **Big Bad Wolf Walker,** Line Mar, late 1940s, litho tin wind-up, 6″ height 50.00   75.00

☐ **Drummer Pig, Fiddler Pig, and Fifer Pig,** Schuco, mid-1930s, felt on tin wind-ups, 6″ height 350.00   400.00

☐ **Fiddler Pig Walker,** Line Mar, late 1940s, litho tin wind-up, 6″ height 50.00   75.00

☐ **Three Little Pigs Acrobats,** Line Mar, 1950s, celluloid and metal (variation of Mickey and Donald Acrobat toy) 150.00   200.00

EDUCATIONAL TOYS

One of the first toy categories specifically designed to be educational was that of alphabet blocks. It was described as early as 1653 in *The Jewel House of Art and Nature,* published in London. It was not until the second half of the 18th century, however, that alphabet blocks were manufactured on any scale for children. By the 1860s in the United States, S.L. Hill Co., New York City, McLoughlin Bros., also of New York, and Jesse Crandall (with his nested blocks), all were producing richly decorated alphabet blocks. Milton Bradley followed with his Kindergarten Alphabet and Building Blocks in 1872; raised-letter blocks were introduced by the Embossing Co. in 1879. Throughout the latter half of the 19th century, F. Richter Co. produced their famous Anchor Box of building stones in three colors.

Construction toys made their appearance as early as the 1860s, when Ellis, Britton, and Eaton of Springfield, Vermont, manufactured hardwood logs with simple locking devices. Charles Crandall developed several toys employing an ingenious finger joint—his building blocks and acrobats. W.E. Crandall, another member of the famous toy making clan, devised toy building blocks which were the forerunner of the Lego units developed in plastic by Gottfried Christianson in Denmark, some 60 years ago. The big three—Meccano, A.C. Gilbert, and Tinkertoy—were early 20th-century innovators. The Meccano system originated in England in 1901; A.C. Gilbert designed his first Erector Set in 1913; Tinkertoy sets were first sold in 1914. Take-apart toys, including lithograph paper-on-wood trains, boats, and tiny buildings, were popular children's fare in the late 19th century as W.S. Reed and R. Bliss sought to satisfy a primal urge among youngsters to dismantle and reassemble toys.

Card games were common in the early colonies by the 18th century, although they took a strong moralistic tone and were not intended for amusement. In the mid-19th century, things lightened up with such popular card games as Dr. Busby, Yankee Pedlar, and Old Maid. Board games originated with the sole purpose of instructing the child, as in the 1804 "Game of Science and the Sport of Astronomy," or H. and S.B. Ives "The Mansion of Happiness"

in 1843, although the entire family generally participated. George Parker of Parker Brothers produced his first game, "Banking," in 1883. It not only taught youngsters the value of money but had the added benefit of interaction between family members of various ages.

Puzzles in shapes of squares and cubes were brightly lithographed and offered countless combinations. A popular puzzle of the late 19th century cut images of famous Americans into three sections, creating obviously humorous combinations titled "Prominent Americans Sliced." Early picture puzzles were best exemplified as dissected maps. John Wallis, a prominent English cartographer, first produced pictured map puzzles in the 18th century. Ironically, these early picture puzzles were confined primarily to teenagers and adults. It was not until the 1920s, when Playskool began turning out wooden puzzles with few pieces, that younger children could also participate.

An instructional toy category that bears special mention because of its inherent graphic appeal is the Historoscope, an elegant chromolith panorama of famous historic events by which pictures on rollers were moved by turning tiny wooden knobs. Any number of panoramas were available, but one of the most popular dealt with George Washington riding his white charger into battle against the British. The real trick is to find these unusual treasures in presentable condition.

Wind, water, sand, gravity—all natural forces—have powered toys for centuries. Among the most popular of these playthings were optical toys, such as the kaleidoscope, rediscovered by Englishman David Brewster in 1817. The persistence of vision, the principle on which motion pictures are based, was exemplified by the Zoetrope, Phenikistiscope, Praxinoscope, Thaumatrope, and the stereoptican—all designed for family viewing and enjoying. The Zoetrope was perfected in 1867 by Milton Bradley from the Wheel of Life, patented in Britain some seven years earlier. Various interchangeable disks, when spun, taught children color mixing with light.

Electro-magnetic toys and chemistry sets were introduced in America in the late 1890s, with chemistry sets having their heyday in the 1920s.

Within the present time frame, plastic blocks made by Halsam and Kiddiecraft during the 1960s, soft blocks by Creative Playthings and Galt, Fisher Price Activity Centers, and plastic modular kits by Leggo and Playmobile all qualify as educational toy collectibles of the future.

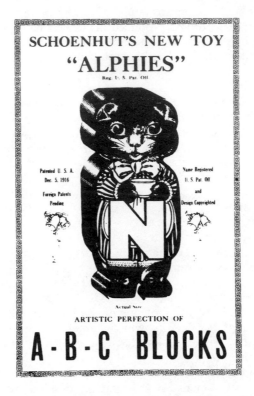

Advertisement for "Alphies" ABC Blocks by Schoenhut, dated 1916. These whimsical educational toys range from $600 to $700 for a set of 26 blocks.

The following is a brief sampling of the hundreds of highly collectible educational toys.

	Price Range	
☐ **Alphabet of Country Scenes,** McLoughlin, 1887, color litho paper on wood	125.00	150.00
☐ **Alphie's ABC Blocks,** A. Schoenhut, 1916	200.00	225.00
☐ **Around the World Trunk,** R. Bliss, 1911, litho paper-on-wood trunk with ABC blocks	100.00	150.00

Price Range

☐ **Beasts and Birds Novelty Blocks,** Lyman Whitney Publishers, Leominster and Boston, Massachusetts, 1874, printed paper on wood 125.00   150.00

☐ **Boy Contractor,** Cruver, Chicago, circa 1900, metal forms, sandstone, cement, plaster 100.00   150.00

☐ **Boy's Union Tool Chests #725 B,** Bliss, 1911 .... 50.00   75.00

☐ **Cardhouse,** designed by Charles Eames, late 1950s 25.00   35.00

☐ **Chemistry Lab,** A.C. Gilbert, 1950s 50.00   60.00

☐ **Chiromagica,** McLoughlin, circa 1870, wood, glass, printed cardboard 150.00   200.00

☐ **Cob House Blocks,** McLoughlin, circa 1887, litho paper on wood 100.00   150.00

☐ **Crandall's Acrobats,** Charles Crandall, circa 1875, painted wood 200.00   250.00

☐ **Crandall's Building Blocks,** Charles Crandall, 1867 .... 200.00   225.00

☐ **Crandall's Wide-Awake Alphabet,** Charles Crandall, 1867 .... 150.00   175.00

☐ **Deluxe Erector Set,** A.C. Gilbert, metal, magnet 50.00   75.00

☐ **Farmyard Puzzles,** Milton Bradley, circa 1900, color litho paper on cardboard 75.00   100.00

☐ **Goodie Two Shoes Spelling Game,** McLoughlin, 1870, wood stenciled with letters and numbers 200.00   225.00

☐ **Great East River Suspension Bridge,** Stirn and Lyons, New York, wood, metal, circa 1880s 250.00   300.00

☐ **Illustrated Cubes Spelling Blocks,** Embossing Co., Albany, New York, 1870 ..... 100.00   150.00

☐ **Jackstraws,** Bone, handmade, 1820s 150.00   200.00

	Price Range	
☐ **Junior Printing House,** Baumgarten, Baltimore, 1883, wood, rubber letter and number stamps	100.00	125.00
☐ **Kaleidoscope,** McLoughlin, circa 1870, wood, glass, metal	250.00	300.00
☐ **Life of George Washington Puzzle,** manufacturer unknown, circa 1860, handpainted paper-on-wood picture puzzle	100.00	125.00
☐ **Lincoln Logs,** John Lloyd Wright Design, 1930s	50.00	75.00
☐ **Log Cabin Playhouse,** Ellis, Britton and Eaton, circa 1865	200.00	225.00
☐ **Marriage of Jenny Wren to Cock Robin Story Blocks,** J.A. Crandall, 1881	150.00	200.00
☐ **Masquerade Blocks,** Charles Crandall, circa 1870	75.00	150.00
☐ **Meccano Set,** Mecanno Ltd., Liverpool, England, designed by Frank Hornby, 1901	50.00	75.00
☐ **Mr. Machine Plastic Figure,** Ideal Toys, 1950s	15.00	25.00
☐ **Nest of Pictures and ABC Blocks,** McLoughlin Bros., circa 1885	100.00	150.00
☐ **Ninth "Gift" Rings For Ring Laying,** Friedrich Froebel, 1826	100.00	125.00
☐ **Organ of Constructiveness,** Edward Wallis, London, 1820s, construction toy	200.00	225.00
☐ **Playtime Animal Object and Alphabet Blocks,** Milton Bradley, 1910, cardboard litho pictures	75.00	100.00
☐ **Praxinoscope,** ER, Paris, circa 1880, litho paper strips	450.00	500.00
☐ **Prominent Americans,** patented by Walter Stranders, 1881 litho paper on cardboard ..	100.00	125.00
☐ **Roman Architect Wood Cubes,** German, 1870s	85.00	125.00

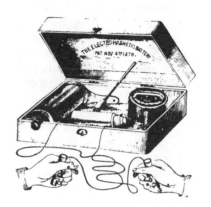

Educational toys, 1890s, Crandall's Sectional ABC Blocks, $250–$300 a set; Weeden Steam Engines, double is $200–$250, single is $150–$200; Electric Battery, $75–$85.

	Price Range	
☐ **Scrabble,** Selchow and Righter, New York, 1953	15.00	25.00
☐ **S.L. Hill's Kindergarten Building Blocks,** 1860s printed paper on wood	150.00	200.00
☐ **Steam Engine,** manufacturer unknown, 1870s, brass, tin, glass	75.00	100.00
☐ **Tinkertoy,** designed by Charles A. Pajeau, 1914	75.00	100.00
☐ **Utopian School Master,** manufacturer unknown, circa 1840, wood litho paper-on-cardboard spelling aid	175.00	200.00
☐ **Victorian Hand Shadow,** manufacturer unknown, projector, 1870s	110.00	125.00
☐ **Zoetrope,** Milton Bradley, circa 1870	350.00	400.00

ETHNIC TOYS

For a number of years ethnic toys, black toys in particular, were kept under wraps by dealers and collectors for fear that patrons might be offended by the derogatory names and roles associated with them. More recently, however, with the TV mini-series *Roots* and the inception of the institute of Black Studies, black collectibles are regarded in a new light, as artifacts of history. The fact of their existence is undeniable, despite the controversy over their aesthetic presentation. Some of the leading collectors, dealers, and authorities in this field are themselves blacks. (Ron Rooks of Baltimore and P.J. Gibbs of Nashville, Tennessee, are two names that immediately come to mind.) Ms. Gibbs has recently published a fine comprehensive book, *Black Collectibles Sold in America*. A monthly *Guide to Buyers, Sellers, and Traders of Black Collectibles* is also available. Write CGL, Box 158472, Nashville, Tennessee 37215, for information.

Often overlooked in the ethnic toy field are those toys, largely from the late 19th century, that depicted Irish, German, and Chinese immigrants in anything but a flattering manner. From 1850 on, Chinese laborers flooded into California; their cheap labor was much in demand in those days to work on the first transcontinental railroad. When hard times came in the late 1870s, strong anti–Chinese sentiment prevailed, leading to the Chinese Exclusion Act of 1882. An Ives cap pistol, "Chinese Must Go," shows a Coolie being pulled by his pigtail and booted out of the country by an immigration official—typical of the defamatory nature of a number of like toys and banks. The Irishman, too, did not escape the satirical barbs of toy makers, as witness the Ives "Irish Woodchopper" clockwork toy, featuring a woodsman with decidedly simian features. "Paddy and His Pig," clearly a lampoon of the company kept by the shanty Irish, was replicated by Lehmann, Stock, and F. Strauss over the years. It depicts a crude-looking bumpkin astride a pig. Many toys showed Germans performing the most menial of tasks and the famed "Katzenjammer Kids" comic toys portrayed Hans and Fritz as nasty little brats.

What may have been lacking in taste was often redeemed by clever and amusing animation. Ethnic toys reflect a fascinating part of our culture and are increasingly in demand these days.

Three minstrel-inspired clockwork toys: Brudder Bones, Fiddler, and the Banjo Player (Poor Old Joe), all three attributed to J.B. Secor, and all from the late 1870s. The three clockwork toys are extremely rare, $2000 plus; the Crandall Donkey and Rider are $800–$1000.

BLACKS

Price Range

☐ **Alabama Coon Jigger,** Strauss, 1910, lithographed tin, wind-up, also known as Tombo, a variation of the Lehmann jigger "Oh My" (Lehmann made the toy for Strauss) 300.00   350.00

Two humorous black toys produced over 30 years apart. *Left:*
Unfortunate African, maker unknown, 1885, wood, tin and cloth pull
toy, $1200–$1400. *Right:* "Oh My" (or Alabama Coon Jigger),
Lehmann, 1914; Strauss made an identical toy called "Tap Tap" which
apparently Lehmann produced for them. "Oh My" is $450–$550.

	Price Range
☐ **Alligator With Rider,** patented by Edward Ives and Joseph Pilkington, 1893, cloth-covered tin, black rides jointed gator, 22″ length	5000.00 plus
☐ **Amos n' Andy** (see "Comic and Character Toys")	
☐ **Automatic Toy Boxers,** patented by Maguire & Gallot, New Jersey and New York, 1876, painted tin with cloth clockwork on wood platform box, fighters give realistic sparring motion	2000.00 plus
☐ **Automatic Toy Dancers,** patented by H. L. Brower, 1873, painted tin with cloth, clockwork, scenic backdrop in wood	2000.00 plus
☐ **Banjo Player (Poor Old Joe),** Secor, 1880s, clockwork, painted tin with cloth	2000.00 plus

Price Range

☐ **Black Couple,** German, 1910–1912, lithographed tin, 8″ height, each 200.00   250.00

☐ **Black Dancers,** German, 1910, clockwork musical lithographed painted tin, 6″ height 350.00   400.00

☐ **Black Dandy Dancing Toy,** German, 1900s 300.00   350.00

☐ **Black Dude,** German, 1900s, with moving glass eyes, lithographed tin wind-up, 6¾″ height 200.00   250.00

☐ **Black Girl Leading Elephant,** German, 1910, 4½″ length 250.00   300.00

☐ **Black Man Playing Bass,** Gunthermann, 1900s, painted tin clockwork, man in big hat seated on stool plays violin with both hands and feet, bright colors, 8½″ height ... 450.00   500.00

☐ **Black Man Pushing Cart,** German, 1900s, 6½″ height 150.00   200.00

☐ **Black Musicians,** Gunthermann (German), banjo and tambourine men, 8¾″ width, 8″ height 1000.00   2000.00

☐ **Black One-Man Band,** German, 1910, lithographed tin, wind-up, 8½″ height 275.00   350.00

☐ **Black "Yellow Kid" in Goat Cart,** early 1900s, identical to Yellow Kid version by Kenton except for black color and red vs. yellow nightshirt, 7½″ length 100.00   150.00

☐ **Brudder Bones,** Secor, 1882, painted tin, clockwork .... 2000.00 plus

☐ **Busy Bootblack,** German, early 1900s, painted tin wind-up, 6″ height 600.00   700.00

☐ **Cakewalk Dancer (Hero of the Cakewalk),** variation of J. M. Cromwell patent, 1879, dapper "gentleman of color" in swallowtail coat dances on platform that has hanging backdrop overhead, 9½″ height (see also "Shoo Fly Champion Dancers") .... 2000.00 plus

	Price Range	
☐ **Charleston Trio,** Marx, 1920s, lithographed tin wind-up, includes dancer, violinist and performing poodle	250.00	300.00
☐ **Colored Dancers,** German, circa 1910, painted tin mechanical, couple appears to be waltzing in circles	250.00	300.00
☐ **Crow's Patent American Negro Dancing Toy,** German, 1910, 9″ height	350.00	400.00
☐ **Dancer With Fan,** H. P. German, 1910, lithographed tin, black lady, 7″ height	250.00	300.00
☐ **Dapper Dan (The Jigging Porter),** Marx, 1920s, lithographed tin wind-up, Dan wears porter's cap	250.00	300.00
☐ **Darktown Battery** (see "Mechanical Banks" listing)		
☐ **Darktown Dude,** German, 1910, painted tin mechanical	500.00	600.00
☐ **Darky With Alligator,** Gong Bell, 1903, cast-iron pull toy, black pulls bell on chain with alligator at opposite end, 7½″ length ..	2000.00 plus	
☐ **Darky Ball Toss,** German, 1900s, hand-painted composition and cloth, ball toss with darky's mouth open as target, 20″ height ...	2500.00	3000.00*
☐ **Darky Banjo Player,** German, 1910, painted tin wind-up, 6¾″ height	450.00	550.00
☐ **Darky Boy and Dog,** German, 1924, painted tin	200.00	250.00
☐ **Darky in Rocking Chair,** German, 1900s, painted tin, known for scary, distorted features of man who rocks back and forth	250.00	300.00
☐ **Disappearing Darky (Jack-in-Box),** German, 1910, composition and wood, black thumbs nose as he pops up out of chimney, 4½″ height	250.00	300.00

*Sold for $3300.00 at Opfer Christmas Auction, December 1985.

Price Range

☐ **Freedman's Bank** (see "Political and Patriotic Toys" listing) ....

☐ **Frightened Coon,** German, 1910, black riding pig, painted tin wind-up 650.00   750.00

☐ **Funny Fire Fighters,** Marx, 1920s, lithographed tin and celluloid, pair black fighters with boxing gloves in crazy car type with ladder, 8″ length 200.00   250.00

☐ **"Gely,"** German, 1920s, lithographed tin wind-up, female driver with large earrings driving car, celluloid windshield, 6½″ length 150.00   200.00

☐ **Ham and Sam,** Strauss, 1920s, one of scores of piano toys produced by Strauss and arch competitor, Louis Marx, lithographed tin wind-up, Ham is at piano while Sam plays banjo, 8½″ height 300.00   350.00

☐ **Ham and Sam,** Linemar, 1950s, pair behind blackboard, 5″ height 400.00   450.00

☐ **Happy Jack and Happy James Dancers,** W.K., German, 6½″ height 400.00   500.00

☐ **Happy Jack Dancer,** W.K., German, tin crank lithographed, 8″ height 300.00   350.00

☐ **Hercules Jazz Band,** Chein, 1920s, lithographed tin wind-up, group of four black musicians, 11½″ height, 12″ width 125.00   150.00

☐ **Hey Hey the Chicken Snatcher,** Marx, 1920s, lithographed tin wind-up, 8½″ height 350.00   400.00

☐ **Hot n'Tott,** Strauss, 1925, lithographed tin wind-up, more uncommon variation of above, 8″ height, 7¾″ width 650.00   700.00

☐ **Initiation First Degree,** Stevens, 1890, mechanical bank, goat butts black who deposits coin in frog's mouth ....   2000.00 plus

☐ **Jazzbo Jim,** Strauss, 1920s, lithographed tin wind-up, 10″ height 300.00   350.00

Price Range

☐ **Jazzbo Jim Dancer on Roof,** Unique Art, 1920s, 8" height 400.00   450.00

☐ **Jazzbo Jim and His Friends,** Strauss, 1925 .... 400.00   450.00

☐ **Jolly Nigger Mechanical Bank,** England, 1900s, cast metal 100.00   150.00

☐ **Lady With Basket,** German, 1910, painted tin mechanical, 7½" height 250.00   300.00

☐ **Lenox Avenue and 125th Street,** Japanese, 1950s, lithographed tin wind-up with celluloid and cloth, black man dances in front of street sign (the Savoy, Cotton Club, and Lenox Club were all located on this celebrated avenue in New York's Harlem) 150.00   200.00

☐ **Male Evangelist,** Ives, 1880s, composition, tin, cloth clockwork .... 2000.00 plus

☐ **Mammy's Boy,** German, 1929, lithographed tin mechanical, 11" height 200.00   250.00

☐ **Maude and Sam,** All Fair Toys, 1920s, lawn cart, lithographed tin, 9" height 300.00   400.00

☐ **Microphone Dancer,** National Comp. Inc., 1920s, composition and tin, black leans against lamppost, toy is activated by speaking through small attached microphone, 12" height 650.00   700.00

☐ **Negro Boy and Cat,** N.A. Hill, 1905, cast-iron bell toy, boy pulls cat tail, 6½" length 350.00   450.00

☐ **Negro Nursemaid With White Child,** Excelsior Toy Co., 1880s, painted composition with cloth .... 2000.00 plus

☐ **Negro With Three-Wheeler,** German, 1910, painted tin, rider doffs hat in greeting motion as vehicle moves 700.00   800.00

☐ **Negro Woman Shopper,** German, 1910, painted tin mechanical, 6½" height 200.00   250.00

Price Range

☐ **"Oh My"** (Lehmann version of Alabama Coon Jigger, which see) ....

☐ **"Old Aunt Chloe,"** Ives, 1880s, composition with cloth, clockwork, scrubs over washboard ....   2000.00 plus

☐ **"Old Black Joe,"** Ives, 1880s, clockwork, painted composition with cloth ....   2000.00 plus

☐ **"Old Susannah" Musical Crank Toy,** German, 1910, plays tune when cranked, black strumming banjo pictured, 4½" height 200.00   250.00

☐ **One-Man Band,** Muller & Kadeder, drummer with cymbals, painted tin mechanical, 7½" 650.00   700.00

☐ **Plantation Mechanical Bank,** Weeden, 1888, cast iron, dancer and banjo player ...   700.00   800.00

☐ **Porter With Rollo Chair** (see "Lehmann Toys" listing) ....

☐ **Pushcart With Black,** Fernand Martin, French, 1920s, painted tin clockwork, black leans into pushcart loaded with fruit and pushes from rear ....   5000.00 plus

☐ **Rastus and His Mother,** Gong Bell, 1903, mammy and son hold bell between them on chain, bell pull toy, 7½" length ....   2000.00 plus

☐ **Red Cap Porter,** Strauss, 1927, lithographed tin mechanical, 6½" height 250.00   300.00

☐ **Red Cap Porter With Handcart,** Strauss, 1920s, lithographed tin mechanical, dog leaps out of steamer trunk as porter pushes, 6½" length 250.00   300.00

☐ **Sambo Special,** manufacturer unknown, 1920s, lithographed wood, painted toy, 8" height 50.00   75.00

☐ **Seesaw With Clown and Darky,** Gong Bell, 1903, cast-iron pull toy, 6½" length 800.00   900.00

Top: A pair of clockwork toys from the 1880s. "Old Nursemaid and Child" is made by Excelsior Toy Company. The doll's head is of German China, the maid's head is composition, Double Dancers by Ives. Both are rarities, and clearly belong in the $2000 plus range.

Price Range

☐ **Shoo Fly Champion Dancers,** patented by
J. M. Cromwell, late 1870s, tin clockwork,
figures advance, retreat, pousette and per-
form variety of antics, 9½ " height .... 2000.00 plus

☐ **Stump Speaker,** Stevens, 1900s, cast-iron
mechanical bank 600.00   700.00

☐ **Sweeping Mammy,** Lingstrom, 1920s,
lithographed tin mechanical, 9 " height 75.00   100.00

☐ **Tom Bones Marionette,** maker unknown,
painted wood, minstrel dummy, 13 " height
.... 2500.00 3000.00*

☐ **"Two Coons,"** Gong Bell, 1903, cast-iron
bell pull toy, black and possum gaze at each
other from opposite ends of hollow log,
8½ " length .... 2000.00 plus

☐ **Watermelon Bell Toy,** N. H. Hill, 1905,
cast-metal pull toy, black boys slice watermelon on platform with cross-cut saw as toy
is pulled across floor 850.00   950.00

☐ **Woman's Right or Suffragette Clockwork
Toy** (see "Political and Patriotic Toys" listing) ....

OTHERS

☐ **Automated Tea Drinker,** manufacturer unknown, early 1900s, Mandarin raises cup to
lip, clockwork, tin mechanical .... 2000.00 plus

☐ **Chinaman in Boat,** possibly James Bailey,
lead, mechanical bank, place coin on tray
and raise Chinaman's pigtail, he raises arm
and flips coin, 4½ " height .... 2000.00 plus

☐ **The Chinaman Walker,** patented by Arthur Hotchkiss, Ives, 1876, composition
with cloth clockwork (toy inspired by movement begun in 1850s to exclude Chinese
from immigrating to the United States) 8000.00 10000.00

*Sold for $3850.00 at Riba-Mobley auction in November 1986.

Price Range

☐ **Chinese Boxers,** early 1900s, possibly German, 4 boxers in each corner of ring, 5th is tossed in blanket, pair of dice and ball also accompanied toy (may well have been used as gambling game, see also Lehmann version of toy) ....   2000.00 plus

☐ **Chinese Roly-Poly,** Schoenhut, 1910, composition, with turning head, 15″ height (Schoenhut made toy in several other sizes) 350.00   400.00

☐ **Dancing Dutch Couple,** Martin, 1910, painted tin mechanical, 6½″ height 400.00   450.00

☐ **Dutch Boy Roly-Poly,** Schoenhut, 1910, papier-mache 300.00   350.00

☐ **Dutch Girl Roly-Poly,** Schoenhut, 1910, papier-mache 300.00   350.00

☐ **Dutch Jolly Jiggers,** Schoenhut, papier-mache, wood and cloth, jiggers are on bent wires and dance when platform below is squeezed, 16″ height, 22″ length 1200.00 1400.00*

☐ **Indian Bust Still Bank,** manufacturer unknown, 1910, cast iron, 3¾″ height 150.00   200.00

☐ **Indian (Hindu) Roly-Poly,** Schoenhut, 1910 ....   500.00   600.00*

☐ **Indian on Horse,** German, 1920s, two-dimensional handoperated squeeze action, tin, Indian has sharp, stylized features, 6½″ length 100.00   125.00

☐ **Indian Rowing Canoe,** manufacturer unknown, 1920s, painted tin wind-up, 8″ length 200.00   250.00

☐ **Irish Woodchopper,** Ives, 1882, composition clockwork, Irishman with pipe chops log ....   2000.00 plus

*Sold for $2800.00 at Atlanta Toy Museum Auction, October 1986.
*Sold for $1100.00 at Atlanta Toy Museum Auction, October 1986.

Irish Woodcutter, Ives, 1880s, clockwork mechanical, $2000 plus.

	Price Range	
☐ **Irishman With Pigs,** German, 1914, painted tin mechanical, chases two pigs with stick, 7½″ length	300.00	350.00
☐ **Jiggs in His Jazz Car,** Maggie and Jiggs (see "Comic and Character Toys" listing)		
☐ **Polite Chinaman,** German, early 1900s, painted tin clockwork, Mandarin with pigtails seesaws on high pole, 13″ height	350.00	400.00
☐ **Sax Player,** German, 1930s, lithographed tin squeeze toy, cymbals on feet, eyes roll, arms move and cymbals clash, 6½″ height	150.00	200.00
☐ **Scotchman on Scooter,** Nifty, 1929, lithographed tin mechanical, 8″ length	200.00	250.00

Price Range

☐ **Sister Lucinda at the Play,** Secor, 1880s, composition clockwork with cloth, fans self and shakes head and body from side to side ....   10000.00 plus

☐ **Spic and Span,** Strauss, 1924, lithographed tin wind-up, another jigger toy, 10″ height 250.00   300.00

☐ **Squaw and Papoose,** in bas relief bust, dark finish with gold trim 350.00   450.00

☐ **Three Musicians,** patented by Henry Mencke, tin glass sand toy 1000.00   1500.00

☐ **Two-Faced Indian,** manufacturer unknown, 1900s, cast-iron still bank, Chief with full headdress back-to-back bust figure, 4¼″ height 250.00   350.00

☐ **"Woman's Right Advocate"** (see "Political and Patriotic Toys" listing) ....

GAMES

W.B. and S.B. Ives made the first moves on these shores to bring board games into the social milieu in 1843 with the highly moralistic "Mansion of Happiness" (see "Educational Toys" listing for additional background). The real triumverate among game board manufacturers, however, proved to be McLoughlin Brothers, Parker Brothers, and Milton Bradley (with Selchow and Righter a not too distant fourth). The exciting and colorful chromolithography that typifies late 19th-century mass-produced board games has caught the eye of a growing legion of games people. Noel Barrett, co-manager of the Atlanta Toy Museum series of auctions, cites board games as one of the most active categories in the hobby today, and prices realized from their October 1986 auction clearly bear him out.

COMIC STRIP GAMES

	Price Range	
☐ **Andy Gump, His Game,** licensed by Sidney Smith Corp., 1924	75.00	100.00
☐ **Beetle Bailey, The Old Army Game,** Milton Bradley, 1963	25.00	35.00
☐ **Charlie McCarthy Question and Answer Game,** Whitman Pub., 1938	25.00	35.00
☐ **Charlie McCarthy Topper Game,** Whitman Pub., 1938	35.00	40.00
☐ **Dick Tracy Detective Game,** Whitman Pub., 1937	35.00	50.00
☐ **Dick Tracy Playing Card Game,** Whitman Pub., 1937	25.00	35.00
☐ **Donald Duck's Party Game For Young Folks,** Parker Bros.	50.00	75.00
☐ **Eddie Cantor's Tell It to the Judge,** Parker Bros., 1938	35.00	50.00
☐ **Ed Wynn, The Fire Chief,** Selchow and Righter, 1937	25.00	35.00

	Price Range	
☐ **Fibber McGee and the Wistful Vista Mystery Game,** Milton Bradley	25.00	35.00
☐ **High Spirits, With Calvin and the Colonial,** Milton Bradley, 1920s	25.00	35.00
☐ **Hi-Way Henry Cross-Country Auto Race,** circa late 1920s	250.00	300.00
☐ **Little Orphan Annie Game,** Milton Bradley, 1927	50.00	75.00
☐ **The Nebbs, Adventures of,** Milton Bradley, 1925–1927	35.00	50.00
☐ **Oh Blondie,** 1940, Whitman Pub. Game (played like Bingo)	25.00	35.00
☐ **Popeye Playing Card Game,** circa 1934, Whitman Pub.	15.00	25.00
☐ **Smitty Game,** Milton Bradley, circa 1930	50.00	75.00
☐ **Snow White and the Seven Dwarfs,** Milton Bradley, 1937	75.00	100.00
☐ **Toonerville Trolley Game,** Milton Bradley, 1927	75.00	100.00
☐ **Uncle Remus Game,** Zip, Parker Bros., circa 1930	50.00	75.00
☐ **Uncle Wiggily,** Milton Bradley, 1918	35.00	50.00
☐ **Walt and Skeezix Gasoline Alley Game,** Milton Bradley, circa 1920	50.00	75.00
☐ **Yellow Kid,** maker unknown, late 1890s ..	100.00	125.00

HISTORICAL GAMES

☐ **Admiral Byrd's South Pole Game,** Parker Bros., 1934	100.00	150.00
☐ **American History in Pictures,** Interstate School Educational Game	15.00	25.00
☐ **Captain Kidd Treasure Game,** Parker Bros., 1890s	100.00	125.00
☐ **Columbus Puzzle,** Milton Bradley, 1890s	35.00	50.00

	Price Range	
☐ **Comical History of America,** Parker Bros., 1920s	25.00	35.00
☐ **Defenders of the Flag,** Noble and Noble Pub., 1920s	25.00	35.00
☐ **Dewey's Victory,** Parker Bros., 1900	100.00	150.00
☐ **Flag Game,** McLoughlin Bros., 1880s	35.00	50.00
☐ **Flight to Paris,** Milton Bradley, 1927	125.00	150.00
☐ **Game of American History,** Parker Bros., 1890s	20.00	30.00
☐ **Game of Buffalo Bill,** Parker Bros., 1980s	20.00	30.00
☐ **Game of Politics** (see "Political and Patriotic Toys" listing)		
☐ **Game of Rough Riders,** Clark and Sowdon, early 1900s	100.00	125.00
☐ **Game of '76 (or The Lion and the Eagle),** Noyes and Snow, 1876	50.00	75.00
☐ **Game of the Transatlantic Flight,** circa 1924, Milton Bradley	125.00	150.00
☐ **Game of World's Fair,** Star Pub., card game, 1923	50.00	75.00
☐ **George Washington's Dream Reading Game,** Parker Bros., late 1890s	25.00	35.00
☐ **Heroes of America, Games of Nations Series,** Paul Educational Games, card game, 1920s	15.00	25.00
☐ **Historical Game of Cards,** A. Flanagan, 1800s	15.00	25.00
☐ **History of Up To Date,** Parker Bros., card game, early 1900s	15.00	25.00
☐ **Home History Game for Boys and Girls,** Milton Bradley, card game, 1910	20.00	30.00
☐ **Hood's War Game,** C. I. Hood, Spanish American War, circa 1900	30.00	40.00

	Price Range	
☐ **In the White House,** Fireside Game Co., card game, 1896	30.00	40.00
☐ **Lindy Flying Game,** Parker Bros., card game, 1927	25.00	30.00
☐ **Mayflower,** Cincinnati Game Co., card game, 1890s	25.00	30.00
☐ **Naval Engagement,** McLoughlin Bros., Civil War, 1870	50.00	75.00
☐ **North Pole Game,** Milton Bradley, 1907 ..	150.00	175.00
☐ **Panama Canal Puzzle Game,** U. S. Playing Cards Co., 1910	50.00	100.00
☐ **Pyramids,** Knapp Electric, 1930s	25.00	30.00
☐ **Race for the North Pole,** Milton Bradley, 1900s	15.00	25.00
☐ **Royal Game of Kings and Queens,** McLoughlin Bros., 1890s	50.00	75.00
☐ **Siege of Havana,** Parker Bros., late 1890s ..	200.00	250.00
☐ **Strat: The Great War Game,** Strat Game Co., World War I, 1915	35.00	50.00
☐ **War of Nations,** Milton Bradley, World War I, 1915	35.00	50.00
☐ **The Way to the White House, Electing the President,** All-Fair	25.00	50.00
☐ **Yankee Doodle,** Cadaco-Ellis, circa 1940	15.00	25.00

NURSERY RHYME GAMES

☐ **Aesop's Fables Cube Puzzles,** McLoughlin Bros., 1800s	150.00	200.00
☐ **Beauty and the Beast,** Milton Bradley, 1900s	25.00	50.00
☐ **Black Sambo,** Samuel Gabriel and Sons, circa 1939	125.00	150.00
☐ **Bo Peep,** McLoughlin Bros., 1890s	150.00	200.00
☐ **Cinderella,** Milton Bradley, card game, 1900s	15.00	25.00

	Price Range	
☐ **Cinderella/Hunt the Slipper,** McLoughlin Bros., variation of Old Maid, 1887	15.00	25.00
☐ **Cock Robin and His Tragical Death,** McLoughlin Bros., card game, 1880s	15.00	25.00
☐ **Dr. Busby St. Nicholas Series Game,** J. Ottmann Lithograph Co. 1890s	15.00	25.00
☐ **Game of Fox and Geese,** J. H. Singer, card game, 1870s	15.00	25.00
☐ **Game of Little Jack Horner,** McLoughlin Bros., card game, 1880s	25.00	50.00
☐ **Game of Old King Cole,** McLoughlin Bros., card game, 1880s	25.00	35.00
☐ **Game of Old Mother Hubbard,** Milton Bradley, board game, 1890s	50.00	75.00
☐ **Game of Red Riding Hood,** Parker Bros, board game, 1895	50.00	75.00
☐ **Game of Red Riding Hood, Adventure Series,** Parker Brothers, board game, 1895 ...	125.00	150.00
☐ **Game of Robinson Crusoe,** Parker Bros., card game, 1895	15.00	25.00
☐ **Game of Sambo,** Parker Bros., target game, 1920s	75.00	100.00
☐ **Game of Three Blind Mice,** Milton Bradley, board game, 1920s	35.00	50.00
☐ **Game of Tom Sawyer,** Milton Bradley, board game, 1930s	50.00	75.00
☐ **Game of Treasure Island,** Gem Publishing Co., board game, 1920s	35.00	50.00
☐ **Game of Visit of Santa Claus,** McLoughlin Bros., board game, 1899	250.00	300.00
☐ **Hickety-Pickety,** Parker Bros., board game, 1920s	35.00	50.00
☐ **Ivanhoe,** Parker Bros., card game, 1890s ..	25.00	35.00
☐ **Jack and the Beanstalk,** Parker Bros., board game, 1890s	35.00	50.00

	Price Range	
☐ **Jack and Jill,** Milton Bradley, board game, 1909	35.00	50.00
☐ **Little Bo Peep,** Parker Bros., card game, 1895	15.00	25.00
☐ **Little Boy Blue,** Milton Bradley, board game, early 1900s	35.00	50.00
☐ **Little Jack Horner,** Milton Bradley, board game, 1900s	50.00	75.00
☐ **Little Mother Goose,** Parker Bros., card game, 1890	25.00	50.00
☐ **Old Woman Who Lived in a Shoe,** Parker Bros., board game	175.00	225.00
☐ **Owl and Pussycat,** E. O. Clark, board game, 1890s	75.00	100.00
☐ **Peter Rabbit,** Milton Bradley, board game, 1910	75.00	100.00
☐ **Pollyanna, The Glad Game,** Parker Bros., board game, circa 1914	35.00	50.00
☐ **Raggedy Ann's Magic Pebble Game,** Milton Bradley, board game, 1940	35.00	50.00
☐ **Red Riding Hood and the World,** McLoughlin Bros., board game, 1890s	50.00	75.00
☐ **Robinson Crusoe,** McLoughlin Bros., board game, 1890s	25.00	50.00
☐ **Santa Claus Game,** Milton Bradley, board game, 1920s	75.00	100.00
☐ **Santa Claus Puzzle Box,** Milton Bradley, picture puzzles, 1920s	85.00	110.00
☐ **Tortoise and the Hare,** U. S. Playing Card Co., board game, 1900s	35.00	50.00
☐ **Winnie the Pooh,** Steven Slesinger Inc., board game, 1933	75.00	100.00
☐ **Wonderful Game of Oz,** Parker Bros., board game, 1921	125.00	150.00

SPORTS GAMES

	Price Range	
☐ **Amateur Golf,** Parker Bros., 1928	50.00	75.00
☐ **Babe Ruth's Baseball Game,** Milton Bradley, 1926	150.00	200.00
☐ **Baseball Game,** Parker Bros., 1913, card game	50.00	75.00
☐ **Big Six: Christy Mathewson, Indoor Baseball Game,** Piroxloid Products Corp., 1922	150.00	200.00
☐ **Bowling,** Parker Bros., 1896, board game ...	50.00	75.00
☐ **Boy's Own Football Game,** McLoughlin Bros., 1800s	200.00	250.00
☐ **Championship Baseball Parlor Game,** Grebnelle Novelty Co., 1914	150.00	200.00
☐ **Classic Derby,** Doremus-Schoen Co., circa 1930s, race track board	35.00	50.00
☐ **Cross-Country Marathon,** Milton Bradley, 1930s	50.00	75.00
☐ **Derby Day,** Parker Bros., circa 1900, card game	25.00	50.00
☐ **Derby Steeplechase,** McLoughlin Bros., 1890	75.00	100.00
☐ **Diamond Game of Baseball,** McLoughlin Bros., circa 1885	75.00	100.00
☐ **Dog Race,** Transogram Co. Inc., circa 1930s	35.00	50.00
☐ **Favorite Steeplechase,** J.H. Singer, circa 1895	35.00	50.00
☐ **Foot Race,** Parker Bros., circa 1900	25.00	35.00
☐ **Fox Hunt,** Milton Bradley, 1905	35.00	50.00
☐ **Game of Baseball,** McLoughlin Bros., 1886	500.00	600.00
☐ **Game of Bicycle Race,** McLoughlin Bros., 1891	200.00	300.00

	Price Range	
☐ **Game of Football,** George Childs, Brattleboro, Vermont, 1895	100.00	125.00
☐ **Game of Gold,** Clark and Snowdon, circa 1900s	75.00	100.00
☐ **Game of Steeple Chase,** Milton Bradley, circa 1910	35.00	50.00
☐ **Game of Tobogganing at Christmas,** McLoughlin Bros., 1899	300.00	350.00
☐ **Grande Auto Race,** U.S. Playing Card Co., circa 1910	50.00	75.00
☐ **Hialeah Racing Game,** Milton Bradley, 1940	50.00	75.00
☐ **Horse Race Game,** Marks Bros. Co., circa 1930, Belmont Park	50.00	75.00
☐ **Hurdle Race,** Milton Bradley, 1905	75.00	100.00
☐ **Kentucky Derby Racing Game,** Whitman Pub., 1930s	35.00	50.00
☐ **Major League Baseball Game,** Philadelphia Game Co., circa 1910, spinner skill game	200.00	300.00
☐ **National-American Baseball Game,** Parker Bros., 1930s	75.00	100.00
☐ **New Game of Hunting,** McLoughlin Bros., 1904	300.00	400.00
☐ **Official Radio Basketball Game,** Toy Creations, 1930s	35.00	50.00
☐ **Official Radio Football Game,** Toy Creations, 1939	35.00	50.00
☐ **Open Championship Golf Game,** Beacon Hudson Co., 1920s	50.00	75.00
☐ **Outboard Motor Race,** Milton Bradley, 1920s	35.00	50.00
☐ **Par Golf Card Game,** National Golf Service Co., 1920s	50.00	75.00
☐ **Peg Baseball,** Parker Bros., 1924	35.00	50.00

	Price Range	
☐ **Races,** Milton Bradley, circa 1880	25.00	35.00
☐ **Saratoga Race Horse Game,** Milton Bradley, 1920s	25.00	50.00
☐ **Spedem Auto Race,** Alderman-Fairchild, 1922	50.00	75.00
☐ **Speed Boat Race,** Milton Bradley, 1930s ...	35.00	50.00
☐ **Star Basketball,** Star Paper Box Co., circa 1920s, bagatelle game	35.00	50.00
☐ **Steeple Chase,** C.M. Clark, 1910	100.00	125.00
☐ **Steeple Chase,** J.H. Singer, circa 1890s ...	35.00	50.00
☐ **Table Croquet,** Milton Bradley, circa 1890s, skill game	50.00	75.00
☐ **Traps and Bunkers, A Game of Golf,** Milton Bradley, circa 1930	25.00	50.00
☐ **World's Championship Baseball Game,** National Indoor Game and Novelty Co., 1900s	50.00	75.00
☐ **Yacht Race,** Milton Bradley, circa 1905 ...	35.00	50.00
☐ **Yachting,** Parker Bros., circa 1895	35.00	50.00

TARGET GAMES

☐ **Big Game Hunters,** Schoenhut, 1924, target game featuring large buffalo (five variations) with Buffalo Bill-type hunters that spring up when target is hit, varnished natural colors, wood base, 12″ width x 10¼″ height, other combinations: rhino and Hindu, bear and Indian, lion and deer with jungle hunters, 13½″ length gun included with eight wood cartridges	300.00	350.00
☐ **Brownie Nine Pins,** McLoughlin Bros., 1892, Palmer Cox Brownies including Uncle Sam, policeman, eskimo, Dutchman, lithograph on wood, 11¾″ height	450.00	550.00

	Price Range	

☐ **Buster Brown Beanbag Toss,** Bliss, 1900s, lithograph on wood, Buster, Tige, and Buster's girl friend, 24″ wide 350.00   400.00

☐ **Columbia Ring Toss Game,** maker unknown, 1890s, lithograph paper on wood, three metal hoops, 19½″ height 500.00   600.00

☐ **Columbus Marble Pool Game,** believed made by Bliss, circa 1893 (in celebration of Columbian Exposition), lithograph paper on wood, coiled metal spiral tower with lithograph alphabet blocks, Columbus figure with Spanish flag stands atop tower, 58″ height 1200.00   1400.00

☐ **Darkie Ring Toss Game,** maker unknown, 1890s, painted cast-iron stained wood, seven black figures, 8⅝″ wide 200.00   250.00

☐ **French Boy Marble Game,** maker unknown, 1890s, lithograph paper on wood, boy is 8½″ length with hole in stomach from which marble rolls toward recessed target area, 22″ length 300.00   350.00

☐ **Jolly Marble Game,** W. S. Reed, 1892, lithograph paper on wood, tivoli game, four of five clowns with animated legs which kick when activated, 21″ height 300.00   350.00

☐ **Le Moulin Game,** French, 1890s, lithograph paper on cardboard, marble target game, two painted tin carts with boy drivers alternately climb ramp to retrieve marble, then roll back down to dump in scoring field as windmill turns 350.00   450.00

☐ **LeNouveau Toboggan Game,** French, 1890s, lithograph paper on wood and cardboard, spring-activated tin cars move down ramp in tower to tip trays, releasing marbles into scoring field, 25½″ height 1200.00   1400.00

Price Range

□ **Mother Goose Target Game,** maker unknown, 1890s, lithograph paper on wood, ball roll target game, when knobs are hit five targets pop up, 18¼" wide 500.00   600.00

□ **Old Guard Ten Pins,** Ives, 1890s, lithograph paper on wood, 10 soldiers, 14" height 700.00   800.00

□ **Punch and Judy Skittles,** maker unknown, 1900s, painted wood and papier-mache, nine figural skittles in shapes of Punch and Judy and other brightly painted characters, on weighted wooden bases, two wooden balls .. 2000.00 plus

□ **Pussy Cat Bean Bag Game,** maker unknown, 1890s, lithograph on wood, wire stand, 15" height 100.00   150.00

□ **Rubber Ball Shooting Gallery,** Schoenhut, 1920s, lithograph paper on wood, popgun and nine targets includes clowns, negro, rabbit, and clay pipes 350.00   400.00

□ **Three Blacks Target Game,** maker unknown, 1800s, paper lithograph on wood, rubber band gun, rubber missile spins black figures on wood dowels, 9½" wide 200.00   250.00

□ **Trick Mule Target Game,** W. S. Reed, lithograph on wood, clown rides mule on wood platform, roll ball to hit target and unseat clown, 22" length 1200.00 1400.00

□ **Uncle Sam and John Bull Marble Roll,** lithograph paper on wood, figures have movable arms, uses regular marbles, 15" height 450.00   500.00

TRAVEL GAMES

□ **Account of Peter Coddle's Visit to New York,** Milton Bradley, 1890s 15.00   20.00

□ **Across the Continent,** Parker Brothers, circa 1935 .... 50.00   75.00

	Price Range	
☐ **Across the Yalu,** Milton Bradley, circa 1905	50.00	75.00
☐ **Aeroplane Race,** McDowell Mfg. Co. (No. 60), 1930s	50.00	75.00
☐ **Airship Card Game,** Parker Bros., 1916 ..	50.00	75.00
☐ **Amusing Game of Innocence Abroad,** Parker Bros., 1888	125.00	150.00
☐ **Auto Game,** Milton Bradley, 1906	75.00	100.00
☐ **Billy Bumps' Visit to Boston,** George S. Parker, circa 1887	25.00	35.00
☐ **Cousin Peter's Trip to New York (Game of),** McLoughlin Bros., 1898	15.00	25.00
☐ **Crazy Travelers,** Parker Bros., circa 1920, skill game	35.00	50.00
☐ **Crossing the Ocean,** Parker Bros., circa 1893	50.00	75.00
☐ **Down the Pike With Mrs. Wiggs at the St. Louis Exposition,** Milton Bradley, 1904 ...	25.00	35.00
☐ **Excursion to Coney Island,** Milton Bradley, circa 1880s	25.00	35.00
☐ **Fast Mail,** Milton Bradley, circa 1900s	150.00	200.00
☐ **North Pole by Airship (Game of),** McLoughlin Bros., 1897	150.00	200.00
☐ **Ocean to Ocean Flight Game,** Wilder Mfg., circa 1927	50.00	75.00
☐ **Peter Coddle and His First Trip to New York,** Milton Bradley, circa 1925 (there were several offshoots of this game)	15.00	25.00
☐ **Pike's Peak or Bust,** Parker Bros., circa 1895	35.00	50.00
☐ **Round the World With Nelly Bly (Game of),** McLoughlin Bros., circa 1890	100.00	125.00
☐ **Street Car Game,** Parker Bros., 1892	75.00	100.00
☐ **Through the Locks to the Golden Gate,** Milton Bradley, circa 1905	50.00	75.00

Price Range

☐ **Toll Gate (Game of)**, McLoughlin Bros.,
circa 1890 .... 100.00   125.00

☐ **Touring, automobile card game**, Wallie
Dorr Co., 1926 .... 25.00   50.00

☐ **Tourist, railroad game**, Milton Bradley,
circa 1900 .... 50.00   75.00

☐ **Train For Boston**, Parker Bros., circa 1900
.... 150.00   175.00

☐ **Transatlantic Flight (Game of)**, Milton
Bradley, circa 1924 .... 125.00   150.00

☐ **Travel (Game of)**, Parker Bros., circa 1894
.... 100.00   125.00

☐ **Trip Around the World**, Parker Bros., circa
1920 .... 25.00   35.00

☐ **Trip Around the World (Game of)**, Mc-
Loughlin Bros., 1897 .... 250.00   300.00

☐ **Trip Through Our National Parks, Game
of Yellowstone**, Cincinnati Game Co., circa
1910 .... 25.00   35.00

☐ **Trips of Japhet Jenkens and Sam Slick**,
Milton Bradley, circa 1871 .... 25.00   35.00

☐ **Trips Railroad Game**, Trips Card Co.,
1905 .... 50.00   75.00

☐ **Trolley Ride (Game of)**, Hamilton-Myers
Co. Pub., 1890s 35.00   50.00

☐ **Voyage Around the World (Game of)**, Mil-
ton Bradley, circa 1930s 100.00   125.00

☐ **Wide World Game**, Parker Bros., 1933 ... 50.00   75.00

GLASS FIGURAL CANDY CONTAINERS

More and more toy collectors are encroaching on the sacred soil of glass collectors in recent years in quest of fascinating figural candy containers in shapes of animals, transportation vehicles, household items, and comic characters. Although candy containers have enjoyed a recent revival in certain gift shops and confectionaries, it is the pre–World War II vintage containers that are so eagerly pursued, particularly varieties dating back as early as 1912.

Considering their rarefied standing today, it is difficult to conceive of containers as mere trinkets, available for 10 to 12 cents at any local five-and-dime store. Once emptied of their treasure of tiny hard candy pellets, a surprisingly large quantity of these containers were preserved as decorative objects. Most containers were of clear glass, although there are examples in ruby, blue, and even milk glass. Frequently, they were painted in vivid colors. The value of the glass toy is enhanced if it has the original paper or tin closure, and if it has retained the original paint. Chips and cracks, of course, quickly send the value plummeting.

Most of the following candy containers were offered in one of the largest collections of such items to be offered in recent memory, that of Florence Main, at the Lloyd W. Ralston Auction in Fairfield, Connecticut, in April, 1981. We've included descriptive material on each lot. The price estimates given are a partial reflection of gaveled prices. To list actual prices realized would be misleading, since all types of grading variations came into play that profoundly affected bidding.

Where available, references are given to two authoritative guides in this highly esoteric specialty. For example, (AE577) on the Upright Piano Bank refers to *American Glass Candy Containers* or *More American Glass Containers*, both by George Eikelberner and Serge Agadjanian, 1967 and 1970. Reference two (S778) is *A Century of Glass Toys* by Mary Louise Stanley, 1971.

Price Range

☐ **Alligator Purse** (AE599–S550), 4¼″ length 250.00 300.00

☐ **American Locomotive With Tin Lithographed Closure** (AE496–S712), 4⅛″ length 25.00 50.00

☐ **Amos n' Andy** (AE21–S1257), 4½″ length 450.00 500.00

☐ **Anchor Condiment Set** (AE385–S353), 5¾″ height 15.00 25.00

☐ **Armored Tank** (AE721–S1137), 4¼″ length 50.00 66.00

☐ **Army Bomber With Paper Propeller** (AE6–S27), 4⅛″ length, each 15.00 25.00

☐ **Auto Lamp** (AE396–S637), 5¾″ overall ... 50.00 75.00

☐ **Babe Ruth on the Bag** (AE78–S315), 4⅛″ height 600.00 650.00

☐ **Baby Ben Alarm Clock** (AE161–S259), 3½″ height 100.00 125.00

☐ **Barney Google**, 3⅝″ height 150.00 200.00

☐ **Barney Google With Apple** (AE72–S294), 3⅞″ height, no paint; **Spark Plug** (AE699–S295), 4⅛″ length, each 150.00 200.00

☐ **Baseball Player and Bat Barrel Bank** (AE77), 3¼″ height 500.00 550.00

☐ **Battleship** (AE97–S221), original paper closure, C6, 3⅝″ length 50.00 75.00

☐ **Battleship on Waves**, (AE96–S220), 5¼″ length 75.00 100.00

☐ **Boston Kettle** (AE355), leather handle, 2″ height 50.00 75.00

☐ **Br'er Rabbit** (AE614), 5⅛″ height 50.00 60.00

☐ **Bugle With Tin Whistle** (AE312–S762), 6¾″ height 75.00 100.00

☐ **Bull Dog** (S404), 4¼″ height 50.00 75.00

	Price Range	
☐ **Camera on Tripod** (AE121–S590), original bulb, 4½" height	150.00	200.00
☐ **Candy Swing** (AE69–S13), 6¾" width overall	500.00	600.00
☐ **Cannon on Golden Tin Carriage** (AE124–S270), 4¾" length; **Cannon on Red Tin Carriage** (AE123–S274), 3¾" length, each	225.00	250.00
☐ **Carrot** (AE609–S850), 4½" height, each ..	25.00	50.00
☐ **C.D. Kenny Co.**, dime savings bank with slatted tin top, 2¾" height	35.00	50.00
☐ **Charlie Chaplin**, Borgfeldt, 2⅞" length ...	150.00	200.00
☐ **Charlie Chaplin Barrel Bank** (AE137–S307), 3¾" height	150.00	200.00
☐ **Charlie Chaplin Barrel Bank**, Smith (AE138–S308), 4⅛" height	250.00	300.00
☐ **Chevrolet** (AE34–S65), 5" length, each ...	20.00	30.00
☐ **Chick in Cracked Eggshell Driving Auto** (AE144–S186), 4¼" length	250.00	300.00
☐ **Chicken on Nest** (AE149–S187), 5" length	50.00	75.00
☐ **Chicken on Rope Top Basket** (AE147–S189), 3½" length	50.00	75.00
☐ **Chrysler Airflow** (AE57–S49), 5" length ..	75.00	100.00
☐ **Clambroth Coupe** (AE51–S36), 5¼" length	50.00	70.00
☐ **Convertible Auto 10 Cents** (AE640–S92), 3¾" length	20.00	30.00
☐ **Cottage** (AE324–S446), chipped chimney, 2¾" length	200.00	250.00
☐ **Crowing Rooster** (AE151–S201), 5½" height	100.00	150.00
☐ **Dirigible Los Angeles** (AE176–S20), 6" length	100.00	125.00

Price Range

☐ **Dog by Barrel,** screw cap, missing eyes, painted, 4″ length 100.00   125.00

☐ **Dolly Sweeper** (AE133–S517), 6½″ height, C3; **Baby Sweeper** (AE132–S3), 7³/₄″ height, each 250.00   300.00

☐ **Don't Park Here Traffic Sign** (AE196–S1147), 4⅝″ height 100.00   150.00

☐ **Drinking Mug** (S790), 4⅛″ height 15.00   25.00

☐ **Duck** (AE198–S194), 3¾″ length 50.00   60.00

☐ **Duck With Large Bill** (AE199–S193), 4⅝″ length 75.00   100.00

☐ **Duck on Sagging Basket** (AE197–S192), rough edges on base, C4, 3¾″ length 75.00   100.00

☐ **Dutch Windmill** (AE843–S1150), 4⅞″ height 75.00   100.00

☐ **880 Locomotive** (AE482–S725), 5″ length 150.00   200.00

☐ **888 Locomotive** (AE485–S708), 5″ length 15.00   25.00

☐ **Electric Car** (AE48–S67), 3⅜″ length 35.00   50.00

☐ **Electric Car** (AE48–S68), 3½″ length; **Ford Hearse** (AE39–S79), 4⅜″ length, each 75.00   100.00

☐ **Electric Car** (AE49–S69), 3⅜″ length 25.00   50.00

☐ **Electric Coupe No. 1,** embossed under running boards, stamped tin closure, 2⅝″ height 50.00   75.00

☐ **Electric Iron** (AE343–S520), 4⅜″ length .. 15.00   25.00

☐ **Embossed Baby Jumbo Pencil** (AE567), 6″ length 15.00   25.00

☐ **Essex** (AE38–S66), 4¾″ length 100.00   125.00

☐ **Felix the Cat Barrel Bank** (AE211–S268), 3½″ height 450.00   500.00

☐ **Fire Engine** (AE217), 4¼″ length 15.00   25.00

☐ **Fire Engine** (AE220), 5¼″ length 15.00   25.00

☐ **Fire Engine** (AE223), 5″ length 35.00   50.00

	Price Range	
☐ **Fire Engine #2** (AE212–S436), 4¾" length	15.00	25.00
☐ **Fire Truck** (AE215–S426), 5" length	15.00	25.00
☐ **Flossie Fishers Bureau** (AE237), litho tin, 3" width	300.00	350.00
☐ **Ford,** high rounded hood (AE59–S767), 4⅛" length	50.00	60.00
☐ **Ford Hearse,** (AE40–S77), corrugated hood, 4¼" length	75.00	100.00
☐ **Gas Pump** (AE240–S1130), 4½" height ...	150.00	200.00
☐ **Gobbler Turkey Standing** (AE790–S206), 3½" height	75.00	100.00
☐ **Gold Drum Mug** (AE543–S784), 2³/₈" height	15.00	20.00
☐ **Green Taxi** (AE46), lithographed tin roof, 4⅛" length	100.00	125.00
☐ **Greyhound Bus** (AE113–S44,) 5" length ..	100.00	150.00
☐ **Happy Fats on Drum** (AE208–S301), 4½" height	150.00	200.00
☐ **Hen on Sagging Basket** (AE148–S183), 3½" length	50.00	75.00
☐ **Horn** (AE313–S763), Dutchboy, opal glass, 5½" height	75.00	100.00
☐ **Horn Trumpet,** milk glass with painted-on bears, screw closure, 5½" height	50.00	75.00
☐ **Hurricane Lamp** (AE371–S586), 4⅝" height	15.00	25.00
☐ **Independence Hall Bank** (AE342–S441), 7¼" height	250.00	300.00
☐ **Indian Motorcycle With Sidecar** (AE522–S1269), 5" length	350.00	400.00
☐ **Jack O'Lantern** (AE349–S470), wire bale, 3⅞" height	25.00	50.00
☐ **Jackie Coogan** (AE345–S313), clear glass, 5" height	850.00	900.00

Price Range

☐ **Jitney Bus** (AE114–S1134), 4¼" length ...   200.00   250.00

☐ **Jolly Santa Claus** (AE674–S892), plastic head, 5¾" height 15.00   25.00

☐ **Kewpie Doll Barrel Bank** (AE359–S303), 3⅛" height 75.00   100.00

☐ **Kiddie Car** (AE360–S503), hobbyhorse head, 4½" length 75.00   100.00

☐ **Knapp Pig,** missing cap, 4" length 75.00   100.00

☐ **Ladder Fire Truck** (AE216–S45), 5" length 100.00   150.00

☐ **Lantern,** ruby flashed with gold trim, twist on closure, 4⅜" height 50.00   75.00

☐ **Lantern With Chain** (AE438–S645), 3⅛" height 35.00   50.00

☐ **Large Suitcase** (AE707–S538), painted opal glass, C5, 4" height 75.00   100.00

☐ **Letters U.S. Mail** (AE521–S486), 3¼" height 100.00   125.00

☐ **Liberty Bell** (AE85), pink champagne, wire bale, 3⅜" height 50.00   60.00

☐ **Limousine** (AE42–S39), 4⅛" length 75.00   100.00

☐ **Lindbergh Spirit of Good Will** (AE8–S18), 4⅞" length 50.00   75.00

☐ **Lynne Type Telephone** (AE740), 4¾" height 25.00   35.00

☐ **Mantel Clock Bank** (AE164–S258), 3⅞" height 75.00   100.00

☐ **Miniature Dial Telephone** (AE739–S922) ..   75.00   100.00

☐ **Miniature Fire Engine** (AE213–S427), 5" length; **Fire Truck, Chemical Bottles** (AE214–S439), 5¼" length 25.00   50.00

☐ **Miniature Locomotive** (AE489), 3⅞" length; **888 Locomotive** (AE482–S710), 4⅞" 25.00   35.00

	Price Range	
☐ **Miniature Railroad Lantern** (AE394), ribbed base, C6, 4½" height	50.00	60.00
☐ **Miniature Streamline Auto**, cardboard push closure, 3⅝" length	35.00	50.00
☐ **Miniature War Tank** (AE724–S1138), 4⅛" length	15.00	20.00
☐ **Mutt Dog Barrel Bank** (AE190–S405), 3¼" height	75.00	100.00
☐ **999 American Locomotive** (AE487–S7419), 4⅝" length	100.00	125.00
☐ **Nursery Lamp, Pair** (AE374–S1267), waxed paper shades, 4⅝" height	300.00	325.00
☐ **1028 Locomotive** (AE492–S740), 5⅛" length	15.00	25.00
☐ **1028 Locomotive** (AE492–S748), 5⅛" length	15.00	25.00
☐ **Opera Glasses** (AE558–S535), 3" height ..	75.00	100.00
☐ **Opera Glasses With Brass Frame**, 3½" height	35.00	50.00
☐ **Owl Perched on Branch** (AE566–S176), 4½" height	100.00	150.00
☐ **Peep Peep Baby Chick** (AE145–S185), 3½" height	50.00	75.00
☐ **Penny Trust Co. Safe** (AE661–S511), clear, 2⅞" height	25.00	35.00
☐ **Peter Rabbit** (AE618–S844), 6½" height ..	50.00	60.00
☐ **Phonograph** (AE574–S776), glass record, tin horn, 4½" height	250.00	300.00
☐ **Pierced Metal Lantern** (AE449–S627), 5¾" height	15.00	25.00
☐ **Pocket Watch** (AE823), leather strap with American eagle fob, 2¾" height	250.00	300.00
☐ **Policeman With Search Light and Billy Club** (AE592–S471), 4⅞" height	550.00	600.00

Price Range

☐ **Powder Horn** (AE589–S1223), plain glass, 5″ length; **Six Shooter,** 5½″ length; **Space Gun,** 3¾″ length; each 20.00   30.00

☐ **Pumpkin-Head Witch,** original paint with closure, 4⅜″ height 100.00   125.00

☐ **Rabbit,** basket on arm, painted, screw closure, 4½″ height 75.00   100.00

☐ **Rabbit Carrying Basket** (AE606–S854), 4½″ height 15.00   25.00

☐ **Rabbit With Collar,** screw-type closure, 5½″ height 75.00   100.00

☐ **Rabbit Crouching,** slide closure, body smooth, 3″ height 100.00   125.00

☐ **Rabbit in Egg Shell,** screw-on closure, rabbit gilded, 5⅜″ height 125.00   150.00

☐ **Rabbit Emerging From Cracked Egg Shell** (AE608–S842), 5¼″ height 50.00   60.00

☐ **Rabbit Family,** marked, missing closure, 4¾″ height 100.00   125.00

☐ **Rabbit Nibbling Carrot,** missing closure, 4½″ height 75.00   100.00

☐ **Rabbit Pushing Baby Chick in Buggy** (AE602–S861), 4″ length 250.00   275.00

☐ **Rabbit Pushing Cart,** 4″ height 75.00   100.00

☐ **Rabbit Pushing Wheelbarrow** (AE601–S838), 4⅛″ height 125.00   150.00

☐ **Rabbit Reclining** (AE615–S864), 3½″ length 50.00   60.00

☐ **Rabbit Rectangular Base** (AE616–S859), 4½″ height 25.00   35.00

☐ **Rabbit Sitting** (AE612), feet and paws extended, 5½″ height 50.00   75.00

☐ **Rabbit Sitting** (AE617–S852), 4½″ height; **Nibbling Carrot** (AE609–S850), 4½″ height; each 25.00   50.00

	Price Range	
☐ **Rabbit Sitting on Egg** (AE607–S48), 4½″ height	100.00	150.00
☐ **Racer With Helmeted Driver** (AE641), #4 on front grill, 3⅝″ length	50.00	60.00
☐ **Radio With Speaker** (AE643–S778), 4½″ height	75.00	100.00
☐ **Railroad Lantern** (AE447–S674), 5″ height	15.00	25.00
☐ **Rapid-Fire Gun** (AE129–S2), 7⅜″ length	175.00	200.00
☐ **Reo** (AE62–S43), rough under closure, 4¼″ length	400.00	450.00
☐ **Republican Elephant GOP** (AE206–S369), C2, 3½″ length	100.00	125.00
☐ **Rocking Horse With Clown Rider** (AE652–S502), 4⅜″ length	200.00	250.00
☐ **Rocking Horse With Saddle** (AE652–S498), 4½″ length	100.00	125.00
☐ **Rocking Settee** (AE653–S514), 2½″ height	75.00	100.00
☐ **Running Rabbit on Log** (AE603–S863), 4¼″ length	100.00	125.00
☐ **Safety First New Year's Baby Barrel Bank** (AE668–S306), 3¾″ height	450.00	500.00
☐ **Santa Claus Descending Chimney** (AE673–S882), 5″ height	75.00	100.00
☐ **Santa Claus With Folded Arms** (AE671–S891), 4½″ height	75.00	100.00
☐ **Santa Claus With Folded Arms and Stern Face** (AE670), green glass, 5¼″ height	100.00	150.00
☐ **Santa Claus Standing Next to Brick Chimney** (AE672–S889), 3⅝″ height	250.00	300.00
☐ **Shelf Clock Bank** (AE163–S262), 3⅞″ height	75.00	100.00
☐ **Sideboard With Mirror** (AE112–S513), 4″ height	75.00	100.00

	Price Range	
☐ **Signal Lantern** (AE398-S622), 5⅛″ height; **Lantern** (AE441-S647), 4½″ height; each ..	50.00	75.00
☐ **Signal Lantern** (AE404-S633), C1, 5¼″ height; **Signal Lantern** (AE405-S634), 5¼″ height	25.00	35.00
☐ **Signal Lantern,** C2, 5¼″ overall; **Signal Lantern** (S623), 6″ height; each	15.00	25.00
☐ **Skookum,** embossed figure, 3½″ height ...	75.00	100.00
☐ **Skookum Tree Stump Bank** (AE681-S310), 3⅝″ height	100.00	125.00
☐ **Soldier on Monument Base** (AE682-S878), 5⅝″ height	400.00	500.00
☐ **Soldier and Tent** (AE688), 3⅜″ height	1500.00	1700.00
☐ **Souvenir Shelf Clock** (AE162-S263), 3¼″ height	100.00	150.00
☐ **Spinning Top** (AE776-S555), wood winder, 3¾″ height	100.00	125.00
☐ **Spirit of St. Louis** (AE90-S30), pink glass and tin, 4⅜″ length	200.00	250.00
☐ **SS Colorado** (AE102-S207), C2, 6½″ length	325.00	350.00
☐ **Stern-Faced Santa Claus** (AE669-S886), 5⅛″ height	100.00	150.00
☐ **Stop and Go Traffic Sign** (AE706-S1132), 4¼″ height	100.00	150.00
☐ **Submarine With Periscope** (AE101-S208), 5⅛″ length	200.00	250.00
☐ **Suitcase,** tin slide closure, 3⅝″ length	50.00	60.00
☐ **Swan Boat With Rabbit and Chick in Egg** (AE713), 4¼″ length	550.00	600.00
☐ **Telephone** (AE731), 1¾″ height	25.00	35.00
☐ **Telephone** (AE735), 4⅛″ height	50.00	75.00
☐ **Telephone** (AE736-S917), clear, 4½″ height	25.00	50.00
☐ **Telephone** (AE742-S901), 6½″ height	200.00	250.00

Price Range

☐ **Telephone** (AE753–S918), 5″ height 25.00 50.00
☐ **Telephone,** Redlich's No. 4, 4⅜″ height ... 35.00 50.00
☐ **Tiny Auto** (AE32–S81), 3″ length 15.00 20.00
☐ **Toonerville Trolley** (AE767–S1262), 3¾″
height 400.00 450.00
☐ **Top Hat** (AE301–S479), 2⅛″ height 25.00 35.00
☐ **Toy Village,** five different houses, litho-
graphed tin 300.00 325.00
☐ **Toy Village,** six different buildings 100.00 150.00
☐ **Trophy,** ruby flashed with gold trim, screw-
on base, 3¾″ height 50.00 75.00
☐ **Trunk** (AE789–S539), opal glass, 2¾″
length 75.00 100.00
☐ **Tubular Lantern** (AE426), 6″ height 15.00 25.00
☐ **Tubular Lantern** (AE427–S638), 6¼″
overall 15.00 25.00
☐ **Uncle Sam Barrel Bank** (AE801–S300),
chip on base, 3⅞″ height 250.00 300.00
☐ **Uncle Sam's Hat Bank** (AE303–S475),
2½″ height 50.00 60.00
☐ **Upright Piano Bank** (AE577–S768), 2⅞″
height 200.00 250.00
☐ **Victory Lines Bus** (AE115–S1144), 5″
length 50.00 75.00
☐ **Victrola and Tin Horn** (AE575–S773),
missing record, 4¾″ height 100.00 150.00
☐ **Volkswagen** (AE58–S84), 6″ length 15.00 25.00
☐ **Wagon** (AE822–S35), 3⅛″ length 75.00 100.00
☐ **Water Wagon Pulled by Mule** (AE539–
S121), 4½″ length 50.00 75.00
☐ **West Brothers Co. Limousine,** with tin
pierced wheels and tin slide top, 4″ length
.... 35.00 50.00
☐ **Westmoreland Specialty Co.,** limousine
with tin pierced wheels, 2½″ height 25.00 35.00

	Price Range	
☐ **Wheelbarrow** (AE832–S1175), 6⅛″ length, ...	50.00	75.00
☐ **Windmill** (AE840), Pfeiffers moonface and eagle head, 6″ height	500.00	550.00
☐ **Windmill** (AE845), Teddy and flag, 6″ height	500.00	550.00
☐ **Windmill With Performing Bear** (AE83–S168), 4½″ height	200.00	250.00
☐ **Witch With Broom** AE594–S463), 4⅝″ height	300.00	350.00
☐ **Woody Station Wagon** (AE56–S73), 4⅞″ length	20.00	30.00
☐ **Yellow Taxi** (AE36–S75), 4¾″ length	75.00	100.00

HOLIDAY TOYS

Of all the myriad folk symbols associated with holiday celebrations, Santa Claus is the most universally beloved. Toys in his image head the Christmas list of an ever-widening circle of followers. Once a thin, dour-looking old gentleman, the transformation took place when Thomas Nast characterized Santa as a plump, jolly old elf, based on the Clement Moore poem, *The Night Before Christmas.* Sharing top billing with Santa toys are those depicting reindeer and the Christmas tree, an old German custom which spread worldwide during the 19th century. Christmas related collectors specialize not only in toys, but seek out early Dresden, paper and figural glass ornaments, papier-mache and composition candy containers, and jack-in-the-boxes.

Until recently, many of the countless other holiday playthings were ignored. Today, however, holidays such as Easter, Halloween, Valentine's Day, St. Patrick's Day, and even Washington's birthday yield fascinating and highly decorative relics of the past that are highly collectible. Of all the topical categories in the hobby, there is none more fanciful, or created in any wider range of materials, than Holiday keepsakes. For further insight into the field, we recommend *Christmas Ornaments, A Festive Study,* and *Holidays Toys and Decorations,* both by Margaret Schiffer.

CHRISTMAS

	Price Range	
☐ **Buckaroo Santa,** Kriger Novelty, 1924 patented, composition and wood, push-pull toy, 7½" height	200.00	300.00
☐ **Father Christmas and Reindeer Pull Toy,** German, early 1900s papier-mache, moss and wood platform with metal wheels, Santa is pulled by four reindeer, 6" height	1000.00	1200.00
☐ **Reindeer,** German, 1915, handpainted tin mechanical, 9" length, rides behind two large (6" height) wheels	150.00	200.00

Price Range

☐ **Santa Acrobat on Stick,** maker unknown, 1904, painted wood with Christmas tree and voice box 200.00   250.00

☐ **Santa Claus,** E. S. Peck, sold by New York Stationery and Envelope Co., 1886, stuffed figure based on Thomas Nast cartoon of Santa, 16½″ height 350.00   450.00

☐ **Santa Claus,** German, 1900s, painted chalk, very early solemn looking version with hands tucked in sleeves, 22″ height .... 5000.00★

☐ **Santa Claus,** Strauss, 1920s, lithograph tin mechanism, Santa figure has high pointed hat, drawn by two reindeer which bob up and down when activated, 12″ length 350.00   400.00

☐ **Santa Claus at Chimney,** mechanical bank arm drops coin down slot in chimney, 6″ height 700.00   800.00

☐ **Santa Claus Sleigh,** Hubley, 1921, cast-iron pull toy, pulled by two reindeer (another version shows only one), 13″ length 700.00   800.00

☐ **Santa Claus Wagon,** German, circa 1910, wood with fabric-covered composition, horses on wheels, painted stencilled sign in red/yellow, "St. Claus Dealer in Good Things," pull toy, 28″ length .... 900.00 1000.00★

☐ **Santa Claus Walker,** Arthur Hotchkiss patented, Ives, 1882, composition with cloth clockwork, 10″ height .... 5000.00 plus

☐ **Santa With Galloping Reindeer,** R. Bliss, circa 1890s, lithograph with wood cutouts, Bliss logo on back panel, Santa in sleigh drawn by two reindeer, 18″ length 550.00   650.00

★Sold for $5500.00 at December 1986 Christmas Auction at Rick Opfers in Timoniom, Maryland. It was missing chalk tree.
★Toy minus leather tacking brought $1400.00 at Atlanta Toy Auction in October 1986.

Santa Claus, one of the most popular walking toys patented by Arthur Hotchkiss of Cheshire, CT, in 1875, who sold the rights to Ives. The above cut appeared in an 1893 Ives catalog. Note the price of $2.75 which was several days pay for the average laborer in the 1890s. $2000 plus range.

	Price Range
☐ **Santa in Goat-Drawn Sleigh,** Althof Bergman, 1890s, lithograph tin clockwork, drawn by pair of goats (a classic Santa toy), 9″ height × 18″ length	2000.00 plus
☐ **Santa Handcar With Mickey Mouse in Pack,** Lionel, 1937, composition and pressed steel, ...	2000.00 plus
☐ **Santa Jack-in-the-Box,** composition and wood, German, 1900s, 5″ height	150.00 200.00

Price Range

☐ **Santa With Pack,** 1890s, cast iron with Santa before big safelike rectangle, 5″ height, 2½″ width 450.00   550.00

☐ **Santa in Roadster,** Karl Bubb, early 1920s, lithograph tin mechanism, superb lithography and detail designate this as one of the classic Santas, 11″ length × 10″ height 1200.00   1500.00

☐ **Santa on Rocking Horse,** German, 1915, painted wood and composition, dappled horse rocks and Santa rings bell, 7″ height mechanism 450.00   550.00

☐ **Santa Roly-Poly,** Schoenhut, 1915, composition, 9″ height 350.00   450.00

☐ **Santa and Sleigh,** possibly Scandanavian, circa 1910, composition and wood, pulled by one reindeer (sleigh looks very Nordic), 3″ height 750.00   850.00

☐ **Santa in Sleigh,** Kyser & Rex, 1880s, cast iron, 13″ length 1000.00   1200.00

☐ **Santa Sleigh With Goats,** Althof Bergman, 1890s, painted tin clockwork, considered to be rarest and most desirable of all Santa Claus toys, 9″ height × 18″ length .... 5000.00 plus

☐ **Santa Standing,** still bank, 1890s, cast iron, 5½″ height 200.00   250.00

☐ **Santa With Tree,** still bank, 1890s, cast-iron figure, tree is wood with metal pine needles, 7″ height 350.00   450.00

☐ **Santa With Tree,** still bank, 1890s, cast iron, 5½″ height, variation of bank but with Christmas tree in one arm 200.00   250.00

☐ **Santa Walker,** Japan, 1960s, celluloid and tin wind-up, 6″ height 50.00   60.00

☐ **St. Nicholas Standing Figure,** German, 1915, painted tin mechanism, carries branch in one hand, 7½″ height 850.00   950.00

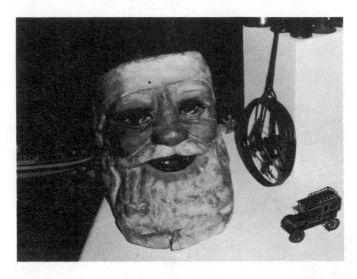

Turn-of-the-century Santa mask in papier-mâché, maker unknown, shares honors with a push hoop toy and tinplate auto, c. 1910, at the booth of Bill Holland, noted collector and photographer, at the Allentown, PA, Antique Show, November, 1986.

	Price Range	
☐ **Walking Santa,** Chein, 1930s, lithograph tin mechanism, 6″ height	250.00	300.00

EASTER

Note: There are a wide variety of papier-mache and composition candy containers featuring Easter rabbits, chickens, eggs, and other Easter items that do not readily identify as toys, but are nonetheless often in specialty collections.

☐ **Bunny Express,** Marx, 1936, Easter Rabbit Express, scale model train toy, large tin rabbit with glass eyes, engine pulls two hopper cars, originally sold at Easter filled with jelly beans, 18″ length 600.00   700.00

☐ **Chanticleer Card with Rabbit** (see "Lehmann Toys" listing) ....

Rabbit in Rabbit Cart, Ideal Toy Co., Detroit, Michigan, 1890s, painted cast iron, 5½″ height, $500-$600; Ideal Rabbit Chariot, 1890s, painted cast iron, 9¼″ length, also came in gilt, $750-$850.

	Price Range	
☐ **Peter Rabbit Chickmobile,** Lionel, 1935, yellow hand car, steel and tin and composition, rabbit is on one end and Easter basket on other, 9½″ length	800.00	900.00
☐ **Pumpkin-Head Walker,** German, 1910, composition, cloth clockwork, 7″ height ..	600.00	650.00
☐ **Rabbit Balance Toy,** German, 1910, papier-mache rabbit with steel and cast-iron balance, figure 3″ height	250.00	300.00
☐ **Rabbit Bowling Game,** German, 1870s, papier-mache with glass eyes, also believed to be a pull toy, 24″ length	1000.00	1200.00
☐ **Rabbit Driving Car,** German, circa 1910, papier-mache rabbit with moss-covered open roadster, glass eyes, 8″ height	750.00	850.00

Price Range

☐ **Rabbit in Tin Roadster,** French, 1900s, lithograph tin mechanical, composition rabbit with cloth, raises and lowers spectacles as car moves along, 16″ length × 16″ height 1500.00   2000.00

☐ **Spook Bank,** maker unknown, contemporary, cast aluminum, pumpkin-headed figure with black cat, 6″ height 50.00   75.00

☐ **Witch Riding Goose,** Strauss, 1920s, lithograph tin wind-up 100.00   125.00

LEHMANN TOYS, 1895–1930

Originating in Brandenburg, Germany, and later in Nuremburg, Earnest Paul Lehmann continues its toy operation to this day. American collectors generally think of Lehmann's glory years as extending from 1895 to 1929. After 1933, Lehmann exported toys to the United States on a sporadic basis. The unprecedented popularity of Lehmann toys on these shores may be attributed to their attractive lithography and patina, their attention to detail, and the infinite variety of animation and mechanical action in both friction and clockwork. Animals, tricycles, bicycles, motorcycles, and comic and serious human figures all comprise a small cosmos, more than justifying a separate category in this guide. Lehmann toys were sold in the United States through jobbers, i.e., Butler Brothers, Baltimore Bargain House, George Broadway Rouss, H. Wolf, and others. Montgomery Ward was a major mail-order outlet for Lehmann.

Note: The date 1881 is occasionally found on a Lehmann specimen; it has no bearing on its date of manufacture and is simply the date the firm was founded. Lehmann toys were targeted to England, France, the United States, and to their own country. Alternate names varied in accordance with these markets. Lehmann was not one to give up on a good thing. The popular Balky Mule and Climbing Miller were offered in the Lehmann catalog over a span of 25 years. All Lehmann toys were trademarked on both the box and the toy itself, with the exception over a brief period of time of the Climbing Monkey, where the mark appears on the box only. The simulated green velvet jacket immediately identifies it as Lehmann.

	Price Range	
☐ **Adam,** porter, baggage truck, separate trunk of chocolates, 1912–1914	700.00	800.00
☐ **African Mail,** ostrich pulling two-wheel cart and native driver, 1892–1926 (later issues have "Kamerun," "Zulu," "Afrika"), 5″ height	350.00	450.00
☐ **AHA,** closed delivery van, 1911, same body as "Karitas," 1911 (550)	200.00	300.00

Lithographic art on the original boxes of Lehmann toys, although seldom accurately depicting the toy contained therein, is so colorful and aesthetically appealing as to clearly enhance the value of a toy. Note that a number of boxes bear patents of as many as four different countries, with Great Britain and the United States clearly the major markets for these whimsical toys.

Price Range

☐ **AJAX,** acrobat, figure with club, 1912,
9½″ height (659) 400.00   500.00

☐ **ALSO,** automobile, red or green variations,
friction, same as OHO, 4.1″ length (700) ... 200.00   500.00

☐ **AM POL,** tricycle, Amundsen, monkey,
map, South Pole, very similar to "New
Century" cycle, orates Amundsen trip,
1912, 4.9″ length (681) 700.00   800.00

☐ **AUTIN,** boy drives soap box delivery wagon, wagon same as cat. 98, The American
Boy, 6″ length 200.00   250.00

☐ **Autobus,** double deck 5th Avenue bus, red
and yellow, 1907–1915, also yellow and
brown version, 8″ length (590) 700.00   800.00

☐ **Autohouette,** garage with galop, 6″ length
(771/760) 350.00   450.00

☐ **Autohouette,** garage with sedan, (771/765)
.... 350.00   450.00

☐ **Autohouette,** garage with galop, sedan,
(772) 300.00   400.00

☐ **Auto-Post,** mail van, similar to Royal Mail,
(575) 400.00   500.00

☐ **Baldur,** taxi-limo, with Lehmann banner as
hood ornament, 1920, 10″ length (739) 400.00   500.00

☐ **Balky Mule,** clown in cloth dress and balking mule, no name on toy, "The Comical
Clown," "Stoerrischer Esel," 1902–1926,
8″ length 175.00   225.00

☐ **Bear,** in man's dress, 1910–1912 .... 250.00   350.00

☐ **Berolina,** cabriolet automobile, nonme-
chanical, 1924 (749) 350.00   400.00

☐ **Boxer,** four Chinese tossing Chinaman in
blanket, "Tossing The Heathen Chinee,"
"Diligent Chinese" ....   2000.00 plus

☐ **Brennabor,** automobile, two lamps, 1929
(777) 300.00   400.00

Price Range

☐ **Broncho,** horse and cowboy, 1907–1924, "Wild West" (625) 400.00 500.00

☐ **BV Aral,** tank wagon (835) 250.00 300.00

☐ **Captain of Kopenick,** tin and cloth, 7½" height 350.00 650.00

☐ **Chanticleer Cart,** rooster pulls rabbit in Easter egg, 1898–1917, 6½" height, also see DUO 300.00 400.00

☐ **Climbing Mice,** tin gravity, 15" height 100.00 200.00

☐ **Climbing Miller,** miller climbing pole topped with windmill with flour sack on head, name not on toy, also known as Guston, 18½" height 175.00 225.00

☐ **Coco,** Negro climbing coconut tree, same action as climbing miller, 1894–1904 .... 450.00 550.00

☐ **Columbia,** dancing sailor, "Brandenburg," "Mars," 1910–1912, 7½" height (535) 300.00 400.00

☐ **Crawling Beetle,** wings unfold, no name on toy, 1914 .... 100.00 200.00

☐ **Crocodile,** litho tin mechanical, 9" length (442) 300.00 400.00

☐ **Daedalus,** British airplane, 1939 .... 400.00 500.00

☐ **Dancing Darky,** two-dimensional jointed 8" figure 200.00 300.00

☐ **Dancing Doll,** tin, 1914, 9" height 150.00 200.00

☐ **Deutsche Reichpost,** mail truck, red and gold with navy interior, 1927–1933, 7¼" length (786) 650.00 750.00

☐ **Dowle Garage,** "Galop," racer and sedan .. 450.00 550.00

☐ **DUO,** rooster, rabbit in cart, rabbit's ears move up and down when activated, friction and clockwork, 1904 (722) 400.00 500.00

☐ **DUO,** rooster, rabbit in egg-shaped cart, friction, framed around cart, 1904–1913 ... 450.00 550.00

☐ **Echo,** motorcycle and rider, brown clothing, 1923, 4" length (725) 750.00 850.00

Price Range

	Price Range	
☐ **EHE and Co.**, open or auto dray truck and driver, 1910, 6¾" length (570)	350.00	450.00
☐ **Emden**, cruiser, Count Von Luckner's raider, 1917 (729)	400.00	500.00
☐ **EMGEH**, machine gun (735)	100.00	150.00
☐ **EPL, I**, dirigible, gold with red fins (Los Angeles), 1912, 9¾" length (651)	450.00	550.00
☐ **EPL, II**, dirigible, 1915, 9¾" length (652)	350.00	450.00
☐ **Express**, white porter pulling two-wheel baggage truck, 1886–1925, 4¾" height	300.00	400.00
☐ **Express**, man pulling cart (770)	200.00	250.00
☐ **Fatzke**, auto two figures, clockwork, "Naughty Boy," "Ruppliger Junge," 1904 (495)	400.00	500.00
☐ **Flying Bird**, bird flies on string, tin with paper wings, name not on toy, 1895, 11" wing span	350.00	450.00
☐ **Futurus**, chime on two wheels, the chime is a munitions part left over from World War I, 1918–1925 (740)	100.00	200.00
☐ **Gala**, automobile, 1929 (780)	150.00	250.00
☐ **Galop**, racing car, 1925, 5½" length (760)	200.00	250.00
☐ **GNOM** truck, Shell	150.00	200.00
☐ **GNOM**, trailer	100.00	150.00
☐ **GNOM**, garage with two cars (806/807) ...	125.00	175.00
☐ **GNOM**, set of three small cars (807A)	100.00	150.00
☐ **GNOM**, set of three small racing cars (807B)	100.00	150.00
☐ **GNOM**, set of three racing cars (808)	100.00	150.00
☐ **GNOM**, filling station (809)	100.00	150.00
☐ **GNOM**, racing car (810)	75.00	125.00
☐ **GNOM**, cabriolet (836)	75.00	125.00

	Price Range	

☐ **GNOM,** heavy truck (837) 100.00 125.00
☐ **GNOM** fire engine (815) 125.00 150.00
☐ **GNOM,** Auto Union racing car (816) 150.00 200.00
☐ **GNOM,** sports car (811) 150.00 250.00
☐ **GNOM,** car with clockwork (812) 150.00 250.00
☐ **GNOM,** truck (813) 150.00 200.00
☐ **Going to the Fair,** lady in boardwalk-type chair pushed by man, friction toy, name not on toy, lady has moving fan, fan sometimes dated 1889, 1889–1894, 4¾" height × 6¼" length 600.00 700.00
☐ **Hail Columbia,** spiral sailor, "Jolly Jack Tar," "Patriot Toy," "Blitzmatrose," 1892–1926 (440) 500.00 600.00
☐ **HALLOH,** motorcycle, rider, 1934 (683) ... 750.00 850.00
☐ **HAUPTMANN,** captain (soldier) walking (580) 400.00 500.00
☐ **Hawkshaw the Detective,** walking man, cane, cloth coat, no name on toy, 1910 ..... 600.00 700.00
☐ **HE 70,** French military plane 350.00 450.00
☐ **HE 70,** airplane, 1937 (817) 200.00 250.00
☐ **HE 70,** German military plane 350.00 450.00
☐ **HE 111,** airplane, 1939 (831) 250.00 300.00
☐ **HE 111,** Shell gasoline truck (830) 100.00 150.00
☐ **HE 111,** bomber (833) 250.00 300.00
☐ **HE 111,** bomber (834) 250.00 300.00
☐ **HEVELLA,** automobile, 1929 (778) 275.00 350.00
☐ **ICARUS,** airship, World War I-type, 1913 (653) 600.00 700.00
☐ **ICARUS,** airplane (818) 350.00 450.00
☐ **IHI,** meat van with cloth drop curtains, 1907, 6¾" length 650.00 750.00
☐ **ITO,** sedan, black and red, 1923, 6¾" length (679) 400.00 500.00

A selection of Lehmann toys.

Price Range

☐ **Jandorf (LU LU),** delivery van, double door in deep green, 1913–1914, 7.3″ length (763) 350.00   450.00

☐ **KADI,** see Peking 400.00   500.00

☐ **Karitas,** see AHA, Red Cross ambulance, 1915 (727) 350.00   450.00

☐ **La LA,** delivery van, 1907 (620) 275.00   350.00

☐ **LANA,** automobile (776) 275.00   350.00

☐ **LILA,** hansom cab, four moving figures and dog, also known as auto sisters, 1908 (520) 650.00   750.00

☐ **LOLO,** auto and driver, uniformed driver in open car, same as "Naughty Boy" but friction, 1906 (540) 250.00   350.00

☐ **London,** police tower (791) 175.00   225.00

☐ **Luxus,** automobile, 3 lamps, 1927 (785) ... 300.00   350.00

☐ **Magic Ball Dancer,** ballerina, gyroscope top, name not on toy, "Die Magisch Kugel Tanzerin" 200.00   300.00

☐ **Maikaefer,** crawling beetle, same as No. 20, 1930 (823) 150.00   200.00

☐ **Mandarin,** Chinese in Mandarin costume being carried in covered palaquin chair, 1895 (565) 650.00   750.00

☐ **Mars,** man driving three-wheeler, 1910–1912, 4.7″ length 200.00   250.00

☐ **Mars,** tank, camouflaged 150.00   200.00

☐ **Mars,** tank, gray 125.00   150.00

☐ **Mars,** propeller toy, Aerial Flyer, three propellers, has date 1881, "Archimedes," 1905–1924 .... 500.00   600.00

☐ **Masuyama,** rickshaw, Japanese lady pulled by coolie, fan, revolving, friction and clockwork, 1910–1927, 5″ height 750.00   850.00

☐ **Mensa,** delivery van, three wheels, self-guiding, 1907 (688) 550.00   650.00

Price Range

☐ **Mikado family,** ricksha, Japanese lady with rocking baby, 1895–1906, 7″ length 400.00   500.00

☐ **Minstrel Man,** litho pull toy, flat, 7″ height 150.00   200.00

☐ **Motorkutsche,** motor coach and driver, made in two (perhaps three) sizes, 1904–1921, 4.9″ length 200.00   300.00

☐ **Mundus,** globe top, German text, 1923, 4″ height (757) 200.00   250.00

☐ **NA OB,** small cart, mule, driver, 1922, 6″ length (680) 150.00   250.00

☐ **Nanni,** man on tricycle pulling lady in trailer, lady waves handkerchief, "Frightened Bride," "Anxious Bride," 1903, 8.5″ length (470) 650.00   750.00

☐ **Naughty Boy,** auto, boy driver, Buster Brown suit, flywheel-propelled car, no name on toy, orange car, same as "Ruppinger Junge Fatze," 1911, 4.9″ length 450.00   550.00

☐ **New Century Cycle,** three-wheel vehicle, man, umbrella, monkey driver, front rig holds American flag on tin pole, name not on toy, "ONKEL," "AUTO UNCLE," 1910 ....   650.00   750.00

☐ **Nina,** flocked cat and mouse, 1932, 11″ length (790) 650.00   750.00

☐ **Nixtum,** man with self-made car, "Mordskerl," three-wheel vehicle, 1927–1934 (775) 350.00   450.00

☐ **NU NU,** one Chinaman and tea cart, friction and clockwork, 1904–1907 (733) 450.00   550.00

☐ **OHO,** auto, uniformed driver, clown on three-wheeled vehicle, clockwork, green car, 1911, 4″ length 350.00   450.00

☐ **ONO ORBIS,** four-wheel truck, driver, globe top, English text, 1923 (762) 250.00   300.00

	Price Range	
☐ **PAAK PAAK,** duck, cart, ducklings, quack, quack, 1910, 7½" length (645)	300.00	400.00
☐ **Paddy's Dancing Pig,** Irishman riding pig, may be same as No. 38, 1912, 7½" height (500)	400.00	500.00
☐ **Panne,** touring car, red and silver with silk flag (687)	550.00	650.00
☐ **Peking,** two Chinese carrying sea chest (KADI), friction and clockwork (723)	500.00	600.00
☐ **Performing Sea Lion,** or performing seal, flippers move, 7½" length, 1907 (445)	200.00	275.00
☐ **Pilotto,** airplane roulette	100.00	150.00
☐ **Pretzel Vendor,** or Baker, pair fighting on tricycle, 5" length, 1905 (450)	650.00	750.00
☐ **Primus,** roller skater, 1910–1922 (670)	1150.00	1250.00
☐ **Quex,** motorcyclist, 1934 (800)	800.00	900.00
☐ **RARA AVIS,** bird	100.00	150.00
☐ **Red Cycle,** man on tricycle, 1903 (471), same tricycle as Cat. 470 (Mars)	350.00	400.00
☐ **RIGI,** cable car, 1929 (795)	150.00	250.00
☐ **ROON,** motorcycle and rider, rider wears black clothing, 1923 (726)	700.00	800.00
☐ **ROTA,** perpetual mobile with ring (805) ..	200.00	250.00
☐ **St. Vincent,** naval cruiser, 1926 (672)	600.00	700.00
☐ **SALUS,** automobile (734)	250.00	300.00
☐ **Shenandoah,** dirigible, also made with name "Los Angeles" (766)	500.00	550.00
☐ **SKIRLOF,** skiing man, 1929 (781)	1500.00	1600.00
☐ **SNICK SNACK,** man walking pair of dogs (724)	850.00	950.00
☐ **TAKU,** naval cruiser (671)	350.00	450.00
☐ **TAM TAM,** top, 3" diameter, 1914 (677)	75.00	125.00
☐ **TAP TAP,** man pushing wheelbarrow, 6½" length × 5" height, 1885–1906 (560)	250.00	300.00

A selection of Lehmann toys.

Price Range

☐ **Taxi,** yellow sedan, 1922 (755) 350.00   450.00

☐ **Terra,** touring sedan, 9.6″ length, 1913–1928 (720) 500.00   600.00

☐ **Titania,** automobile, two lamps, 1929 (779) 500.00   600.00

☐ **Tom,** "JOCKO," climbing monkey on string, 1903–1910 (385) 100.00   150.00

☐ **Truck and Driver,** yellow with European postal insignia, 5¼″ length (585) 300.00   400.00

☐ **TUT TUT,** auto driver in white suit and hat, squeak horn, 6.7″ length, 1904–1926 (490) 600.00   700.00

☐ **TYRAS,** walking dog, 1905 (432) 300.00   400.00

☐ **UHU,** amphibian auto with celluloid windscreen, paddles on wheels, driver swivels, 9.4″ length, 1906–1922 (555) 800.00   900.00

☐ **Valleda,** touring sedan with folding seats (730) 550.00   650.00

☐ **Vinetta,** monorail car with gyroscopic mechanism, red, green with gold trim, 9¾″ length 550.00   650.00

☐ **Walking Down Broadway,** Mr. and Mrs. Lehmann, couple strolling with dog; 6¼″ length; 1889–1894 .... 750.00   850.00

☐ **ZICK-ZACK,** two figures, one black, one white, on two-wheeled carnival (Zig Zag) carriage, 4.9″ length, 1907–1914 (640) 650.00   750.00

☐ **ZIKRA,** Mexican cart with driver pulled by zebra, 1913, U.S. patented, "Dare Devil," NA-NA, variation of "Balky Mule" 200.00   300.00

☐ **ZULU,** ostrich, two-wheel cart, driver, 1926, later version of "African Mail," friction and clockwork, 7″ length (721) 400.00   500.00

A selection of Lehmann toys.

MARBLES

Few toys evoke any fonder recollection of childhood days than marbles. Dating back to as early as Roman times, they reached the height of their popularity during the Victorian Age. Mention of "knuckle down to your taw, aim well, shoot away," is included in 18th-century America children's books. Charles Francis, of New York, writing in *The Boy's Own Book* in 1829, graded various marble types. The Dutch marbles of glazed clay received the lowest rating, those of yellow stone with spots of black and brown followed in ascending order, while the taws of red-veined pink marble ranked supreme. Marble manufacturing in the United States centered in Ohio, with Samuel Dyke of South Akron a leading purveyor of clay marbles in the 1880s (marbles had been imported primarily from Europe until the mid-19th century). The National Onyx Marble and the Navarre Glass Marble Co. of Navarre, Ohio, and M.B. Misler of Ravenna were leading makers into the 20th century. Many marbles of brown or blue glazed clay were fashioned at Bennington, Vermont, and in potteries in Ohio, Indiana, and Pennsylvania. Mongomery Ward was one of the leading distributors of marbles in the 1890s.

The most coveted marbles today are the pricey and rare sulfides of clear glass with encased white figures of animals, birds, flowers, political figures, and comic characters. Glass marbles of the Venetian swirl variety, often called "glassies," feature colored glass in a clear glass marble, much akin to paperweights produced by leading glass companies.

Marbles comprise such an esoteric area of specialization, with a language all its own, that we hesitate to describe and price these items. We do know that the sulfides featuring leading personalities and comic characters can range from $200 to $300 and up. Latticino Swirls, each with their own unique design that defies description and ranging in diameter from 1¾" to 2", often command prices of $100 on up, and wide-banded core marbles also are highly desirable and on the expensive side.

For further exploration of this subject, we recommend *Collecting Antique Marbles*, by Paul Bauman (see Bibliography). More information is also available through the *Marble Collectors Society of America* (see "Collecting Organizations" listing) which publishes a newsletter, *Marble Mania*.

NAUTICAL TOYS

As was the case with aviation toys, the topical category of boats and ships is clearly monopolized by European makers. Obvious exceptions would include Messrs. Ives, Fallows, Reid, and Bliss with their classic early painted and lithographed tin, paper-on-wood and cardboard fleet of colorful sidewheelers and Noah's Arks. Then too, there are the highly uncommon Ives oarsmen in painted tin and the cast-iron sculls by Ives and Wilkins, which attract topical sports collectors as well. "Ruling the waves" in nautical playthings are the German makers Maerklin, Bing, Planck, Carette, Schoenner, and Radiguet, whose golden era extended from the early 1900s to World War I. Superbly enameled tinplate pacquette boats and warships with clockwork mechanisms produced in this span have recently brought outrageous prices at auction. The record-breaking price of $28,600 for a beautifully scaled replica of the liner *Lusitania* by Maerklin, believed to be unique, was achieved at a Sotheby Collector's Carousel in 1983 and may stand up for some time to come.

PAINTED AND LITHOGRAPHED TIN AND WOOD

	Price Range	
☐ *"Adirondack"* **Sidewheeler,** Dent Hardware, 1920s, approximately 10″ length	300.00	350.00
☐ *America* **Clipper Ship,** W.S. Reed, 1877, 42″ length	1200.00	1500.00
☐ *Atlanta* **Steam Yacht,** Ives, 1893, with or without whistle, three cast-iron wheels, 19″ and 23″ length sizes		2000.00 plus
☐ *Brooklyn* **Torpedo Boat,** German, circa 1905, 30″ length, painted tinplate		2000.00 plus
☐ *City of New York,* Wilkins, 1900, cast iron, 15½″ length	500.00	600.00
☐ *Columbia,* **Sidewheeler,** W.S. Reed, 1800s, lithographed wood, 24″ length	1200.00	1500.00
☐ *Crescent,* George W. Brown, 1870, painted tin, 14½″ length	1500.00	2000.00

Battleship, Ideal, Detroit, Michigan, lithograph paper on wood pull toy, 20″ length, $1200-$1400. "Gem of the Ocean" attributed to R. Bliss, early 1900s, lithograph paper on wood, 27″ length, $1800-$2000.

Price Range

☐ *Dime Boat,* maker unknown, 1880s, lithographed wood, tugboat, 6″ length 800.00   900.00

☐ **Diving Submarine,** A.C. Gilbert, 1920s, tin clockwork, 12″ length 200.00   250.00

☐ *Gem of the Ocean,* R. Reed, 1880s, lithographed wood, sidewheeler, 24″ length 1000.00   1200.00

☐ *General Taylor,* maker unknown, circa 1880, handpainted tin 1000.00   1200.00

☐ **Gunboat,** Earnst Planck (German), circa 1900, painted sheet metal, 16⅝″ length 450.00   550.00

☐ **Gunboat,** German, 1910, 7″ length, red and white body, black and green stripes 150.00   200.00

☐ **Gunboat With Airplanes,** Carette, circa 1914, painted tinplate clockwork, 17″ length ....   2000.00 plus

☐ *H. M. S. Blake,* R. Bliss, British war cruiser, bright blue, 19″ length 300.00   350.00

☐ *Indiana* **Battleship,** Morton Converse, patented in 1900, lithographed tinplate, wood, 32″ length 900.00   1100.00

☐ *Leviathan* **Oceanliner,** Bing, circa 1925, painted tinplate, clockwork, 39″ length ....   2000.00 plus

☐ **Live Steam Launch,** Weeden, 1915, painted tin, 20″ length 350.00   400.00

☐ **Merchant Marine Ship,** Ives, 1920s, painted tin mechanical, 11″ length 200.00   250.00

☐ *Missouri* **Battleship,** German, circa 1913, painted tinplate clockwork, 28″ length .....   2000.00 plus

☐ *New Mexico* **Battleship,** S. Orkin, 1920, painted tinplate, 25″ length 800.00   1000.00

☐ **Ocean Liner,** Arnold, lithographed tin mechanical, 1920s, 11½″ length 250.00   300.00

☐ **Ocean Liner,** Kingsbury, circa 1920s, painted steel, red, white and buff, gilt rails, clockwork mechanical, adjustable rudder ..   250.00   300.00

Price Range

☐ **Ocean Liner,** Marx, 1929, lithographed tin, 11½″ length 350.00   400.00

☐ *Ocean* **Passenger Liner,** Greppert & Kelch, 1920, lithographed tin clockwork, 12″ length 250.00   350.00

☐ *Orobar* **Ocean Liner,** German, 1920s, painted tinplate, battery-operated lights, 12″ length 350.00   450.00

☐ **Pacquet Boat,** Maerklin, 1914, painted tinplate, clockwork, winding mechanism on second stack, 8″ and 10″ length sizes 1200.00   1500.00

☐ **Paddlewheeler,** Carette, 1910, painted tin mechanical 550.00   650.00

☐ *Providence,* W.S. Reed, 1880s, lithographed wood 1200.00   1500.00

☐ *Puritan* **Sidewheeler,** Harris, circa 1903, cast iron, white with red trim, gray roof, black stack, 10¾″ length 250.00   300.00

☐ *Puritan* **Sidewheeler,** Wilkins, 1895, painted cast iron, white with red trim, orange roof, black stack, 10⅜″ length 275.00   325.00

☐ *Schwaben* **Gunboat,** German, circa 1910, painted tinplate, 16″ length .... 2000.00 plus

☐ *Sirene,* Meltete at Parent, France, 1890s, paddlesteamer clockwork, 29½″ length 1200.00   1400.00

☐ **Speedboat,** Hess, 1920s, lithographed tin friction, 12″ length 150.00   200.00

☐ **Speedboat,** Lionel, 1930s, lithographed tin mechanical, two passengers, 18″ length 250.00   300.00

☐ **Steamboat,** maker unknown, 1892, cabin with awning, 20″ length 1200.00   1400.00

☐ **Steamboat,** Mathias Hess (German), 1908, painted tin, three-wheeler floor toy, 10½″ length 1200.00   1400.00

☐ **Steam Launch,** Weeden, 1920s, tinplate, 15½″ length 200.00   250.00

Four Sidewheel Steamer toys. *Top left:* "St. Johns," $2000 plus; *Top right:* "Pacific," $2000 plus; *Center:* "Water Witch," $2000 plus. Top two toys attributed to George W. Brown, third, maker unknown.

	Price Range	
☐ **Submarine,** Ives, 1900s, painted tinplate, gray with red trim, 10½" length	250.00	300.00
☐ **Submarine,** maker unknown, 1936, steel, clockwork, actually dives and rises, 10" and 13" length sizes	350.00	400.00
☐ **Two-Masted Sailing Ship,** W.S. Reed, 1877, lithographed wood clockwork, 38" length	300.00	350.00
☐ *Union* **Ferry Boat,** Bing, circa 1917, painted tinplate clockwork, 21" length	2000.00 plus	

A catalog page from a premier toy boat maker, Gebruder Maerklin, c. 1915. These handsomely enameled tinplate toys featured long-running clockwork mechanisms and copied the original down to the last-minute detail. Unfortunately, the prices on Maerklin toy boats have escalated to a range of what you might expect to pay for a real yacht.

	Price Range	
☐ *Union*, R. Bliss, 1880s, lithographed wood, sidewheeler, 24″ length	1200.00	1400.00
☐ *Vixen* Racing Yacht, Ives, 1920s, painted tin mechanical, 13″ length	100.00	125.00

Pacquet boat, Maerklin, 1911, enameled tinplate, $2000. Deep Sea Diver, Bing, 1915, $350–$400.

	Price Range	
☐ *Volunteer IXL*, Fallows, late 1890s, painted, stained and stenciled tin clockwork, 16″ length	1200.00	1400.00
☐ **Warship,** Dayton, tin pressed-steel friction toy, 15½″ length	600.00	700.00
☐ **Warship,** maker unknown, tin mechanical friction wheeled toy, 15½″ length	200.00	250.00

CAST-IRON BOATS

☐ *Chris Craft,* Hubley, 1920s painted cast-iron cabin cruiser, with anchor, Chris-Craft embossed on bow, 11″ length	350.00	400.00
☐ *City of New York* **Sidewheeler,** Harris, 1900s, painted cast iron, name embossed along side of paddlewheel	250.00	300.00
☐ *Showboat,* Arcade, 1928, painted cast iron with Showboat painted across side, 11″ length	350.00	400.00

A popular spinoff among nautical toys, and actually a collecting specialty in itself, is the Noah's Ark. Lithograph paper on wood and tin with wooden figures. American, maker unknown, 1890s, $650–$750.
Lithograph paper on wood, Noah's Ark, German, 1880s, $1200–$1400.

	Price Range	
☐ **Sidewheeler,** Dent, 1910, painted sidewheeler, unidentified, 11″ length	200.00	250.00
☐ *Static* **Speed Boat,** Hubley, 1920s, with driver, painted cast iron, three wheels, 10″ length	300.00	350.00

PENNY TOYS

Penny toys originated in late Victorian and Edwardian England, receiving their name because they sold for a bargain price of a penny, a ha'penny, or a tuppenny. Because they brought to even the poorest child's home the wonders of leverage, flywheels, friction, springs, and crankshafts, they soon found popularity in America and France as well.

The major manufacturing centers from 1890 to World War I were Kienberger & Co., Johann Philipp Meier, Johann Distler, and Walter Stock in Nuremberg for tin and lead models and Sonnenberg for wood. Penny toys were also manufactured in Japan, France, and the United States, plus a limited number in the United Kingdom. A between-the-wars phase of celluloid versions proved short-lived because of the fragility and inflammability of that material.

In recent years, penny toys have been fervently pursued by miniaturists, Victorian doll house collectors, as well as toy enthusiasts. These once paltry geegaws, to quote Leslie Daiken, founder of the British Toy Museum, are vivid embodiments of fashion and custom, travel and pleasure, trade and child's play.

	Price Range	
☐ **Aeronautical,** German, lihtographed tin, 7″ height	100.00	125.00
☐ **Alligator,** German, 5″ length	75.00	100.00
☐ **Armored Car,** German, 1910, camouflaged lithographed tin, 2⅞″ length	75.00	100.00
☐ **Auto,** Gesch, German, 1910, earliest auto penny toy, stained tin	150.00	200.00
☐ **Baby Carriage,** German, 1900s, lithographed tin, with baby, 2½″ height	100.00	150.00
☐ **Battleship,** J. Ph. Meier, 1900–1914, three-deck ship bears name "Thunderer," triple stack belches smoke with crosscut using sawhorse on platform, 3½″ length	150.00	200.00
☐ **Beetle,** German, 1900s, 3″ length	50.00	75.00

Price Range

☐ **Billiard Player,** Kienberger & Co. (German), circa 1920s, lithographed tin, spring-loaded wire rod pool mechanism, 4″ length   100.00   150.00

☐ **Bird Cage on Stand,** German, 1900s, lithographed tin with bellows, 8″ height 75.00   100.00

☐ **Boattail Race Car,** GF, German, 1910, lithographed tin 100.00   125.00

☐ **Boxers,** Ferman, CKO, 1900, squeeze toy   35.00   50.00

☐ **Boy on Sleigh,** Johann Philipp Meier, 1920s, two pairs disk wheels, lithographed tin pull toy, 2¾″ height 300.00   400.00

☐ **Brown Horse on Wheeled Platform,** Sonneberg, Germany, 1900s, pull toy, brown with red and yellow trim, 5″ height 150.00   200.00

☐ **Butcher's Cart,** German, lithographed tin ..   75.00   100.00

☐ **Child in Highchair,** German, 1890s, lithographed tin, 2½″ height 150.00   175.00

☐ **Chinaman With Umbrella,** German, 1900s, Chinaman rides on small wagon, 3″ length 150.00   200.00

☐ **City of London Police Ambulance,** German, 1900s, flywheel mechanical, lithographed tin, 4″ length 250.00   300.00

☐ **Clown in Barrel,** Stock, German, 1910, lithographed tin, 3″ length 350.00   400.00

☐ **Clown Prodding Donkey,** German, 1920s, lithographed tin leverage toy, clown tries to persuade donkey to budge with stick, 4″ length 150.00   200.00

☐ **Dancing Man,** German, 1900s, 4″ height ..   50.00   75.00

☐ **Dancing Minstrel,** Johann Distler (German), late 1920s, lithographed tin, jointed tin black figure dances on platform, crank mechanical (miniaturized version of Tombo, Dapper Dan, et al.), 3½″ height 125.00   175.00

☐ **Delivery Van,** German, 1920, lithographed tin 100.00   125.00

Price Range

☐ **Dirigible,** German, early 1920s, lithographed tin, string toy, four-bladed propellor spins, 3″ length 150.00   200.00

☐ **Doll's Baby Carriage,** German, 1910, painted molded lead, 3″ length 150.00   200.00

☐ **Electric Omnibus,** German, 1900s, lithographed tin, passengers ride in open air on roof as well as inside omnibus, hollow tin driver is seated in open cab, flywheel mechanical, 4½″ length 250.00   275.00

☐ **Elephant Clicker,** German, 1900s, lithographed tin 50.00   75.00

☐ **Express Boy,** German, 1920s, bellhop sits on trunk...   25.00   50.00

☐ **Express Parcel Delivery Truck,** German, 1920s 100.00   150.00

☐ **Fire Engine,** C. K. O., lithographed tin, 5½″ height 50.00   75.00

☐ **Fire Truck With Firemen,** German, 1890s, lithographed and nickeled tin mechanical, 4½″ length 175.00   200.00

☐ **Fleecy Lamb,** German, circa 1870, wood with real wool, 2½″ length 200.00   250.00

☐ **Garage,** German, 1900s, lithographed tin with gas pump, 4″ length 75.00   100.00

☐ **Garage With Two Cars,** German, 1900s, 2½″ height 50.00   75.00

☐ **Girl Feeding Rooster,** German, 1920s, wheeled platform 250.00   275.00

☐ **Girl on Swing,** German, 1900s, lithographed tin 200.00   225.00

☐ **Grand Hotel Wagon,** German, 1930s, lithographed tin, horse-drawn carriage, bright red and yellow, gilded spoke wheels, 5¼″ length 250.00   300.00

☐ **Hansom Cab With Driver,** German, 1915, lithographed tin, pulled by dappled horse   200.00   250.00

Price Range

☐ **Hay Wagon,** German, 1920s, horse-drawn, lithographed tin 100.00   150.00

☐ **Hens and Chicks on Nest,** German, 1915, lithographed tin 200.00   250.00

☐ **Hook and Ladder Truck,** German, 1900s, two helmeted passengers seated back to back, overhead ladder in open truck, fire bell, flywheel mechanical, lithographed tin, 4½″ length 250.00   300.00

☐ **Horse and Cart,** German, painted tin, ¾″ length 50.00   75.00

☐ **Horse and Cart,** German, 1910, lithographed tin 75.00   100.00

☐ **Horse-Drawn Hanson Cab,** German, 1900s, lithographed tin 100.00   125.00

☐ **Horse on Platform,** J. M., German, 1900, 3″ height 50.00   75.00

☐ **Hot Air Balloon,** German, early 1920s, lithographed tin, two-pulley string mechanical, single revolving propellor above air bag plus tiny anchor, 2½″ height 175.00   200.00

☐ **Jack-in-the-Stove,** English, circa 1910, spring-operated lithographed tin, man's head pops out of top of parlor stove, 4″ height 200.00   250.00

☐ **Knight on Horseback,** German, 1900s, lithographed tin, 4″ length 75.00   100.00

☐ **Landau Roadster,** German, lithographed tin 100.00   125.00

☐ **Limousine,** German, 1900s, lithographed tin, 2½″ length 50.00   75.00

☐ **Locomotive,** German, 1900s, stained tin, earliest locomotive penny toy, friction drive 125.00   150.00

☐ **Locomotive,** KiCo, German, 3¾″ length ... 50.00   75.00

☐ **Man and Twirler,** German, 1920s, lithographed tin, 7″ height 35.00   50.00

Price Range

☐ **Merry-Go-Round,** German, lithographed tin mechanical, 4½" height 75.00   100.00

☐ **Monkey Climbing Ladder,** German, 1920s, 6¾" length 75.00   100.00

☐ **Monoplane,** German, circa 1915, lithographed tin mechanical, large propellor, oversized pilot sits in open cockpit, 5" length 200.00   250.00

☐ **Mother Pushing Girl in Sleigh,** German, 1890, lithographed tin 150.00   200.00

☐ **Mule Cart,** German, 1910, lithographed tin, 6" length 200.00   225.00

☐ **Nodding Goose,** 1920s, lithographed tin, platform toy 100.00   150.00

☐ **Oarsman,** German, 1900s, 2 men in scull on wheels, lithographed tin, 6½" length 100.00   150.00

☐ **Ocean Liner,** German, 1910, lithographed tin wheeled pull toy 150.00   200.00

☐ **Open Touring Car,** German, 1900s, lithographed tin, 4½" length 75.00   100.00

☐ **Pool Player,** German, 1910, 4" length 50.00   75.00

☐ **Pug Dog,** English, 1900s, hollow tin, painted, 2" length 125.00   150.00

☐ **Pumper Fire Engine,** pale blue, 4" length 100.00   150.00

☐ **Quarter Moon,** German, 1915, lithographed tin 175.00   200.00

☐ **Race Car With Driver,** German, 1920s, lithographed tin, 2½" length 50.00   60.00

☐ **Racing Car,** CFO, German, lithographed tin 100.00   125.00

☐ **Roosters,** German, CKO, 1900, squeeze toy 50.00   60.00

☐ **Rotating Ferris Wheel,** English, 1900s, lithographed tin with cars covered with tin awnings, 4" height 150.00   200.00

Price Range

☐ **Scale,** German, 1900s, 3″ length 50.00   75.00

☐ **Sedan,** German, 1890s, lithographed tin,
4½″ length 75.00   100.00

☐ **Sewing Machine,** German, lithographed tin
with drawer, 3″ height 75.00   100.00

☐ **Skier,** German, 1920s, lithographed tin,
wheeled toy 175.00   200.00

☐ **Squirrel on Treadmill,** French, 1910, lithographed tin mechanical 50.00   75.00

☐ **Submarine,** German, 1930s 35.00   50.00

☐ **Sulky,** German, 1920s, lithographed tin 200.00   225.00

☐ **Swordsmen,** German, CKO, 1900s, squeeze
toy 35.00   50.00

☐ **Tank Truck,** German, 1920s, lithographed
tin 75.00   100.00

☐ **Taxi,** German, circa 1910–1915, driver
seated in front, open section, lithographed
tin with nickeled wheels, friction mechani-
cal 150.00   175.00

☐ **Tin-Top Jitney Bus,** glass chassis, tin
wheels, approximately 3½″ length 250.00   300.00

☐ **Toonerville Trolley,** German (Cracker
Jack) 300.00   350.00

☐ **Torpedo Touring Car,** German, 1920s,
lithographed tin 50.00   75.00

☐ **Touring Car,** J. M., German, 1900s,
lithographed tin, 3¼″ length 75.00   100.00

☐ **Town Car,** Johann Philip Meier, German,
1920s, open limousine with brightly lithographed details including headlamps,
spoked wheels, tin, 3⅜″ length 125.00   150.00

☐ **Toy Airplanes on Pole,** German, 1900s,
spring action, 6″ height 100.00   150.00

☐ **Train,** Japan, lithographed tin 50.00   75.00

☐ **Train Car,** German, 1900s, lithographed
tin, 2½″ length 50.00   75.00

Price Range

☐ **Trolley,** French, lithographed tin, 3″ length 50.00   75.00

☐ **Truck,** JD, German, 1910, lithographed tin friction 75.00   100.00

☐ **Two Ducks,** German, 1915, lithographed tin 50.00   75.00

POLITICAL AND PATRIOTIC TOYS

POLITICAL AND PATRIOTIC TOYS INNER CIRCLE

The following is a selection of the most elite toys in the political-patriotic category:

Abraham Lincoln or Gideon Weeles, Garrard Calgani, 1860s, automated sand toy.

Benjamin Harrison, maker unknown, 1888, Grover Cleveland bisque scale toy.

General Butler Walker, Ives, 1880s, clockwork or Tilden the Statesman, Ives, 1880, clockwork.

General Grant Smoking Cigar, Ives, circa 1876, clockwork.

Moody-Sanky, maker unknown, 1880s, still bank, cast iron.

Rocking American Eagle Bell Ringer, maker unknown, 1890s.

Uncle Sam and the Don, Gong Bell, 1903, bell ringer cast metal.

Uncle Sam on Velocipede, Ives, 1890s, clockwork.

U. S. Capitol, W.S. Reed, 1884, lithographed wood histograph.

William H. Taft "Egg" Still Bank, cast iron, 1908.

Woman Suffragette, Automatic Toy Works, 1875, wood clockwork or Political Stump Speaker, Ives, 1882, wood clockwork.

HONORABLE MENTION: Theodore Roosevelt Teddy and the Bear, and Teddy and the Lion mechanical banks, J. & E. Stevens, early 1900s; Magic General Grant and General Butler Wood, A. A. Davis, 1880s, glass novelty jigglers; Teddy Roosevelt Nodder, maker unknown, 1900s, composition; Uncle Sam and John Bull, Gong Bell, 1900s, bell ringer; Uncle Sam's Chariot, Kenton, 1929, cast-iron pull toy; Uncle Sam Mechanical Bank, Shephard, 1886; Windfield Shay Bottling Up Cervera, bottle bank, origin unknown, 1898.

POLITICAL TOYS

Sulfide marbles are known to have appeared with presidents' images for the following candidates: William McKinley, Theodore Roosevelt, Alton Parker, and William Howard Taft. They are highly

Magic General Grant, A.A. Davis, Nashua, NH, 3″ diameter novelty toy, lithograph on paper figure of Grant jiggles when glass-covered wooden ring is shaken, $500–$600. Visiting Statesman, Ives, clockwork mechanical walker, 1880s, $2000 plus.

prized by both political and marble collectors alike, and they often command prices ranging from several hundred dollars and up.

John F. Kennedy inspired two board games, the P. T. 109 and JFK's New Frontier, both by Parker Bros. and valued at $10–$12 and $15–$20, respectively. Parker Bros. also produced a Presidential Election Board Game in 1892, which the company has periodically updated. The early version is $25–$50.

The political toys listed in this section are in chronological sequence of a presidency and/or campaign. Our section of political toys begins with the administration of Rutherford B. Hayes.

Reference numbers appearing in parentheses at the end of some listings are identifiable in Ted Hakes political catalog.

Rutherford B. Hayes

Price Range

☐ **Rutherford Hayes Mechanical Bank,** J. & E. Stevens, 1870s, cast iron, may have been prototype, only one example known, 8″ height .... 2000.00 plus

Benjamin Harrison

Price Range

☐ **Benjamin Harrison vs. Grover Cleveland Balance Scale,** maker unknown, circa 1888, bisque figures of pair swathed in American flags hang from opposite ends of wood and tin scale balance. Figures are 2½″ height, balance is 5½″ length (Hake 3149) 600.00   700.00

☐ **Harrison vs. Blaine Blocks of Five Administration Puzzle,** circa 1884, *New York Herald,* wood tiles within wood frame, 4″ × 4″. James Blaine was Harrison's Secretary of State who himself obviously aspired for the nomination as president (Hake 3011) ..   50.00   75.00

☐ **Harrison vs. Cleveland Arm Wrestling,** maker unknown, 1800s, wood and composition on string, 6″ height 350.00   450.00

Grover Cleveland

☐ **Cleveland or Harrison Campaign Egg,** maker unknown, 1888, brass rooster pops out of composition egg, slogan: "Crow for Cleveland" (or Harrison) 250.00   300.00

☐ **Grover Cleveland Political Euchre Card Game,** maker unknown, 1880s, caricatures of various candidates appear in lieu of Kings, Queens, Jacks (Hake 3043) 100.00   125.00

William McKinley

☐ **McKinley/Hobart Spinning Top,** Gibbs, 1896, wood and metal with gold paper band depicting both Republican candidates, slogan: "On Top, Protection, Sound Money, Prosperity," 2″ height (Hake 3034) 150.00   200.00

Theodore Roosevelt

☐ **Roosevelt Bear on Bicycle,** maker unknown, 1900s, lithographed tin (flat) on steel sheet bicycle, with iron weight 200.00   250.00

Price Range

☐ **Roosevelt on Safari,** Schoenhut, circa 1910, wood-jointed figure, 6 ″ height (part of Teddy's Adventures in Africa set) 600.00   700.00

☐ **Standing Teddy Roosevelt Nodder,** German, 1910, composition 300.00   350.00

☐ **Teddy Bear Still Bank,** maker unknown, 1900s, cast iron, "Teddy" appears on side, 2½ ″ height 150.00   200.00

☐ **Teddy Dexterity Puzzle,** German, 1900s, lithographed tin and glass, small white marbles, object is to place balls in indentations for Teddy's prominent teeth, 3 ″ diameter   100.00   150.00

☐ **Teddy and the Lion Vanish Puzzle,** maker unknown, 1900s, 3 ″ width, 4 ″ height (vanish puzzles comprised a geometric paradox whereby figures are dissected and rearranged and a portion of the original appears to have disappeared) 75.00   100.00

☐ **Teddy Puzzle,** maker unknown, 1908, lithographed tin and cardboard and metal balls, object is to place metal balls within center of shallow tin cups that serve as eyeglasses 150.00   200.00

☐ **Teddy Roosevelt "Knock Him Out" Novelty Toy,** Scientific Toy Co., Hartford, Connecticut, patented 1893, wood mechanical, lithograph paper-on-wood figure of Teddy pops up via spring mechanism, paper label (black on red) reads "For Parker Nit-Knock Him Out; We Want Roosevelt" (could there possibly be a Parker mate to this one?) 450.00   500.00

☐ **Teddy Roosevelt Rough Rider,** German, 1900s, painted tin wind-up, 7 ″ width, 7 ″ height 350.00   400.00

☐ **Teddy Roosevelt Rough Rider,** maker unknown, 1900s, cast-iron still bank, gold with silver and black trim, 5 ″ height 100.00   150.00

	Price Range	
☐ **Teddy Roosevelt Rough Rider,** Gong Bell, 1903, cast-iron pull toy	250.00	300.00
☐ **Teddy's Teeth Tin Whistle,** Teddy's Teeth Co., Chicago, Illinois, lithograph tin, made shrill blast, "more noise than a horn," the ultimate in political kitsch, 3″ length ..	35.00	50.00

William Howard Taft

☐ **"Billy Possum" Still Bank,** maker unknown, 1908, cast iron, silver on black base, slogan reads "Billy Possum" and "Possum and Taters" on opposite sides of base	250.00	300.00
☐ **Peaceful Bill/Smiling Jim Still Bank,** maker unknown, 1908, cast iron, bust masks of successful running mates William Taft and James Sherman appear back to back, bronze finish, 4″ height, ...	250.00	300.00
☐ **Taft "Bill the Beamer" Roly-Poly,** Bill the Beamer Co., New York, circa 1909, white composition, figure holds baseball in right hand, 4½″ height, 3″ diameter (Taft was the first President to officially throw out the first baseball at a World Series)	150.00	200.00
☐ **Taft "Billy Possum" Prosperity Still Bank,** maker unknown, 1908, ceramic, caricature of Taft's head on possum's body, 5″ height (Hake 3021)	150.00	200.00
☐ **Taft "The Egg" Still Bank,** J. & E. Stevens, 1908, cast iron, egg-shaped caricature with top hat on figure, very common bank, 3½″ height	900.00	1000.00
☐ **Taft "Happy Billy Possum's Prosperity Puzzle,"** National Novelty Co., Worcester, Massachusetts, 1908, lithographed cardboard game with marbles, object is to send marbles through dimensional image of William Howard Taft and into White House Gate, 6″ square	150.00	200.00

"Bill the Beamer" (William Howard Taft) roly-poly composition figure,
Bill the Beamer Company, New York, c. 1909, 4½" height, 3" diameter.
Taft was the first president to officially toss out the first baseball at a
World Series game. (Note the ball in right hand.) The portly Taft
inspired a number of roly-poly toys. $150–$200.

Price Range

☐ **Taft Roly-Poly,** maker unknown, 1900s, celluloid, stained black, green, and tan, 1½" height 150.00   200.00

☐ **William Howard Taft Roly-Poly,** maker unknown, 1900s, papier-mache, 5¼" height   200.00   250.00

Woodrow Wilson

☐ **Woodrow Wilson/Thomas Marshall Coin Bank,** maker unknown, 1916, oval celluloid, slogan appears: "Our Country. Our Flag. Our President. Help Re-Elect Woodrow Wilson," with cameo portraits of Wilson and Marshall, red, white, and blue colors, 3" length 300.00   350.00

Warren G. Harding

☐ **Warren Harding Still Bank,** maker unknown, 1920s, cast metal in bronze finish, 4½" height (many savings banks began issuing still banks in likenesses of presidents, beginning in the 1920s; most often, they were of cast metal with bronze finish and featured advertising from the local money lender) 35.00   50.00

Calvin Coolidge

☐ **Calvin Coolidge Still Bank,** maker unknown, 1924, pottery, brown-toned, slogan: "Do as Coolidge Does . . . Save," 4" height (Hake 2047) 75.00   100.00

Herbert Hoover

☐ **Al Smith Whistling Figure,** German, late 1920s, wood-carved with clockwork mechanism and bellows, Al Smith with famed derby hat, whistles tune "Happy Days Are Here Again," 12" height (Smith ran on the "Wet" anti-prohibition platform in 1928 against Hoover) ....   400.00   500.00★

★This toy, akin to the Charlie Chaplin Whistler toy, sold for $1100 at an auction in 1985.

Price Range

□ **"Al Smith Wins, Here's How,"** puzzle, Cahoes Novelty Co., Cahoes, New York, 1928, cardboard with wood tiles, $5^{1}/_{2}"$ square 50.00   75.00

□ **Herbert Hoover Elephant Still Bank,** maker unknown, 1932, white with Hoover and Curtis embossed in black trim on side, $4^{3}/_{4}"$ height, 7″ width (Hake 2127) 100.00   150.00

□ **"Herbert Hoover, Wins, Prove It!"** puzzle, Cahoes Novelty Co., Cahoes, New York, 1928, cardboard with wood tiles, $5^{1}/_{2}"$ square 50.00   75.00

Franklin D. Roosevelt

□ **Alf Landon Elephant Still Bank,** maker unknown, 1936, gray with red blanket and gold letters "Land On Roosevelt, 1936," 5″ height (Hake 2121) 100.00   150.00

□ **FDR Bust Still Bank,** maker unknown, 1930s, molded and painted cloth body with oilcloth shirt and shoes, floppy hat, pair of canes 200.00   300.00*

□ **"New Deal" Safe FDR Still Bank,** Kenton, 1936, cast iron, 5″ height 75.00   100.00

□ **Roosevelt (FDR) "Happy Days" Barrell Still Bank,** Chein, 1936, tin with slot in top, 4″ height 15.00   25.00

□ **Thomas Dewey Metal Figure,** maker unknown, 1944, cast metal, painted, name embossed on base, 4″ height (Hake 2004) 15.00   25.00

*Brought $500 at Atlanta Toy Museum Auction, October 1986.

"I Like Ike" elephant, Linemar, 1950s, battery-operated walker, $75–$100.

Dwight D. Eisenhower

Price Range

☐ **Dwight D. Eisenhower Bust Still Bank,** maker unknown, 1950s, cast metal with bronze finish, 4¹/₂″ height. (Note: These banks were rarely campaign oriented and are thus less desirable among political collectors) 15.00   25.00

☐ **"I Like Ike" Walking Elephant,** Linemar, 1952, felt over tin battery-operated toy, elephant holds "I Like Ike" banner in trunk, waving back and forth as he walks, 6″ length 75.00   100.00

Lyndon B. Johnson

☐ **Lyndon Johnson and Barry Goldwater Nodder Figures,** maker unknown, 1964, plastic, 3″ height (Hake 2257 and 2290), each 15.00   25.00

Richard M. Nixon

	Price Range	
☐ **Humphrey/Muskie '68 Donkey Still Bank,** maker unknown, 1968, cast iron, plain finish, 4″ height	25.00	50.00
☐ **Nixon/Agnew '68 Elephant Still Bank,** maker unknown, 1968, cast iron, plain finish, 4″ height	25.00	50.00

Ronald Reagan

☐ **Ronald Reagan Jellybean White House Ceramic Still Bank,** 4⅝″ height × 5½″ width	15.00	25.00

PATRIOTIC TOYS

☐ **Freedom Bell Ringer,** Gong Bell, 1880, tin and cast-iron pull toy, kneeling black figure in tin with bell and American Flag, 6″ length	900.00	1000.00
☐ **Independence 1776–1876,** Gong Bell, 1876, nickel-plated steel pull toy with cloth flag, features bronze eagle perched on Liberty Bell, 9½″ length	800.00	900.00
☐ **John Bull and Uncle Sam,** Watrous Mfg. Co., 1905, cast iron and steel, 7″ length ...	450.00	550.00
☐ **Rocking Eagle Bell Toy,** maker unknown, circa 1890, cast iron, eagle on rockers holds large Liberty Bell in beak, 4¾″ length	650.00	750.00
☐ **Uncle Sam Accordion Toy,** German, 1920s, papier-mache with firecrackers that come out of head, cloth and paper-covered wood box	250.00	300.00
☐ **Uncle Sam and the Don Bell Toy,** Gong Bell, 1903, Uncle Sam and Spanish Don engage in sword duel with bells at end of swords, 7½″ length	1000.00	1200.00

"Uncle Sam Going to the World's Fair" (left), Ives, 1875. Same velocipede was also ridden by a monkey, clown, a girl, a boy, black or white, in other Ives variations, $2000 plus. "Stump Speaker," Ives, 1882, bows and scrapes in his red, white, and blue checked trousers, $2000 plus.

	Price Range	
☐ **Uncle Sam Going to the Fair Velocipede,** Ives, 1875, tin and wood, clockwork three-wheeler, 9″ length (other Ives variations featured little girl, both black and white, monkey and clown)	5000.00 plus	
☐ **Uncle Sam Mechanical Bank,** C. G. Shepherd, 1886, cast iron, Uncle Sam puts coin in his satchel, beard moves up and down, 8½″ height	650.00	750.00
☐ **Uncle Sam Three-Coin Register Bank,** Durable Toy and Novelty Co., 1900s, tin, a popular bank with youngsters over the years but not necessarily with collectors	25.00	50.00

Price Range

☐ **Uncle Sam Waving Hat,** maker unknown, 1916, lithograph wood and cloth, he flips hat from one hand to the other 10½" height 100.00   150.00

☐ **Uncle Sam's Chariot,** Kenton, 1929, cast-iron pull toy, Uncle Sam rides in eagle-shaped chariot drawn by two horses, 12" length 750.00   850.00

☐ **Uncle Sam's Hat Bank,** Chein, 1930s, lithograph tin, 5" height 25.00   50.00

SOFT TOYS

Soft Toy Collecting Tips: It is often possible to estimate a soft toy's vintage by its pile. Rayon pile, for example, was used during the 1920s; synthetic pile came to the fore in the late 1940s. Steiff toys carried an identifying mark, the hexagonal metal button in the ear, from 1905 to date. Often the ear tags are missing but check the left ear for a hole that might have been left by the tag. The most prized Teddy Bears are those from Steiff and Ideal Novelty and Toy Co., especially those covered with mohair. Straw, kapok, and excelsior were the more common stuffings in older Teddy Bears.

IDEAL, STEIFF, AND MISCELLANEOUS SOFT TOYS

Ideal Novelty and Toy Co., Brooklyn, NY

	Price Range	
☐ **Teddy Bear,** 1903–1906, yarn nose and mouth, felt-padded paws, diagonal stitching from ear to nose, light cinnamon color mohair, 13″ height	150.00	200.00

Steiff

☐ **Antelope,** 1950s, 8½″ height	50.00	60.00
☐ **Baby Chick,** 1950s, mohair, 4″ height	15.00	20.00
☐ **"Bambi" Deer,** circa 1960s, velvet, 5″ height	25.00	35.00
☐ **Black Shirt Cadet,** 1900s, black hat with fringe, swivel neck, gray pants, black shirt, 8¼″ height	800.00	1000.00
☐ **"Boy" Cowboy,** 1950s, rubber head, felt body and limbs, 8″ height	150.00	200.00
☐ **Bulldog,** circa 1960s, mohair, 6″ height	25.00	35.00
☐ **Camel,** 1950s, mohair, with ear tag	15.00	20.00

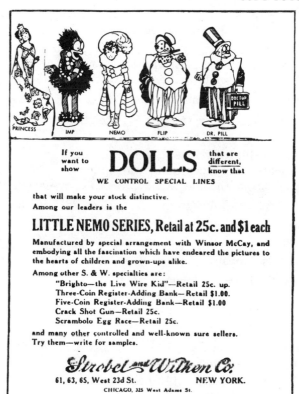

Comic enthusiasts bemoan the lack of toys inspired by that most
imaginative of early comic strips, "Little Nemo in Slumberland."
Created by Winsor A. McCay, it was as if he discovered the nightmare as
an art form. Dolls featuring characters from the strip advertised by
Strobel and Wilken can command prices in the $500 range.

	Price Range	
☐ **Chef Doll,** 1900s, swivel neck with center seam, blue glass eyes, chef's hat, jointed body, 10″ height	800.00	1000.00
☐ **Chimp,** 1950s, 9½″ height	50.00	60.00
☐ **Cocker Spaniel,** circa 1960s, mohair, 6″ height	25.00	35.00

Price Range

☐ **Donkey,** 1950s, plush and mohair, 5½″ height 50.00   60.00

☐ **Donkey,** circa 1960s, plush, glass eyes and ear buttons, 8″ height 25.00   35.00

☐ **Duckling,** 1950s, mohair, 4″ height 15.00   20.00

☐ **Elephant,** 1950s, straw stuffing, 6½″ height 25.00   35.00

☐ **Elf Boy,** 1910, swivel neck, center seam, brown glass eyes, green outfit with brown leather shoes, 8″ height 800.00   1000.00

☐ **Fawn,** 1950s, 7½″ height 50.00   60.00

☐ **"Flossy" Goldfish,** 1950s, straw stuffing, 4¾″ height 25.00   35.00

☐ **Fox,** 1950s, mohair, 6″ length 20.00   25.00

☐ **French Legionnaire,** 1900s, swivel neck, jointed body, long blue coat, red pants, blue glass eyes, mustache, ribbon on sleeve, 10¾″ height 1200.00   1400.00

☐ **Frog,** 1950s, mohair, 4″ height 20.00   25.00

☐ **Gendarme,** early 1900s, velvet hands and feet, felt body and limbs, 14″ height (a center seam in their faces and prominent noses are telltale features of turn-of-the century Steiff soft toys) 200.00   300.00

☐ **German Foot Soldier,** circa 1915, plush mohair and felt, 13½″ height 50.00   75.00

☐ **Giraffe,** 1950s, 11½″ height 50.00   60.00

☐ **Goat,** 1950s, mohair, 8″ length 20.00   25.00

☐ **Green Tiger,** mohair, with ear tag 15.00   20.00

☐ **"Grissy" Donkey,** 1950s, straw stuffing, 7½″ height 25.00   35.00

☐ **Ground Hog,** 1950s, mohair, 5″ height ... 20.00   25.00

☐ **Halloween Cat,** 1950s, 7″ height 20.00   25.00

☐ **"Hucky" Crow,** 1950s, mohair, 4″ length 15.00   20.00

Very rare runabout, most likely made by Carette in
Germany, circa 1900. Painted tin.
(Photo courtesy of Carl Burnett)

Woman and child in shoe, most likely made by Ives or
Althof Bergman, circa 1880s. Made of tin and cloth.
(Photo courtesy of Carl Burnett)

From the collection of Carl Burnett: a Schoenhut roly-poly clown; a Dayton pressed steel friction toy duck; a Kenton cast-iron Happy Hooligan in cart; a complete layout of track with Ives trains. (Photo courtesy of Carl Burnett)

Quartet of teddy bears, circa 1900-1910. *From left to right:*
Steiff $800-$1000; German Mohair $200-$250;
Steiff $800-$900; Cinnamon Plush $450-$550.

Teddy Bear driving Steelcraft Chrysler pedal car, 1931,
51″ (length), $1500–$2000 (car); Teddy Bear—Steiff,
circa 1905, beige mohair, fully jointed, 30″ (height),
$1000–$1200. (Photo courtesy of Linda Mullin)

Girl and hoop toy, made by George Brown, 1880s.
Valued at $2000 or more. (Photo courtesy of
Robert W. Skinner Auctions)

Pig-drawn, two-wheel cart, made by Gunthermann in the
1890s. Painted tin. Valued at $700-$800.
(Photo courtesy of Robert W. Skinner Auctions)

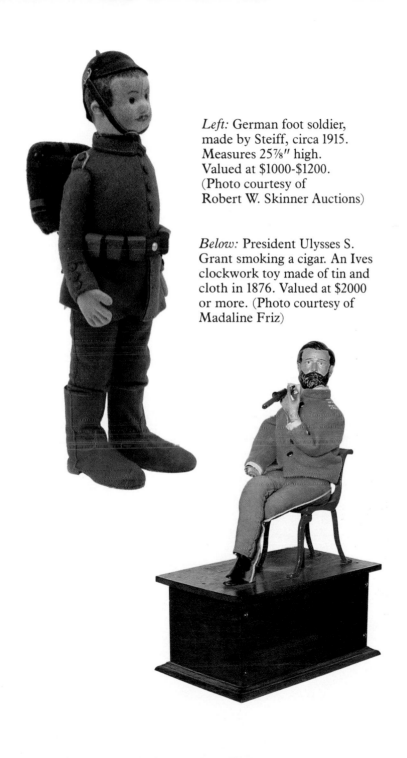

Left: German foot soldier, made by Steiff, circa 1915. Measures 25⅞″ high. Valued at $1000-$1200. (Photo courtesy of Robert W. Skinner Auctions)

Below: President Ulysses S. Grant smoking a cigar. An Ives clockwork toy made of tin and cloth in 1876. Valued at $2000 or more. (Photo courtesy of Madaline Friz)

Painted tin train, made by Stevens & Brown,
circa 1880s. Valued at $2000 or more.
(Photo courtesy of Robert W. Skinner Auctions)

Whistler locomotive, made by Ives in the 1880s.
Painted and stenciled tin. Valued at $1500-$1700.
(Photo courtesy of Carl Burnett)

Left: Teddy bear shares the spotlight with the Seven Dwarfs plush, stuffed dolls, maker unknown. Made in 1938. Valued at $50-$60 each.

Below: Grouping of 1950s-1960s Steiff stuffed animals. Valued at $50-$60 each. (Photo courtesy of Robert W. Skinner Auctions)

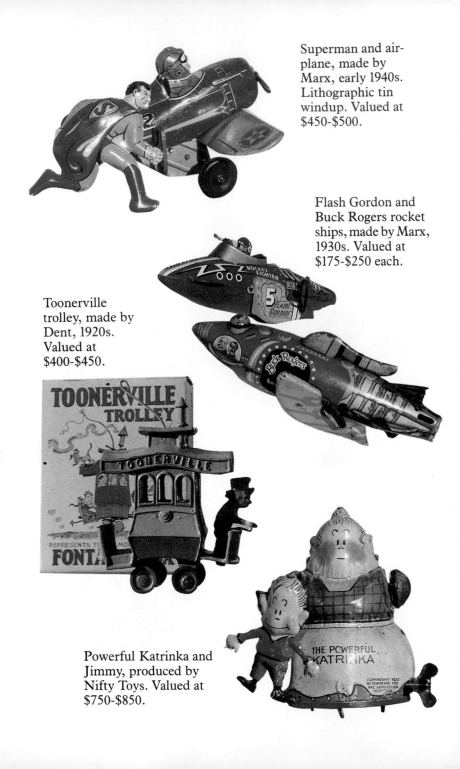

Superman and airplane, made by Marx, early 1940s. Lithographic tin windup. Valued at $450-$500.

Flash Gordon and Buck Rogers rocket ships, made by Marx, 1930s. Valued at $175-$250 each.

Toonerville trolley, made by Dent, 1920s. Valued at $400-$450.

Powerful Katrinka and Jimmy, produced by Nifty Toys. Valued at $750-$850.

Price Range

☐ **Indian Doll,** 1900s, swivel neck with center seam, beaded eyes, black mohair wig, brown fringed "Buckskins," orange vest, 16″ height 1200.00   1400.00

☐ **Kitten,** 1950s, 7″ height 20.00   25.00

☐ **Koala Bear,** circa 1960s, mohair, glass eyes and ear buttons, 8″ height 35.00   50.00

☐ **Lamb on Wheels,** 1925, pull toy, woolly coat, felt ears, muzzle and legs, glass eyes, metal platform with wooden wheels, ear button, 13″ length 300.00   350.00

☐ **Llama,** circa 1960s, mohair, 6¾″ height .. 35.00   50.00

☐ **Man in Tuxedo,** 1900s, swivel head with center seam, beaded eyes, black knee britches, red coat with tails, black leather shoes, 16″ height 1600.00   1800.00

☐ **"Mat Sailor,"** 1950s, rubber head, felt body and limbs, sailor plays accordion, 8″ height 150.00   200.00

☐ **"Maxi" Mole,** 1950s, mohair, no tag or button, 4¾″ height 25.00   35.00

☐ **"Michi" and "Michmu" Porcupines,** 1930s, wearing costumes, 20½″ height 250.00   300.00

☐ **Okapi,** 1950s, mohair, 8″ length 20.00   25.00

☐ **Orangutan,** 1950s, 5″ height 20.00   25.00

☐ **Pair Peasant Boy and Girl,** circa 1910, swivel necks, boy has blue glass eyes, blue shirt, brown pants, 13″ height, girl has center facial seam, bead eyes, white mohair wig, jointed felt body, 12½″ height 800.00   1000.00

☐ **Peasant Girl,** 1900s, swivel neck with center seam, blond mohair wig, red skirt and weskit, 15½″ height 1000.00   1200.00

☐ **"Peggy" Penguin,** 1950s, 8½″ height 50.00   60.00

☐ **Penguin,** 1950s, mohair, no tag or button, 6½″ height 25.00   35.00

	Price Range	
☐ **"Perry" Squirrel,** circa 1960s, mohair, 5″ height	25.00	35.00
☐ **"Pieps" Mouse,** 1950s, mohair, 3″ height	15.00	20.00
☐ **Piglet,** 1950s, mohair, 6″ length	15.00	20.00
☐ **"Pinky" Pekinese,** circa 1960s, mohair, 6″ height	25.00	35.00
☐ **Pony With Saddle,** 1950s, straw stuffing, 4¾″ height	25.00	35.00
☐ **Poodle on Wheels,** circa 1910, fine plush, glass eyes, on four cast-iron wheels, 13″ length	500.00	600.00
☐ **Rabbit Puppet,** circa 1960s, mohair, 12″ height	25.00	35.00
☐ **Rabbit on Wheels,** 1950s, plush and mohair, 3½″ height	50.00	60.00
☐ **Reclining Poodle,** circa 1960, 8″ height ...	50.00	75.00
☐ **Reindeer,** 1950s, 9½″ height	50.00	60.00
☐ **"Robby" Small Seal,** circa 1960s, mohair, 4½″	35.00	50.00
☐ **Rooster,** 1950s, mohair, 6″ height	15.00	20.00
☐ **Seated Puppy,** circa 1960s, mohair, 6″ height	25.00	35.00
☐ **Sheep,** 1910, mohair and velour, glass eyes, 37″ length	500.00	600.00
☐ **"Slo" Turtle,** 1950s, mohair, no tag or button, 7″ length	25.00	35.00
☐ **Small Owl,** circa 1960s, mohair, 4½″ height	35.00	50.00
☐ **"Snobby" Poodle,** circa 1960s, mohair, 6″ height	25.00	35.00
☐ **Spotted Pony,** circa 1960s, mohair, cream and brown, 8″ height	35.00	50.00
☐ **Squirrel,** circa 1960s, mohair, 5″ height ...	25.00	35.00

Price Range

☐ **Sunny Jim,** attributed to Steiff, circa 1910, cloth head stitched in two sections, beaded eyes, felt orange jacket, yellow vest, top hat, 11¾" height (a good example where lack of positive Steiff identification drastically affects price) 250.00 300.00

☐ **Teddy Bear,** 1903–1910, paws with felt padding, rounder face than Ideal version, light cinnamon color mohair, 13" height .. 400.00 500.00

☐ **Teddy Bear,** circa 1906, black shoe-button eyes, hump, 16" height, light golden color 800.00 1000.00*

☐ **Teddy Bear,** 1906, golden mohair, black shoe-button eyes, hump, felt pads, 15½" height 900.00 1000.00

☐ **Turkey,** 1950s, plush and mohair, 6" height 60.00 70.00

Miscellaneous

☐ **Bear,** German, 1950s, unjointed, velveteen lower body, 22" height 75.00 100.00

☐ **Calico Cat,** maker unknown, 1890s, patent printed 20.00 25.00

☐ **Cobbler Doll,** Lenci, 1900s, swivel head, jointed body with brown pants, checkered shirt, black cap with tassel, green neckerchief, 17" height 400.00 500.00

☐ **Dog on Wheels,** German, 1950s, St. Bernard type with glass eyes, mohair fur, steel frame and rubber wheels, 21" length 50.00 75.00

☐ **Oriental Silk Tiger Cat Pin Cushion,** maker unknown, 1890s 30.00 35.00

☐ **Rabbit Squeak Toy,** German, 1890s, glass eyes, pink bow, ears wiggle when bellows are squeezed, mohair, 7" height 125.00 150.00

*Sold for $1100.00 at Skinner Auction, December 1985.

	Price Range	
☐ **Seated Dog,** German, 1900s, yellow fur with cinnamon chest and head, glass eyes, 11½″ height	75.00	100.00
☐ **Stuffed Dog,** maker unknown, United States, 1910–1920, pearl button eyes, rounded face, straw stuffed, after 1920 this type of toy was stuffed with cotton, 4″ height	25.00	30.00
☐ **Teddy Bear,** English, 1930s, brushed wool flannel, 16″ height	200.00	250.00
☐ **Teddy Bear,** German, 1910, black, shoe-button eyes, hump, cinnamon plush, 14¼″ height	500.00	600.00
☐ **Teddy Bear,** German, early 1920s, long snout, small hump, mohair fur, 20″ height	150.00	200.00
☐ **Teddy Bear,** German, maker unknown, circa 1930, mohair, "Winnie The Pooh" type, 12″ height	75.00	100.00
☐ **Teddy Bear,** Shuco, circa 1930, mohair, 10″ height	100.00	150.00
☐ **Teddy "Crowler" Bear,** Germany, circa 1920, straw stuffed, 16½″ height	500.00	600.00
☐ **Velvet Rabbit,** maker unknown, 1890s, black and rust color	35.00	40.00

COMIC AND CHARACTER SOFT TOYS

☐ **Billiken Doll,** E. I. Horsman & Co., New York City, 1909–1911, composition head, plush body, The Billiken Co., 11″ height (originally created by Florence Pretz of Kansas City, Missouri)	125.00	175.00
☐ **Charlie Chaplin,** Louis Amberg & Son, New York City, 1915, cloth body with composition head and hands, by special arrangement with Essanay Film Co., cloth label features Indian Chief emblem of Amberg, 14″ height	200.00	250.00

Price Range

☐ **Donald Duck,** Knickerbocker Toy Co., 1938–1940, wears felt red tunic and furry black hat of drum major or band leader, 16″ height 150.00   200.00

☐ **Dopey,** England, Chad Valley, circa 1939, all cloth body, velvet slippers, 6″ height .. 100.00   125.00

☐ **Dopey,** Knickerbocker Toy Co., 1939, velvet stuffed body with composition face, approximately 8″ height 100.00   150.00

☐ **Ferdinand the Bull,** Knickerbocker Toy Co., 1940s, plush figure, felt flower in mouth, 10″ height 100.00   150.00

☐ **Fred Flintstone,** T. M., Japan, circa 1960s, 10½″ licensed under "Hanna Barbera Productions 1962," vinyl and cloth, 10½″ height 25.00   50.00

☐ **Grumpy,** Knickerbocker Toy Co., 1939, velvet stuffed body with composition face, approximately 8″ height 100.00   150.00

☐ **Ignatz Mouse,** Knickerbocker Toy Co., New York City, 1931, Ignatz seems to be spitting image of Mickey Mouse, including the saucer-pie eyes, big shoes on feet, round ears, and pointed snout, 12″ height 250.00   350.00

☐ **Krazy Kat,** Averill Mfg. Co., New York City, 1916, Krazy has long carrot-shaped nose, high, almost sticklike upright ears, big bow ribbon around neck, fabric shoes, 20″ height 350.00   500.00

☐ **Krazy Kat,** Knickerbocker Toy Co., New York City, 1931, 12″ height 250.00   350.00

☐ **Little Pixie People,** Victoria Toy Works, England, circa 1940, cotton heads, velvet and felt bodies, tag reads "I'm one of Norah Wellings' Little Pixie People," tag hangs around neck, marked similarity to Palmer Cox Brownies, 9¼″ height, each ... 25.00   50.00

The surreal comic strip "Krazy Kat" by George Herriman predated Walt Disney's Mickey Mouse by over a decade, but an Ignatz Mouse doll by Knickerbocker featured in this 1930s advertisement bears a remarkable resemblance to the Disney creation, clearly flirting dangerously with copyright infringement. All this does is further enhance the doll's value among crossover collectors in today's market. Ignatz/Mickey, $350–$500; Krazy Kat, $200–$250.

Price Range

☐ **Mickey Mouse,** Ann Wilkinson Designs, England, 1980, cotton stuffed, designed and made in England for Bloomingdale's Department Store, New York City, 9″ height 50.00   75.00

Price Range

☐ **Mickey Mouse,** Charlotte Clark design for Walt Disney Enterprises, 1930, the FIRST stuffed Mickey doll, bright red pants, 12″ height 500.00   600.00

☐ **Mickey Mouse,** Dean's Rag Book Co., London, 1932–1935, cotton and velvet plush, standing, toothy grin, pointed snout, floppy ears, round painted eyeballs encased in clear plastic with floating pupils, 9″ height 150.00   200.00

☐ **Mickey Mouse,** Margarete Steiff & Co., New York City, 1931, 4¼″ height, felt; 6½″, 8¼″, 10½″, 12½″, and 16¾″ height sizes, velvet (price range depending on size) 250.00   650.00

☐ **Mickey Mouse,** Margarete Steiff & Co., 1931, purple pants, yellow gloves and bright orange shoes, distributed by George Borgfeldt Corp., New York City, 19″ height ...   400.00   500.00

☐ **Mickey Mouse Tricycle,** Steiff, circa early 1930s, stuffed, jointed Mickey, velvet fabric, long whiskers on Mickey's snout, seated on bellows squeaker, tricycle (actually it's a four-wheeler) of wood with steel wire, pull toy, 8½″ height 600.00   700.00

☐ **Mickey the Cowboy,** Knickerbocker Toy Co., 1936, designed by Charlotte Clark, 10″ height 350.00   500.00

☐ **Minnie Mouse,** Ann Wilkinson Designs, England, 1980, cotton stuffed, designed and made in England for Bloomingdale's Department Store, New York City, 9″ height 50.00   75.00

☐ **Minnie Mouse,** Knickerbocker Toy Co., mid-1930s, stuffed velvet, Minnie wears lace pantaloons under red polka dot skirt, bright orange shoes, 14″ height 250.00   300.00

Price Range

☐ **Minnie Mouse,** Margarete Steiff & Co., New York City, 1931, 4¼″ height, felt; 6½″, 8¼″, 10½″, 12½″, and 16¾″ height sizes, velvet (price range depending on size) 250.00   650.00

☐ **Pinocchio,** Knickerbocker Toy Co., 1939–1940, mostly composition, jointed with felt outfit and hat, 14″ height 200.00   250.00

☐ **Pinocchio Hand Puppet,** Crown Toy, early 1940s, "Walt Disney Ent." incised on neck, composition head, mohair body, 9″ height 50.00   75.00

☐ **Popeye,** maker unknown, circa 1930–1950, cloth head and body, smokes corncob pipe, large plastic buttons on blue tunic, 16″ height 150.00   200.00

☐ **Raggedy Ann,** Georgene Novelties, New York City, 1930–1950, designed by John Gruelle, original creator of these classic rag dolls, cloth-stuffed doll with reddish brown yarn hair, black button eyes, triangular red painted-on nose, 20″ height 100.00   150.00

☐ **Snow White,** Knickerbocker Toy Co., 1940s, composition face and limbs, cloth body, 12″ height 100.00   150.00

☐ **Two-Gun Mickey,** Knickerbocker Toy Co., 1936, designed by Charlotte Clark, 12″ height 350.00   500.00

CELEBRITY DOLLS

☐ **The Brownies,** Arnold Print Works, North Adams, Massachusetts, 1892, cotton sheet, figures of Soldier, Irishman, and Indian which were to be cut out and stuffed with cotton, straw, etc., designed by originator of The Brownies, Palmer Cox, also featured Uncle Sam, Dude, John Bull, Highlander, and others, 12 figures in all appeared in each yard of fabric, 8″ height 350.00   450.00

Price Range

☐ **The Captain and Katzenjammer Kids** (set of three), Knickerbocker Toy Co., circa 1925, cloth dolls with painted and applied features, bulbous noses, cloth costumes, Hans: 14″ height, Fritz: 16″ height, The Captain: 18″ height 500.00   600.00

☐ **Fritz (Katzenjammer)**, Saalfield Publishing Co., 1914, printed cloth-stuffed doll 200.00   250.00

☐ **Gunga Din Nodder**, maker unknown, 1939, composition and cloth stuffed, all white native uniform, inspired by the movie, although this doll in no way resembles Sam Jaffe who played the waterboy, Gunga Din, 18″ height 75.00   100.00

☐ **Jerry Mahoney**, maker unknown, 1950s, ventriloquist doll, composition face, cloth body, TV kiddie star of the 1950s, 25″ height 100.00   150.00

☐ **Katzenjammer Kids** (each), Samstag & Hilder Bros., 1908, cloth dolls, Hans and Fritz 250.00   300.00

☐ **Mammy Doll**, George Borgfeldt & Co., New York City, 1930s, designed by Tony Sarg, cloth body with composition head and limbs, red print bandanna on head, big white apron, black mohair wig, one of the most desirable of scores of Mammy dolls that have appeared in a variety of material since 1850, 20″ height, white baby, 8″ height 250.00   300.00

☐ **Nancy and Sluggo** (each), Georgene Novelties, 1940s, licensed by Ernie Bushmiller, United Artists Synd., Sluggo: 14½″ height, Nancy: 14″ height (the comic strip "Nancy" by Ernie Bushmiller originated in the early 1920s) 100.00   200.00

☐ **Topsy-Turvy Doll,** maker unknown, 1880, linen and cotton, originated in post–Civil War South, called topsy-turvy or double-enders because doll could be flipped from black to white as long black skirt revealed desired side, 14″ height 200.00   250.00

☐ **W. C. Fields,** Effanbee (Fleischaker & Baum), New York City, circa 1930, cloth body with composition head, shoes, limbs, "An Effanbee product" inscribed on back of shoulder, wears felt coat, white beaver top hat, white felt spats over black shoes, mouth moves as per ventriloquist's dummy, string from back of neck works jaw when pulled, 18″ height (the W. C. Fields Effanbee doll has gone as high as $500.00 at auction within the past year) 150.00   200.00

SPORTS AND RECREATION

One popular and topical collecting category that requires little stimulation from crossover specialists in toy banks, games, and clockwork tins is that of Sports and Recreation. Virtually every athletic endeavor, from gymnastics to bowling, has been recreated in some highly animated toy form. Probably the pinnacle of perfection in this field is the coveted Calamity (or Football) mechanical bank, in which one can almost feel the impact of colliding players as the coin is inserted. Probably the most fiercely contested subcategory among sports toy enthusiasts is that of bicycling, with billiards, of all things, represented in infinite variety by any number of manufacturers including Lilliputian-sized Cracker Jack giveaways).

BASEBALL

	Price Range	
☐ **Baseball Batter Still Bank,** A. C. Williams, early 1909, 5¾" height	200.00	250.00
☐ **Batsman,** Gong Bell, 1913, bell pull toy, bat strikes bell as toy rolls along	850.00	950.00
☐ **Crossed Bats and Ball Still Bank,** early 1900s, 5" height	250.00	300.00
☐ **Home Run King,** Strauss, 1924, lithographed tin mechanical, 6½" height	350.00	400.00

BICYCLING

☐ **Bicycle Race,** French, 1900s, painted tinplate clockwork on wooden base, three riders complete via steel shafts attached to hub, might be a gambling game, 9.6" width	1500.00	2000.00

Single Oarsman, Ives, 1869, patented by Nathan S. Warner, the second earliest Ives listing. Painted tin with wooden oars, $1100-$1300. Bicycle Rider, Ideal, early 1900, painted tin mechanical, $1200-$1400.

	Price Range	
☐ **Bicycle Race,** Muller and Kadeder, 1880s, painted tin clockwork, two riders on steel rods race around central hub, 6″ height ...	1000.00	1500.00★
☐ **Bicyclist,** German, early 1900s, painted tin blown figure, 11″ length	1200.00	1500.00
☐ **Bicyclists,** manufacturer unknown, 1930s, five aluminum figures, 12″ length	50.00	75.00
☐ **Four Cyclists on Tandem Bike,** Ives, 1890, cast-iron pull toy	2000.00 plus	
☐ **Steam Tricycle,** French, 1900s, soldered tin, steam powered, 7.9″ length	700.00	800.00

★Sold for $1300.00 at Ralston Auction in 1981.

Price Range

☐ **Tricyclist,** German, 1910, lacquered tin-
plate, push toy, 4.7" height 350.00   400.00

☐ **Tricyclist on Highwheeler,** French, 1900s,
painted tin, clockwork, 4.7" length 650.00   750.00

☐ **Tricyclists,** French, early 1900s, painted
tin, clockwork, pair of riders in bright uni-
forms, bell rings each time wheel turns full
cycle, 11" length ....   2000.00 plus

BILLIARDS

☐ **Great Billiard Champ,** KiCo, 1895, painted
tin mechanical, 6⅜" length 450.00   550.00

☐ **Pool Player,** German, 1910, lithographed
tin mechanical, 14½" length 400.00   450.00

☐ **Pool Player,** Gunthermann, lithographed
tin mechanical, mustachioed player, 7½"
length 300.00   350.00
Note: There are scores of variations on the Pool Player toy, mostly
German, from the 1920s.

BOATING AND SAILING

☐ **Cat Boat Sailing Bank,** cast-iron still bank,
13" height 200.00   250.00

☐ **Oarsmen,** Ives, 1882, painted and stenciled
tin clockwork, blue and red trim, 12"
length ....   2000.00 plus

☐ **Racing Scull,** U.S. Hardware, 1890s, cast
iron, four oarsmen and coxswain, 9" length
.... 1500.00   2000.00

☐ **Racing Scull,** U.S. Hardware, 1910, cast
iron, eight oarsmen and coxswain, 14½"
length ....   2000.00 plus

☐ **Racing Scull,** Wilkins, 1890s, cast iron,
four oarsmen and coxswain, 10½" length ... 1000.00   1200.00

	Price Range	
☐ **Skiff Trainer,** Fernand Martin, 1910, painted tin mechanical, 7″ length	500.00	600.00

FISHING

☐ **Boy Fishing,** New Hampshire Hill Brass, Co., 1905, cast iron, bell pull toy, boy reeling in fish, 6½″ length × 5½″ height	450.00	500.00
☐ **Fisherman,** mechanical bank, manufacturer unknown, contemporary, cast iron, 12″ length	200.00	225.00

FOOTBALL

☐ **Football Player,** still bank, cast iron, player kneeling with large football on shoulders, 5¾″ height	250.00	300.00
☐ **Football Player,** still bank, manufacturer unknown, cast iron, gold finish, player holds football under one arm, 5¾″ height	150.00	200.00
☐ **Football Players,** Secor, 1923, lithographed tin, cloth, 8″ width × 2″ height	300.00	400.00
☐ **Harvard Football Player,** German, 1904, tin figure with celluloid ball, mechanical, 9″ height	900.00	1000.00
☐ **Sandy Andy Fullback,** Strauss, 1920s, lithographed tin mechanical, 6½″ length ..	250.00	300.00
☐ **Touchdown,** Gong Bell, 1913, cast-iron pull toy, two boys kick ball to each other through posts with bell in middle, 6″ length	900.00	1000.00

GOLF

☐ **Golfer,** Strauss, 1924, lithographed tin mechanical with chute for balls, 6¾″ height ..	200.00	250.00
☐ **Hole in One,** Japan, 1960s, lithographed battery-operated mechanical bank, small lever sends penny into 18th hole, 6½″ height	150.00	200.00

"Batsman," Gong Bell, 1913, $1200-$1400; "Touchdown," Gong Bell, 1913, $1000-$1200. Football- and baseball-related toys are increasingly in demand from specialty collectors.

	Price Range	
☐ **Play Golf,** Strauss, 1930s, lithographed tin mechanical, 11½″ length	250.00	300.00
☐ **Set of Golfers,** Schoenhut, 1920s, painted wood figures on metal shafts, balls, boundary markers, bunkers, sandtraps, greens, felt, figures on shafts are 36″ length	500.00	600.00*

GYMNASTICS

☐ **Acrobats,** Ives, 1893, composition clockwork	2000.00 plus	
☐ **Acrobats Bell Toy,** Gong Bell, 1903, cast-iron pull toy, 6¾″ length	1000.00 plus	
☐ **Balance Swing,** Gibbs, 1910, painted tin and steel, 14½″ height	150.00	200.00
☐ **Gymnast on Trapeze,** Wyandotte, 1940s, lithograph tin mechanical, 9″ height	75.00	100.00
☐ **Little Acrobat,** Fernand Martin, 1910, painted tin mechanical	350.00	450.00
☐ **Tic Tac,** Marx, 1930s, lithographed tin mechanical acrobat, 12″ height	125.00	150.00
☐ **Triple Acrobats,** Marx, 1935, nickeled finish wind-up, 19″ height	250.00	300.00

HORSE RACING AND HORSEBACK RIDING

☐ **Horse and Driver,** Watrous, 1905, bell pull toy, cast iron, 7″ length	400.00	500.00
☐ **Horse and Jockey,** German , 1910, painted tin, on wheeled platform, 4″ height	250.00	300.00
☐ **Horseback Riders,** Fallows, 1895, painted tin	1500.00	2000.00
☐ **Horses and Jockey Ring Toy,** German, 1910, painted tin, 6½″ diameter	325.00	350.00
☐ **Jockey and Horse,** German, 1904, painted tin, 6½″ height	450.00	500.00

*Sold for $1210.00 at Atlanta Toy Museum Auction in October 1986.

Price Range

☐ **Jockey and Horse,** manufacturer unknown, 1920s, tin lithographed and cast-iron balance toy, 9″ height 200.00   250.00

☐ **Jockey Riding Horse,** German, 1900s, lithographed tin penny toy, 2½″ width 75.00   100.00

☐ **Rider and Sulky,** German, manufacturer unknown, 1920, cast iron, 8¾″ height 250.00   300.00

ICE SKATING

☐ **Skating Mechanical Bank,** Kyser & Rex, 1880s, cast iron, four skaters (two fallen on ice), when coin is inserted two figures move around to a figure in rear who awards a girl skater a wreath, 4½″ height ....   5000.00 plus

MISCELLANEOUS

☐ **Bowler,** manufacturer unknown, mechanical bank, contemporary, cast iron, 11″ length 200.00   225.00

☐ **Boy Flying Kite,** German, 1910, painted tin mechanical, 13½″ height 350.00   400.00

☐ **Boy Juggling Balls,** German, 1910, painted tin mechanical with celluloid balls, wears light blue sailor suit 250.00   300.00

☐ **Boy on Stilts,** German, 1904, painted tin mechanical, 9″ height 500.00   600.00

☐ **Hunter,** German, 1915, painted tin mechanical, man with big hat and gun, 9″ height 200.00   250.00

☐ **Hunter,** New Hampshire Hill Brass Co., 1905, bell ringer, cast iron, hunter aims gun at rabbit, 6″ length × 5″ height 850.00   950.00

☐ **Matador and Bull,** German, 1904, matador rides bull, tin lithograph 400.00   500.00

Price Range

☐ **Matador and Bull,** German, 1920s, lithographed tin mechanical, the pair face each other across long steel shaft which undulates as toy is activated (similar to Maggie and Jiggs toy by Nifty), 7″ length 200.00   250.00

☐ **Soccer Player,** German, 1920s, tin, spring cocking mechanism, kicker, 7″ height 250.00   300.00

☐ **Tennis Player,** mechanical bank, manufacturer unknown, contemporary, cast iron, 10⅝″ wide 200.00   225.00

PRIZE FIGHTING

☐ **Knockout Prize Fighter,** Strauss, 1920s, lithographed tin wind-up, 6½″ height 500.00   600.00

ROLLER SKATING

☐ **Boy on Roller Skates,** German, 1914, tin mechanical with hair wig, boy skates on one foot 350.00   400.00

SKIING

☐ **Skier,** Chein, 1930s, lithographed tin mechanical, 6″ height 200.00   225.00

☐ **Ski Jumper,** Schoenhut, 1920, wood, ski track with skier coming down steep ramp to vault over goal post, 26½″ length 350.00   400.00

SLEDDING

☐ **Double Ripper Sled,** New Hampshire Hill Brass Co., 1905, bell pull toy, cast iron, four figures on bobsled, 9″ length, 4″ height .. 750.00   800.00

☐ **Gyro Coaster,** 1924, 9″ length 200.00   250.00

Price Range

☐ **Sled Rider,** Dayton, 1914, pressed-steel tin
friction toy, 9″ length 200.00   250.00

SURFING

☐ **Beach Patrol,** Hubley, 1932, cast-iron pull
toy, advertising Jantzen swimsuits, male
figure on surfboard, 8″ height 800.00   900.00

☐ **Surf Girl,** Hubley, 1932, cast-iron pull toy,
girl on surfboard advertising Jantzen swimsuits, companion to Beach Patrol toy, 8″
height 800.00   900.00

TIN TOYS

There are any number of purists among tin toy collectors who prefer to remain frozen in time in the glory days of the late 19th century. This marked the era when Ives, George Brown, William Fallows, Hall & Stratford, and Althof Bergmann excelled with delicately sculptured hoop toys, animals, and human figures acting out little tableaus on wheeled platforms. Without question, 19th-century classic tins bring out the very best among American toy makers in terms of patina, superb craftsmanship, and an unerring eye for detail in recapturing a glorious "coming of age" for this nation of ours. Never before have so few toys been desired by so many.

Two highly coveted clockwork toys from the 19th century: "The Boxers" was patented in 1876 by William Maguire and Julius Gallot of New Jersey and New York. "The Old Lady Jig Dancers" was produced by E.R. Ives in the early 1890s. Both toys were produced in such limited quantities that they rarely appear on the market. $2000 plus.

IVES (A Chronological Listing)

Price Range

☐ **Chinese Must Go Cap Pistol,** 1879 (see "Cap Pistols and Cap Bombs" listing) .....

☐ **Clown on Powder Keg, Mule and Clown,** 1880s (see "Cap Pistols and Cap Bombs" listing) ....

☐ **Cuzner's Trotter,** 1871, patented by J. B. Cuzner, horse has moving legs with jointed hoofs that distinguish it from most other early horse-drawn tins, 12″ length ....   2000.00 plus

☐ **Double Humpty Dumpty Cap Explorer** (see "Cap Pistols and Cap Bombs" listing) ....

☐ **Double Oarsmen,** 1869, 19″ length (also featured a parlor model with wheels) ....   2000.00 plus

☐ **General Grant Smoking Cigar,** 1876 (see "Political and Patriotic Toys" listing) ......

☐ **Horse and Cart,** 1880s, cast-iron red cart, legs with wires activate single foot gait .....   2000.00 plus

☐ **Irish Lady Dancer** (see "Ethnic Toys" listing) ....

☐ **Irish Woodchopper,** 1882 (see "Ethnic Toys" listing) ....

☐ **Locomotive and Tender** (see "Trains" listing) ....

☐ **Mechanical Horse and Buggy With Whipping Driver,** 1874, two sizes: 12″ length and 17″ length ....   2000.00 plus

☐ **Monkey Churning,** 1874, plush-covered wooden body with metal feet, wood churn, wood platform, 11½″ height ....   2000.00 plus

☐ **The Old Nurse (Old Nursemaid and Child),** licensed to Excelsior Toy Co., New York City, black nurse rocks small white doll to and fro on clockwork platform, 9½″ height ....   2000.00 plus

Price Range

☐ **Punch and Judy Cap Pistol,** 1882 (see "Cap
Pistols and Cap Bombs" listing) ....

☐ **Single Acrobat,** 1875, patented by Henry
L. Brower, New York City, woman in cloth
"jumper" on cross-bar, clockwork mechanism goes in complete or partial revolutions
....   2000.00 plus

☐ **Stump Speaker,** 1882 (see "Political and
Patriotic Toys" listing) ....

☐ **Two Men on Bar,** 1880s, tin clockwork ...   2000.00 plus

☐ **Uncle Sam on Velocipede,** 1875 (see "Political and Patriotic Toys" listing) ....

☐ **The Union Locomotive,** 1880s, yellow cab
with painted black windows, tin clockwork,
7½" length ....   2000.00 plus

☐ **Victory Locomotive,** 1870, red and black
with cast-iron wheels that can turn in front,
clockwork mechanism, stenciled name, 9"
length ....   2000.00 plus

☐ **Walking Horse Cart,** 1873, cast iron and
pressed steel, 10¼" length 500.00   600.00

☐ **Walking Santa,** 1880s (see "Holiday Toys"
listing) ....

☐ **Whistler Locomotive,** 1880, painted tin,
12½" length ....   2000.00 plus

☐ **Whistler Steam Yacht,** 1880 (see "Nautical
Toys" listing) ....

ROLLING HOOP TOYS

The classic and elegant hoop toys of the 1870–1890 era were
small, usually not exceeding 6" or 7" diameter, and encircled various human as well as familiar animal figures. They were part of
the standard repertoire of Althof Bergmann, as well as James Fallows, George Brown, and Merriam Mfg.

An array of toys that can readily be viewed as sculptural art. Although the jobber made no mention of maker by name, these painted and stenciled tin platform and hoop toys are possibly George Brown, Althof Bergmann, or Hull and Stafford, c. 1880s, and would rate in the $1000–$2000 and up stratosphere.

	Price Range
☐ **Boy With Hoop,** Stevens and Brown (speculative), 1870s, bell chime is attached at hub of hoop, wire rods connect chime with handle of two-wheel cart on which running boy figure is attached	2000.00 plus
☐ **Boy Riding Dog,** Althof Bergmann, 1874, boy waves and holds dogs collar with other hand, 4¾″ length	1000.00 1200.00

Price Range

☐ **Boy With St. Bernard,** Althof Bergmann, 1874, boy with dog on leash, dog carries bucket in jaws, 4¾" and 6½" length 1200.00   1400.00

☐ **Dog in Hoop,** Stevens and Brown, 1872, pointer-type running with high curled tail, 6" diameter 1500.00   2000.00

☐ **Hoop With Boy or Girl,** Althof Bergmann, 1874, 6½" and 8" diameter 800.00   900.00

☐ **Hoop With Elephant,** Althof Bergmann, 1874, 6¼" and 8" diameter 800.00   900.00

☐ **Rabbit in Hoop,** Merriam, 1870s, blown-tin white rabbit, one of the most uncommon of all rolling hoops .... 2000.00 plus

☐ **Shepherd and Flock Platform Toy,** Althof Bergmann, 1890s, shepherd with crook, dog, goat, and four sheep, 13⅓" length ... 1500.00   1600.00

☐ **Two Musicians and Menagerie Platform Toy,** Althof Bergmann, 1890, drummer and fifer lead parade of two lions, two bears, and elephant, 11½" length (variations included horse with monkey rider, elephant and dog, 9" length; also 7"-length version of three sheep and a goat) .... 2000.00 plus

☐ **White Horse in Hoop,** attributed to George Brown, 1870s, hoop of corrugated tin, 8" diameter .... 2000.00 plus

TOY TRAINS

Trains comprise the most widely collected single classification in the world of toys. There are toy trains constructed in whole or in part, of tin, brass, pressed steel, and cast iron. They may be powered by clockwork, steam, electricity and friction, or simply pushed or pulled along the parlor floor by youngsters on imaginary track. The major foci in Railroadiana, however, are the locomotives, tenders, boxcars, and rolling stock, plus everything manufactured to help make an entire electric railroad system complete, including stations, signals, bridges, tunnels, crossings, water towers, and seemingly endless track footage. Trains of the same gauge can hook up to each other, even if they were produced in different years and by different makers. Shortly after World War II, a system was established to standardize gauge by the following measurements:

"0" = 1¾"
"1" = 1¾"

Whether you were good, passably good, or a very good boy dictated the size of an Althof Bergmann Union locomotive to be found under the Christmas tree. Toys pictured in this Althof Bergmann 1874 catalog today would bring prices from $1200 to $2000 plus.

"2" = 2″
"Standard" = 2⅛″

Although the intent was to allow collectors to "freewheel it," most railroad buffs remained fiercely loyal to one company or another.

The child-powered tin trains had their heyday in the United States from 1860–1890 with Ives, Althof Bergmann, Hull & Stafford, Francis Field and Francis, James Fallows, and Union Mfg. dominating the field.

The first American maker to introduce tin trains with a clockwork mechanism is reputed to be George W. Brown & Co. of Forestville, Connecticut, dating back to 1856. Two major lithograph-on-wood or cardboard toy train makers, R. Bliss of Rhode Island and Milton Bradley of Springfield, Massachusetts, capitalized on what was almost exclusively a U.S. method to bring excitement and color to what had been a pretty drab (basic black) presentation. Youngsters clamored for the lithographed trains, almost to a fault, as the survival rate was not high. These rank in the highly prized category.

Another American monopoly centered on trackless cast-iron train pull toys. Ives paved the way in the 1880s, quickly followed by Kenton, Arcade, Dent, Carpenter, Ideal, Hubley, J. & E. Stevens, Pratt & Letchworth, and Wilkins. Cast-iron trains remained in production until the 1930s.

THE TOY RAILROAD SYSTEM

The revolution in toy trains really came when Maerklin introduced the track and gauge system at the Leipzig Toy Fair in 1891. Not only did Maerklin display a figure of eight-track plan, but an attractive enameled tin station and other accessories were added to provide realism. Issmayer, Carette, Bing, and other German makers soon got into the act, adding embellishments of their own.

Early in the 20th century, the United States ended Germany's dominance of the toy train system market, with Ives again leading the way with the first clockwork train to run on tracks. When a fire destroyed the Ives factory in 1900, the founders, Edward and Harry Ives, used the insurance money to equip a new plant with the latest machinery to turn out clockwork tin trains and tinplate sectional track. The firm accorded the honor of being the first successful maker of electrically powered toy trains was not Ives but Carlisle & Finch of Cincinnati, Ohio, in 1897. Other American manufacturers soon took up the challenge. They included Knapp Electric & Novelty Co., Voltamp Electric Mfg. Co, Baltimore, and most notably, American Flyer of Chicago.

THE BIG FOUR: IVES, AMERICAN FLYER, LIONEL, AND MARX

After all is said and done, American train collectors concentrate most heavily on the Big Four listed in this guide under their own catalog or model numbers. Ives led the way from the early 1900s until the 1920s, an era regarded by railroad cognoscenti as the glory years, with Lionel emerging as an archrival. The Depression, as well as Lionel, caught up with Ives, and in 1930 Lionel bought out the venerable firm that had been producing top-of-the-line toys and trains for over 60 years. American Flyer and Lionel vied for top honors through another fast-paced innovative era of the 1940s and 1950s until management problems crippled American Flyer and Lionel bought *them* out in 1966.

Marx managed to remain aloof from the competitive fray during these years, largely because they concentrated on the lower end of the line. For the price, the quality was surprisingly good. Marx's plastic line of trains attracted considerable attention in the 1950s and has since amassed a sizeable following of its own. It is certainly easier to build up a sizeable complex of Marx equipment since it is still more within reach than their die-cast counterparts. Marx ceased production in 1980. Lionel has diversified, concentrating on scientific toys and spinning off its dwindling train operation to General Mills in 1969.

TRAINS AND TROLLEYS (Floor and Carpet Toys)

	Price Range	
☐ **Bay Window Switcher Locomotive,** Wilkins, 1890s, painted black cast iron, 7½" length	100.00	150.00
☐ **Locomotive "Gloria,"** German, 1900s, stained and litho tin friction, 6½" length ..	200.00	250.00
☐ **Locomotive #999,** Kenton, 1900s, tender, two stock cars, M.C.R.R. caboose, 43" length, cast iron	450.00	550.00

Gebruder Maerklin #1 gauge electric Schnellbake track with Laurel Line car and accessories was priced at $12,500 by a Pennsylvania dealer at the Allentown Antique Show and Sale in November, 1986. A tinplated model of the 19th-century steam-fired Stevenson's Rocket, also by Maerklin, set a record for toy trains at Sotheby's May, 1985, sale in London, peaking at $39,270.

	Price Range	
☐ **Locomotive #999,** Kenton, circa 1890s, same as above except has M.C.R.R. name embossed, red, white and blue gondolas, 48″ length	400.00	500.00
☐ **"Rosita" New York Central Railroad Train Set,** cast iron, engine, tender, three passenger cars, 50″ length	500.00	600.00

Price Range

☐ **Streetcar,** German, circa 1910, horse-drawn, stained and litho tin 300.00   350.00

☐ **Summer Trolley,** Morton Converse, 1915, painted pressed steel, says "City Hall Park #175," 16″ length 350.00   400.00

☐ **Train,** locomotive #49, manufacturer unknown, 1910, tender, painted cast iron, 25″ length 75.00   125.00

☐ **Train,** locomotive #152, Ideal Mfg., 1910, tender, two passenger cars, cast iron, 24″ length 100.00   150.00

☐ **Train,** locomotive, manufacturer unknown, 1890s, tender, flat car, P. & L. RR, painted cast iron and pressed steel 75.00   125.00

☐ **Train #7148,** German, 1915, litho tin mech, engine and passenger car, 12″ length 200.00   250.00

☐ **Train Set,** American Flyer, 1915, painted cast iron and litho tin, locomotive, tender, four freight cars 200.00   250.00

☐ **Trolley,** Bing, 1920, double-decker summer platform, litho tin clockwork, 0 gauge, 6¼″ length 200.00   250.00

☐ **"Union" Locomotive and Pennsylvania Coach,** Ives, 1880s, painted and stenciled tin clockwork, bell 700.00   800.00

☐ **"Wilkins' Largest Train Set,"** Wilkins, 1900s, painted cast iron, American style, locomotive, tender and two passenger cars, 55″ overall 900.00   1000.00

AMERICAN FLYER

Narrow Gauge

Train Sets

☐ **No. 1312, The Vanguard,** locomotive #3100, pullman car #3141, observation car #3142, train length 21″, circular track, 88″ circumference 75.00   100.00

Price Range

☐ **No. 1314, The Dixie Queen,** locomotive #3105, baggage car #3150, pullman car #3151, observation car #3152, train length 32″, oval track 51″ × 31″ 100.00   150.00

☐ **No. 1316, The Clipper,** locomotive #3103, sand car #3103, automobile car #3012, caboose #3014, train length 31″, oval track 41½″ × 31″ 100.00   150.00

☐ **No. 1319, The Iron Horse,** locomotive and tender #3192, baggage car #3150, pullman car #3151, observation car #3152, train length 34″, oval track 51″ × 31″ 150.00   175.00

☐ **No. 1321, The Old Dominion,** locomotive and tender #3192, log car #3046, sand car #3016, automobile car #3015, caboose, #3017, train length 44″, oval track 51″ × 31″ 200.00   250.00

☐ **No. 1324, The Discoverer,** locomotive #3109, sand car #3207, automobile car #3208, caboose #3211, train length 40″, oval track 61″ × 31″ 200.00   250.00

☐ **No. 1326, New Potomac,** locomotive #3109, two pullman cars, both #3171, observation car #3172, train length 36″, oval track 61″ × 31″ 300.00   350.00

☐ **No. 1328, The New Bluebird,** locomotive #3107, baggage car #3150, pullman car #3161, observation car #3162, train length 31″, oval track 61″ × 31″ 350.00   400.00

☐ **No. 1329, Major Leaguer,** locomotive and tender #3193, tank car #3018, sand car #3016, automobile car #3015, caboose #3017, train length 45″, oval track 61″ × 31″ 300.00   350.00

☐ **No. 1332, The Little American,** locomotive #1094, pullman car #1123, observation car #1124, train length 21″, curved track 83″ 450.00   550.00

Price Range

☐ **No. 1333, The Explorer,** locomotive #3110, baggage car #1204, pullman car #1203, observation car #1209, train length 31½", oval track 37" × 27" 150.00   200.00

☐ **No. 1338, The Bluebird,** locomotive #3113, baggage car #1205, pullman car #1286, observation car #1287, train length 31", oval track 27" × 57" 150.00   175.00

☐ **No. 1339, The Commodore,** locomotive and tender #3194, club car #3180, pullman car #3181, observation car #3182, train length 41", oval track 61" × 31" 600.00   700.00

☐ **No. 1344, The Potomac,** locomotive #3116, club car #3180, pullman car #3181, observation car #3182, train length 36½", oval track 27" × 57" 650.00   750.00

☐ **No. 1346, The Jeffersonian,** locomotive #3115, club car #3280, pullman car #3281, observation car #3282, oval track 32" × 57" 1100.00   1200.00

☐ **No. 1347, The Merchant,** locomotive #3115, machinery car #3206, sand car #3207, automobile car #3208, caboose #3211, train length 52", oval track 33" × 67" 1200.00   1300.00

☐ **No. 1348, The Ambassador,** locomotive #3117, club car #3380, pullman car #3381, observation car #3382, oval track 45" × 74" 1100.00   1200.00

☐ **No. 1349, The Steel Mogul,** locomotive and tender #3194, log car #3216, sand car #3207, automobile car #3208, caboose #3211, train length 56", oval track 71" × 31" 1200.00   1350.00

☐ **No. 1351, The Man-O-War,** locomotive and tender #3194, club car #3380, pullman #3381, observation car #3382, train length 51", oval track 71" × 31" 1100.00   1200.00

	Price Range	
☐ **No. 1384, The Potomac,** with remote control reversing locomotive, locomotive #3186, club car #3180, pullman car #3181, observation car #3182, train length 36½", oval track 27" × 57"	1000.00	1100.00
☐ **No. 1386, The Jeffersonian,** with remote control reversing locomotive, locomotive #3185, club car #3280, pullman car #3281, observation car #3282, oval track 32" × 57"	1600.00	1800.00
☐ **No. 1387, The Merchant,** with remote control reversing locomotive, locomotive #3185, machinery car #3206, sand car #3207, automobile car #3208, caboose #3211, train length 52", oval track 33" × 67"	1500.00	1600.00
☐ **No. 1388, The Ambassador,** with remote control reversing locomotive, locomotive #3187, club car #3380, pullman car #3381, observation car #3382, oval track 45" × 74"	1500.00	1700.00

Locomotives

☐ **No. 1093 Locomotive,** runs forward only, headlight and brass trim, two-tone green, 7"	100.00	125.00
☐ **No. 3100 Locomotive,** runs forward only, red , 7½"	125.00	150.00
☐ **No. 3103 Locomotive,** runs forward only, brass trim, red, 8"	100.00	125.00
☐ **No. 3105 Locomotive,** runs forward only, blue, 3½"	100.00	125.00
☐ **No. 3109 Locomotive,** manual control reverse, 9"	150.00	250.00
☐ **No. 3115 Locomotive,** track switch reverse, two headlights, 10¼"	150.00	250.00

	Price Range	
☐ **No. 3185 Locomotive,** remote control reverse, two headlights, 10¼″	150.00	200.00
☐ **No. 3187 Locomotive,** remote control reverse, twin headlights, brass trim, two-tone red, 10¼″	150.00	175.00
☐ **No. 3192 Locomotive and Tender,** runs forward only, single headlight, black with brass trim, 12″	100.00	125.00
☐ **No. 3194 Locomotive and Tender,** manual control reverse, tender has eight wheels, 14¾″	125.00	150.00
☐ **No. 3195 Locomotive,** runs forward only, single headlight, black with brass trim	100.00	125.00
☐ **No. 3198 Locomotive,** manual control reverse, black with brass trim	150.00	250.00

Rolling Stock

☐ **No. 1106 Log Car,** four wheels (single truck), 6½″	10.00	15.00
☐ **No 1109 Sand Car,** four wheels (single truck), 5½″	10.00	12.00
☐ **No. 1110 Box Car,** four wheels (single truck), 5½″	10.00	12.00
☐ **No. 1111 Caboose,** four wheels (single truck), 5½″	10.00	12.00
☐ **No. 1112 Box Car,** four wheels (single truck), 6½″	10.00	15.00
☐ **No. 1113 Sand Car,** four wheels (single truck), 6½″	10.00	15.00
☐ **No. 1114 Caboose,** four wheels (single truck), 6½″	10.00	15.00
☐ **No. 1115 Automobile Car,** red, 6½″	15.00	20.00
☐ **No. 1116 Sand Car,** various colors, 6½″ ..	15.00	20.00
☐ **No. 1117 Caboose,** emerald green roof, red, 6½″	15.00	20.00

	Price Range	
☐ **No. 1118 Tank Car,** ends and dome nickel plated, battleship gray, 6½″	15.00	20.00
☐ **No. 1119 Stock Car,** four wheels (single truck), 5½″	15.00	20.00
☐ **No. 1141 Log Car,** four wheels (single truck), 5½″	5.00	10.00
☐ **No. 1146 Log Car,** with solid pine logs, bottom and side braces in black enamel, 6½″	5.00	10.00
☐ **No. 3012 Automobile Car,** four wheels (single truck), 6½″	15.00	20.00
☐ **No. 3013 Sand Car,** four wheels (single truck), 6½″	12.00	15.00
☐ **No. 3014 Caboose,** four wheels (single truck), 6½″	15.00	20.00
☐ **No. 3015 Automobile Car,** eight wheels (double truck), 6½″	20.00	25.00
☐ **No. 3016 Sand Car,** eight wheels (double truck), 6½″	20.00	25.00
☐ **No. 3017 Caboose,** eight wheels (double truck), 6½″	20.00	25.00
☐ **No. 3018 Tank Car,** eight wheels (double truck), 6½″	20.00	25.00
☐ **No. 3045 Wrecking Car,** eight wheels (double truck), 6½″	20.00	25.00
☐ **No. 3046 Log Car,** eight wheels (double truck), 6½″	20.00	25.00
☐ **No. 3141 Pullman Car,** brass trim, 6½″ ..	15.00	20.00
☐ **No. 3142 Observation Car,** brass trim, 6½″	15.00	20.00
☐ **No. 3171 Pullman Car,** etched nameplate, brass trim, 8¼″	30.00	35.00
☐ **No. 3172 Observation Car,** etched nameplate, brass trim, 8¼″	35.00	45.00

Price Range

☐ **No. 3206 Machinery Car,** golden orange
and dark blue, 9½″ 30.00   35.00

☐ **No. 3207 Sand Car,** eight wheels (double
truck), 9½″ 35.00   40.00

☐ **No. 3208 Automobile Car,** sliding doors,
tan body, turquoise blue roof, 9½″ 30.00   35.00

☐ **No. 3210 Tank Car,** polished metal tank
ends and dome cap, blue, 9½″ 35.00   45.00

☐ **No. 3211 Caboose,** lighted, eight wheels
(double truck), 9½″ 45.00   55.00

☐ **No. 3216 Log Car,** eight wheels (double
truck), 9½″ 20.00   30.00

☐ **No. 3280 Club Car,** sliding door, brass
trim, blue, 9½″ 40.00   45.00

☐ **No. 3281 Pullman Car,** brass trim, blue
9½″ 40.00   45.00

☐ **No. 3282 Observation Car,** brass platform
railing, blue, 9½″ 40.00   45.00

Standard Gauge

Train Sets

☐ **Freight Set,** diesel locomotive #4680 engine
with tender, tank car #4010, mechanic's car
#4022, caboose #4017 ....   1200.00   1400.00

☐ **Freight Set,** electric locomotive #4692 with
golden state tender, cattle car #4020, gon-
dola #4017, boxcar #4018, caboose #4021 ....   1600.00   1800.00

☐ **Freight Set,** Hiawatha locomotive with
tender, lumber, crane, gondola, tank and
caboose 750.00   850.00

☐ **Passenger Set,** electric locomotive #4000,
with baggage #4040, American coach,
Pleasantview observation car, green, yellow,
black, and white 800.00   900.00

	Price Range	
☐ **Passenger Set,** electric locomotive #4643 0-4-0, American coach, Pleasantview observation, green	400.00	450.00
☐ **Passenger Set,** Franklin locomotive 4-4-0, with two coaches #20, overland express baggage car #30	250.00	300.00
☐ **Passenger Set,** locomotive and tender, Columbus baggage #24773, Hamilton vista dome #24813, Washington observation #24833, silver cars with red stripe	200.00	250.00
☐ **Passenger Set,** #356 silver bullet locomotive, with two coaches, original silhouette stripes	275.00	325.00
☐ **Pocohontas Set,** diesel locomotive #4692 with tender, baggage #4340, pullman #4341, observation #4342, pullman #4343, caboose	2000.00 plus	

Locomotives

☐ **No. 88 Franklin Locomotive,** with tender	85.00	100.00
☐ **No. 290 Electric Locomotive,** 4-6-2	75.00	100.00
☐ **No. 300 Reading Lines Locomotive,** tender	50.00	75.00
☐ **No. 301 Reading Lines Locomotive,** with tender	35.00	50.00
☐ **No. 302 Reading Lines Locomotive,** plastic body	35.00	50.00
☐ **No. 303 Electric Locomotive,** 4-4-0, plastic body	50.00	75.00
☐ **No. 307 Reading Lines Locomotive,** with tender, plastic body	50.00	75.00
☐ **No. 312 Electric Locomotive,** 4-6-2, with tender	35.00	50.00
☐ **No. 322 New York Central Locomotive,** 4-6-4, with 12-wheel tender	150.00	175.00

	Price Range	
☐ **No. 360A Diesel Locomotive,** with tender 364B	150.00	175.00
☐ **No. 370 Diesel Locomotive,** twin motor, with tender	75.00	100.00
☐ **No. 812 Texas Pacific Switcher**	200.00	250.00
☐ **No. 21206 San Francisco Diesel AA**	100.00	150.00
☐ **No. 21573 New Hampshire Diesel AA**	300.00	325.00
Rolling Stock		
☐ **No. 20 Western-Type Franklin Coach**	40.00	50.00
☐ **No. 30 Western-Type Franklin Car**	40.00	50.00
☐ **No. 38 Overland Express**	50.00	60.00
☐ **No. 40 Western-Type Baggage Express Car**	40.00	50.00
☐ **No. 625G Gulf Tank Car**	25.00	35.00
☐ **No. 628 Lumber Car,** W.L., metal base ..	15.00	20.00
☐ **No. 629 Cattle Car,** Maroon	20.00	25.00
☐ **No. 630 Caboose,** with lights	10.00	12.00
☐ **No. 630 Caboose,** dark red	15.00	20.00
☐ **No. 631 T & P Gondola,** green	10.00	15.00
☐ **No. 632 Hopper,** dark gray	10.00	12.00
☐ **No. 633 B & O Box Car,** red and white ..	15.00	30.00
☐ **No. 634 Searchlight Car**	15.00	25.00
☐ **No. 636 Depressed Center Cable Car,** 12 wheel	25.00	30.00
☐ **No. 637 Katy Box Car,** yellow and black ...	30.00	35.00
☐ **No. 637 Katy Box Car,** light yellow	35.00	45.00
☐ **No. 638 Caboose,** A.F.L., red	10.00	12.00
☐ **No. 639 Box Car,** light yellow	30.00	35.00
☐ **No. 639 Box Car,** dark yellow	25.00	30.00
☐ **No. 640 Hopper,** gray, 4 hoppers	10.00	12.00
☐ **No. 640 Wabash Hopper,** black	25.00	35.00

	Price Range	
☐ **No. 640 Hopper,** light gray	30.00	35.00
☐ **No. 642 Box Car,** red and white	30.00	35.00
☐ **No. 642 Box Car,** brown and white	30.00	40.00
☐ **No. 644 A.F. Industrial Brown Hoist,** 12 wheel, red cab	100.00	125.00
☐ **No. 644 Box Car,** black and blue	50.00	60.00
☐ **No. 645A Work Caboose,** no railings	15.00	20.00
☐ **No. 650 New Haven Coach,** green and white trim	65.00	75.00
☐ **No. 651 Baggage,** red	20.00	30.00
☐ **No. 653 Pullman**	60.00	75.00
☐ **No. 654 Observation Car,** 12-wheel trucks, dark green	50.00	75.00
☐ **No. 660 Baggage, chrome**	40.00	60.00
☐ **No. 714 Lumber Car,** gray	30.00	40.00
☐ **No. 716 Dump Car,** automatic	15.00	20.00
☐ **No. 717 Lumber Car,** automatic	20.00	30.00
☐ **No. 718 Railway Express Car,** red	35.00	45.00
☐ **No. 732 Automatic Car**	45.00	55.00
☐ **No. 734 Automatic Car,** red	30.00	40.00
☐ **No. 734 Automatic Car,** brown	30.00	40.00
☐ **No. 740 Automatic Handcar**	75.00	100.00
☐ **No. 802 I. C. Box Car**	12.00	15.00
☐ **No. 804 Gondola**	20.00	25.00
☐ **No. 806 Caboose,** red	10.00	15.00
☐ **No. 906 Crane**	35.00	45.00
☐ **No. 911 Gondola**	10.00	15.00
☐ **No. 914 Log Unloading Car**	40.00	50.00
☐ **No. 916 Gondola**	20.00	25.00
☐ **No. 921 Hopper,** brown and white, with coal pile	25.00	35.00

Price Range

☐ **No. 923 I. C. Refrigerator Car** 20.00   30.00

☐ **No. 924 Covered Hopper** 12.00   15.00

☐ **No. 925 Gulf Tank Car** 12.00   15.00

☐ **No. 929 Cattle Car,** maroon 10.00   15.00

☐ **No. 935 Bay Window Caboose** 100.00   125.00

☐ **No. 937 Caboose,** yellow 40.00   50.00

☐ **No. 938 Caboose** 10.00   15.00

☐ **No. 942 Silver Meteor Seaboard** 25.00   35.00

☐ **No. 970 Seaboard Box Car** 35.00   45.00

☐ **No. 24039 Rio Grande Cookie Box Car** .. 60.00   75.00

☐ **No. 24057 Mounds Box Car** 30.00   35.00

☐ **No. 24065 N.Y.C. Box Car,** green, white,
and black 60.00   75.00

☐ **No. 24110 Gondola** 10.00   12.00

☐ **No. 24125 Gondola,** gray and red 10.00   12.00

☐ **No. 24125 Gondola,** gray and maroon 10.00   12.00

☐ **No. 24127 Gondola,** maroon 20.00   25.00

☐ **No. 24127 Gondola,** gray and maroon 15.00   20.00

☐ **No. 24422 G.N. Reefer,** green and white 30.00   35.00

☐ **No. 24533 Depressed Center Service Car**
.... 40.00   60.00

☐ **No. 24549 Generator Car,** with search-
light, yellow and brown 30.00   40.00

☐ **No. 24549 Searchlight Car** 12.00   15.00

☐ **No. 24549 Industrial Brown Hoist** 30.00   40.00

☐ **No. 24569 Crane** 35.00   50.00

☐ **No. 24575 Borden Container Car** 40.00   50.00

☐ **No. 24579 Flat Car** 5.00   10.00

☐ **No. 24603 Caboose** 15.00   20.00

☐ **No. 24631 Radio-Equipped Caboose,** yel-
low, silver, and red 30.00   40.00

	Price Range	
☐ **No. 24634 Bay Window Caboose**	75.00	100.00
☐ **No. 24636 Caboose**	10.00	12.00
☐ **No. 24638 Bay Window Caboose**	75.00	100.00
☐ **No. 25052 Bay Window Caboose,** with man	100.00	125.00
☐ **No. 42597 C.N.W. Lumber Car**	40.00	60.00

Wide Gauge

Train Sets

☐ **No. 1460, The Pioneer,** locomotive and tender #4664, sand car #4017, automobile car #4018, caboose #4021, train length 72″, oval track 3′9″ × 6′1″	900.00	1100.00
☐ **No. 1463, The Pathfinder,** locomotive #4635, sand car #4017, stock car #4020, caboose #4021, train length 5′3″, oval track 3′9″ × 6′1″	600.00	800.00
☐ **No. 1469, The Frontier Town,** locomotive #4654, two pullman cars both #4151, observation car #4152, train length 61″, oval track 3′9″ × 6′1″	900.00	1000.00
☐ **No. 1470, The New Lone Scout,** locomotive #4633, club car #4250, pullman car #4251, observation car #4252, train length 61″, oval track 3′9″ × 6′1″	800.00	1000.00
☐ **No. 1471, The Trail Blazer,** locomotive #4644, sand car #4017, caboose #4011, train length 48″, oval track 3′9″ × 4′11″	300.00	350.00
☐ **No. 1472, The New Eagle,** locomotive #4644, passenger car #4151, observation car #4152, train length 48″, oval track 3′9″ × 4′11″	550.00	650.00
☐ **No. 1473, The Statesman,** locomotive #4654, two pullman cars, both #4151, observation car #4152, train length 61″, oval track 3′9″ × 6′1″	650.00	750.00

Price Range

☐ **No. 1480, The New Lone Scout,** with remote control reversing locomotive, locomotive #4683, club car #4250, pullman car #4251, observation car #4252, train length 61″, oval track 3′9″ × 6′1″ 800.00   1000.00

☐ **No. 1481, The Trail Blazer,** with remote control reversing locomotive, locomotive #4684, sand car #4017, caboose #4011, train length 48″, oval track 3′9″ × 4′11″ 500.00   600.00

☐ **No. 1482, The New Eagle,** with remote control reversing locomotive, locomotive #4684, passenger car #4151, observation car #4152, train length 48″, oval track 3′9″ × 4′11″ 600.00   700.00

☐ **No. 1483, The Statesman,** with remote control reversing locomotive, locomotive #4684, two pullman cars, both #4152, observation car #4152, train length 61″, oval track 3′9″ × 6′1″ 800.00   900.00

☐ **No. 1484, The Hamiltonian,** locomotive #4678, club car #4340, pullman car #4341, observation car #4342, train length 61″, oval track 3′9″ × 7′3″ 900.00   1100.00

☐ **No. 1485, The Mountaineer,** locomotive #4637, machinery car #4022, sand car #4017, automobile car #4018, tank car #4010, caboose #4021, train length 94″, oval track 3′9″ × 7′3″ 1000.00   1200.00

☐ **No. 1487, The Pocahontas,** locomotive #4637, club car #4340, pullman car #4341, dining car #4343, observation car #4342, train length 79″, oval track 4′11″ × 7′3″
.... 1100.00   1300.00

☐ **No. 1489, The President's Special,** locomotive #4689, club car #4390, dining car #4393, pullman car #4391, observation car #4392, train length 100″, oval track 4′11″ × 9′7″ .... 2000.00 plus

Price Range

☐ **No. 1490, The Pioneer,** with remote control reversing locomotive, locomotive #4694, sand car #4017, automobile car #4018, caboose #4021, train length 71″, oval track 3′9″ × 6′1″ 1200.00   1400.00

☐ **No. 1492, The Iron Monarch,** locomotive and tender #4694, club car #4340, pullman car #4341, observation car #4342, train length 72″, oval track 3′9″ × 7′3″ 1200.00   1400.00

☐ **No. 1493, The Pathfinder,** with remote control reversing locomotive, locomotive #4685, sand car #4017, stock car #4020, caboose #4021, train length 5′3″, oval track 3′9″ × 6′1″ 800.00   900.00

Locomotives

☐ **No. 4633, St. Paul,** manual control reverse, 13½″ 150.00   175.00

☐ **No. 4637, Shasta,** remote reverse, 15″ 140.00   160.00

☐ **No. 4644, New Haven,** manual control reverse, 12½″ 125.00   150.00

☐ **No. 4654, Daniel Webster,** manual reverse, 12¼″ 135.00   150.00

☐ **No. 4664, Steam Type,** with tender, manual control reverse, 25″ 150.00   175.00

☐ **No. 4678, Daniel Boone,** remote reverse, 15″ 150.00   175.00

☐ **No. 4683, St. Paul,** remote control reverse, 13½″ 150.00   175.00

☐ **No. 4684, Daniel Webster,** remote reverse, 12¼″ 175.00   200.00

Price Range

☐ **No. 4686, The Ace,** remote reverse, 18½″
.... 150.00   175.00

☐ **No. 4689, New York Central,** deluxe model, 12 wheels, ringing bell, light blue, 18½″ 175.00   200.00

IVES
0 Gauge

Electrical Train Sets

☐ **No. 500 Locomotive #3250,** baggage car #550, chair car #51, round setup, track length 96″ 550.00   600.00

☐ **No. 501 Steel Locomotive #3251,** with headlight, baggage car #550, chair car #551, parlor car #552, oval setup, track length 126″ 450.00   500.00

☐ **No. 502 Steel Locomotive #3252,** with headlight and reverse, baggage car #70, two parlor cars #72, oval setup, track length 145″ 450.00   500.00

☐ **No. 503 Steel Locomotive #3253,** with headlight and reverse, buffet car #130, parlor car #129, oval setup, track length 130″
.... 1000.00   1100.00

☐ **No. 504 Steel Locomotive #3253,** with headlight, reverse, buffet car #130, two parlor cars #129, oval setup, track length 160″
.... 1200.00   1300.00

☐ **No. 505 Locomotive #3250,** baggage car #50, chair car #51, round setup, track length 96″ 500.00   600.00

☐ **No. 506 Locomotive #3250,** stock car #53, caboose #56, round setup, track length 76″
.... 600.00   650.00

☐ **No. 510 Locomotive #3251,** gravel car #563, merchandise car #561, caboose #567, oval setup, track length 125″ 700.00   750.00

Price Range

☐ **No. 511 Locomotive #3252,** tank car #66, merchandise car #61, caboose #67, oval setup, track length 126″ 750.00   800.00

☐ **No. 515 Locomotive #3253,** merchandise car #125, caboose #67, oval setup, track length 126″ 1000.00   1100.00

☐ **No. 516 Locomotive #3253,** stock car #127, gravel car #128, caboose #67, oval setup, track length 84″ 1400.00   1500.00

☐ **No. 570, The Yankee Clipper,** locomotive #3258, electric type, with electric headlight, chair car #552 with windows, observation car #558, round setup, train length 22½″, track length 96″ 1400.00   1500.00

☐ **No. 571, The County Freight,** locomotive #3258, box car #564, gravel car #563, caboose #562, round setup, train length 30½″, track length 96″ 1800.00   2000.00

☐ **No. 572, The Blue Vagabond,** locomotive #1125 with electric headlight, tender #17, baggage car #550, chair car #552, oval setup, train length 35″, track length 160″ 1200.00   1400.00

☐ **No. 572F, The Traders Fast Freight,** steam-type locomotive #1125, merchandise car #564, gondola car #563, caboose #562, oval setup, train length 35″, track length 160″ .... 2000.00 plus

☐ **No. 573, The Knickerbocker,** locomotive #3261 with hand reverse and headlight, two parlor cars #133, observation car #134, oval setup, train length 36¼″, track length 132″ 1100.00   1200.00

☐ **No. 574F, The Patriot,** electric-type locomotive #3255 with double headlights, two parlor cars #135, observation car #136, oval setup, train length 37½″, track length 140″ 1100.00   1200.00

☐ **No. 574R,** as above with automatic reverse 1400.00   1500.00

Price Range

☐ **No. 575, Midwest Fast Freight,** Atlantic-
type locomotive #25 with lens-equipped
headlight, die-cast ender #25, merchandise
car #125, gravel car #128, caboose #121, all
cars are equipped with automatic couplers
and journal boxes; eight wheels and two
trucks, oval setup, train length 47″, track
length 160″ 1600.00   1800.00

☐ **No. 575R,** as above with automatic reverse
.... 1600.00   1800.00

☐ **No. 576, The Commodore Vanderbilt,**
steam-type electric locomotive #1122, tender
#25, two parlor cars #135, observation car
#136 with lights, oval setup, train length
44″, track length 210″ 1800.00   2000.00

☐ **No. 577, The Columbian,** St. Paul electric
locomotive #3257; double headlights, hand
reverse, two pullman cars #141, observation
car #142, oval setup, train length 45″, track
length 225″ .... 2000.00 plus

☐ **No. 577R,** as above; automatic reverse ..... 2000.00 plus

☐ **No. 579, The Black Diamond,** locomotive
#1122 with hand reverse, tender #25, two
pullman cars #141, observation car #142,
oval setup, train length 56″, track length
225″ .... 2000.00 plus

☐ **No. 579R,** as above with automatic reverse
.... 2000.00 plus

☐ **No. 590, Universal Fast Freight,** locomotive #1122 with lens-equipped headlight,
tender #25, refrigerator car #124, lumber car
#123, merchandise car #125, gravel car
#128, stock car #127, tank car #122, ca-
boose #121, oval setup, train length 90″,
track length 250″ .... 2000.00 plus

☐ **No. 590R,** as above with automatic re-
verse .... 2000.00 plus

☐ **No. 610 Locomotive #3251,** baggage car #550, parlor car #552, with station and tunnel, round setup, track length 76″ .... 2000.00 plus

☐ **No. 1102 Locomotive #1100,** tender #11, chair car #551, round setup, track length 96″ 1000.00   1100.00

☐ **No. 1105 Iron Locomotive #1116,** with headlight, tender #11, baggage car #550, parlor car #552, oval setup, track length 125″ 600.00   700.00

☐ **No. 1105X Iron Locomotive #3216,** with headlight, baggage car #550, parlor car #552, oval setup, track length 130″ 700.00   800.00

☐ **No. 1112 Iron Locomotive #1116,** with headlight, tender #11, baggage car #550, chair car #551, parlor car #552, oval setup, track length 176″ 700.00   800.00

☐ **No. 1112X Iron Locomotive #3216,** with headlight, baggage car #550, chair car #551, parlor car #552, oval setup, track length 220″ 1000.00   1100.00

☐ **No. 1113 Iron Locomotive #1118,** with headlight and reverse, tender #17, chair car #61, oval setup, track length 120″ 1100.00   1200.00

☐ **No. 1114 Iron Locomotive #1118,** with headlight and reverse, tender #17, baggage car #60, chair car #61, oval setup, track length 146″ 900.00   1000.00

☐ **No. 1114X Iron Locomotive #3218,** with headlight and reverse, baggage car #60, chair car #61, oval setup, track length 136″ 900.00   1000.00

☐ **No. 1115X Iron Locomotive #3218,** with headlight and reverse, baggage car #60, parlor car #62, chair car #61, oval setup, track length 176″ 1000.00   1100.00

Price Range

☐ **No. 1126 Iron Locomotive #1125,** with headlight and reverse, tender #25, combination car #130, oval setup, track length 176″ 1100.00   1200.00

☐ **No. 1127 Iron Locomotive #1125,** with headlight and reverse, tender #25, combination car #130, parlor car #129, oval setup, track length 154″ 1100.00   1200.00

☐ **No. 1127X Iron Locomotive #3238,** with headlight and reverse, combination car #130, parlor car #129, oval setup, track length 154″ 800.00   900.00

☐ **No. 1128 Iron Locomotive #1125,** with headlight and reverse, tender #25, combination car #130, two parlor cars #129, oval setup, track length 210″ 1000.00   1100.00

☐ **No. 1128X Iron Locomotive 3238,** with headlight and reverse, combination car #130, two parlor cars #129, oval setup, track length 210″ 900.00   1000.00

☐ **No. 1130X Iron Locomotive #3239,** with headlight and reverse, combination car #71, drawing room car #72, oval setup, track length 210″ 1200.00   1300.00

☐ **No. 1131X Iron Locomotive #3239,** with headlight and reverse, combination car #71, drawing room car #72, observation car #73, oval setup, track length 210″ 1600.00   1800.00

☐ **No. 1150 Iron Locomotive #1129,** with headlight and reverse, tender #40, merchandise car #7345, caboose #7546, oval setup, track length 184″ 900.00   1000.00

☐ **No. 1151 Iron Locomotive #1129,** with headlight and reverse, tender #40, tank car #7849, coal car #7648, caboose #7546, oval setup, track length 184″ 950.00   1050.00

Price Range

☐ **No. 1152 Iron Locomotive #1129,** with headlight and reverse, tender #40, coal car #7648, stock car #7446, merchandise car #7345, caboose #7546, oval setup, track length 256″ 1500.00   1700.00

Electrical Locomotives

☐ **No. 1100 Locomotive,** length 6½″ 175.00   200.00

☐ **No. 1100-1 Locomotive,** length 7″ 200.00   210.00

☐ **No. 1116 Locomotive,** with headlight, length 7″ 200.00   210.00

☐ **No. 1117 Locomotive,** length 7½″ 300.00   320.00

☐ **No. 1118 Locomotive,** steam type, with headlight and reverse, length 7¾″ 100.00   110.00

☐ **No. 1125 Locomotive,** steam type, with electric headlight, coal tender #17, overall length 12″ 200.00   220.00

☐ **No. 1125 Locomotive,** with reverse, headlight with resistance, length 8¾″ 250.00   270.00

☐ **No. 1129 Locomotive,** with headlight and reverse, length 13½″ 1600.00   1800.00

☐ **No. 3200 Locomotive,** New York Central type, length 6¾″ 160.00   170.00

☐ **No. 3216 Locomotive,** with headlight, length 8″ 200.00   210.00

☐ **No. 3217 Locomotive,** New York Central type, length 7¾″ 300.00   350.00

☐ **No. 3218 Locomotive,** New York Central type, reverse, headlight with resistance, length 7¾″ 200.00   225.00

☐ **No. 3218 Locomotive,** with headlight and reverse, length 8″ 250.00   300.00

☐ **No. 3238 Locomotive,** New York Central type, eight wheels, reverse, headlight with resistance, length 9¼″ 225.00   250.00

☐ **No. 3250 Locomotive,** plain finish, length 8″ 150.00   175.00

Price Range

☐ **No. 3251 Locomotive,** with headlight, nickel trimmed, length 8 " 150.00   175.00

☐ **No. 3252 Locomotive,** with headlight and reverse, nickel trimmed, length 8 " 140.00   160.00

☐ **No. 3253 Locomotive,** with headlight and reverse, nickel trimmed, length 9 " 150.00   200.00

☐ **No. 3255 Locomotive,** New York Central type, with hand reverse, brass rails, journal boxes and name, length 10 " 300.00   350.00

☐ **No. 3255R,** same as #3255, with automatic reverse instead of hand reverse 350.00   400.00

☐ **No. 3257 Locomotive,** Chicago, Milwaukee, and St. Paul type, brass trimmed, with double headlights, whistle and pantograph, length 10¼ " 350.00   400.00

☐ **No. 3258 Locomotive,** New York, New Haven, and Hartford type, with headlight and whistle, length 7½ " 500.00   550.00

☐ **No. 3261 Locomotive,** New York, New Haven, and Hartford type, with electric headlight, pantograph and hand reverse, length 8¾ " 350.00   400.00

Mechanical Train Sets

☐ **No. 0 Passenger Train,** locomotive #2, tender #1, passenger car #051, track length 96 " 500.00   550.00

☐ **No. 1 Passenger Train,** locomotive #5, tender #1, passenger car #52, track length 96 " 500.00   550.00

☐ **No. 2 Passenger Train,** locomotive #5, tender #1, baggage car #50, passenger car #51, track length 110 " 400.00   450.00

☐ **No. 3 Passenger Train,** locomotive #6, tender #1, baggage car #50, passenger car #51, parlor car #52, track length 126 " 500.00   550.00

☐ **No. 4 Passenger Train,** locomotive #11, tender #11, baggage car #551, passenger car #551, length 110" 400.00   450.00

☐ **No. 5 Freight Train,** locomotive #5, tender #1, lumber car #57, caboose #55, track length 100" 400.00   450.00

☐ **No. 6 Freight Train,** locomotive #6, tender #1, freight car #53, stock car #55, caboose #56, track length 126" 500.00   550.00

☐ **No. 7 Freight Train,** locomotive #11, tender #11, gravel car #553, caboose #557, track length 110" 400.00   450.00

☐ **No. 9 Freight Train,** locomotive #17, tender #11, two gravel cars #63, caboose #67, track length 126" 425.00   450.00

☐ **No. 10 Freight Train,** locomotive #17, tender #11, refrigerator car #68, stock car #65, merchandise car #64, caboose #67, track length 156" 500.00   550.00

☐ **No. 11 Passenger Train,** locomotive #17, tender #11, baggage car #60, passenger car #61, track length 124" 400.00   450.00

☐ **No. 12 Passenger Train,** locomotive #17, tender #11, baggage car #60, passenger car #61, parlor car #62, track length 126" 425.00   475.00

☐ **No. 13 Passenger Train,** locomotive #17, tender #11, baggage car #60, passenger car #61, parlor car #62, track length 210" 450.00   475.00

☐ **No. 14 Passenger Train,** locomotive #17, tender #11, baggage car #60, passenger car #61, parlor car #62, track length 225" 600.00   650.00

☐ **No. 15 Passenger Train,** locomotive #20, tender #25, baggage car #131, parlor car #129, buffet car #130, track length 156" ..   650.00   700.00

☐ **No. 16 Passenger Train,** locomotive #25, tender #25, baggage car #131, parlor car #129, buffet car #130, track length 156" ..   700.00   750.00

Price Range

☐ **No. 17 Iron Locomotive #25,** with brake and reverse, tender #25, combination car #130, parlor car #129, track length 156″ ..   700.00   750.00

☐ **No. 18 Iron Locomotive #25,** with brake and reverse, tender #25, combination car #130, two parlor cars #129, track length 225″ 500.00   550.00

☐ **No. 19 Freight Train,** locomotive #20, tender #25, merchandise car #125, gravel car #128, caboose #67, track length 156″ 600.00   650.00

☐ **No. 19R Freight Train,** locomotive #25, tender, two gravel cars #128, caboose #67, track length 126″ 550.00   600.00

☐ **No. 20 Iron Locomotive #6,** tender #11, baggage car #50, chair car #51, track length 126″ 550.00   600.00

☐ **No. 20R Passenger Train,** locomotive #25, tender, combination car #130, track length 130″ 600.00   700.00

☐ **No. 21 Steel Locomotive #30,** baggage car #550, chair car #551, track length 110″ 700.00   800.00

☐ **No. 21R Passenger Train,** locomotive #25, tender, combination car #130, drawing room car #129, track length 162″ 700.00   800.00

☐ **No. 22 Electric-Type Locomotive #31,** with brake, full nickel trim, baggage car #70, two parlors cars #72, track length 104″ 600.00   700.00

☐ **No. 22R Passenger Train,** locomotive #25, tender, combination car #130, drawing room car #129, track length 176″ 600.00   700.00

☐ **No. 23 Locomotive #32,** with brake, combination #130, two parlors cars #129, track length 156″ 450.00   500.00

☐ **No. 23R Passenger Train,** locomotive #25, tender, baggage car #131, drawing room car #129, track length 184″ 500.00   550.00

	Price Range	
☐ **No. 24R Passenger Train,** locomotive #25, tender, baggage car #131, combination car #130, drawing room car #129, track length 380″	500.00	550.00
☐ **No. 30 Freight Train,** locomotive #25, tender #25, refrigerator car #124, lumber car #123, caboose #67, track length 165″	500.00	550.00
☐ **No. 30R Freight Train,** locomotive #25, tender, lumber car #123, merchandise car #125, caboose #67, track length 330″	600.00	650.00

Mechanical Locomotives

☐ **No. 1 Steam Type,** with brake, length 6½″	125.00	150.00
☐ **No. 2 Locomotive**	160.00	170.00
☐ **No. 5 Locomotive**	300.00	325.00
☐ **No. 6 Steam Type,** with brake, length 6½″	180.00	190.00
☐ **No. 17 Steam Type,** with brake, length 7″	125.00	135.00
☐ **No. 17 Locomotive,** with brake, length 7½″	135.00	145.00
☐ **No. 19 Steam Type,** with brake, length 7⅝″	100.00	110.00
☐ **No. 20 Speed-Governed,** reverse, length 9″	120.00	130.00
☐ **No. 25 Speed-Governed,** reverse, length 9″	300.00	320.00
☐ **No. 30 Electric Type,** with brake, length 8″	325.00	350.00
☐ **No. 31 Electric Type,** with brake, nickel trimmed, length 8″	100.00	110.00

Rolling Stock

☐ **No. 50 Baggage Car,** with doors, separate roof, body, platform, couplers, four wheels, length 5⅛″	75.00	85.00

	Price Range	

☐ **No. 51 Chair Car,** separate roof, body, platform, couplers, four wheels, length 5⅛" 100.00 110.00

☐ **No. 52 Parlor Car,** separate roof, body, platform, couplers, four wheels, length 5⅛" 85.00 100.00

☐ **No. 53 Merchandise Car,** separate roof, body, platform, couplers, four wheels, length 5⅛" 50.00 60.00

☐ **No. 54 Gravel Car,** open, roomy, complete with separate platform, couplers, four wheels, length 5⅛" 30.00 40.00

☐ **No. 55 Stock Car,** a realistic slatted car, separate roof, sides, platform, couplers, four wheels, length 5⅛" 30.00 35.00

☐ **No. 56 Caboose Car,** with cupola, length 5" 40.00 45.00

☐ **No. 57 Lumber Car,** with separate lumber, chains, stakes, platform, couplers, four wheels, length 5⅛" 35.00 45.00

☐ **No. 60 Baggage Car,** length 6¾" 40.00 50.00

☐ **No. 61 Passenger Car,** length 6¾" 40.00 50.00

☐ **No. 63 Gravel Car,** with eight wheels, two trucks, automatic couplers, journal boxes, length 6¼" 40.00 50.00

☐ **No. 64 Merchandise Car,** says "New York, New Haven and Hartford Railroad," with sliding doors, automatic couplers to double trucks of eight wheels, journal boxes, length 6½" 80.00 90.00

☐ **No. 64,** says "Santa Fe 64396" 90.00 100.00

☐ **No. 64,** says "Atlantic Coast Line 67389" .. 90.00 100.00

☐ **No. 64,** says "Rock Island 151370" 90.00 100.00

☐ **No. 64,** says "Erie 85829" 90.00 100.00

☐ **No. 64,** says "Union Line" 100.00 110.00

	Price Range	
☐ **No. 64,** says "Illinois Central Railroad 641506"	100.00	110.00
☐ **No. 64,** says "L.V. 64158"	100.00	110.00
☐ **No. 64,** says "New York Central Lines" ..	115.00	120.00
☐ **No. 64,** says "Baltimore & Ohio RR 64385"	115.00	120.00
☐ **No. 64,** says "Northern Pacific 64348"	100.00	110.00
☐ **No. 64,** says "Refrigerator Burlington Route"	120.00	130.00
☐ **No. 64,** says "Pennsylvania Lines 64160"	100.00	110.00
☐ **No. 65 Stock Car,** with sliding doors, two trucks, eight wheels, journal boxes, automatic couplers, length 6½"	140.00	150.00
☐ **No. 66 Tank Car,** eight wheels, two trucks, journal boxes, length 6½"	200.00	210.00
☐ **No. 67 Caboose,** length 6½"	50.00	60.00
☐ **No. 68 Observation Car,** large brass observation platform, separate roof, eight wheels, two trucks, journal boxes, automatic couplers, length 6½"	90.00	100.00
☐ **No. 69 Lumber Car,** complete with lumber, six stakes, three guy chains, two trucks, journal boxes, automatic couplers, length 6½"	40.00	50.00
☐ **No. 70 Caboose Car,** with brass-trimmed platform, number plates, eight wheels, two trucks, automatic couplers, journal boxes, length 6½"	90.00	100.00
☐ **No. 71 Combination Car,** imitation glass windows, length 12"	90.00	100.00
☐ **No. 72 Drawing Room Car,** imitation glass windows, length 12"	100.00	110.00
☐ **No. 73 Refrigerator Car,** length 11½"	105.00	115.00
☐ **No. 74 Stock Car,** length 11½"	100.00	110.00
☐ **No. 75 Caboose,** length 11½"	115.00	125.00

		Price Range

☐ **No. 76 Coal Car,** length 11¼″ 120.00 130.00

☐ **No. 77 Lumber Car,** length 11½″ 130.00 140.00

☐ **No. 121 Steel Caboose,** with a cupola, heavy brass-trimmed platforms, automatic couplers, brass name and number plates, two trucks, eight wheels, length 9″ 135.00 145.00

☐ **No. 122 Tank Car,** with name in brass, number plates, ladder, handrail; two trucks, eight wheels; automatic couplers; length 9″ 110.00 120.00

☐ **No. 123 Lumber Car,** with eight sticks of lumber, removable, upright rods and four brass chains, two trucks, eight wheels, length 9″ 90.00 100.00

☐ **No. 124 Refrigerator Car,** M.D.T. design, roomy, two trucks, eight wheels, equipped with sliding doors, automatic couplers and journal boxes, length 9″ 90.00 100.00

☐ **No. 125 Merchandise Car,** says "Salt Lake Route 12584," with sliding doors, two trucks, eight wheels, journal boxes, various designs and heralds, length 9″ 80.00 90.00

☐ **No. 125,** says "Frisco Lines 12582" 100.00 110.00

☐ **No. 125,** says "Union Pacific System 12578" 80.00 90.00

☐ **No. 125,** says "Chicago Corn Belt Route Great Western 12585" 80.00 90.00

☐ **No. 125,** says "Union Line" 90.00 100.00

☐ **No. 125,** says "Wabash 12580" 95.00 105.00

☐ **No. 125,** says "MK and T Southwest" 110.00 120.00

☐ **No. 125,** says "Cotton Belt Route" 80.00 90.00

☐ **No. 126 Caboose,** length 8″ 55.00 65.00

☐ **No. 127 Stock Car,** with open slats, sliding doors, cars finished in brilliant orange, two trucks, eight wheels, length 9″ 50.00 60.00

Price Range

☐ **No. 128 Gravel Car,** open car, gray with New York Central markings and herald, two trucks, eight wheels, length 9″ 50.00   60.00

☐ **No. 129 Pullman Car,** electrically lighted, two trucks, brass journal boxes, lithographed sides, eight wheels, length 9″ 50.00   60.00

☐ **No. 130 Club Car,** electrically lighted, two trucks, brass journal boxes, lithographed sides, eight wheels, length 9″ 80.00   90.00

☐ **No. 131 Baggage Car,** lithographed baggage car, four sliding doors, two on each side, automatic couplers, journal boxes, two trucks, eight wheels, length 9″ 80.00   90.00

☐ **No. 132 Observation Car,** electrically lighted, rear platform, brass journal boxes, lithographed sides, two trucks, eight wheels, length 9″ 100.00   110.00

☐ **No. 133 Parlor Car,** heavy steel interlocking grip construction, enamel finish, eight wheels, two trucks, brass name and window plates, length 8″ 95.00   100.00

☐ **No. 141 Parlor Car,** with lights, eight brass name and number plates, window trim and window panes, outside vestibules, brass steps, length 11″ 180.00   200.00

☐ **No. 142 Observation Car,** with two lights, eight brass name and number plates, window trim and window panes, outside vestibules, brass steps, brass observation platform 200.00   210.00

☐ **No. 181 Buffet Car,** with automatic couplers, eight wheels, swivel trucks, windows, length 14¾″ 120.00   130.00

☐ **No. 550 Baggage Car,** with sliding doors, separate roof, sides, platform, couplers, four wheels, length 6½″ 50.00   60.00

Price Range

☐ **No. 551 Chair Car,** assorted colors, separate sides, roof, platform, couplers, four wheels, length 6½ " 50.00   60.00

☐ **No. 552 Caboose Car,** deluxe, brass plates and trim, cupola, separate windows, couplers, four wheels, length 6½ " 50.00   60.00

☐ **No. 553 Gravel Car,** strong open car with turned edges, separate platform, separate couplers, four wheels, length 6½ " 45.00   55.00

☐ **No. 554 Merchandise Car,** a true in detail box car with separate roof, sides, sliding doors, couplers, platform, four wheels, length 6½ " 50.00   60.00

☐ **No. 555 Stock Car,** with slats, sliding doors, separate top, platform, couplers, four wheels, length 6½ " 45.00   55.00

☐ **No. 556 Tank Car,** with brass, separate platforms, couplers, four wheels, length 6½ " 50.00   60.00

☐ **No. 557 Caboose Car,** with couplers, sliding doors, separate platform, cupola, four wheels, length 6½ " 60.00   70.00

☐ **No. 558 Observation Car,** with brass-trimmed observation platform, separate roof, sides, platform, couplers, four wheels, length 6½ " 70.00   80.00

☐ **No. 559 Lumber Car,** eight sticks of lumber, two guy wires, separate platform and couplers, four wheels, length 6½ " 55.00   65.00

☐ **No. 563 Gravel Car,** length 6½ " 45.00   50.00

☐ **No. 564 Merchandise Car,** length 6½ " ...   35.00   45.00

☐ **No. 565 Stock Car,** length 6½ " 40.00   50.00

☐ **No. 566 Tank Car,** length 6 " 25.00   35.00

☐ **No. 567 Caboose,** length 6½ " 35.00   40.00

1 Gauge

Mechanical Train Sets

Price Range

☐ **No. 30, The Mohican,** passenger train, locomotive #00, coal tender #9, two cars #51, train length 23½", track length 82" ....   2000.00 plus

☐ **No. 31, The Seneca,** locomotive #00, tender #11, baggage car #50, two passenger cars #51, oval setup, train length 29¼", track length 105" ....   2000.00 plus

☐ **No. 32, The Pequot,** locomotive #10, tender #11, two cars #551, round setup, train length 26", track length 96" ....   2000.00 plus

☐ **No. 33, The Apache,** locomotive #176, tender #12, parlor car #551, observation car #558, oval setup, train length 26¼", track length 105" ....   2000.00 plus

☐ **No. 34, The Sioux,** locomotive #66, tender with coal #12, merchandise car #53, gravel car #54, caboose #56, oval setup, train length 29½", track length 125" ....   2000.00 plus

☐ **No. 35, The Iroquois,** locomotive #176, baggage car with doors #550, chair car #551, observation car with brass-trimmed observation platform #558, oval setup, train length 33¾", track length 136" ....   2000.00 plus

☐ **No. 42 Passenger Train,** locomotive #40, tender #40, combination car #71, track length 140" ....   2000.00 plus

☐ **No. 43 Passenger Train,** locomotive #40, tender #40, combination car #71, drawing room car #72, track length 210" ....   2000.00 plus

☐ **No. 44 Passenger Train,** locomotive #40, tender #40, baggage car #70, combination car #71, drawing car #72, track length 210" ....   2000.00 plus

☐ **No. 45 Freight Train,** locomotive #41, tender #40, lumber car #77, caboose #75, track length 144" ....   2000.00 plus

Price Range

☐ **No. 46 Freight Train,** locomotive #41, tender #40, two gravel cars #76, caboose #75, track length 126″ 1600.00   1800.00

☐ **No. 47 Freight Train,** locomotive #41, tender #40, stock car #74, refrigerator car #73, lumber car #77, caboose #75, track length 124″ .... 2000.00 plus

Standard Gauge

Train Sets

☐ **No. 612 Locomotive #3253,** buffet car #130, two parlor cars #129, with station, tunnel, signal telegraph poles, oval setup, track length 160″ .... 2000.00 plus

☐ **No. 700 Locomotive #3241,** four wheels, headlight and reverse, buffet car #184, observation car #186, oval setup, train length 52″, track length 132″ .... 2000.00 plus

☐ **No. 701 Locomotive #3244,** one wheel, headlight and reverse, buffet car #181, parlor car #185, observation car #186, oval setup, train length 52″, track length 156″ 950.00   1050.00

☐ **No. 702 Locomotive #3242,** four wheels, two headlights and reverse, buffet car #187, observation car #189, oval setup, train length 52″, track length 180″ 900.00   1000.00

☐ **No. 704 Locomotive #3244,** 12 wheels, two headlights and reverse, buffet car #187-3, observation car #187-3, all cars lighted, oval setup, train length 67″, track length 310″ 900.00   1000.00

☐ **No. 711 Locomotive #3241,** four wheels, headlight and reverse, flat car #196, caboose #195, round setup, track length 110″ 1000.00   1200.00

Price Range

☐ **No. 712 Locomotive #3241,** four wheels, headlight and reverse, flat car #196, coke car #191, merchandise car #192, caboose #195, oval setup, track length 125 " 850.00   900.00

☐ **No. 713 Locomotive #3242,** four wheels, two headlights and reverse, two flat cars #196, coke car #191, merchandise car #192, stock car #193, caboose #195, oval setup, track length 210 " 1100.00   1200.00

☐ **No. 1071, The Tiger,** #3236 New York, New Haven, and Hartford electric-type locomotive with steel cab, hand reverse, two headlights, whistle, and pantograph, parlor car #185, observation car #186, oval setup, train length 40 ", track length 196 " .... 2000.00 plus

☐ **No. 1072, The Local Freight,** #3236 New York, New Haven, and Hartford type, with double headlights and hand reverse, gondola car #198, caboose #195, oval setup, train length 40¾ ", track length 156 " 1600.00   1700.00

☐ **No. 1072R,** same as above with automatic reverse .... 2000.00 plus

☐ **No. 1073, The Skyliner,** New York City electric-type locomotive #3242, with hand reverse, pantograph and brass trim, combination baggage club car #184, pullman car #185, observation car #186, oval setup, train length 56 ", track length 210 " .... 2000.00 plus

☐ **No. 1073R,** same as above with automatic reverse .... 2000.00 plus

☐ **No. 1075, The Merchants Fast Freight,** locomotive #1134, with lens-equipped headlight, hand reverse, pilot truck, rear trailer, tender #40, merchandise car #192, gondola car #198, caboose #195, oval setup, train length 66¼ ", track length 210 " .... 2000.00 plus

☐ **No. 1075R,** same as above, with automatic reverse .... 2000.00 plus

Price Range

☐ **No. 1076, The Westerner,** steam-type locomotive #1134, with lens-equipped headlight, tender #40, club car with baggage compartment #184, parlor car #185, observation car #186, with brass-trimmed lighted platform, oval setup, train length 66", track length 200" .... 2000.00 plus

☐ **No. 1076R,** same as above with automatic reverse .... 2000.00 plus

☐ **No. 1077, The Chief,** steam-type locomotive #1134, tender #40, club car #247, chair car #248, oval setup, train length 81", track length 200" .... 2000.00 plus

☐ **No. 1091, The Domestic Freight,** steam-type locomotive #1134, gravel car #198, tank car #190, merchandise car #192, lumber car #197, caboose #195, oval setup, train length 97", track length 200" .... 2000.00 plus

☐ **No. 1091R,** same as above with automatic reverse .... 2000.00 plus

Locomotives

☐ **No. 1132 Steam-Type Locomotive,** four wheels, headlight and reverse, nickel trimmed, length 12½" 425.00   450.00

☐ **No. 1134 Steam-Type Locomotive,** pilot truck, four driving wheels, two-wheel trailer, lens-equipped headlight, length 14¾" 1500.00   1700.00

☐ **No. 1134R,** same as above with automatic reverse 1400.00   1600.00

☐ **No. 3236 New York, New Haven, and Hartford Electric Locomotive,** with pantograph, double headlights, brass handrails, flag holders, brass name, number plates and window frames, length 11¾" 700.00   800.00

Steam type #1134, $1000–$1500.

	Price Range	
☐ **No. 3236R,** same as above with automatic reverse	800.00	900.00
☐ **No. 3237 Chicago, Milwaukee, and St. Paul Type,** with double headlights and pantograph, eight brass hatches, brass name and number plates and trim, length 10¼″	800.00	900.00
☐ **No. 3237R,** same as above with automatic reverse	850.00	900.00
☐ **No. 3241 New York Central Type,** with reverse, headlight, and partial nickel trim, length 13¼″	800.00	850.00
☐ **No. 3242 New York Central Type,** two pantographs, double headlights, brass doors, windows, rails, flag holders and name and number plates, length 13¼″	800.00	850.00
☐ **No. 3242R,** same as above with automatic reverse	850.00	900.00
☐ **No. 3243 Locomotive,** with two headlights and reverse, full nickel trim, length 16″ ...	800.00	900.00
☐ **No. 3245 Chicago, Milwaukee and St. Paul Type,** with two full four-wheel pilot trucks, four driving wheels with brass springs, tanks, journal boxes, with double headlights, pantographs, hand reverse, length 18″		2000.00 plus
☐ **No. 3245R,** same as above with automatic reverse		2000.00 plus

Accessories

	Price Range	

☐ **No. 80 Scenery,** six sections displaying pastoral scene, sections 20" × 15" 250.00   260.00

☐ **No. 86 Telegraph Poles,** 12 poles with connection wire 85.00   100.00

☐ **No. 87 American Flag,** on pole, square base, flag can be raised or lowered 100.00   125.00

☐ **No. 89 Water Tank,** spill spout, steel construction and cross beams, height 11" 225.00   250.00

☐ **No. 90 Bridge,** brick work design, two sections, 0 gauge, mechanical train, length 31"
.... 165.00   175.00

☐ **No. 90-3 Bridge,** brick work, two sections, 1 gauge, electric, length 21" 215.00   230.00

☐ **No. 91 Bridge,** brick work, double arch, three sections, 0 gauge, mechanical, length 31" 160.00   175.00

☐ **No. 91-2 Bridge,** brick work, double arch, three sections, 0 gauge, electrical, length 31" 215.00   225.00

☐ **No. 92 Bridge,** brick work, triple arches, four sections, 0 gauge, for mechanical, length 42" 275.00   300.00

☐ **No. 92-3 Bridge,** brick work, triple arches, four sections, 0 gauge, for electrical, length 42" 275.00   300.00

☐ **No. 97 Swing Drawbridge,** opens side-to-side, three sections, length 31" 350.00   400.00

☐ **No. 98 Single Trestle Bridge,** three sections, 0 gauge, length 31" 200.00   225.00

☐ **No. 98-1 Single Trestle Bridge,** three sections, 1 gauge, mechanical, length 42" 200.00   210.00

☐ **No. 98-3 Single Trestle Bridge,** three sections, 0 gauge, electric, length 31" 200.00   210.00

☐ **No. 98-1-3 Single Trestle Bridge,** three sections, 1 gauge, electric, length 31" 200.00   210.00

	Price Range	
☐ **No. 99 Double Trestle Bridge,** four sections, 0 gauge, mechanical, length 41″	200.00	210.00
☐ **No. 99-1 Double Trestle Bridge,** four sections, 1 gauge, mechanical, length 51″	275.00	300.00
☐ **No. 99-3 Double Trestle Bridge,** four sections, electric, length 41″	275.00	300.00
☐ **No. 99-1-3 Double Trestle Bridge,** four sections, electric, length 56″	275.00	300.00
☐ **No. 100 Bridge,** arch base, two sections, 0 gauge, length 21″	275.00	300.00
☐ **No. 100-2 Bridge,** arch base, two sections, 1 gauge, length 28″	250.00	275.00
☐ **No. 101 Bridge,** three sections, aquaduct base, 0 gauge, length 31″	225.00	250.00
☐ **No. 101-1 Bridge,** three sections, aquaduct base, 1 gauge, length 42″	250.00	275.00
☐ **No. 102 Bridge,** roller lift, drops as train approaches, length 31″	250.00	275.00
☐ **No. 103 Tunnel,** mountain style, length 6½″	325.00	350.00
☐ **No. 105 Tunnel,** mountain style, length 11″	120.00	130.00
☐ **No. 106 Tunnel,** mountain formation, length 14″	120.00	130.00
☐ **No. 106E Tunnel,** mountain style, length 16″	150.00	160.00
☐ **No. 107 Signal,** single arm, with track check, 0 gauge	90.00	100.00
☐ **No. 107D Signal,** two arms, pedestal base ..	100.00	110.00
☐ **No. 107S Signal,** one arm, pedestal base ..	100.00	110.00
☐ **No. 108 Signal,** single arm, with track check, 1 gauge	95.00	105.00
☐ **No. 109 Semaphore,** double arm, height 11½″	160.00	175.00
☐ **No. 110 Bumper,** 0 gauge	30.00	35.00

Price Range

☐ **No. 110-1 Bumper,** 1 gauge	30.00	35.00
☐ **No. 111 Elevating Post,** pedestal base, rectangular top	90.00	100.00
☐ **No. 112 Danger Sign,** for railroad crossing gates	50.00	60.00
☐ **No. 113 Passenger Station,** sidewalk base, windows and doors 13½″ × 9¾″	250.00	275.00
☐ **No. 114 Station,** doors and windows, passenger, 13½″ × 6″	250.00	275.00
☐ **No. 115 Station,** one door, freight dock, 10″ × 5½″	160.00	175.00
☐ **No. 116 Passenger Station,** one side of the track, windows and doors, 18½″ × 8″	200.00	225.00
☐ **No. 117 Covered Platform,** eight posts, two facing benches, 19″ × 7½″	200.00	225.00
☐ **No. 118 Covered Platform,** one post	125.00	150.00
☐ **No. 119 Station,** two posts on sidewalk with roof, 11½″ × 3½″	160.00	175.00
☐ **No. 120 Covered Platform,** four posts, trellis fence, 18½″ × 4″	160.00	170.00
☐ **No. 121 Glass Dome,** canopy supported by six posts, brick-work sidewalk, 18½″ × 9½″	240.00	260.00
☐ **No. 122 Glass Dome Station,** one building, glass dome supported on other side by four posts, 18½″ × 16½″	450.00	500.00
☐ **No. 123 Glass Dome Station,** two buildings connected over the track by glass canopy, 18½″ × 22¼″	1200.00	1400.00
☐ **No. 140 Crossing Gates,** automatic, with guard house, 0 gauge, length 20½″	800.00	900.00
☐ **No. 140-3 Crossing Gates,** with guard house and sign, for 2¼″ track	800.00	900.00
☐ **No. 145 Turntable,** handturned, diameter 10¼″	500.00	550.00
☐ **No. 215 Crossing Gate,** no guard house ..	500.00	550.00

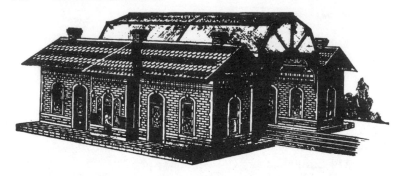

Glass dome station, $1000–$1200.

	Price Range	
☐ **No. 220 Freight Station,** lithographed sides, length 9″	250.00	300.00
☐ **No. 221 Passenger Station,** lithographed and painted, length 9″	400.00	450.00
☐ **No. 225 Way Station,** lighted, arched windows, length 8½″	400.00	450.00
☐ **No. 226 Suburban Station,** lighted, double chimney, length 8½″	500.00	550.00
☐ **No. 226 Suburban Station,** lighted, double chimney, length 10¼″	450.00	500.00
☐ **No. 228 Station,** four benches facing, six posts supporting roof, open air	300.00	325.00
☐ **No. 230 Town Station,** lighted, working doors and windows, steel construction, length 14″	500.00	550.00
☐ **No. 349 Crossing Signal,** flashes, cross design, wrought iron base	100.00	110.00
☐ **No. 350 Traffic Signal,** blinks, small and globular, used in cityscapes	110.00	120.00
☐ **No. 601-4 Lamppost,** double bulb, 3½ volts, scroll design	70.00	80.00
☐ **No. 601-8 Lamppost,** double bulb, 8 volt, scroll design	80.00	90.00

Electric locomotive, c. 1903, rare.

	Price Range	
☐ **No. 630 Signal Set,** single arm, double arm, water tank, danger signal	110.00	120.00
☐ **No. 631 Signal Outfit,** lamppost, single arm flag	200.00	225.00
☐ **No. 632 Signal Outfit,** double arm, double light, flag	200.00	225.00

LIONEL

Lionel Early Years

Train Sets

☐ **Amtrak Set,** #8466A locomotive, #8467A dummy, #8475B unit, five Williams Amtrak aluminum coaches, vista dome, two coaches, baggage, observation, plastic	575.00	625.00
☐ **Channelmaster Set,** #243 locomotive with tender, giraffe car #3376, gondola #6162, fireman and ladder car #3512, track maintenance #6812, accessories and track	450.00	500.00

☐ **Freight Set,** #226E locomotive, with tender #2226W, dump car #3859, floodlight car #3820, merchandise car #3814, caboose #2817 .... 1500.00   1700.00

☐ **Freight Set,** #19142-100, #242 locomotive and tender, flat car says "VAN CAMP PORK AND BEANS", #638-2361, turbo missile car #3309, caboose 125.00   135.00

☐ **Freight Set,** #261 locomotive and tender, cattle car #806, hopper #803, lumber car #831, accessories and track 650.00   700.00

☐ **Freight Set,** #261 locomotive with tender, gondola #717, box car #719, caboose #722, transition line 525.00   550.00

☐ **Freight Set,** #262 locomotive and tender, oil car #804, gondola #902, caboose #807, with circuit breaker and accessories 600.00   650.00

☐ **Freight Set,** #262E engine with tender, tank car #654, hopper #653, gondola #652, box car #655, caboose #607, all cars nickel trimmed 650.00   700.00

☐ **Freight Set,** #263E locomotive with 263W Vanderbuilt tender, tank car #2815, hopper #2816, crane car #2810, caboose #2817, all cars trimmed with nickel ....   2000.00 plus

☐ **Freight Train Set,** #1054, #1681 engine and tender, tank car #1680, gondola #1677, caboose #1682, lithographed 300.00   325.00

☐ **Freight Set,** #166E locomotive with tender, Baby Ruth box car #2679, caboose #2682 .... 175.00   200.00

☐ **General Set,** #1862 locomotive with tender, coach with whistle #1875, mail car #1876, horse car #1877 .... 600.00   650.00

☐ **General Set,** #1862 locomotive with tender, #1865 coach, #1866 baggage 300.00   325.00

☐ **Mail Train,** pre-war, ... 150.00   175.00

Price Range

☐ **Passenger Set,** #263E locomotive with #2263W tender, coach #2613, observation #2614, baggage #2615 .... 2000.00 plus

☐ **Passenger Set,** #675 locomotive with 2466W tender, two pullmans #2442, observation car #2443, brown with gray detail ..

☐ **Passenger Set,** #752 locomotive with tender, coach #753, observation car #754 .. 850.00 900.00

☐ **Passenger Set,** #2026 locomotive and #6466W tender, two pullmans #2440, observation car #2441, green with yellow trim 350.00 370.00

☐ **Pre-War Set,** #259E locomotive with tender, tank car #804, caboose #807 .... 100.00 110.00

☐ **Railway Express Passenger Set,** locomotive and tender, baggage #2530, tail car #2531, silver buff coach #2534 .... 250.00 275.00

☐ **Red Devil Set,** #264E locomotive with #265 tender, two coaches #603, observation #604, baggage #615, track and accessories .... 2000.00 plus

☐ **San Francisco,** #2383AA locomotive, baggage car #2530, observation car #2531, vista dome #2533, coach #2532 .... 650.00 700.00

☐ **Sears Set,** #1862 locomotive, with #1862 tender, coach #1885, baggage #1886, baggage #1876, horse car #1887 .... 650.00 700.00

☐ **Sears Special Set,** #1861 locomotive with #1862 tender, horse car with corral and horses #1887, mail car #1886, coach #1885, rare set 1100.00 1300.00

Locomotives

☐ **No. 10E Electric,** with steam wheels, black, chrome and brass trim 200.00 210.00

☐ **No. 21D Texas Special AA,** without motor 30.00 35.00

☐ **No. 201 Union Pacific AA,** orange 25.00 35.00

	Price Range	
☐ **No. 204 Santa Fe AA,** blue and yellow	60.00	70.00
☐ **No. 205 Missouri Pacific Steam Type,** large apron	25.00	35.00
☐ **No. 208 Sante Fe AA,** with horn	80.00	90.00
☐ **No. 212 Sante Fe AA,** two-way reverse, no magnetraction, horn, red and silver	45.00	55.00
☐ **No. 215 Santa Fe AA,** with double-axle magnetraction, orange	95.00	105.00
☐ **No. 218 Santa Fe AA,** with horn, battery pack	40.00	50.00
☐ **No. 221 Santa Fe AA,** two-way reverse, rubber tires, olive green	110.00	120.00
☐ **No. 222 Rio Grande AA,** yellow	35.00	45.00
☐ **No. 227 Canadian National,** without reverse, green with yellow lettering	50.00	60.00
☐ **No. 229 Minneapolis and St. Louis AA,** battery pack	50.00	60.00
☐ **No. 230 Chesapeake and Ohio AA,** blue ...	40.00	50.00
☐ **No. 231 Rock Island AA,** with reverse and magnetraction	40.00	50.00
☐ **No. 232 New Haven AA,** without reverse or magnetraction	45.00	55.00
☐ **No. 238 Pennsylvania Torpedo,** with tender	300.00	325.00
☐ **No. 246 Steam Type,** 2-42, with scout tender	30.00	35.00
☐ **No. 246 Steam Type,** with #1130T tender	15.00	25.00
☐ **No. 251 Lionel Lines,** diesel, rare	600.00	650.00
☐ **No. 258 Steam Type,** three-position E unit	50.00	60.00
☐ **No. 259 Steam Type,** pre-war	70.00	80.00
☐ **No. 259E Locomotive,** with #1689T tender, gun metal	40.00	50.00
☐ **No. 263 Tin Pilot,** red	15.00	20.00

	Price Range	
☐ **No. 263W Tender,** with whistle, six-wheel gun metal	140.00	150.00
☐ **No. 264E Steam Type,** with tender, red and orange	250.00	275.00
☐ **No. 400 Budd Car,** diesel	210.00	220.00
☐ **No. 520 Electric Locomotive**	125.00	135.00
☐ **No. 622 Switcher,** diesel motor	175.00	200.00
☐ **No. 628 Northern Pacific,** 44-ton switcher, diesel	110.00	120.00
☐ **No. 634 A.T. & S. F.,** switcher	70.00	80.00
☐ **No. 671 Reading Lines,** steam type, 6-8-6, with #2671W tender, 12 wheel	350.00	375.00
☐ **No. 671 Reading Lines,** steam type, with #2046-W-50 tender, red	200.00	220.00
☐ **No. 675 Baldwin Drivers,** steam type, with #2466W tender	125.00	135.00
☐ **No. 675 Steam Type,** with #6466W tender	115.00	125.00
☐ **No. 726 Steam Type,** with #2426 whistle tender, 12 wheels, steel rimmed	400.00	450.00
☐ **No. 736 Berkshire,** with 2046W whistle tender	300.00	350.00
☐ **No. 746 Norfolk and Western Steam Type,** with tender, striped cab, rare	800.00	850.00
☐ **No. 746 Steam Type,** with tender, long and ornate	650.00	700.00
☐ **No. 1045 Flagman,** with flag, brown suit and blue arms	20.00	25.00
☐ **No. 1055 Texas Special AA,** without reverse, red	25.00	30.00
☐ **No. 1061 Steam Type,** 2-4-2, with slope back tender	25.00	30.00
☐ **No. 1656 Switcher,** steam type, with #6403B tender, with bell	200.00	250.00
☐ **No. 1664 Steam Type,** with tender	175.00	200.00

	Price Range	
☐ **No. 2020 Steam Type,** no tender	140.00	160.00
☐ **No. 2023 Union Pacific,** twin AA's, yellow, gray, and red	125.00	150.00
☐ **No. 2024 Chesapeake and Ohio AA**	45.00	55.00
☐ **No. 2026 Steam Type,** 2-6-4, with tender ..	85.00	95.00
☐ **No. 2031 Rock Island AA,** with horn	125.00	135.00
☐ **No. 2037 Steam Type,** 2-6-4, with tender ..	75.00	85.00
☐ **No. 2056 Locomotive,** with #2046W tender, nonmagnetraction, 1952	140.00	160.00
☐ **No. 2060 Locomotive,** with reverse, boiler and cab	25.00	35.00
☐ **No. 2321 Lackawanna,** diesel, "C.N.W." colors	225.00	250.00
☐ **No. 2322 Diesel,** Virginian double motor ...	325.00	350.00
☐ **No. 2339 Wabash,** electric	175.00	200.00
☐ **No. 2340 Lionel Lines,** twin motor GG-1, maroon	600.00	650.00
☐ **No. 2345 Western Pacific,** twin AA, rare ..	550.00	600.00
☐ **No. 2349 Northern Pacific GP9,** diesel switcher, with horn	100.00	110.00
☐ **No. 2350 New Haven,** electric	225.00	250.00
☐ **No. 2360 Lionel Lines,** twin motor, striped cab, GG-1, with original box	900.00	1000.00
☐ **No. 2365 C & O, diesel**	200.00	210.00
☐ **No. 2367 Wabash F3,** diesel, twin AA motor with horn	250.00	260.00
☐ **No. 2383 Western Pacific,** dummy A	200.00	210.00
☐ **No. 6110 Steam Type,** 2-4-2, with tender ..	50.00	60.00
☐ **No. 7890 Northern Pacific,** diesel, #7890B motor, green, yellow, and silver	200.00	210.00
☐ **No. 8040 Steam Type,** with plastic tender	30.00	40.00
☐ **No. 8561 Jersey Central,** shell and cab	30.00	40.00

Rolling Stock

	Price Range	
☐ **No. 112 Gondola,** says "Rock Island" with black trucks, gray body	30.00	35.00
☐ **No. 113 Cattle Car,** pea green with black trucks	35.00	40.00
☐ **No. 114 Box Car,** orange with black trucks	50.00	60.00
☐ **No. 117 Caboose,** with trucks, black and maroon	50.00	60.00
☐ **No. 164 Log Loader,** chain drive, with roof, silver	150.00	170.00
☐ **No. 175 Rocket Launcher,** with tower and rocket, spring action	90.00	100.00
☐ **No. 460 Transport Set,** piggyback style, flat car with two green vans	60.00	70.00
☐ **No. 511 Lumber Car,** stakes and load, dark green	35.00	40.00
☐ **No. 513 Cattle Car,** olive drab and orange detail	60.00	70.00
☐ **No. 514 Box Car,** says "Union Pacific," yellow and brown trim	75.00	85.00
☐ **No. 514 Reefer,** with air vents, blue and silver	100.00	110.00
☐ **No. 514 Reefer,** with air vents, red	95.00	105.00
☐ **No. 515 Tank Car,** terra cotta	55.00	65.00
☐ **No. 516 Hopper,** with coal load, brass trim	120.00	130.00
☐ **No. 517 Caboose,** with working windows, pea green and orange, brass trim	40.00	45.00
☐ **No. 603 Coach,** red with black roof	45.00	50.00
☐ **No. 604 Observation Car,** orange	15.00	20.00
☐ **No. 652 Gondola,** burnt orange and white, rubber stamped	95.00	105.00
☐ **No. 653L Hopper,** says "Minneapolis and St. Louis," quad type	10.00	15.00

Price Range

☐ **No. 655 Box Car,** cream and brown	10.00	15.00
☐ **No. 655 Box Car,** yellow and maroon	40.00	45.00
☐ **No. 657 Caboose,** red with tuscan roof	10.00	15.00
☐ **No. 657 Caboose,** red with yellow roof	5.00	10.00
☐ **No. 671 Turbine,** with tender, #2671W motor	150.00	160.00
☐ **No. 752W Union Pacific Streamliner,** whistle model, with observation deck saying "Lionel Lines"	550.00	600.00
☐ **No. 804 Tank Car,** four wheel, silver	15.00	20.00
☐ **No. 804 Tank Car,** says "Shell," ladders decal, red and yellow	20.00	25.00
☐ **No. 804 Tank Car,** says "Sunoco," silver with red and yellow detail	15.00	20.00
☐ **No. 805 Box Car,** pea green and orange ...	15.00	20.00
☐ **No. 806 Stock Car,** orange and maroon ...	25.00	35.00
☐ **No. 807 Caboose,** nickel plated, red	15.00	20.00
☐ **No. 807 Caboose,** red and peacock blue ..	10.00	15.00
☐ **No. 810 Crane Car,** with cab and swivel waste	5.00	10.00
☐ **No. 812 Gondola,** giraud style, green	10.00	15.00
☐ **No. 812 Gondola,** mojave green	15.00	20.00
☐ **No. 813 Cattle Car,** orange and brass trim	95.00	105.00
☐ **No. 814 Box Car,** yellow and orange, automobile furniture	95.00	105.00
☐ **No. 815 Sunoco Tank,** silver	95.00	105.00
☐ **No. 816 Hopper,** red with nickel trim	120.00	130.00
☐ **No. 817 Caboose,** two-tone green	25.00	30.00
☐ **No. 820 Searchlight Car,** orange and black, rubber stamped, says "Illinois Central & Missouri Valley Route R.R."	85.00	90.00
☐ **No. 831 Lumber Car,** giraud green	20.00	25.00

Price Range

☐ **No. 831 Log Car,** with load, stakes, and rail green	10.00	15.00
☐ **No. 1004 Box Car,** says "Baby Ruth," orange and blue	15.00	20.00
☐ **No. 1005 Tank Car,** says "Sunoco," gray ..	15.00	20.00
☐ **No. 1514 Box Car,** says "Baby Ruth," wind-up series, tile red	30.00	35.00
☐ **No. 1615 Tender,** black with red lettering	5.00	10.00
☐ **No. 1666 Locomotive,** with 2466T tender with steam-type motor	45.00	50.00
☐ **No. 1679 Box Car,** says "Baby Ruth," cream and blue	15.00	20.00
☐ **No. 1680 Tank Car,** lithographed, gray ...	5.00	10.00
☐ **No. 1682 Caboose,** red	15.00	20.00
☐ **No. 1690 Coach Car,** dark red and brown	50.00	60.00
☐ **No. 1691 Observation Car,** dark red and brown	50.00	60.00
☐ **No. 1717 Gondola**	35.00	45.00
☐ **No. 1719 Box Car**	35.00	45.00
☐ **No. 1722 Caboose**	20.00	25.00
☐ **No. 1722 Caboose,** lithographed	35.00	45.00
☐ **No. 1766 Coach,** transition series, brass fittings, maroon and terra cotta	300.00	325.00
☐ **No. 1777 Gondola,** lithographed	50.00	60.00
☐ **No. 2235 Tender,** with whistle	25.00	50.00
☐ **No. 2257 Caboose,** says "Southern Pacific," red	10.00	15.00
☐ **No. 2357 Caboose,** deluxe with tools, ladders, silver and blue	15.00	20.00
☐ **No. 2400 Passenger Car,** says "Maplewood," green and gray	25.00	30.00

Price Range

☐ **No. 2432 Donee Car,** says "Clifton," silver and red 35.00 45.00

☐ **No. 2436 Observation Car,** says "Moose Heart," silver and red 35.00 45.00

☐ **No. 2442 Passenger Car,** with lights, brown with gray trim 30.00 40.00

☐ **No. 2442 Tank Truck,** says "Clifton," double dome 35.00 45.00

☐ **No. 2443 Passenger Car,** with lights, brown with gray trim 30.00 40.00

☐ **No. 2444 Coach,** says "Newark," window stripe, red 30.00 40.00

☐ **No. 2445 Coach,** says "Elizabeth," window stripe, red 35.00 45.00

☐ **No. 2452 Gondola,** says "Pennsylvania," 027 .... 10.00 15.00

☐ **No. 2454 Box Car,** says "Baby Ruth" 15.00 20.00

☐ **No. 2456 Hopper,** says "Lehigh Valley," black 15.00 20.00

☐ **No. 2458 Box Car,** black metal 5.00 10.00

☐ **No. 2458 Box Car,** says "Pennsylvania," tuscan and maroon, 1946 .... 15.00 20.00

☐ **No. 2460 Crane,** 12 wheel, black 50.00 60.00

☐ **No. 2465 Tank Car,** says "Sunoco," double-dome, silver 10.00 15.00

☐ **No. 2472 Caboose,** without light, all die cast 20.00 25.00

☐ **No. 2555 Tank Car,** says "Sunoco," with decal 30.00 35.00

☐ **No. 2651 Lumber Car,** with load 20.00 25.00

☐ **No. 2652 Gondola,** burnt orange 15.00 20.00

☐ **No. 2654 Tank Car,** says "Shell" 15.00 20.00

☐ **No. 2655 Box Car,** rubber stamped, cream and brown 15.00 20.00

	Price Range	
☐ **No. 2657 Caboose**	15.00	20.00
☐ **No. 2657 Caboose,** tuscan roof	15.00	20.00
☐ **No. 2675 Tank Car,** says "DuPont," single dome	15.00	20.00
☐ **No. 2677 Gondola,** brown, white, and black	40.00	50.00
☐ **No. 2679 Box Car,** says "Baby Ruth," maroon and red lettering	40.00	50.00
☐ **No. 2682 Caboose**	5.00	10.00
☐ **No. 2812 Gondola,** burnt orange	15.00	20.00
☐ **No. 2812 Gondola,** pea green, nickel trim	95.00	105.00
☐ **No. 2814 Box Car,** cream and maroon	60.00	70.00
☐ **No. 2817 Caboose,** two-tone green	15.00	20.00
☐ **No. 3349 Jet Car,** with turbo rocket, spring mechanism on deck	10.00	15.00
☐ **No. 3356 Horse Car Set,** with corral and horses, and ramp	40.00	50.00
☐ **No. 3357 Maintenance Car,** hydraulic platform	5.00	10.00
☐ **No. 3360 Crane Car,** burro type, black ...	125.00	150.00
☐ **No. 3376 Zoo Car,** says "Bronx Zoo," with giraffe, blue railings	15.00	20.00
☐ **No. 3386 Zoo Car,** says "Bronx Zoo"	25.00	30.00
☐ **No. 3419 Chopper Car,** with wind-up wheel	15.00	20.00
☐ **No. 3444 Cop and Hobo,** Erie Set	60.00	70.00
☐ **No. 3451 Lumber Car,** black	25.00	30.00
☐ **No. 3662 Milk Car,** says "San Francisco," custom painted	30.00	35.00
☐ **No. 5464 Hopper,** gray and black, with cover and latches	45.00	50.00
☐ **No. 5464-46 Hopper,** gray and black, with cover and latches	35.00	40.00

Price Range

☐ **No. 5464-46 Hopper,** gray	5.00	10.00
☐ **No. 6012 Gondola,** black	5.00	10.00
☐ **No. 6014 Box Car,** says "Baby Ruth," white and orange	5.00	10.00
☐ **No. 6014 Box Car,** says "Chung King," plastic and die cast	60.00	70.00
☐ **No. 6014 Box Car,** says "Ship it on Frisco," white and red	5.00	10.00
☐ **No. 6017 Caboose,** says "Boston and Maine," blue and white	10.00	15.00
☐ **No. 6017 Caboose,** tile red with silver decor	3.00	5.00
☐ **No. 6017 Caboose,** says "A.T.S.F.," gray	25.00	30.00
☐ **No. 6017 Caboose,** tile red with silver decor	5.00	10.00
☐ **No. 6024 Box Car,** says "Nabisco Shredded Wheat"	30.00	35.00
☐ **No. 6025 Box Car,** says "Gulf Lines," with catwalk, black	5.00	10.00
☐ **No. 6025 Tank Car,** says "Gulf Oil," double tank, orange	5.00	10.00
☐ **No. 6032 Gondola,** black	5.00	10.00
☐ **No. 6035 Tank Car,** says "Sunoco," gray ..	5.00	10.00
☐ **No. 6037 Caboose,** brown	5.00	10.00
☐ **No. 6042 Gondola,** blue	5.00	10.00
☐ **No. 6042 Gondola,** blue and white	5.00	10.00
☐ **No. 6044 Box Car,** says "Airex," with catwalk and rails	20.00	30.00
☐ **No. 6045 Tank Car,** says "Cities Services," double dome with catwalk	30.00	35.00
☐ **No. 6047 Caboose,** red, rare	5.00	10.00
☐ **No. 6050 Box Car,** savings bank with teller window	5.00	10.00

	Price Range	
☐ **No. 6050 Box Car,** says "Libbey's Tomato Juice"	5.00	10.00
☐ **No. 6057 Caboose,** says "Long Island Railway," red	5.00	10.00
☐ **No. 6059 Caboose,** says "Minneapolis and St. Louis," red plastic	10.00	15.00
☐ **No. 6062 Gondola,** with cable reels, black and white	5.00	10.00
☐ **No. 6111 Flat Car,** with log load, red	5.00	10.00
☐ **No. 6111 Flat Car,** with log load, stamped steel gray	5.00	10.00
☐ **No. 6112 Gondola,** black, with containers	15.00	20.00
☐ **No. 6112-86 Gondola,** blue	5.00	10.00
☐ **No. 6119 DL & W Work Caboose,** red and gray	25.00	30.00
☐ **No. 6119 Work Caboose**	15.00	25.00
☐ **No. 6141 Gondola,** black	5.00	10.00
☐ **No. 6142 Gondola,** green and white	5.00	10.00
☐ **No. 6162 Gondola,** says "New York Central," with three canisters, blue	5.00	10.00
☐ **No. 6176 Hopper,** light yellow and black lettering	30.00	40.00
☐ **No. 6257 Caboose,** light brown	10.00	15.00
☐ **No. 6257 Caboose,** tile red	5.00	10.00
☐ **No. 6282 Wheel Car,** red	25.00	30.00
☐ **No. 6315 Tank Car,** says "Gulf," tangerine	25.00	30.00
☐ **No. 6315 Tank Car,** says "Lionel Lines," orange and yellow	20.00	30.00
☐ **No. 6342 Culvert Car**	20.00	30.00
☐ **No. 6343 Flat Car,** barrel type with manually-operated ramp, red	5.00	10.00

	Price Range	
☐ **No. 6346 Hopper,** says "Alcoa Aluminum"	45.00	55.00
☐ **No. 6357 Caboose,** with light, maroon	5.00	10.00
☐ **No. 6357 Caboose,** tuscan and red	5.00	10.00
☐ **No. 6404 Flat Car,** with load of boats, gray and blue	45.00	55.00
☐ **No. 6405 Flat Car,** with yellow van, brown	25.00	35.00
☐ **No. 6405 Horse Car,** says "Lionel Lines"	20.00	30.00
☐ **No. 6413 Mercury Capsule,** metal platforms, silver	5.00	10.00
☐ **No. 6414 Auto Loader,** super cars, special paint	20.00	25.00
☐ **No. 6414 Auto Car,** with four cars, blue and white	20.00	25.00
☐ **No. 6414 Auto Loader,** with four cars, red and gray	20.00	25.00
☐ **No. 6414 Auto Loader,** with four cars, yellow and turquoise	30.00	35.00
☐ **No. 6414 Auto Loader,** with red and black cars, yellow body	30.00	35.00
☐ **No. 6415 Tank Car**	30.00	35.00
☐ **No. 6415-25 Caboose**	25.00	35.00
☐ **No. 6417 Caboose**	35.00	45.00
☐ **No. 6418 Girder Car,** with U.S. steel girder load, straps and rails, gray	30.00	40.00
☐ **No. 6424 Flat Car,** with cars, red and white	20.00	25.00
☐ **No. 6425 Gulf Tank Car,** triple dome	15.00	20.00
☐ **No. 6427 Caboose**	20.00	25.00
☐ **No. 6428 Mail Car,** says "U.S. Mail"	25.00	30.00
☐ **No. 6428 Railway Post Office**	150.00	160.00
☐ **No. 6434 Poultry Dispatch**	65.00	75.00

Price Range

☐ No. **6436-25 Hopper,** red	35.00	45.00
☐ No. **6436-110 Hopper**	20.00	30.00
☐ No. **6437 Caboose,** says "Pennsylvania" with herald	50.00	60.00
☐ No. **6446 Hopper,** painted blue, no road name	15.00	20.00
☐ No. **6446 Hopper,** says "Jack Frost Cane Sugar"	30.00	35.00
☐ No. **6446-14 Covered Hopper,** covers and latches	65.00	75.00
☐ No. **6446-25 Hopper,** covered, missing three latches, black	30.00	35.00
☐ No. **6446-25 Hopper,** black	30.00	35.00
☐ No. **6446-25 Hopper,** gray	35.00	45.00
☐ No. **6448 Target Car,** red and white	40.00	50.00
☐ No. **6452 Gondola,** black	5.00	10.00
☐ No. **6454 Box Car,** says "New York Central," terra cotta with tuscan doors	40.00	50.00
☐ No. **6454 Box Car,** says "Pennsylvania," tuscan and red trim	20.00	25.00
☐ No. **6454 Box Car,** says "Southern Pacific," #027, with decal	30.00	35.00
☐ No. **6456 Hopper,** says "Lehigh Valley," maroon	15.00	20.00
☐ No. **6457 Caboose,** deluxe model, with smoke stack, tools, ladders, red	15.00	20.00
☐ No. **6460 Crane Car,** red cab	40.00	50.00
☐ No. **6460 Crane Car,** swivel base, hook and wire, gray	50.00	60.00
☐ No. **6462 Gondola,** says "New York Central" with load of barrels	10.00	15.00
☐ No. **6462-25 Gondola,** red	25.00	35.00
☐ No. **6464 Great Northern Box Car**	35.00	45.00

	Price Range	
☐ No. 6464-1 Western Pacific, silver and blue	35.00	45.00
☐ No. 6464-50 Minneapolis and St. Louis Box Car	75.00	100.00
☐ No. 6464-75 Rock Island Box Car	30.00	40.00
☐ No. 6464-225 Southern Pacific Box Car, black, red, and yellow	110.00	120.00
☐ No. 6464-275 State of Maine	45.00	55.00
☐ No. 6464-375 Central of Georgia	200.00	220.00
☐ No. 6464-400 B & O Box car	55.00	65.00
☐ No. 6464-425 New Hampshire Box Car ..	40.00	50.00
☐ No. 6464-450 Great Northern, green, yellow and orange	75.00	85.00
☐ No. 6464-475 B & M Box Car, blue and black	45.00	55.00
☐ No. 6464-525 Minneapolis and St. Louis Box Car	20.00	25.00
☐ No. 6464-725 New Hampshire Box Car ..	175.00	180.00
☐ No. 6465 Tank Car, says "Lionel Lines," double dome, orange	5.00	10.00
☐ No. 6465 Tank Car, says "Sunoco," double dome, silver	5.00	10.00
☐ No. 6468 Box Car, says "Baltimore and Ohio," working doors and ramp, tuscan ...	225.00	250.00
☐ No. 6473 Horse Transport, with red lettering	10.00	15.00
☐ No. 6476 Hopper, says "Lehigh Valley," red	5.00	10.00
☐ No. 6511 Flat Car, with load of four pipes, tile red	15.00	25.00
☐ No. 6517 Caboose, with bay window, yellow	30.00	40.00
☐ No. 6518 Transformer Car, with insulators, 16 wheels	25.00	30.00

Price Range

☐ **No. 6519 Passenger Coach,** says "Allis Chalmers"	5.00	10.00
☐ **No. 6560 Crane Car,** plastic frame	25.00	35.00
☐ **No. 6561 Cable Reel Car,** with two spools, gray	30.00	40.00
☐ **No. 6572 Reefer,** says "REA," green	35.00	45.00
☐ **No. 6650 Missile Launch,** spring action and crane, white rocket	15.00	25.00
☐ **No. 6656 Stock Car,** bright yellow	20.00	30.00
☐ **No. 6801 Boat Car,** with boat, yellow and white	20.00	30.00
☐ **No. 6801 Boat Car,** with cradle and blue boat	15.00	25.00
☐ **No. 6802 Girder Car,** red	5.00	10.00
☐ **No. 6803 Flat Car,** military load	5.00	10.00
☐ **No. 6805 Waste Car,** says "Caution: Radioactive"	30.00	40.00
☐ **No. 6812 Track Maintenance Car,** red and yellow	40.00	50.00
☐ **No. 6814 Caboose,** working style	5.00	10.00
☐ **No. 6819 Flat Car,** no load, red	5.00	10.00
☐ **No. 6821 Flat Car,** with load of crates, red	5.00	10.00
☐ **No. 6822 Searchlight Car,** swivel base, light blue	10.00	15.00
☐ **No. 6825 Trestle Car,** black	15.00	20.00
☐ **No. 6826 Flat Car,** with load of Christmas trees, with steps	40.00	50.00
☐ **No. 9161U Caboose,** says "Canadian National NSC," black trucks	15.00	20.00
☐ **No. 36621 Milk Car,** with cans and frame design	40.00	50.00
☐ **No. 63561 Stock Car,** says "New York Central," yellow	25.00	35.00

	Price Range	
☐ **No. 64173 Caboose**, says "Lionel Lines," orange and black	15.00	20.00
☐ **No. 64173 Caboose**, says "Lionel Lines" ..	10.00	15.00
☐ **No. 64273 Caboose**, says "Lionel Lines," with porthole	15.00	20.00
☐ **No. 336155 Log Car**, 0 gauge, with tip tray, magnetic action	10.00	15.00
☐ **No. 536417 Caboose**, says "Pennsylvania NSC," New York zone type	10.00	15.00
☐ **No. 611925 Work Caboose**, says "D.L.W.," orange	10.00	15.00
☐ **No. 643625 Hopper**, says "Lehigh Valley," maroon	20.00	25.00
☐ **No. 646825 Box Car**, says "New Haven," orange with black lettering	35.00	50.00

Accessories

☐ **No. 025 Bumper**	5.00	10.00
☐ **No. 068 Railroad Crossing Sign**	10.00	15.00
☐ **No. 069 Railroad Crossing Signal**	10.00	15.00
☐ **No. 6 Whistle Controller**	15.00	20.00
☐ **No. 45 Gateman**, automatic, with signal ..	15.00	20.00
☐ **No. 65 Whistle Controller**	15.00	20.00
☐ **No. 78 Train Control**, automatic, with lights	25.00	35.00
☐ **No. 81 Rheostat**	10.00	15.00
☐ **No. 91 Circuit Breaker**	30.00	40.00
☐ **No. 97 Coal Loader**, with scoop and drawer, shoot action	150.00	160.00
☐ **No. 99N Train Control**, automatic	50.00	60.00
☐ **No. 122 Station**, chimney lighted, benches, dome	150.00	160.00
☐ **No. 126 Station**, one chimney, base	90.00	100.00
☐ **No. 140 Swinging Banjo Signal**	20.00	30.00

Price Range

☐ **No. 145 Gateman**, automatic action	15.00	20.00
☐ **No. 153C Contractor**	5.00	10.00
☐ **No. 175 Rocket Launcher**, spring action ...	125.00	135.00
☐ **No. 191 Villa**, white with green roof	250.00	275.00
☐ **No. 200 Turntable**, standard gauge	900.00	1000.00
☐ **No. 270 Single-Span Bridge**, standard gauge	150.00	160.00
☐ **No. 280 Bridge**, standard gauge	150.00	160.00
☐ **No. 300 Hilgate Bridge**	1100.00	1300.00
☐ **No. 310 Billboard**, says "B.P."	3.00	5.00
☐ **No. 364 Log Loader**, crane and hook	85.00	95.00
☐ **No. 394 Beacon**, metal construction, red ...	10.00	15.00
☐ **No. 394 Beacon,** swivel action, blue	5.00	10.00
☐ **No. 397 Coal Loader**, shoot and door	100.00	110.00
☐ **No. 397 Coal Loader**, spring action, with conveyor belt	50.00	60.00
☐ **No. 440C Panel Board**	185.00	195.00
☐ **No. 440N Signal Bridge,** standard gauge ..	250.00	260.00
☐ **No. 442 Diner**, aluminum style, simulated windows	350.00	375.00
☐ **No. 455 Oil Derrick**, movable arms	110.00	120.00
☐ **No. 456 Coal Ramp**, with hopper	150.00	160.00
☐ **No. 465 Dispatching Station**, with whistle	160.00	170.00
☐ **No. 840 Power Station**, standard gauge, large green base, steps, rare	2000.00 plus	
☐ **No. 2214 Girder Bridge**, two piece	5.00	10.00
☐ **No. 2786 Freight Station**, plastic	10.00	15.00
☐ **No. 3472 Milk Cans for Car and Platform**	35.00	45.00
☐ **No. 5021 Left Hand-Switch**	15.00	20.00
☐ **No. 5122 Right Hand-Switch**	15.00	20.00

Model Products Company, 1970 to Present

Train Sets

Price Range

☐ **No. 1050, New Englander Set**, #8007 DC locomotive, #6026W style tender, tender lettered NY, NH & H, locomotive is 2-6-4 with #9346 NY, NH & H square window caboose, #9036 Mobil gas tank, 9140 Burlington gondola and #9035 Conrail box 125.00   150.00

☐ **No. 1052 Chesapeake and Ohio Set**, 8008 DC die cast locomotive, #6026 style tender, #9307 Conrail box, #9036 Mobil gas tank, #9017 Wabash gondola, #9038 B & O hopper and #9381 Chessie caboose 140.00   160.00

☐ **No. 1053, James Gang Set**, #8005 red DC General locomotive and tender, #9306 flat with fences, #9035 cattle with good and bad guys, and #9541 ATSF REA baggage car 100.00   125.00

☐ **No. 1054, Royal Limited Set**, #8061 Western Maryland Chessie U36C, all die-cast truck cars, #9818 Western Maryland Reefer, #9234 radioactive waste cars, #9344 Citgo tank, #9328 Chessie bay window caboose, #9432 Cowan 100th Anniversary of Birth Post-war Years, #9329 Chessie crane car ...   450.00   475.00

☐ **No. 1071, Mid-Atlantic Set**, with new body style #8063 SD9 Seaboard locomotive, #9369 Sinclair chemical tank, #9233 16-wheel transformer car, #9371 Atlantic sugar hopper, #9372 Seaboard bay window caboose, #9370 Seaboard gondola and the #9433 Cowan 100th anniversary birthday car 350.00   37500

Price Range

□ **No. 1072, Cross-Country Set,** #8066 Toledo, Peoria & Western GP20, #9374 Reading hopper, #9232 Allis Chalmers reactor car, #9428 TPW box car in green and ivory, #9373 Getty oil chemical tanks, #9379 Santa Fe gondola and #9309 TPW bay window caboose, together with a #2303 Santa Fe manual gantry crane 250.00   260.00

□ **No. 1280, Kickapoo Set,** mixed colors of cars 100.00   110.00

□ **No. 1350, Canadian Pacific Service Station Special Set,** with #8365 and #8366 Canadian Pacific AAF3, #9113 N & W hopper, #9723 WP box, #9725 No pac box, #9163 CP N5C, #9725 MKT stock 500.00   550.00

□ **No. 1387, Milwaukee Passenger Set** 220.00   235.00

□ **No. 1387, Milwaukee Passenger Car Set**   200.00   210.00

□ **No. 1450, Rio Grande SSS Service Station** 240.00   250.00
Special Set, with Rio Grande F3 AA and other cars 110.00   120.00

□ **No. 1453, Coca Cola Set,** with switcher, three box cars, caboose, no track or transformer 110.00   120.00

□ **No. 1453, Coca Cola Set,** with 75th anniversary logo on the Tab, Fanta and Sprite box cars, commemorating 75th anniversary of Coca Cola, logo is a square overprint to the left of the car door 85.00   95.00

□ **No. 1460, Grand National Set,** with #8470 Chessie U36B, no track or transformer 200.00   210.00

□ **No. 1487, Broadway Ltd. Passenger Set** ... 300.00   325.00

□ **No. 1577, Liberty Special Set,** with Alco A, three box cars, caboose, patriotic set 150.00   160.00

□ **No. 1584, Spirit of America Set,** #8559, Norfolk & Western, GP9 and cars, #1776 NSC caboose, locomotive with stars on cab side 260.00   275.00

	Price Range	

☐ **No. 1585, 75th Anniversary Set**, with U36B, box, hoppers, reefers and caboose .. 300.00 310.00

☐ **No. 1587, Capital Limited Baltimore and Ohio Passenger Set** 260.00 275.00

☐ **No. 1587U, Capital Limited Set** 220.00 235.00

☐ **No. 1663, Amtrak Passenger Car Set**, with Alco A locomotive and former #027 style cars 200.00 210.00

☐ **No. 1664, Illinois Central U36B Set**, with drawbridge, from 1976 .... 250.00 260.00

☐ **No. 1665, New York Central Empire State Express Set** 275.00 300.00

☐ **No. 1672, Northern Pacific GP Service Station Special Set**, with all cars having sprung die-cast trucks except the caboose, which has regular bay window trucks 250.00 275.00

☐ **No. 1760, Steel Hauler Set**, DC with trucks, cranes, etc., one only, #8769 switcher 60.00 70.00

☐ **No. 1764, Heartland Express Set**, with NP Pig Palace car available only in this set, and GM&O #GP20 .... 225.00 250.00

☐ **No. 1765, Rocky Mountain Special**, with tender GN U36B, and a string of cars including the GN bay window caboose 275.00 300.00

☐ **No. 1766, Budd Car Set**, 1966 service station special set consisting of three Budd cars 225.00 250.00

☐ **No. 1776, Bicentennial Locomotive**, #U36B with #7600 caboose, box cars #7601-7613, #7610 Virginia car 600.00 625.00

☐ **No. 1860, Workin' RR Timberline Set**, with log loader 60.00 70.00

☐ **No. 1866, Great Plains Express Set**, with CP rail #GP9 and #9417 CP rail black box car with gold lettering (1979) 180.00 190.00

Price Range

☐ **No. 1867, Milwaukee Limited Set,** new #SD18 locomotive, all die cast 240.00   250.00

☐ **No. 1868, 1978 Service Station Special Set** 180.00   190.00

☐ **No. 1960, Midnight Flyer Set,** DC motor .. 80.00   90.00

☐ **No. 1970, Southern Pacific Limited Set,** die-cast truck cars 300.00   320.00

☐ **No. 1980, LCCA 10th Anniversary Convention,** #GP20 locomotive for Des Moines, Iowa, lettered "The Rock," two passenger cars 140.00   150.00

Locomotives

☐ **No. 8001 Nickel Plate 2-6-4 Locomotive and Tender,** 1980, DC 80.00   90.00

☐ **No. 8002 Union Pacific Berkshire 2-8-4,** magnetraction, electronic whistle, sound of steam, gray elephant ears, #9811 reefer, #9419 box car, #9367 tank, #9366 hopper and #9368 bay window caboose, #9383 Union Pacific flat with two vans 400.00   420.00

☐ **No. 8003 Chessie Steam Special 2-8-4 Berkshire,** with five Chessie steam special #027 passenger cars numbered #9581 through #9585 .... 440.00   460.00

☐ **No. 8004 Rock Island and Peoria Chrome General Locomotive and Tender** 160.00   170.00

☐ **No. 8005 James Gang Red General Locomotive,** with tender 80.00   90.00

☐ **No. 8007 New Englander,** New York, New Haven, and Hartford, plastic body, old #2035, style 2-6-4 locomotive, DC 85.00   95.00

☐ **No. 8021 Santa Fe B Unit** 30.00   40.00

☐ **No. 8022 Santa Fe A,** unit powered, dark blue, J.C. Penney special set locomotive ... 60.00   70.00

☐ **No. 8022 Santa Fe Double AA,** J. C. Penney special 90.00   100.00

	Price Range	
☐ **No. 8025 Canadian National AA Diesel**, orange and black stripes	85.00	95.00
☐ **No. 8025 Canadian National Power A**, units only	70.00	80.00
☐ **No. 8030 Illinois Central GP9**, early model with metal stakes	90.00	100.00
☐ **No. 8030 Illinois Central GP9**, plastic handrails, double pickup	80.00	90.00
☐ **No. 8030 Illinois Central GP9**	60.00	70.00
☐ **No. 8031 Canadian National GP7**, with metal handrails	110.00	120.00
☐ **No. 8031 Canadian National GP7**, plastic handrails	80.00	90.00
☐ **No. 8041 New York Central Pacemaker**, steam, 1970 version	70.00	80.00
☐ **No. 8042 Grand Trunk and Western**, die-cast steam, #6026T style tender	80.00	90.00
☐ **No. 8042 Grand Trunk and Western**, with #6026T style tender	65.00	75.00
☐ **No. 8050/8051 Delaware and Hudson U36C**, combination power and dummy units sold as pairs only	200.00	210.00
☐ **No. 8054 Burlington Texas Zephyr F3AA**, plus aluminum passenger cars #9576–#9580 with "silver" names, one-unit train	600.00	650.00
☐ **No. 8056 Chicago and Northwestern Fairbanks Morse Double Motor**, magnetraction diesel	280.00	300.00
☐ **No. 8057 Burlington SW1 Switcher**, three-way reverse	80.00	90.00
☐ **No. 8059 Pennsylvania B Unit**, Brunswick green	200.00	225.00
☐ **No. 8060 Pennsylvania Tuscan B Units** ..	90.00	100.00
☐ **No. 8061 Western Maryland Chessie System U36C**, Royal Limited set breakups ...	110.00	120.00

Price Range

☐ **No. 8062 Burlington Texas Zephyr B Unit,** chrome 80.00 90.00

☐ **No. 8063 Seaboard SD9 Single-Power Unit**, six-wheel trucks out of the Mid-Atlantic set 110.00 120.00

☐ **No. 8064 Florida East Coast GP9 Diesel Power and Dummy Unit**, as combination only to get power units 130.00 140.00

☐ **No. 8066 Toledo, Peoria and Western** 95.00 105.00

☐ **No. 8071 Des Moines, Iowa 10th Anniversary GP20**, says "The Rock," cab numbered 1980 .... 150.00 160.00

☐ **No. 8071 Virginia Power and #8072 Dummy**, combination 200.00 225.00

☐ **No. 8111 DT & I Switcher**, orange 50.00 75.00

☐ **No. 8140 Locomotive**, 0-4-0, raised white letters on cab, cab has outside shades, old 1060 body style 35.00 50.00

☐ **No. 8141 Pennsylvania Sound of Steam Locomotive**, gray, red stripe, 1971 .... 50.00 60.00

☐ **No. 8142 Chesapeake and Ohio Steam Engine**, die-cast boiler 70.00 80.00

☐ **No. 8142 Chesapeake and Ohio Locomotive and Tender**, die-cast boiler, letters on cab and tender, says "Sound of Steam" ... 65.00 75.00

☐ **No. 8200 Kickapoo Switcher** 60.00 70.00

☐ **No. 8203 Pennsylvania Steam Locomotive and Tender**, SOS and smoke, 1972 .... 100.00 110.00

☐ **No. 8206 Steam Locomotive and Tender**, sound of steam, whistle, New York Central 200.00 225.00

☐ **No. 8206 New York Central Locomotive and Tender** 200.00 225.00

☐ **No. 8209 Dockside Switcher**, 1972 early production 80.00 90.00

	Price Range	
No. 8250 Santa Fe Power and #8255 Dummy	130.00	140.00
No. 8252 Delaware and Hudson AB Diesel, with #8253 tender	75.00	85.00
No. 8254 Illinois Central GP9 Dummy Unit, plastic handrails only on dummy	50.00	60.00
No. 8258 Canadian National GP7 Dummy, plastic handrails only on dummy	50.00	60.00
No. 8304 Baltimore and Ohio Die-Cast Locomotive and Tender, from Capital Ltd. passenger set	90.00	100.00
No. 8304 Rock Island Steam, 4-4-2, die-cast, with Rock Island tender	85.00	95.00
No. 8304 Chesapeake and Ohio, with C & O tender, says "Sound of Steam"	110.00	120.00
No. 8310 Sears Special, 2-4-0 steam switcher, nickel plate road	80.00	90.00
No. 8350 U.S. Steel Industrial Switcher	50.00	60.00
No. 8351 Santa Fe Silver Single-Powered A	50.00	60.00
No. 8352 Powered and Dummy Santa Fe, #8355 dummy with horn	140.00	150.00
No. 8352 Santa Fe GP20 Power Only	100.00	110.00
No. 8353 GT Powered and Dummy Combination, #8356	115.00	125.00
No. 8354 Erie Switcher, three-position E unit	90.00	100.00
No. 8355 Santa Fe GP Dummy, with horn	85.00	95.00
No. 8356 GP7 Dummy Unit	50.00	60.00
No. 8357 Pennsylvania GP9 Power Unit	95.00	100.00
No. 8357 Pennsylvania GP Power and Dummy Unit, #8358	120.00	130.00
No. 8359 Chesapeake and Ohio, special new 50th anniversary	110.00	120.00

	Price Range	
☐ **No. 8360 Long Island Power and Dummy Unit**, with horn	130.00	140.00
☐ **No. 8361 Western Pacific AB #027 Diesel**	75.00	85.00
☐ **No. 8363 Baltimore and Ohio AA Diesel,** single motor	210.00	220.00
☐ **No. 8364 Baltimore and Ohio ABA F3 Combination**	225.00	235.00
☐ **No. 8365 Canadian Pacific AA Diesel**	310.00	320.00
☐ **No. 8367 Long Island GP20 Dummy**, with horn	90.00	100.00
☐ **No. 8452 Erie AB Alco Diesel Combination** #027, with dummy #8453	85.00	95.00
☐ **No. 8453 Erie Alco B Unit Only**, boxed ..	50.00	60.00
☐ **No. 8454 Rio Grande Power and Dummy,** #8455	115.00	125.00
☐ **No. 8455 Rio Grande GP7 Dummy Unit** ..	30.00	35.00
☐ **No. 8460 Switcher**, red and white	70.00	80.00
☐ **No. 8463 Chessie GP20 Switcher**, limited production, 1974 engine	80.00	90.00
☐ **No. 8463 Chessie GP20 Switcher**	85.00	95.00
☐ **No. 8464 Denver and Rio Grande F3 AA Units**	195.00	205.00
☐ **No. 8465 Rio Grande F3 Diesel AA Combination**	225.00	235.00
☐ **No. 8466 Amtrak F3 Power A**	160.00	170.00
☐ **No. 8467 Amtrak F3 AA Power and Dummy**	175.00	185.00
☐ **No. 8468 Baltimore and Ohio B Unit**	80.00	90.00
☐ **No. 8469 Canadian Pacific B Unit**	85.00	95.00
☐ **No. 8470 Chessie U36B Diesel**	85.00	95.00
☐ **No. 8470 Chessie U36B Matched Combination**, power pak	120.00	130.00
☐ **No. 8471 Pennsylvania Switcher**, heavy switcher, 3-position E unit	300.00	320.00

	Price Range	
☐ **No. 8473 Coca Cola Switcher Only**, single step on side of body	60.00	70.00
☐ **No. 8473 Coca Cola Switcher Only**, 2 steps on side of body	40.00	50.00
☐ **No. 8473 Coca Cola Switcher Only**, 2 steps on side of body, no box	50.00	60.00
☐ **No. 8474 Rio Grande B Unit for F3 AA** ...	70.00	80.00
☐ **No. 8475 Amtrak F3 Style B Unit**	65.00	75.00
☐ **No. 8500 Pennsylvania Locomotive and Tender 2-4-0,** 1130T-size tender has roller that says "Sound of Steam"	20.00	30.00
☐ **No. 8506 Pennsylvania Switcher 0-4-0**	110.00	120.00
☐ **No. 8550 Jersey Central Combination GP9**	125.00	135.00
☐ **No. 8551 Pennsylvania Electric Locomotive,** says "Little Joe"	95.00	105.00
☐ **No. 8552 Southern Pacific ABA Alco**	145.00	155.00
☐ **No. 8555 Milwaukee F3 AA Diesel**	210.00	220.00
☐ **No. 8556 Baltimore and Ohio Chessie Switcher,** 3-way E unit	95.00	105.00
☐ **No. 8558 Milwaukee Road EP5 Electric** ..	100.00	110.00
☐ **No. 8559 Norfolk and Western Locomotive,** GP9 with circle of stars	120.00	130.00
☐ **No. 8560 Chessie U36B Dummy Units** ...	60.00	70.00
☐ **No. 8561 Jersey Central GP9 Dummy Units**	60.00	70.00
☐ **No. 8562 Missouri Pacific GP20 Combination**	125.00	135.00
☐ **No. 8563 Rock Island Alco Locomotive,** power A only, red with white letters, yellow stripe and nose under headlight, 1975	60.00	70.00
☐ **No. 8564 Union Pacific U36B Diesel**	180.00	190.00
☐ **No. 8566 Southern F3 AA Diesel**	300.00	310.00
☐ **No. 8568 F3 Single-Powered A Unit,** preamble press, single powered A	90.00	100.00

Price Range

☐ **No. 8569 Soo Switcher**	80.00	90.00
☐ **No. 8570 Liberty Special Alco A**	80.00	90.00
☐ **No. 8571 Frisco Power and Dummy**	120.00	130.00
☐ **No. 8572 Frisco U36B Dummy Only**	65.00	75.00
☐ **No. 8573 Union Pacific**	200.00	210.00
☐ **No. 8575 Milwaukee Road F3B Unit**	95.00	105.00
☐ **No. 8576 Penn Central GP7 Switcher**	70.00	80.00
☐ **No. 8600 Steam Locomotive and Tender,** 4-6-4 Hudson, silver boiler front, NYC tender	200.00	210.00
☐ **No. 8603 Chesapeake and Ohio Steam** ...	35.00	45.00
☐ **No. 8604 Jersey Central Boiler and Cab,** tender is black Jersey Central and has roller sound of steam	120.00	130.00
☐ **No. 8650 Burlington Northern U36B Power and Dummy,** #8651	200.00	210.00
☐ **No. 8652 Santa Fe F3 Power and Dummy AA,** #8653	120.00	130.00
☐ **No. 8654 Boston and Maine Power and Dummy,** combination, #8655	120.00	130.00
☐ **No. 8654 Boston and Maine Power Unit** ..	100.00	120.00
☐ **No. 8656 Canadian National Alco,** combination	150.00	160.00
☐ **No. 8659 Virginian Rectifier Electric**	135.00	145.00
☐ **No. 8660 Rail Switcher,** diesel	90.00	100.00
☐ **No. 8661 Southern F3B Unit**	80.00	90.00
☐ **No. 8665 Jeremiah O'Brien,** 1776	110.00	120.00
☐ **No. 8666 Northern Pacific GP9 Switcher** from 1976 NP SSS set	125.00	135.00
☐ **No. 8668 Northern Pacific GP Dummy,** to match 8666 GP9 from SSS set	105.00	115.00
☐ **No. 8668 Northern Pacific GP Dummy** ...	90.00	100.00
☐ **No. 8669 Illinois Central Gulf U36B**	95.00	105.00

	Price Range	
☐ No. 8701 General Locomotive and Tender	210.00	220.00
☐ No. 8702 Southern Crescent Locomotive and Tender	350.00	360.00
☐ No. 8703 Wabash Locomotive and Tender	60.00	70.00
☐ No. 8750 GP7 Power and Dummy, combination, #8751	125.00	135.00
☐ No. 8753 GG1 Pennsylvania Tuscan, five stripe	450.00	460.00
☐ No. 8754 New Haven Rectifier	110.00	120.00
☐ No. 8755 Sante Fe U36B Combination Dummy, #8756	135.00	145.00
☐ No. 8756 Sante Fe U36B, dummy only ...	70.00	80.00
☐ No. 8757 Conrail GP9 Power Unit	85.00	95.00
☐ No. 8758 Southern GP7 Power and Dummy, #8774	120.00	130.00
☐ No. 8759 Erie Lackawanna Power and Dummy, #8760	120.00	130.00
☐ No. 8760 Erie Lackawanna GP7 Dummy	50.00	60.00
☐ No. 8761 Grand Trunk GT Switcher	65.00	75.00
☐ No. 8762 Great Northern Electric EP5 ...	150.00	175.00
☐ No. 8762 Great Northern EP5	100.00	150.00
☐ No. 8763 Norfolk and Western Powered GP9	85.00	100.00
☐ No. 8764 Budd Baltimore and Ohio, two-unit set	200.00	250.00
☐ No. 8766 Budd Powered RDC4 Baltimore and Ohio	200.00	300.00
☐ No. 8767 Budd Powered RDC4 Plus RDC1 Nonpowered Passenger Car	200.00	225.00
☐ No. 8769 Republic Steel DC Switcher	50.00	75.00
☐ No. 8770 Electromotive Division Switcher	80.00	90.00

	Price Range	
☐ No. 8711 Great Northern U36B Locomotive	95.00	100.00
☐ No. 8772 Gulf Mobile and Ohio GP20, breakup locomotive	95.00	100.00
☐ No. 8773 Mickey Mouse Express Locomotive	180.00	190.00
☐ No. 8775 Lehigh Valley GP9 Power Unit ..	100.00	110.00
☐ No. 8776 Chicago and Northwestern GP20 Power and Dummy, #8779	150.00	160.00
☐ No. 8777 Santa Fe F3B Unit	95.00	105.00
☐ No. 8800 Lionel Lines Die-Cast 4-4-2 Steam Engine	90.00	100.00
☐ No. 8801 Blue Comet Locomotive and #9536-9540 Blue Comet Passenger Cars, with six-wheel die-cast trucks, complete sets	500.00	525.00
☐ No. 8803 Locomotive, Tender, and Throttle, pack out of Workin' RR sets	25.00	35.00
☐ No. 8850 Penn Central, black GG1	300.00	325.00
☐ No. 8851 New Haven F3 Double Motor AA	275.00	300.00
☐ No. 8854 Rail GP9	90.00	100.00
☐ No. 8855 Milwaukee SD18	120.00	130.00
☐ No. 8857 Northern Pacific U36B Combination Power and Dummy, #8858	120.00	130.00
☐ No. 8859 Conrail Rectifier, electric	100.00	110.00
☐ No. 8860 The Rock Switcher, three-position reverse	80.00	90.00
☐ No. 8864 New Haven B Unit	85.00	95.00
☐ No. 8866 GP9 Powered	90.00	100.00
☐ No. 8867 GP9 Dummy, to match 1978 SSS locomotive	80.00	90.00
☐ No. 8866 and MSIL GP9 Combination ...	160.00	170.00

	Price Range	
☐ **No. 8872 Santa Fe SD 18**, blue and yellow combination	175.00	185.00
☐ **No. 8873 Santa Fe SD18 Dummy**	65.00	75.00
☐ **No. 8904 Wabash Steam Locomotive and Tender**, die-cast body	85.00	95.00
☐ **No. 8950 Virginian FM Trainmaster**, double motor, magnetraction	350.00	360.00
☐ **No. 8951 Southern Pacific Trainmaster**, double motor, magnetraction	400.00	410.00
☐ **No. 8952 Pennsylvania AA**, double motor F3, magnetraction, Brunswick green	350.00	360.00
☐ **No. 8955 Southern U36B Power and Dummy, #8956**, combination	130.00	140.00
☐ **No. 8957 Burlington GP20 Power and Dummy, #8958**, combination	115.00	125.00
☐ **No. 8960 Southern Pacific U36C Power and Dummy, #8961** combination	125.00	135.00
☐ **No. 8962 Reading U36B Breakup**, out of Quaker City set	100.00	120.00
☐ **No. 8970 Pennsylvania F3 AA**, double motor, magnetraction, tuscan	225.00	250.00

Rolling Stock

☐ **No. 6315 Pittsburg Convention Orange Chemical Tank Car**, for the 1972 TCA convention	80.00	90.00
☐ **No. 6410, 6411, 6412 Amtrak Coach**, coach and vista to complement the Amtrak boxed passenger set	80.00	90.00
☐ **No. 6436 Clearwater, Florida, Hopper Car**, for 1969 TCA convention	125.00	135.00
☐ **No. 6464-500 Timken**, all orange, made specially for Glen Uhl	90.00	100.00
☐ **No. 6464 1970 Chicago Convention Car**, first convention car made by MPC, yellow body with red letter and red door	80.00	90.00

Price Range

☐ **No. 6517-60 TCA Bay Window Caboose,** orange, for the TCA 1966 Santa Monica convention, light orange, metal truck 500.00   520.00

☐ **No. 6572 REA Reefer,** light green 60.00   70.00

☐ **No. 7600 Bicentennial Caboose** 50.00   60.00

☐ **No. 7700 Uncle Sam Box Car,** red, white and blue 100.00   120.00

☐ **No. 7701 Camel Box Car** 15.00   20.00

☐ **No. 7702 Camel Box Car,** Tobacco Road series 20.00   25.00

☐ **No. 7702 Prince Albert Tobacco Road Box Car** 20.00   25.00

☐ **No. 7702 Prince Albert Box Car** 15.00   20.00

☐ **No. 7703 Beech Nut Box Car,** Tobacco Road Series 15.00   20.00

☐ **No. 7705 Canadian Toy Fair Box Car** 325.00   350.00

☐ **No. 7706 Sir Walter Raleigh,** Tobacco Road car 20.00   25.00

☐ **No. 7707 White Owl Tobacco Road Box** .. 20.00   25.00

☐ **No. 7707 White Owl Tobacco Road Box** .. 20.00   25.00

☐ **No. 7708 Winston Tobacco Road Box** 20.00   25.00

☐ **No. 7709 Salem Tobacco Road Box** 20.00   25.00

☐ **No. 7710 Mail Pouch Tobacco Box** 20.00   25.00

☐ **No. 7711 ElProducto Tobacco Box** 20.00   25.00

☐ **No. 7712 ATSF Great American Box Car** 40.00   50.00

☐ **No. 7800 Pepsi Cola Soda Pop Box Car** .. 15.00   25.00

☐ **No. 7801 A & W Soda Pop Box Car** 15.00   25.00

☐ **No. 7802 Canada Dry Soda Pop Box Car** 15.00   25.00

☐ **No. 7803 Trains 'N' Trucking Box Car,** 1977 .... 60.00   75.00

	Price Range	
☐ **No. 7806 Seasons Greetings Car**, given to dealers as a gift from Lionel in 1976, silver with red and green letters	150.00	175.00
☐ **No. 7808 Northern Pacific Pig Palace**	70.00	80.00
☐ **No. 7809 Vernor's Soda Pop Box Car**	15.00	20.00
☐ **No. 7810 Orange Crush Soda Pop Box Car**	70.00	80.00
☐ **No. 7811 Dr. Pepper Soda Pop Box Car** ...	15.00	20.00
☐ **No. 7812 TCA 1977 Houston Convention Stock Car**	15.00	20.00
☐ **No. 7813 Seasons Greetings Car**, for 1977	15.00	20.00
☐ **No. 7814 Seasons Greetings Car**, for 1978	40.00	50.00
☐ **No. 7815 Toy Fair Box Car**, for 1978	130.00	140.00
☐ **No. 9011 Great Northern #027 Hopper Car**	140.00	150.00
☐ **No. 9011 Great Northern #027 Hopper Car**, blue	140.00	150.00
☐ **No. 9012 T.A.G. #027 Hopper Car**	10.00	15.00
☐ **No. 9012 T.A.G. Hopper Car**, dark blue	10.00	15.00
☐ **No. 9013 Canadian National #027 Hopper Car**, red	10.00	15.00
☐ **No. 9013 Canadian National Hopper Car**, red	10.00	15.00
☐ **No. 9015 Reading Hopper Car #027**, scarcest of #027 hoppers	25.00	35.00
☐ **No. 9016 Chessie Hopper Car**, #027	10.00	15.00
☐ **No. 9017 Wabash Gondola**, red, completely unlettered	10.00	15.00
☐ **No. 9018 D.T. and I. Hopper Car**, #027	15.00	20.00
☐ **No. 9019 Workin' RR Set**, breakup IC crane car	10.00	15.00
☐ **No. 9019 Workin' RR Set**, breakup blue side dump	10.00	15.00

	Price Range	
☐ **No. 9019 Workin' RR Set**, breakup SF work caboose	10.00	15.00
☐ **NO. 9019 Penn Central Box Car**, #027, 4 wheel	10.00	15.00
☐ **No. 9020 Union Pacific Flat Car**, with stakes	10.00	15.00
☐ **No. 9021 Santa Fe 2-in-1 Work Caboose** ..	10.00	15.00
☐ **No. 9022 ATSF Flat Car**, black, with stakes	10.00	15.00
☐ **No. 9023 MKT Flat Car**, with bulkhead ...	10.00	15.00
☐ **No. 9024 C and O Flat Car**, with stakes ..	10.00	15.00
☐ **No. 9025 D T and 12-in-1 Work Caboose**	10.00	15.00
☐ **No. 9026 Republic Steel Flat Car**, blue, with stakes	5.00	10.00
☐ **No. 9027 Soo Work Caboose**, 2-in-1 style	10.00	15.00
☐ **No. 9029 ATSF**, red, with stakes	10.00	15.00
☐ **No. 9029 Union Pacific Flat Car**, yellow, with stakes	10.00	15.00
☐ **No. 9032 Southern Pacific Gondola**, red ...	10.00	15.00
☐ **No. 9033 Penn Central #027 Gondola**, green	10.00	15.00
☐ **No. 9035 Conrail #027 Box Car**, blue	6.00	10.00
☐ **No. 9035 Conrail #027 Box Car**	6.00	10.00
☐ **No. 9036 Mobil Gas Single-Dome Tank Car**, white	6.00	10.00
☐ **No. 9037 Conrail #027 Box Car**, tuscan ...	6.00	10.00
☐ **No. 9037 Conrail Box Car**, tuscan	6.00	10.00
☐ **No. 9038 Chessie #027 Hopper**, blue	6.00	10.00
☐ **No. 9039 Mobil Gas Single-Dome Tank**, red	6.00	10.00
☐ **No. 9040 Wheaties Box Car**	8.00	12.00
☐ **No. 9040 Wheaties #027 Box Car**	8.00	12.00

Price Range

☐ No. 9041 Hershey #027 Box Car	8.00	12.00
☐ No. 9042 Autolite Motorcraft Regular Box Car	10.00	15.00
☐ No. 9042 Autolite Motorcraft Box Car, with no red lettering on side of car	10.00	15.00
☐ No. 9043 Erie Lackawanna Box Car	10.00	15.00
☐ No. 9044 Rio Grande Box Car	10.00	15.00
☐ No. 9045 Toys R Us Box Car, white	50.00	60.00
☐ No. 9046 Tru-Value Tru-Test Paint Box Car, uncataloged special	50.00	60.00
☐ No. 9047 Toys R Us Box Car, white	50.00	60.00
☐ No. 9049 Toys R Us Special Box Car	50.00	60.00
☐ No. 9051 Firestone Tank Car	15.00	20.00
☐ No. 9052 Toys R Us #027 Box Car	50.00	60.00
☐ No. 9054 J.C. Penney 75th Anniversary Box Car, cargo master set only at J.C. Penney	40.00	50.00
☐ No. 9055 Republic Steel Gondola, yellow	10.00	15.00
☐ No. 9057 CP Rail Caboose, Great Plains set breakup	15.00	20.00
☐ No. 9058 Lionel Lines Caboose, orange, came in Black River freight set	15.00	20.00
☐ No. 9060 Nickel Plate Road Caboose, brown	15.00	20.00
☐ No. 9060 Nickel Plate Road Caboose, tuscan	15.00	20.00
☐ No. 9061 Santa Fe Caboose, red	15.00	20.00
☐ No. 9062 Penn Central Caboose, jade green	15.00	20.00
☐ No. 9063 GTW Caboose, maroon, sold only in Canada	15.00	20.00
☐ No. 9064 Chesapeake and Ohio Caboose ..	10.00	15.00
☐ No. 9065 Canadian National Caboose	15.00	20.00

Price Range

☐ **No. 9068 Reading Bobber Caboose**	10.00	15.00
☐ **No. 9068 Reading Bobber Caboose**, lettered for TCA West coast convention	20.00	25.00
☐ **No. 9069 Jersey Central Lines Caboose,** tuscan	15.00	20.00
☐ **No. 9070 Rock Island Route of the Rockets Caboose**, gray, from sets only	15.00	20.00
☐ **No. 9071 ATSF Bobber Caboose**, came from sets	15.00	20.00
☐ **No. 9073 Coca Cola Caboose**	10.00	15.00
☐ **No. 9073 Coca Cola Caboose**, part of coke set only	10.00	15.00
☐ **No. 9076 Liberty Special Caboose**	15.00	20.00
☐ **No. 9078 Rock Island Bobber Caboose,** red	15.00	20.00
☐ **No. 9085 Santa Fe Work Caboose**, 4 wheel	10.00	15.00
☐ **No. 9090 Mini Max Car**	15.00	20.00
☐ **No. 9090 Mini Max Box Car**	15.00	20.00
☐ **No. 9110 Baltimore and Ohio Hopper,** black, uncovered	15.00	20.00
☐ **No. 9111 Norfolk and Western Quad Hopper**, tuscan, uncovered	15.00	20.00
☐ **No. 9113 Norfolk and Western Hopper,** gray, 1973 SSS set car	20.00	25.00
☐ **No. 9113 Norfolk and Western Hopper,** covered, imprinted for three rivers TCA chapter	15.00	20.00
☐ **No. 9114 Morton's Salt Billboard Hopper,** dark blue, yellow roof	15.00	20.00
☐ **No. 9114 Morton's Salt Hopper**	15.00	20.00
☐ **No. 9115 Planter's Peanut Billboard Hopper**, blue, yellow-covered top	15.00	20.00

Price Range

☐ **No. 9116 Domino Sugar Billboard Hopper**, gray, with dark blue cover	15.00	20.00
☐ **No. 9118 LCCA 1974 Convention Car**, Corning glass, gray, gray roof	15.00	25.00
☐ **No. 9119 Detroit and Mackinac Hopper**, red, covered	40.00	50.00
☐ **No. 9119 Detroit and Mackinac Hopper**, imprinted for Detroit-Toledo TCA chapter	40.00	50.00
☐ **No. 9121 L and N Bulldozer and Scraper**, flat, tuscan, two yellow loads	15.00	25.00
☐ **No. 9121 L and N Flat Car**, with two loads	15.00	25.00
☐ **No. 9123 Chesapeake and Ohio Rack Car**, blue	15.00	25.00
☐ **No. 9123 TCA Convention Auto Rack Car**, Detroit	45.00	55.00
☐ **No. 9123 C and O Auto Rack Car**	15.00	25.00
☐ **No. 9124 P and LE Flat with Bunkers and Logs**, green	15.00	25.00
☐ **No. 9126 Chesapeake and Ohio Auto Rack Car**, yellow	15.00	25.00
☐ **No. 9128 Heinz Pickle Car**, gray	15.00	25.00
☐ **No. 9129 Norfolk and Western Rack Car**, tuscan, sets only	15.00	25.00
☐ **No. 9130 Baltimore and Ohio Hopper Car**, covered roof with hatches	15.00	25.00
☐ **No. 9130 Baltimore and Ohio Hopper**	15.00	25.00
☐ **No. 9131 Denver and Rio Grande Gondola**, orange	15.00	25.00
☐ **No. 9132 Libby's Crushed Pineapple**, gray	15.00	25.00
☐ **No. 9132 Libby's Crushed Pineapple**	15.00	25.00
☐ **No. 9133 Burlington Northern TOFC Flat**, with green vans	15.00	25.00

	Price Range	
☐ No. 9133 Burlington Northern TOFC Flat	15.00	25.00
☐ No. 9134 Virginian Hopper, silver, covered	15.00	25.00
☐ No. 9135 Norfolk and Western Hopper, covered, dark blue	15.00	20.00
☐ No. 9135 Norfolk and Western Hopper, royal blue	25.00	30.00
☐ No. 9135 Norfolk and Western Hopper, dark blue	15.00	20.00
☐ No. 9136 Republic Steel Gondola, blue ..	10.00	15.00
☐ No. 9138 Sunoco Three-Dome Tank, SSS set car	30.00	35.00
☐ No. 9139 Penn Rack Car, jade green	15.00	20.00
☐ No. 9140 Burlington Gondola, green	10.00	15.00
☐ No. 9141 Burlington Northern Gondola ..	10.00	15.00
☐ No. 9141 Burlington Gondola, maroon, rare	70.00	80.00
☐ No. 9141 Burlington Northern Gondola, green	10.00	15.00
☐ No. 9142 Republic Steel Gondola, green ...	10.00	15.00
☐ No. 9143 Canadian National Gondola, tuscan	15.00	20.00
☐ No. 9144 Denver and Rio Grande Gondola, black	10.00	15.00
☐ No. 9144 Denver and Rio Grande Gondola	10.00	15.00
☐ No. 9145 Illinois Central Gulf Auto Rack Car, orange	15.00	20.00
☐ No. 9146 Mogen David Wine Vat Car, blue	15.00	25.00
☐ No. 9147 Texaco Texas Oil Company Plated Tank Car, chemical type	15.00	25.00
☐ No. 9148 Dupont Triple-Dome Tank Car, ivory	15.00	25.00

	Price Range	
☐ **No. 9149 CP Rail Flat Car**, with two CP rail piggy vans, red	15.00	25.00
☐ **No. 9150 Gulf Tank**, white	15.00	25.00
☐ **No. 9151 Shell Tank Car**, chemical, single dome, yellow	15.00	25.00
☐ **No. 9152 Shell Tank Car**, orange with black ends	15.00	25.00
☐ **No. 9153 Chevron Tank Car**, silver	15.00	25.00
☐ **No. 9153 Chevron Tank Car**, silver, black tank ends	15.00	25.00
☐ **No. 9154 Borden's Chrome-Plated Tank Car**, single dome, chemical	15.00	25.00
☐ **No. 9154 Borden's Chrome-Plated Tank Car**	15.00	25.00
☐ **No. 9155 LCCA 1975 Convention Car**, Monsanto Chemical Tank Car, white, St. Louis	70.00	80.00
☐ **No. 9156 Mobil Gas Chemical Tank Car**, chrome plated	15.00	20.00
☐ **No. 9156 Mobil Gas Chemical Tank Car** ..	15.00	20.00
☐ **No. 9157 C and O Harnischfeger-Type Crane Kit**, on flat car	15.00	20.00
☐ **No. 9158 Penn Central Power Shovel Kit Car**, jade green	15.00	20.00
☐ **No. 9158 Penn Central Power Shovel Kit Car**	15.00	20.00
☐ **No. 9159 Sunoco Chrome-Plated Tank** ...	30.00	35.00
☐ **No. 9160 Illinois Central N5C Caboose**, porthole style	15.00	30.00
☐ **No. 9161 Canadian National Caboose**, N5C, orange and black	15.00	20.00
☐ **No. 9162 Pennsylvania N5C Caboose**, tuscan	25.00	30.00
☐ **No. 9163 Santa Fe Caboose**, red	20.00	25.00

	Price Range	
☐ **No. 9165 Canadian Pacific N5C Caboose**	25.00	30.00
☐ **No. 9166 Rio Grande Caboose**, yellow and silver	15.00	20.00
☐ **No. 9166 Rio Grande Caboose**	15.00	20.00
☐ **No. 9167 Chessie Caboose**, N5C, yellow, very short supply, Chessie road name	25.00	30.00
☐ **No. 9167 Chessie Caboose**	30.00	40.00
☐ **No. 9168 Union Pacific N5C Caboose**, yellow	15.00	20.00
☐ **No. 9168 Union Pacific N5C Caboose**	15.00	20.00
☐ **No. 9169 Milwaukee Road Caboose**, orange	15.00	20.00
☐ **No. 9170 Norfolk and Western N5C Caboose**	45.00	55.00
☐ **No. 9171 Missouri Pacific Caboose**	15.00	20.00
☐ **No. 9172 Penn Central Caboose**, black ...	15.00	20.00
☐ **No. 9173 Jersey Central Caboose**, red	15.00	20.00
☐ **No. 9174 NYC (P and LE) Bay Window Caboose**	60.00	70.00
☐ **NO. 9175 Virginian N5C Caboose**, blue ..	15.00	20.00
☐ **No. 9177 Northern Pacific Bay Window Caboose**, green and yellow, metal trucks ..	20.00	25.00
☐ **No. 9178 Illinois Central Gulf Caboose** ..	30.00	35.00
☐ **No. 9179 Chessie Caboose**, four-wheel yellow bobber style like the Kickapoo	15.00	20.00
☐ **No. 9180 The Rock N5C Caboose**, blue and white	15.00	20.00
☐ **No. 9181 Boston and Maine N5C Caboose**, blue and white	15.00	20.00
☐ **No. 9182 Norfolk and Western N5C Caboose**, black	15.00	20.00
☐ **No. 9183 Mickey Mouse Express N5C Caboose**	20.00	25.00

Price Range

☐ **No. 9184 Erie Bay Window Caboose**, plastic trucks, red	20.00	25.00
☐ **No. 9184 Erie Bay Window Caboose**, imprinted for North Texas Chapter TCA	35.00	40.00
☐ **No. 9185 Grand Trunk GT N5C Caboose**	15.00	20.00
☐ **No. 9186 Conrail N5C Caboose**, blue and white logo	15.00	20.00
☐ **No. 9187 Gulf, Mobil and Ohio Caboose**, Heartland Express set	20.00	25.00
☐ **No. 9188 Great Northern Bay Window Caboose**, Rocky Mountain set	40.00	50.00
☐ **No. 9189 Gulf Oil Tank Car**, Gulftane LP gas, chemical tank, chrome plated	30.00	35.00
☐ **No. 9200 Illinois Central Box Car**	20.00	30.00
☐ **No. 9200 Illinois Central Box**, narrow letters	25.00	35.00
☐ **No. 9200 Illinois Central Box**, wide letters	25.00	35.00
☐ **No. 9201 Penn Central Box Car**, green, 1970 car	40.00	50.00
☐ **No. 9202 Santa Fe Shock Control Box Car**	40.00	50.00
☐ **No. 9203 Union Pacific Box Car**, yellow ...	50.00	60.00
☐ **No. 9203 Union Pacific Box Car**	50.00	60.00
☐ **No. 9204 Northern Pacific Box Car**, with built date	40.00	50.00
☐ **No. 9204 Northern Pacific Box Car**, without built date	40.00	50.00
☐ **No. 9205 Norfolk and Western Box Car**, dark blue	15.00	20.00
☐ **No. 9205 Norfolk and Western Box Car**, light blue	15.00	20.00
☐ **No. 9206 Great Northern Box Car**, blue ...	15.00	20.00
☐ **No. 9207 Soo Box Car**, Tim Trucks	15.00	20.00

Price Range

☐ **No. 9208 CP Rail Box Car**, Tim Trucks, yellow and black lettering	20.00	25.00
☐ **No. 9208 CP Rail Box**, yellow and black ..	20.00	25.00
☐ **No. 9209 Burlington Northern**, 9700 mold	20.00	25.00
☐ **No. 9209 Burlington Northern Box Car**, Tim Trucks	20.00	25.00
☐ **No. 9209 Burlington Northern Box**	20.00	25.00
☐ **No. 9210 Baltimore and Ohio Auto Box Car**, black, orange doors	35.00	40.00
☐ **No. 9210 Baltimore and Ohio Auto Box Car**, black with dark green doors, no decal	30.00	35.00
☐ **No. 9210 Baltimore and Ohio Auto Box Car**, black, orange doors, TCA Pacific Northwest Division decal	30.00	35.00
☐ **No. 9210 Baltimore and Ohio Auto Box Car**, dark green doors, TCA Pacific Northwest Division decal	30.00	35.00
☐ **No. 9211 Penn Central Box Car**, silver door, jade green	30.00	35.00
☐ **No. 9211 Penn Central Box Car**, jade green	30.00	35.00
☐ **No. 9211 Penn Central Box Car**	30.00	35.00
☐ **No. 9212 SCL Flat**, 1976 LCCA convention car at Atlanta with van loads, flat car body lettered one side	40.00	50.00
☐ **No. 9213 Hopper**	25.00	30.00
☐ **No. 9214 Northern Pacific Box Car**, tuscan	15.00	20.00
☐ **No. 9214 Northern Pacific**, tuscan, 9700 mold	15.00	20.00
☐ **No. 9215 Norfolk and Western**, Bet Trucks, dark blue with silver door	15.00	20.00
☐ **No. 9215 Norfolk and Western Box Car**, no number on end, Tim Trucks	30.00	35.00

	Price Range	
☐ **No. 9216 Great Northern Rack Car**, Milwaukee Limited breakup	30.00	35.00
☐ **No. 9230 Monon Box Car**, tuscan	20.00	25.00
☐ **No. 9230 Monon Box Car**	20.00	25.00
☐ **No. 9231 Reading Bay Window Caboose** ..	20.00	25.00
☐ **No. 9232 Allis Chalmers Reactor Load**, Cross-Country set only	30.00	35.00
☐ **No. 9233 Drop Center 16-Wheel Transformer Car**, Mid-Atlantic set only, Lionel's longest freight car	60.00	70.00
☐ **No. 9234 Radioactive Waste Car**, flat car with two waste containers	50.00	60.00
☐ **No. 9250 Waterpoxy Triple-Dome Tank Car**, white	20.00	25.00
☐ **No. 9259 Southern Bay Window Caboose**, LCCA 1977 convention car	60.00	70.00
☐ **No. 9260 Reynolds Aluminum Hopper Car**, blue	15.00	20.00
☐ **No. 9261 Sun Maid Raisins Hopper Car**, red, yellow roof	15.00	20.00
☐ **No. 9262 Ralston Purina Hopper**, red checkerboard on white, covered	35.00	45.00
☐ **No. 9263 Pennsylvania Hopper Car**, tuscan, covered	20.00	25.00
☐ **No. 9264 Illinois Central Hopper**, orange, covered	15.00	20.00
☐ **No. 9265 Chessie Covered Hopper**, yellow	15.00	25.00
☐ **No. 9266 Southern Hopper**, "Big John" ...	40.00	50.00
☐ **No. 9267 Alcoa Covered Hopper**, metal trucks, 1976 SSS set car	30.00	40.00
☐ **No. 9268 Northern Pacific Bay Window Caboose**, made to match 1976 SSS NP	20.00	25.00
☐ **No. 9269 Milwaukee Bay Window Caboose**, Milwaukee Limited	40.00	50.00

Price Range

☐ No. 9270 Northern Pacific N5C Caboose ..	20.00	25.00
☐ No. 9271 N and STL Bay Window Caboose, 1978 SSS	30.00	40.00
☐ No. 9272 New Haven Bay Window Caboose	20.00	30.00
☐ No. 9273 Southern Bay Window Caboose	30.00	40.00
☐ No. 9274 Santa Fe Red Bay Window Caboose	75.00	85.00
☐ No. 9276 Peabody Coal Hopper, Milwaukee Limited, set	30.00	35.00
☐ No. 9278 Life Savers Tank	20.00	25.00
☐ No. 9279 Magnolia Three-Dome Tan	15.00	20.00
☐ No. 9280 ATSF Horse Transport Car, red	15.00	20.00
☐ No. 9281 ATSF Auto Carrier, red	15.00	20.00
☐ No. 9282 Great Northern Piggy Back Flat	15.00	20.00
☐ No. 9283 Union Pacific Yellow Gondola ...	15.00	20.00
☐ No. 9284 ATSF Gondola	20.00	25.00
☐ No. 9285 Illinois Central Gulf Piggy Back Car, with vans	20.00	25.00
☐ No. 9286 Bessemer, B L and E Hopper Car	20.00	25.00
☐ No. 9287 Southern N5C Porthole Caboose, red	15.00	20.00
☐ No. 9288 Lehigh Valley N5C Caboose, red	15.00	20.00
☐ No. 9289 Chicago and Northwestern N5C Caboose, yellow	15.00	20.00
☐ No. 9289 Chicago and Northwestern Caboose, no box	15.00	20.00
☐ No. 9297 Cities Service Chemical Tank ..	30.00	35.00
☐ No. 9300 Penn Central Operating Dump Car, helium tank load, green	25.00	35.00

	Price Range	
☐ **No. 9300 Penn Central Dump Car**, log load	15.00	20.00
☐ **No. 9300 Penn Central Log Dump Car** ...	15.00	20.00
☐ **No. 9300 Penn Central Log Car**	10.00	15.00
☐ **No. 9301 U.S. Mail Car**, for Sacramento Sierra Division TCA car in 1976	25.00	30.00
☐ **No. 9301 Operating Mail Car**, 1973 regular run	15.00	20.00
☐ **No. 9301 Operating Mail Car**	15.00	20.00
☐ **No. 9302 L and N Searchlight Car**, tuscan	15.00	20.00
☐ **No. 9303 Union Pacific Operating Log Car**, yellow	15.00	20.00
☐ **No. 9303 Union Pacific Operating Log Car**	15.00	20.00
☐ **No. 9304 Chesapeake and Ohio Operating Dump Car**, blue	15.00	20.00
☐ **No. 9305 Outlaw and Sheriff Car**, from James Gang set	30.00	40.00
☐ **No. 9306 ATSF Flat Car**, with fences and horses out of James Gang set	15.00	20.00
☐ **No. 9307 Erie Animated Gondola**, cop and hobo	45.00	55.00
☐ **No. 9309 Toledo, Peoria and Western TPW Bay Window Caboose**, out of Cross-Country set	25.00	30.00
☐ **No. 9310 Santa Fe Log Dump**, red	15.00	20.00
☐ **No. 9311 Union Pacific Coal Dump**, yellow	15.00	20.00
☐ **No. 9312 Conrail Searchlight**, gray motor cover	15.00	20.00
☐ **No. 9312 Conrail Searchlight Car**, with orange motor cover	50.00	60.00

Price Range

☐ **No. 9313 Gulf Triple-Dome Tank Car,** die-cast trucks, from Southern Pacific Limited set 40.00   50.00

☐ **No. 9315 Southern Pacific Gondola,** die-cast trucks 20.00   25.00

☐ **No. 9316 Southern Pacific Bay Window Caboose,** die-cast trucks 50.00   60.00

☐ **No. 9317 Santa Fe Bay Window Caboose,** blue and yellow 30.00   35.00

☐ **No. 9319 TCA 25th Anniversary Convention Silver Bullion Car** 180.00   190.00

☐ **No. 9320 Gold Bullion Car,** die-cast trucks 70.00   80.00

☐ **No. 9321 ATSF Santa Fe Single Dome Tank Car** 50.00   60.00

☐ **No. 9322 ATSF Santa Fe Hopper Car** 50.00   60.00

☐ **No. 9322 ATSF Basic Body Only,** painted and lettered 30.00   40.00

☐ **No. 9323 ATSF Santa Fe Bay Window Caboose** 60.00   70.00

☐ **No. 9324 Tootsie Roll Tank Car** 15.00   20.00

☐ **No. 9325 N & W Flat Car,** with fences ... 10.00   15.00

☐ **No. 9326 Burlington Northern Bay Window Caboose** 20.00   25.00

☐ **No. 9327 Bakelite Three-Dome Tank Car** 15.00   20.00

☐ **No. 9328 Chessie System Bay Window Caboose,** out of Royal Limited set 45.00   55.00

☐ **No. 9329 Chessie System Crane Car,** out of Royal Limited set, yellow, blue and silver 50.00   60.00

☐ **No. 9330 Side Dump Car,** out of Smokey Mountain set, four-wheel dump car 15.00   20.00

☐ **No. 9331 Union 76 Chemical Tank Car,** die-cast trucks 35.00   45.00

	Price Range	
☐ **No. 9332 Reading Crane Car**, die-cast trucks	45.00	55.00
☐ **No. 9333 Southern Pacific Piggy Back with Trailer**	15.00	20.00
☐ **No. 9333 Southern Pacific Flat Car**, with bulldozer kit load, in Black River set, no box loose pack	15.00	20.00
☐ **No. 9334 Humble Oil Single-Dome Tanker**	15.00	20.00
☐ **No. 9336 CP Rail Gondola**, die-cast trucks, from Quaker City Limited	25.00	30.00
☐ **No. 9338 Penn Power and Light Hopper**, die-cast trucks, from Quaker City Limited ..	45.00	55.00
☐ **No. 9339 Great Northern #027 Box Car**, dark green	15.00	20.00
☐ **No. 9340 Illinois Central Gulf #027 Gondola**, red	15.00	20.00
☐ **No. 9341 Atlantic Coast Line Caboose**, square window	15.00	20.00
☐ **No. 9344 Citgo Triple Dome Tank Car**, out of Royal Limited set, die-cast trucks ..	25.00	30.00
☐ **No. 9346 Wabash Caboose**, came only in 1979 Wabash Cannonball set	15.00	20.00
☐ **No. 9347 TTOS 1979 Niagara Falls Convention Car**, blue triple-dome tank car, sprung trucks	60.00	70.00
☐ **No. 9348 Santa Fe Crane Car**, die-cast trucks, spike herald, matches FARR set #1	50.00	60.00
☐ **No. 9349 San Francisco Mint Gold Bullion Car**, maroon	40.00	50.00
☐ **No. 9351 Penn Three-Deck Auto Carrier**, tuscan	15.00	20.00
☐ **No. 9352 Chicago and Northwestern Flat Car**, green with yellow vans	30.00	35.00

	Price Range	
☐ **No. 9353 Crystal Line Tank Car**, red, three dome	20.00	25.00
☐ **No. 9354 Pennzoil Chemical Tank Car,** chrome plated	15.00	20.00
☐ **No. 9355 Delaware and Hudson Bay Window Caboose**, blue and gray	20.00	25.00
☐ **No. 9357 Smokey Mountain Bobber Caboose**	15.00	20.00
☐ **No. 9358 LCCA Sands of Iowa Des Moines Convention Car**, for 1980, robins egg blue, plastic trucks	50.00	60.00
☐ **No. 9359 National Basketball Association #027 Box Car**	35.00	40.00
☐ **No. 9360 National Hockey League #027 Box Car**	35.00	40.00
☐ **No. 9361 Chicago and Northwestern Bay Window Caboose**	20.00	25.00
☐ **No. 9362 Major League Baseball #027 Box Car**	30.00	40.00
☐ **No. 9363 N and W Manual Operating Dump Car**, #9325 on frame	15.00	20.00
☐ **No. 9364 N and W Manual Operating Crane Car**, #9325 on frame	10.00	15.00
☐ **No. 9365 Toys R Us #027 Box Car**	10.00	15.00
☐ **No. 9366 Union Pacific FARR #2 Hopper**	30.00	35.00
☐ **No. 9367 Union Pacific FARR #2 Tank Car**	30.00	35.00
☐ **No. 9368 Union Pacific FARR #2 Bay Window Caboose**	35.00	45.00
☐ **No. 9369 Sinclair Chemical Tank Car,** green, die-cast trucks	30.00	40.00
☐ **No. 9370 Seaboard Gondola**, die-cast trucks	20.00	30.00
☐ **No. 9371 Atlantic Sugar Hopper Car**, yellow, die-cast trucks	30.00	35.00

	Price Range	
☐ **No. 9372 Seaboard Bay Window Caboose**, die-cast trucks	50.00	60.00
☐ **No. 9373 Getty Chemical Tank Car**, white	25.00	30.00
☐ **No. 9374 Reading Black-Covered Hopper**	25.00	30.00
☐ **No. 9379 Santa Fe Gondola**, yellow and black	20.00	25.00
☐ **No. 9380 New York, New Haven, and Hartford Square Window Caboose**, silver	20.00	25.00
☐ **No. 9381 Baltimore and Ohio Chessie System Square Window Caboose**	20.00	25.00
☐ **No. 9382 Florida East Coast Bay Window Caboose**, red and yellow, plastic trucks ...	20.00	25.00
☐ **No. 9383 Union Pacific FARR #2 Flat Car**, with vans	40.00	50.00
☐ **No. 9400 Conrail Box Car**	15.00	20.00
☐ **No. 9401 Great Northern Box Car**	15.00	20.00
☐ **No. 9402 Susquehanna Box Car**	15.00	20.00
☐ **No. 9403 Seaboard Coast Line Box Car** ...	15.00	20.00
☐ **No. 9404 Nickel Plate Road Box Car**	15.00	20.00
☐ **No. 9405 Chatahooche Box Car**	15.00	20.00
☐ **No. 9406 Denver and Rio Grande West Box**	15.00	20.00
☐ **No. 9407 Union Pacific Stock Car**	25.00	30.00
☐ **No. 9408 Lionel Lines Circus Car**, 1978, set SSS	20.00	25.00
☐ **No. 9411 Lackawanna, D L and W, Phoebe Snow Box**	40.00	50.00
☐ **No. 9412 Richmond, Fredericksburg, and Potomac Box**	15.00	20.00
☐ **No. 9413 Naperville Junction Box**	15.00	20.00
☐ **No. 9414 Cotton Belt Box**	15.00	20.00

Price Range

☐ No. 9415 Providence and Worcester Box ..	15.00	20.00
☐ No. 9416 Minnesota, Dakota and Western	15.00	20.00
☐ No. 9417 CP Rail, gold letters, from Great Plains Express set, 1979	70.00	80.00
☐ No. 9418 Feature-End Box Car, for 1979 commemorating Great American railroads	80.00	90.00
☐ No. 9419 Union Pacific Box Car, FARR #2	25.00	30.00
☐ No. 9420 Baltimore and Ohio Sentinel Box Car	15.00	20.00
☐ No. 9421 Maine Central Box Car	15.00	20.00
☐ No. 9422 Elgin, Joliet and Eastern Box Car	15.00	20.00
☐ No. 9423 New York, New Haven and Hartford Box Car	15.00	20.00
☐ No. 9424 Toledo, Peoria and Western Box Car, orange with silver roof	15.00	20.00
☐ No. 9425 British Columbia Railway Auto Box Car, with two-color green auto doors	20.00	25.00
☐ No. 9426 Chesapeake and Ohio Box Car ..	15.00	20.00
☐ No. 9427 The Bay Line Box Car	15.00	20.00
☐ No. 9428 Toledo, Peoria and Western Box, green and ivory	60.00	70.00
☐ No. 9429 Joshua Cowan 100th Anniversary of Birth Box Car, The Early Years ...	60.00	70.00
☐ No. 9430 Joshua Cowan 100th Anniversary of Birth Box Car, The Standard Gauge Years	55.00	65.00
☐ No. 9431 Joshua Cowan 100th Anniversary of Birth Box Car, The Pre-war Years	110.00	120.00
☐ No. 9433 Joshua Cowan 100th Anniversary of Birth Box Car	110.00	120.00

Price Range

☐ No. 9434 Joshua Cowan "The Man" 100th Anniversary of Birth Box Car	95.00	105.00
☐ No. 9500 City of Milwaukee Car	50.00	60.00
☐ No. 9501 Aberdeen Milwaukee Road Passenger Car	15.00	30.00
☐ No. 9501 Aberdeen Milwaukee Road Passenger Car	25.00	30.00
☐ No. 9501 President Washington Observation, Milwaukee road	50.00	60.00
☐ No. 9503 City of Chicago, Milwaukee Passenger Car	50.00	60.00
☐ No. 9504 Tacoma Milwaukee Passenger Car	30.00	40.00
☐ No. 9505 Seattle Milwaukee Passenger Car	30.00	40.00
☐ No. 9506 Milwaukee Road Combination Baggage Car	30.00	40.00
☐ No. 9510 Pennsylvania Combination Baggage Car	25.00	35.00
☐ No. 9511 Minneapolis Special Coupon Car, says "Milwaukee Road"	30.00	35.00
☐ No. 9512 TTOS Convention Car for Summerdale Junction Convention, 1974	40.00	50.00
☐ No. 9513, 9514, 9515 Three Pennsylvania Cars	75.00	85.00
☐ No. 9516 Baltimore and Ohio Mountain Top	50.00	60.00
☐ No. 9520 TTOS Convention Car, for Phoenix convention, 1975	50.00	60.00
☐ No. 9521 Pennsylvania Full Baggage Car ..	125.00	135.00
☐ No. 9522 Milwaukee Full Baggage Car ...	125.00	135.00
☐ No. 9523 Baltimore and Ohio Full Baggate Car	50.00	60.00
☐ No. 9524 Baltimore and Ohio Margaret Corbin Coach, blue	35.00	45.00

	Price Range	
☐ **No. 9525 Baltimore and Ohio Emerald Brook Coach** ....:....................	35.00	45.00
☐ **No. 9526 Convention Car**, for Snobird, Utah, convention 1976, without decal	40.00	50.00
☐ **No. 9526 Convention Car**, for Snobird, Utah, convention 1976, car has decal indicating attendance at the convention	50.00	60.00
☐ **No. 9527 Milwaukee Campaign Observation**, F.D. Roosevelt Car, orange	25.00	35.00
☐ **No. 9528 Pennsylvania Campaign Observation**, H.S. Truman Car, tuscan	25.00	35.00
☐ **No. 9529 Baltimore and Ohio Campaign Observation Car**, D.D. Eisenhower Car, blue	25.00	35.00
☐ **No. 9530 Southern Crescent Car**	25.00	35.00
☐ **No. 9535 TTOS Convention Car**, for Columbus, Ohio, convention 1977	45.00	55.00
☐ **No. 9536 Blue Comet Cars**	45.00	55.00
☐ **No. 9541 ATSF REA Baggage**	25.00	35.00
☐ **No. 9544 TCA Land of Lincoln 1980 Chicago Convention Car**	50.00	60.00
☐ **No. 9551, W and A "General" Baggage** ...	40.00	50.00
☐ **No. 9570 Pennsylvania Congressional Aluminum Passenger Car**	125.00	135.00
☐ **No. 9575 Pennsylvania Thomas Edison Car**	100.00	110.00
☐ **No. 9576 Burlington Zephyr Chrome Plated Aluminum Car**	45.00	55.00
☐ **No. 9581 Chessie Steam Special Passenger**, No. 027, plastic	50.00	60.00
☐ **No. 9588 Burlington Texas Zephyr Silver Dome Car**, aluminum	70.00	80.00
☐ **No. 9600 Chesapeake and Ohio Hi Cube Car**, yellow lettering on blue car	25.00	35.00

	Price Range	
☐ No. 9601 Illinois Central Gulf Hi Cube Box Car, orange	25.00	35.00
☐ No. 9602 Santa Fe Hi Cube, red	25.00	35.00
☐ No. 9603 Penn Central Hi Cube, jade green	25.00	35.00
☐ No. 9604 Norfolk and Western Hi Cube, black	15.00	20.00
☐ No. 9605 New Haven Hi Cube, orange ...	25.00	35.00
☐ No. 9606 Union Pacific Hi Cube, yellow ...	15.00	20.00
☐ No. 9607 Southern Pacific Hi Cube, red ...	15.00	20.00
☐ No. 9608 Burlington Northern Hi Cube, green	15.00	20.00
☐ No. 9610 Frisco Hi Cube Box, case only in Rocky Mountain Set	30.00	35.00
☐ No. 9610 U Frisco Hi Cube	30.00	35.00
☐ No. 9611 TCA Boston Convention Hi Cube Box Car	45.00	55.00
☐ No. 9620 0 Gauge Sports Car	85.00	95.00
☐ No. 9620 Wales Conference 0 Gauge Sports Box Car	15.00	20.00
☐ No. 9621 Campbell Conference 0 Gauge Sports Box Car	15.00	20.00
☐ No. 9622 Western Conference 0 Gauge Sports Box Car	15.00	20.00
☐ No. 9623 Eastern Conference 0 Gauge Sports Box Car	15.00	20.00
☐ No. 9624 Major League Baseball, National League 0 Gauge Sports Box Car ...	15.00	20.00
☐ No. 9625 Major League Baseball, American League 0 Gauge Sports Box Car	15.00	20.00
☐ No. 9669 Mickey Mouse Hi Cube Car	85.00	95.00
☐ No. 9672 Mickey Mouse 50th Anniversary Hi Cube Box Car	200.00	250.00

Price Range

☐ **No. 9678 Hollywood Convention Hi Cube Box Car**, 1978, with decal indicating attendance at the convention 60.00   70.00

☐ **No. 9700 Southern Box Car**, red 15.00   20.00

☐ **No. 9700 1976 "Philadephia"**(misspelled on car) **Convention Box Car** 60.00   70.00

☐ **No. 9701 Baltimore and Ohio Auto Box Car**, silver with light blue doors 35.00   45.00

☐ **No. 9701 Baltimore and Ohio**, black, rare 90.00   100.00

☐ **No. 9701 Baltimore and Ohio**, silver, dark blue doors 40.00   50.00

☐ **No. 9701 Baltimore and Ohio**, silver with light green doors 40.00   50.00

☐ **No. 9701 Baltimore and Ohio**, silver with maroon doors 40.00   50.00

☐ **No. 9701 Baltimore and Ohio**, silver with regular black doors 15.00   20.00

☐ **No. 9701 Baltimore and Ohio Auto Box**, blue doors with Pacific Northwest TCA Division decal 35.00   45.00

☐ **No. 9701 Baltimore and Ohio Auto Box**, dark blue doors with Pacific Northwest TCA Division decal 40.00   50.00

☐ **No. 9701 Baltimore and Ohio Auto Box**, maroon doors with Pacific Northwest TCA Division decal 40.00   50.00

☐ **No. 9701 Baltimore and Ohio Auto Box**, light green doors, with Pacific Northwest TCA Division decal 40.00   50.00

☐ **No. 9702 Soo Line Box Car** 15.00   30.00

☐ **No. 9703 Rail Box Car**, dark red, black lettering, rare 80.00   90.00

☐ **No. 9704 Norfolk and Western Box**, tuscan 25.00   30.00

	Price Range	
☐ **No. 9705 Denver and Rio Grande Box Car**, orange	25.00	20.00
☐ **No. 9706 C and O Box Car**, blue	15.00	20.00
☐ **No. 9707 MKT Cattle Stock Car**	15.00	20.00
☐ **No. 9707 MKT Cattle Stock Car**, no box	15.00	20.00
☐ **No. 9708 New York Toy Fair Car**, 1973 Railway Post Office Car, red, white, and blue	100.00	125.00
☐ **No. 9708 Railway Post Office Car**, red, white, and blue	15.00	20.00
☐ **No. 9709 State of Maine Box Car**, for 1972 SSS set	30.00	40.00
☐ **No. 9710 Rutland Box Car**, from 1972 SSS set	30.00	40.00
☐ **No. 9711 Southern Box Car**, tuscan	15.00	20.00
☐ **No. 9712 Baltimore and Ohio Auto Box** ..	15.00	20.00
☐ **No. 9713 Rail**, green, black letters	25.00	30.00
☐ **No. 9713 Rail**, says "Seasons Greetings" by Lionel, 1974	140.00	150.00
☐ **No. 9714 Denver and Ohio Grande Box Car**, silver	15.00	20.00
☐ **No. 9715 Chesapeake and Ohio Box Car**, black	20.00	25.00
☐ **No. 9716 Penn Central Box Car**, jade green	25.00	30.00
☐ **No. 9717 Union Pacific Box Car**, yellow ...	30.00	40.00
☐ **No. 9718 Canadian National Box Car**, tuscan	30.00	40.00
☐ **No. 9719 New Haven "Coupon" Box Car**	20.00	25.00
☐ **No. 9723 Western Pacific Box Car**, from 1973 SSS set, orange	35.00	40.00

Price Range

☐ **No. 9723 Western Pacific Box**, says "Welcome New York Toy Fair," 1974 by Lionel 125.00   135.00

☐ **No. 9723 Western Pacific Fanta Soda Box Car**, color of orange, variation 60.00   70.00

☐ **No. 9724 Missouri Pacific Eagle Box Car**, CP SSS set car 45.00   55.00

☐ **No. 9725 NKT Stock Car**, yellow 15.00   20.00

☐ **No. 9728 Union Pacific Stock Car**, for LCCA Denver, Colorado, convention 50.00   60.00

☐ **No. 9729 Rail**, black, from Great Plains Express set 60.00   70.00

☐ **No. 9730 Rail Box Car**, black letters, silver car 30.00   40.00

☐ **No. 9730 Rail Box Car**, white letters, silver car 30.00   40.00

☐ **No. 9730 CP Rail Box Car**, black letters, specially hot-pressed letters for the Western Michigan Chapter TCA, Great Lakes Division, overprint in red 30.00   40.00

☐ **No. 9730 CP Rail Box Car**, imprinted for Sacramento Sierra Division Chapter TCA ... 30.00   40.00

☐ **No. 9731 Milwaukee Box Car**, red with white letters 15.00   20.00

☐ **No. 9732 Southern Pacific Box Car**, only in Southern Pacific Limited set, metal trucks 35.00   45.00

☐ **No. 9733 LCCA Wheeling, West Virginia, Convention Car**, 1979, box car 55.00   65.00

☐ **No. 9734 Bangor and Aroostock Box Car**, from Quaker City set, metal trucks 50.00   60.00

☐ **No. 9735 Grand Trunk Box Car**, blue with GT letters 15.00   20.00

☐ **No. 9737 Central of Vermont Box Car**, tuscan 15.00   20.00

	Price Range	
☐ **No. 9739 Denver and Rio Grande Box Car**, yellow	15.00	20.00
☐ **No. 9739 Denver and Rio Grande Box Car**, lettered for No. Texas Chapter of Lone Star Division TCA	30.00	35.00
☐ **No. 9739 Denver and Rio Grande Box Car**	15.00	20.00
☐ **No. 9740 Chesapeake and Ohio Box Car,** yellow	15.00	20.00
☐ **No. 9740 Chesapeake and Ohio Box Car,** imprinted for Great Lakes Division TCA ..	35.00	45.00
☐ **No. 9740 Chesapeake and Ohio Box Car,** yellow	15.00	20.00
☐ **No. 9742 Minneapolis and St. Louis Box Car**, green, overprinted "Season's Greetings," 1973 by Lionel	140.00	150.00
☐ **No. 9742 Minneapolis and St. Louis Box Car**, green, special "coupon" car, uncataloged	35.00	45.00
☐ **No. 9743 Sprite Box Car**, green	15.00	20.00
☐ **No. 9744 Tab Box Car**, magenta, pinkish red	15.00	20.00
☐ **No. 9745 Fanta Box Car**, orange	15.00	20.00
☐ **No. 9747 Chessie System Double-Door Auto Box**, blue	30.00	40.00
☐ **No. 9748 CP Rail Box Car**, white letters ..	20.00	25.00
☐ **No. 9749 Penn Central Box Car**, jade green	15.00	20.00
☐ **No. 9750 D T and I Box Car**, dark green ..	15.00	20.00
☐ **No. 9751 Frisco Box Car**, red	20.00	25.00
☐ **No. 9752 L and N Box Car**	20.00	25.00
☐ **No. 9753 Maine Central Box Car**, NETCA New England Division TCA imprint, 1975	25.00	30.00
☐ **No. 9753 Maine Central Box Car**, yellow ..	15.00	20.00

Price Range

☐ **No. 9754 New York Central,** imprint for
NETCA TCA Division, red and gray 35.00 40.00

☐ **No. 9754 New York Central Pacemaker
Box Car,** red and gray 15.00 20.00

☐ **No. 9755 Union Pacific Box Car,** tuscan ... 30.00 35.00

☐ **No. 9755 NB Union Pacific Box Car,** tuscan 25.00 30.00

☐ **No. 9757 Central of Georgia Box Car** 30.00 35.00

☐ **No. 9758 Alaska Box Car,** blue 20.00 25.00

☐ **No. 9759 Paul Revere, Liberty Bell and
President's Car Set** 80.00 90.00

☐ **No. 9762 1975 Toy Fair Car** 15.00 20.00

☐ **No. 9763 Rio Grande Cattle Car,** orange 20.00 25.00

☐ **No. 9764 Grand Trunk Double-Door Auto
Box** 15.00 20.00

☐ **No. 9767 Rail Box Box Car,** yellow 20.00 25.00

☐ **No. 9768 Boston and Maine Box Car,** blue
.... 15.00 20.00

☐ **No. 9768 Boston and Maine Box Car,** blue
with special imprint metca Division TCA 20.00 25.00

☐ **No. 9769 Bessemer and Lake Erie Box
Car,** orange 15.00 20.00

☐ **No. 9770 Northern Pacific Box Car,** orange 15.00 20.00

☐ **No. 9771 Norfolk and Western Box Car,**
blue 15.00 20.00

☐ **No. 9772 Great Northern Box Car,** tricolor 45.00 55.00

☐ **No. 9773 New York Central Stock Car** ... 35.00 40.00

☐ **No. 9774 TCA Convention Car,** for Orlando, Florida, orange 45.00 55.00

☐ **No. 9775 Minneapolis and St. Louis Box
Car,** set, metal trucks 40.00 50.00

☐ **No. 9776 Southern Pacific Box Car,** metal
trucks, black 45.00 55.00

	Price Range	
☐ **No. 9777 Virginian Box Car**, blue	15.00	20.00
☐ **No. 9779 Philadephia Car**, misspelled	60.00	70.00
☐ **No. 9780 Johnny Cash Box Car**, silver with black roof, 1976 feature-end deal car	70.00	80.00
☐ **No. 9781 Delaware and Hudson Box Car**, yellow	15.00	20.00
☐ **No. 9782 The Rock Box Car**, blue	15.00	20.00
☐ **No. 9783 Baltimore and Ohio Box Car**, blue	15.00	20.00
☐ **No. 9784 ATSF Box Car**, red	15.00	20.00
☐ **No. 9785 Conrail Box Car**, bright blue	15.00	20.00
☐ **No. 9785 Conrail Box Car**, bright blue, overprinted for Sacramento Sierra TCA chapter	35.00	45.00
☐ **No. 9786 Chicago and Northwestern CNW Box**, tuscan	20.00	25.00
☐ **No. 9787 Central Railroad of New Jersey**, black	20.00	25.00
☐ **No. 9788 Lehigh Valley Box Car**, creamy white	20.00	25.00
☐ **No. 9789 Pickens Railroad Box Car**	50.00	60.00
☐ **No. 9789 U Pickens Railroad Box Car**	50.00	60.00
☐ **No. 9801 Sentinel Baltimore and Ohio Standard O Series**, metal trucks	30.00	40.00
☐ **No. 9802 Miller High-Life Beer Standard O Series**, metal trucks	30.00	40.00
☐ **No. 9803 Johnson Wax Box Car**, white and black, standard O, metal trucks	30.00	40.00
☐ **No. 9805 GT Reefer**, standard O series, metal trucks	30.00	40.00
☐ **No. 9806 Rock Island Tuscan**, standard O series, metal trucks	80.00	90.00
☐ **No. 9807 Stroh's Beer Standard O Series**, metal trucks	70.00	80.00

Price Range

☐ **No. 9808 Union Pacific, Standard O Series Box**, metal trucks, yellow, no box 90.00   100.00

☐ **No. 9809 Clark Reefer,** standard O series, metal trucks 40.00   50.00

☐ **No. 9811 Union Pacific FARR #2 Reefer** .. 30.00   35.00

☐ **No. 9812 Arm and Hammer Billboard Reefer** 20.00   25.00

☐ **No. 9813 Ruffles Potato Chip Billboard Reefer** 20.00   25.00

☐ **No. 9814 Perrier Sparkling Water Billboard Reefer** 20.00   25.00

☐ **No. 9816 Brach's Candies Billboard Reefer** 20.00   25.00

☐ **No. 9817 Bazooka Gum Billboard Reefer** .. 20.00   25.00

☐ **No. 9818 Western Maryland Reefer**, out of Royal Limited set 50.00   60.00

☐ **No. 9820 Wabash Gondola**, standard O series, metal trucks 50.00   60.00

☐ **No. 9821 Southern Pacific Gondola**, tuscan, standard O series, metal trucks 50.00   60.00

☐ **No. 9822 Grand Trunk Gondola**, standard O series, metal trucks 50.00   60.00

☐ **No. 9823 Santa Fe Flat**, with load of crates, standard O series, metal trucks 90.00   100.00

☐ **No. 9824 New York Central Gondola**, black, standard O series, metal trucks 50.00   60.00

☐ **No. 9825 Shaeffer's Beer**, standard O series, metal trucks, white 50.00   60.00

☐ **No. 9826 Pittsburgh and Lake Erie Box Car**, jade green, standard O series, metal trucks 50.00   60.00

☐ **No. 9851 Schlitz Reefer**, white 15.00   20.00

☐ **No. 9852 Miller High-Life Beer Reefer**, white 20.00   25.00

☐ **No. 9853 Cracker Jack Reefer**, caramel ... 30.00   35.00

	Price Range	
☐ **No. 9853 Cracker Jack Reefer**, white with brown roof	20.00	30.00
☐ **No. 9853 Cracker Jack Reefer**, white, red roof, correct variation	30.00	40.00
☐ **No. 9853 Cracker Jack Reefer**, white, no box	20.00	25.00
☐ **No. 9854 Baby Ruth Reefer Car**, white, with "R" for registered to right to use "Ruth"	15.00	20.00
☐ **No. 9854 Baby Ruth Reefer Car**, without "R"	25.00	35.00
☐ **No. 9854 Baby Ruth Reefer Car**	10.00	15.00
☐ **No. 9855 Swift Reefer**, aluminum with black roof	20.00	25.00
☐ **No. 9856 Old Milwaukee Beer Reefer**, red	20.00	25.00
☐ **No. 9856 Old Milwaukee Beer Reefer**	20.00	25.00
☐ **No. 9858 Butterfinger Reefer Car**, orange and blue	15.00	20.00
☐ **No. 9859 Pabst Blue Ribbon Beer Reefer Car**, white	15.00	20.00
☐ **No. 9859 Specially Painted Car for Rocky Mountain Division TCA**	35.00	45.00
☐ **No. 9860 Gold Medal Flour Reefer**, white	15.00	20.00
☐ **No. 9860 Gold Medal Reefer**, loose from sets	15.00	20.00
☐ **No. 9861 Tropicana Billboard Reefer**, green, early model in sets only with metal bar on trucks, mounting rod, loose pack	45.00	55.00
☐ **No. 9861 Tropicana Reefer**, boxed, later design truck mount without metal bar	20.00	25.00
☐ **No. 9862 Hamm's Beer Billboard Reefer**, blue body	20.00	25.00
☐ **No. 9862 Hamm's Beer Billboard Reefer**	20.00	25.00

	Price Range	
☐ **No. 9863 REA Express Reefer Car**, green	25.00	30.00
☐ **No. 9864 TCA Convention Car**, for Seattle convention 1974	45.00	55.00
☐ **No. 9866 Coors Golden Reefer Car**, white "R" above "S" in Coors	25.00	30.00
☐ **No. 9866 Coors Golden Reefer Car**, white "R" below "S" in Coors	40.00	50.00
☐ **No. 9866 Coors Golden Reefer Car**, white, variation with no "R" after "S" in Coors ..	30.00	40.00
☐ **No. 9866 Coors Reefer**	20.00	25.00
☐ **No. 9867 Hersheys Milk Chocolate Reefer**, chocolate brown	30.00	40.00
☐ **No. 9869 Santa Fe Reefer**, 1976 SSS car only, metal trucks	40.00	50.00
☐ **No. 9870 Old Dutch Cleanser Reefer**, yellow	15.00	20.00
☐ **No. 9871 Carling Black Label Beer Car** ..	15.00	20.00
☐ **No. 9872 Pacific Fruit Express Reefer**	15.00	20.00
☐ **No. 9873 Ralston Purina Reefer**	15.00	20.00
☐ **No. 9874 Miller Light Reefer**	15.00	20.00
☐ **No. 9875 Atlantic and Pacific Reefer**	15.00	20.00
☐ **No. 9876 Central Vermont Reefer**, Milwaukee Limited breakup	40.00	50.00
☐ **No. 9877 Gerber Baby Food Billboard Reefer**	15.00	20.00
☐ **No. 9878 Good 'n Plenty Billboard Reefer**	15.00	20.00
☐ **No. 9879 Hills Brothers Coffee Billboard Reefer**	15.00	20.00
☐ **No. 9880 ATSF Great American Railroad Reefer with Spike**	55.00	65.00
☐ **No. 9881 Rath Packing Co. Reefer**	25.00	35.00
☐ **No. 9882 New York Central Reefer**, metal trucks	30.00	35.00

	Price Range	
☐ **No. 9883 Nabisco Oreo Reefer**, white	20.00	30.00

Accessories

☐ **No. 2110 Trestle Set**, graduated	15.00	20.00
☐ **No. 2111 All Elevated "A" Piers**, to match #2110 Trestle Set	15.00	20.00
☐ **No. 2122 Extension Bridge and Rock Piers**	20.00	25.00
☐ **No. 2126 Whistling Freight Shed**, use for whistle for nonwhistle locomotives	25.00	30.00
☐ **No. 2127 Diesel Horn Shed**, requires 9V battery cell	25.00	30.00
☐ **No. 2133 Freight Station**, lighted	25.00	30.00
☐ **No. 2140 Banjo Signal**, die cast and metal as old Lionel	25.00	30.00
☐ **No. 2145 Automatic Gateman**	35.00	40.00
☐ **No. 2151 Operating Semaphore**, plastic ..	15.00	20.00
☐ **No. 2152 Crossing Gate**, automatic	15.00	20.00
☐ **No. 2154 Automatic Highway Flasher Signal**	15.00	20.00
☐ **No. 2162 Automatic Crossing Gate and Crossing Signal**	15.00	20.00
☐ **No. 2170 Boxed Set of Three Plastic Street Lamps**	5.00	10.00
☐ **No. 2171 Box of Two Gooseneck Lamps**, old Lionel style #75 decorative plastic, two lamps	10.00	15.00
☐ **No. 2175 Sandy Andy Gravel Loader**	50.00	60.00
☐ **No. 2180 Road Sign Set**, all plastic signs ...	5.00	10.00
☐ **No. 2214 Plate Girder Bridge**, metal base, gray plastic sides	10.00	15.00
☐ **No. 2256 Station Platform**, with picket fences	10.00	15.00

Price Range

☐ **No. 2280 Bumper**, black plastic, unlighted, old #260 shape	10.00	15.00
☐ **No. 2290 Spur Bumpers**, lighted, box of two	10.00	15.00
☐ **No. 2301 Operating Sawmill**, nearly identical to old Lionel #464 mill	65.00	75.00
☐ **No. 2303 Santa Fe Manual Gantry Crane**	50.00	60.00
☐ **No. 2313 Floodlight Tower**, bank of eight lights, similar to old #195	20.00	25.00
☐ **No. 2314 Searchlight Tower**, single spotlight, tall	15.00	20.00
☐ **No. 2317 Drawbridge**, operating, raises and lowers bridge, bell clangs, stops train, low trestle set piers	50.00	60.00
☐ **No. 2319 Watch Tower**, lighted, similar to old #445 building, no operating men	20.00	25.00
☐ **No. 2710 Billboards**, boxed set, signs and cardboard inserts	5.00	10.00
☐ **No. 2717 Short Extension Bridge**, trestle type, packed with plastic sack	5.00	10.00
☐ **No. 2718 Barrel Platform Kit**	5.00	10.00
☐ **No. 2719 Watchman's Shanty Kit**	5.00	10.00
☐ **No. 2720 Lumber Shed Kit**	5.00	10.00
☐ **No. 2784 Freight Station Kit**, boxed	5.00	10.00
☐ **No. 2784 Freight Station Kit**, bagged as came in James gang set	5.00	10.00
☐ **No. 2785 Engine House**, kit boxed, no longer made, box has some tears	50.00	60.00
☐ **No. 2787 Freight Station Kit**	30.00	35.00
☐ **No. 2789 Water Tower Kit**	20.00	25.00

Price Range

- [ ] **No. 2792 Layout Starter Pack**, consists of extension bridge kit, barrel platform kit, lumber shed kit, telephone poles, fourteen road signs, five billboards, track layout book 20.00 25.00
- [ ] **No. 2796 Grain Elevator Kit** 35.00 45.00
- [ ] **No. 2797 Rico Station Kit**, rerun in 1981, but new catalog #2709, different color 50.00 60.00
- [ ] **No. 2900 Lockon** 5.00 10.00
- [ ] **No. 2901 Track Clips**, #027 flat Ives style 5.00 10.00
- [ ] **No. 2909 Smoke Fluid**, large bottle 5.00 10.00
- [ ] **No. 4050 Red 50 Watts**, made before they went to 7.5 VA designation 15.00 20.00
- [ ] **No. 4050 Red 7.5 VA Transformer**, AC .. 15.00 20.00
- [ ] **No. 4060 DC Transformer With AC Posts**, 12 VA as used in New Englander set 15.00 20.00
- [ ] **No. 4065 DC Power Pack AC Posts 5.5 VA**, as used in James gang and Midnight Flyer 10.00 15.00
- [ ] **No. 4870 DC Power Pack**, as used in #8803 Rock Island set 10.00 15.00
- [ ] **No. 4090 90 Watts**, old 1044 style, largest AC transformer the U.S. Government will allow to be made for toy trains, boxed 60.00 75.00
- [ ] **No. 4125 Maroon 25 Watts**, as came in Coca-Cola set, large enough to run an SW1 switcher or small 0-4-0 steam engine 10.00 15.00
- [ ] **No. 4150 Blue 7.5 VA Transformer**, AC, pushbutton reverse 15.00 20.00
- [ ] **No. 4150 Blue 50 Watts**, MPC boxed, lighter blue than 7.5 VA #4150, pushbutton reverse 15.00 20.00
- [ ] **No. 4250 Black 25 VA**, with pushbutton reverse control, size of old Lionel 45 watt ... 12.00 15.00

MARX

MARX

Marx logo.

	Price Range	
☐ **No. 4550 Red Flat DC Power Pack with AC Posts**, came in 1978–1979 sets	12.00	15.00
☐ **No. 5013 #027 New Curved Track**	3.00	5.00
☐ **No. 5014 One-Half Curve #027**, bulk pack	3.00	5.00
☐ **No. 5018 #027 New Straight Track**	3.00	5.00
☐ **No. 5019 One-Half Straight #027**, bulk pack	3.00	5.00
☐ **No. 5020 90-Degree #027 Crossover**	10.00	15.00
☐ **No. 5021 Manual Switch**, left, #027	15.00	20.00
☐ **No. 5022 Manual Switch**, right, #027	15.00	20.00
☐ **No. 5023 45-Degree #027 Crossover**	10.00	15.00

MARX

Locomotives

☐ **Commodore Vanderbilt**, copper nameplate, no tender	15.00	25.00
☐ **Power Car**, #M10005, blue and red	10.00	15.00
☐ **Power Car**, #M10005, snub nose, green and white	15.00	20.00
☐ **REA Car**, #M10005, snub nose, cream colored and white	15.00	20.00

	Price Range	
☐ **"Sparkling Friction RR,"** #242, with tender, rubberized friction action, black ...	15.00	20.00
☐ **Steam Type**, #400, plastic, electric	10.00	15.00
☐ **Steam Type**, #490, with New York Central tender, electric motor, red and gray	15.00	25.00
☐ **Steam Type**, #499, four wheel, with fiberglass side plates	10.00	15.00
☐ **Steam Type**, #666, with Allstate tender, electric, die-cast construction, silver on black	10.00	15.00
☐ **Steam Type**, #999, die-cast construction, with tender	20.00	25.00
☐ **Steam Type**, #1666, tender, slope sided, black lettering on red cab	15.00	20.00
☐ **Steam Type,** #1666, front and rear trucks, headlights, smokes, white numbers on red cab	20.00	25.00
☐ **Steam Type**, #3000, running board, red, silver, back boiler	25.00	20.00

Rolling Stock

☐ **Allstate Motor Oil Tank Car**, trucks, dome tank, blue	7.00	10.00
☐ **Allstate Motor Oil**, triple dome, die-cast wheels, blue	20.00	12.00
☐ **ATSF Caboose**, #4427, die-cast wheels, red	5.00	7.00
☐ **ATSF Caboose**, #4427, stamped steel, tuscan	7.00	10.00
☐ **ATSF Caboose**, working style, die-cast wheels	5.00	7.00
☐ **Baltimore and Ohio Box Car**, #467110, simulated trucks, red and silver	7.00	10.00
☐ **Baltimore and Ohio Box Car**, #467110, simulated four wheel, red with white lettering	5.00	10.00

	Price Range	
☐ **Baltimore and Ohio Gondola**, #241708, four wheel, red and green	5.00	7.00
☐ **Baltimore and Ohio Gondola**, #241708, metal, lithographed, yellow and red	5.00	7.00
☐ **Baltimore and Ohio Gondola**, 241708, steel, red	5.00	7.00
☐ **B.K.X. Car**, #4581, with searchlight, working with generated, red light	20.00	25.00
☐ **Bogata Pullman**, die-cast, blue with white windows	15.00	20.00
☐ **Boston and Maine Box Car**, #77003, diccast wheels, blue	5.00	10.00
☐ **Boston and Maine Car**, #77003 die-cast wheels/plastic body, blue with silver trim	7.00	10.00
☐ **Cable Reel Car**, #4566, die-cast wheels, single gray spool, blue	12.00	15.00
☐ **Caboose**, #956, nickel plate, four wheel, red	5.00	10.00
☐ **C.B. and Q Flat Car**, #5545, die-cast wheels, frame, blue	5.00	10.00
☐ **Cities Services Tank**, #2532, light-wheel type, die-cast wheels, blue and white	5.00	7.00
☐ **Cities Services Tank Car**, #2532, stamped steel	5.00	10.00
☐ **Colorado and Southern Box Car**, #91453, yellow	5.00	7.00
☐ **Crane Car**, #5590, revolving cab, gears, diecast frame and wheels	15.00	20.00
☐ **C.R.I.P. Box Car**, #5526, says "Groceries and Sundries," yellow	10.00	15.00
☐ **C.R.I.P. Gondola**, #552, four wheel, red, green	5.00	7.00
☐ **C.S.O.X. Tanker**, single dome, says "Cities Services," stamped steel trucks	5.00	10.00
☐ **Erie Flat**, #4528, with two wheels, ten wheels	5.00	7.00

	Price Range	
☐ **Erie Gondola**, 51170, fold-down ends, black	10.00	15.00
☐ **Erie Gondola**, #51170, fold-down ends, dark blue	15.00	20.00
☐ **Erie Gondola**, #51170, no ends, die-cast wheels, black	5.00	10.00
☐ **Erie Gondola**, #51170, no ends, die-cast wheels, black	5.00	10.00
☐ **Erie Gondola**, #51170, removable ends, blue	5.00	10.00
☐ **Erie Gondola**, #51170, stamped steel	5.00	10.00
☐ **Hudson Steam Type**, #333, with Santa Fe tender, electric motor	30.00	50.00
☐ **Illinois Central Switcher**, says "Gulf States," electric motor, red and white	20.00	30.00
☐ **Lehigh Valley Gondola**, #552, four wheel, green and silver	5.00	10.00
☐ **Lehigh Valley Hopper**, #21913, simulated four wheel, black with yellow letters	5.00	10.00
☐ **Lehigh Valley Hopper**, #21913, simulated four wheel, white with yellow lettering	10.00	15.00
☐ **Los Angeles Coach**, cream and green	10.00	15.00
☐ **Marlines Box Car**, #249319, die-cast trucks, sliding doors	8.00	10.00
☐ **Middle States Oil Tanker**, #553, four wheels, red and silver	5.00	10.00
☐ **Middle States Tanker**, four wheels, with coupler, silver	5.00	10.00
☐ **Missouri Pacific Cattle Car**, die-cast wheels, operating type, red	10.00	15.00
☐ **Missouri Pacific Stock Car**, #540999, tin wheels, red	5.00	10.00
☐ **Monon Caboose**, #350, with smokestack, die-cast frame, red	15.00	20.00

Price Range

☐ **New York Central Baggage Car,** #5014, lithographed, blue and gray 25.00   30.00

☐ **New York Central Caboose,** #694, black frame, lithographed 10.00   15.00

☐ **New York Central Caboose,** plastic, four wheels, red 5.00   10.00

☐ **New York Central Caboose,** #20102, four wheels, red and gray 5.00   10.00

☐ **New York Central Caboose,** #20102, red and blue 5.00   10.00

☐ **New York Central Caboose,** #556; "Marx" with herald, red and black 5.00   10.00

☐ **New York Central Caboose,** #18326; "Pacemaker," white 5.00   10.00

☐ **New York Central Caboose,** #556, silver and blue 5.00   10.00

☐ **New York Central Caboose,** with smoke-stack, stamped steel, white 5.00   10.00

☐ **New York Central Caboose,** #20102, steel, forked couplers 5.00   10.00

☐ **New York Central Caboose,** #18326, with smokestack, metal and tin wheels, brown ... 5.00   10.00

☐ **New York Central Caboose,** #18326, tus-can red 5.00   10.00

☐ **New York Central Caboose,** #18326, tus-can 5.00   10.00

☐ **New York Central Caboose,** #18326, with smokestack 5.00   10.00

☐ **New York Central Caboose,** with stack, four wheels, simulated eight wheels, ma-genta 5.00   10.00

☐ **New York Central Coffin Tender,** four wheels, gray with silver band 5.00   10.00

☐ **New York Central Coffin Tender,** four wheels, lithographed 5.00   10.00

	Price Range	
☐ **New York Central Gondola**, #715100, plastic, blue	5.00	10.00
☐ **New York Central Gondola**, #715100, simulated four wheels, blue with white lettering	5.00	10.00
☐ **New York Central Pacemaker Caboose**, simulated wheels, school bus yellow	5.00	10.00
☐ **New York Central Pacemaker Caboose**, #20120, steel, four wheels, yellow and white	5.00	10.00
☐ **New York Central Tender**, with coal load, four wheels, black	5.00	10.00
☐ **New York Central Tender**, plastic, four wheels	5.00	10.00
☐ **New York Central Tender**, slope back, with load, black	5.00	10.00
☐ **New York Central Tender**, tin construction, lithographed, silver, blue	5.00	10.00
☐ **Northern Pacific Hopper**, "General Coal Co.," blue, red	10.00	12.00
☐ **Northern Pacific Tender**, #554, "General Coal," red, yellow	5.00	10.00
☐ **Observation Car**, opening doors, lithographed, red	30.00	35.00
☐ **Pacemaker Caboose**, smokestack, four wheels, orange	5.00	10.00
☐ **Pacemaker Caboose**, smokestack, simulated eight wheels, lithographed	5.00	10.00
☐ **Pacific Fruit Express Box**, #43461, catwalks, lithographed	5.00	10.00
☐ **Pacific Fruit Express Closed Car**, #43463, doors and catwalk	5.00	10.00
☐ **Pacific Fruit Express Flat Car**, doors, rails, red, white	5.00	10.00
☐ **Penn Central Caboose**, #18326; smokestack, jade green	5.0	10.00

	Price Range	
☐ **Pennsylvania Gondola**, #347100, steel, gray	5.00	10.00
☐ **Pennsylvania Gondola**, #34170, light gray, white	5.00	10.00
☐ **Pennsylvania Gondola**, #347100, silver	5.00	10.00
☐ **Pennsylvania Merchandise Service Box Car**, #37956, four wheels, barn red	5.00	10.00
☐ **Reading Caboose**, #92812, simulated wheels	5.00	10.00
☐ **Rocket Fuel Tank Car**, #246, simulated four wheels, white	5.00	10.00
☐ **Rock Island Box Car**, #147815, doors and railings, catwalk	5.00	10.00
☐ **Rock Island Caboose**, #17858, die-cast wheels, maroon	5.00	10.00
☐ **Santa Fe Box**, #3280, catwalk and railing, orange, white	5.00	10.00
☐ **Santa Fe Cattle Car**, #13975, catwalk, fence frame, brown	5.00	10.00
☐ **Santa Fe 4 Switcher**, #1998, die-cast frame, electric motor	20.00	15.00
☐ **Santa Fe Stock Car**, #13975, high side, brown	10.00	12.00
☐ **Santa Fe Stock Car**, #13975, die cast, tuscan	5.00	10.00
☐ **Santa Fe Tanker**, "Middle States Oil"	5.00	10.00
☐ **Seaboard Gondola**, #91257, red, black	7.00	10.00
☐ **Southern AA**, #6000, snub nose, "ALCO," orange, silver	20.00	25.00
☐ **Southern Auto Carrier**, 51100, carload, die-cast wheels, rack	10.00	15.00
☐ **Southern Flat Car**, #51100, die-cast wheels, maroon	5.00	10.00
☐ **Southern Flat Car**, #51100, die-cast wheels, white	5.00	10.00

	Price Range	
☐ **Southern Pacific Caboose**, die-cast wheels, tuscan	5.00	10.00
☐ **Southern Pacific**, #1235, blue, red	5.00	10.00
☐ **Union Pacific Box**, #9100, "Challenger," die-cast frame, wheels, black, red	15.00	20.00
☐ **Union Pacific Caboose**, #3900, black, orange	5.00	10.00
☐ **Union Pacific Caboose**, #3824 with bay window, die-cast wheels, tuscan	15.00	20.00
☐ **Union Pacific Caboose**, #3900, stack, orange, red	10.00	12.00
☐ **Union Pacific Caboose**, #4586, working type, overhung roof	5.00	10.00
☐ **Union Pacific Caboose**, #3824, yellow, brown	5.00	10.00
☐ **Union Pacific Caboose**, #3824, yellow, black	5.00	10.00
☐ **Union Pacific Cattle Car**, sliding door, lithographed on brown body	10.00	12.00
☐ **Union Pacific Coffin Tender**, black	5.00	10.00
☐ **Union Pacific Switcher**, #1998, die-cast frame, motor, headlights, white and gray	25.00	30.00
☐ **Union Pacific Switcher**, horns, handrails, electric die-cast frame, wheels	30.00	35.00

TRANSPORTATION VEHICLES

Because the field of toy train collecting is so vast and popular among toy collectors, it has been featured separately in the preceding chapter.

Placing a strong second to trains in overall popular appeal among toy collectors is the vast assembly line of miniature motor-toys produced in the United States or imported from Europe or Japan from 1894 to 1942, the generally acknowledged cut-off date for most purists. So sizeable, so diversified, and so complex is the field, with its substrata of pleasure cars, trucks, taxis, buses, racers, tractors, cranes, and bulldozers—plus miniatures of the same—that each deserves a special guide all its own and, in fact, does often appear in published form. The ultimate in tunnel vision books is the recent opus on *Miniature Emergency Vehicles*. Arcade, Dent, Hubley, Kenton, Kilgore, and Wilkins all produced authentically detailed (down to the last hubcap and hood ornament) fleets of motor toys.

ANIMAL-DRAWN VEHICLES

Clearly dominating the early cast-iron toys of the 19th century were the animal-drawn rigs produced by such leading makers as Ives, Pratt & Letchworth, Carpenter, and Wilkins. From the dawning of the 20th century to the 1950s, horse-drawn phaetons, hansom cabs, drays, and fire pumpers coexisted side by side with the increasingly popular motortoys, with Dent Hardware, Hubley, Arcade, and Kenton the major forces in the field. The combination of power, speed, and grace embodied in these horse-drawn toys makes them the favorites of interior decorators as well as the legion of equine fanciers who collect topically. Major competition also comes from inveterate fire-fighting toy collectors.

Cast Iron Inner Circle

The following is a representative selection of the rarest and most beautiful ever cast:

Four classic Carpenter cast-iron rigs. *Top:* Pony Phaeton, $1200–$1400; *second row:* Double Truck, around $1000; *third row:* Contractor Wagon, $800–$900; *bottom row:* Tally-Ho, $2000 plus. Cuts are from 1892 Carpenter Catalog.

Price Range

☐ **Depot Wagon**, Carpenter, circa 1880, painted cast iron, pair of galloping horses, six removable standing passengers .... 2000.00 plus

☐ **English Trap**, Kenton, 1890s, painted cast iron, four passengers, driver, coachman, Victorian lady with small boy, horse and trap plated in bronze, 15″ length (Trap: from "trappings," symbolizing elegance) ..   800.00   1000.00

☐ **Hansom Cab**, Pratt & Letchworth, late 1890s, painted cast iron, prancing steed, yellow cab, yellow coachman, 12″ length ..   600.00   700.00

☐ **Horse-Drawn Caisson**, Ives, 1890s, painted cast iron, brass cannon, 23″ length 750.00   850.00

☐ **Horse-Drawn Surrey**, Pratt & Letchworth, 1890s, painted cast iron, 16″ length 1000.00   1200.00

☐ **Horse-Drawn Tally-Ho Coach**, Carpenter, 1890s, painted cast iron, two pair rearing horses, seven passengers, 26½″ length .....   2000.00 plus

☐ **Oxford Trap**, Dent Hardware Co., circa 1910, painted cast-iron coachman and woman passenger, single white horse 700.00   800.00

☐ **Spider Phaeton**, Hubley Mfg. Co., circa 1906, painted cast iron, pair horses, woman driver, groom in rear 800.00   1000.00

☐ **Three-Seated Brake**, Hubley, 1890, painted cast iron, pair of horses, six passengers, 18″ length ....   2000.00 plus

☐ **Two-Seated Brake**, Hubley, circa 1900, painted cast iron, three passengers and driver, only a few of this rare specimen are known to exist ....   2000.00 plus

Cast Iron

☐ **Buckboard**, Kenton, 1929, two horses, lines, 12½″ length 250.00   300.00

All of the Horses, Tongues, Shafts and Platforms used in my Toys are guaranteed to be made of MALLEABLE IRON.

No. 7.–GALLOPING HORSE, which is removable from Platform.

Patented Nov. 16th, 1880; May 10th, '81; July 19th '81; and March 20th, '83.

Packed Three dozen in a Case. - - - - - - - Price per dozen

No. 8.–SMALL HORSE & CART, with removable Figure and galloping Horse.

Patented May 25th, 1880; reissued March 14th, '82; patented Nov. 16th, '80; May 10th, '81; July 19th '81; Dec. 20th, '81; Nov. 21st, 82; March 20th, '83; Oct. 23rd, '83; May 13th, '84.

Packed Three dozen in a Case. - - - - - - - Price per dozen

No. 9.–PONY CART, with removable Figures and galloping Horses.

Patented May 25th, 1880; reissued March 14th, '82; patented Nov. 16th '80, May 10th '81, July 19th, '81, Nov. 21st, '82; March 20th '83; October, 23rd, '83; May 13th, 84.

Packed Three dozen in a Case. - - - - - - - Price per dozen

Catalog from 1880s by Francis W. Carpenter, Harrison, Westchester, New York, one of the premier cast-iron and malleable-iron toy makers. Although Carpenter discontinued numbering his toys in consecutive order at some unspecified time, his first dozen toys are well-documented. His very first was a cast-iron freight train with two gondolas, a tender and locomotive. (Secor shared the first patent, on June 8, 1880, of a cast locomotive toy.) The rigs shown here are valued between $1500 and well beyond the $2000 range.

Price Range

☐ **Cairo Express**, Kenton, 1924, elephant
pulling cart with native driver, 10″ length   500.00   600.00

☐ **City Transfer**, Kenton, 1929, covered rig,
30″ length 1500.00   2000.00

☐ **Coal Cart**, Kenton, 1929, small mule and
cart, 10″ length, other sizes 150.00   200.00

☐ **Coal Wagon**, Kenton, 1929, one horse,
painted and decorated, with lines, 16¼″
length, other sizes 300.00   400.00

☐ **Concrete Mixer**, Kenton, 1941, 13⅝″
length 700.00   800.00

☐ **Contractor's Dumping Wagon**, Kenton,
1929, pull lever and three boxes will dump,
hack driver, 16″ length 400.00   450.00

☐ **Coupe Cab**, Kenton, 1929, 10″ length 250.00   300.00

☐ **Covered Wagon**, Hubley, 1928, two horses,
15″ length 350.00   450.00

☐ **Covered Wagon**, Kenton, 1952, removable
cover on wagon, 15⅜″ height 250.00   350.00

☐ **Depot Wagon**, Carpenter, 1880, six remov-
able figures, galloping horses ....   2000.00 plus

☐ **Dray**, Kenton, 1929, four large horses,
traces and lines, with barrels and boxes, 33″
length, ... 1200.00   1400.00

☐ **Dray**, Kenton, 1929, painted, six blocks and
six barrels, 23½″ length 600.00   700.00

☐ **Dray**, Kenton, 1929, three horses, lines and
traces, with barrels, 16½″ length 400.00   500.00

☐ **Dray**, Kenton, 1929, two large horses,
painted lines and traces with six barrels,
16½″ length, other sizes 350.00   400.00

☐ **Express Wagon**, Kenton, 1929, two horses,
lines and traces, 16½″ length, also 12½″
length 350.00   400.00

☐ **Farm Wagon**, Kenton, 1929, painted
14″ length 300.00   325.00

	Price Range	
10¼″ length	325.00	350.00
☐ **Fire Chief**, Kenton, 1929, painted		
14″	300.00	400.00
9¼″ length	250.00	300.00
☐ **Fire Patrol**, 1904, two galloping horses, driver and five firemen in blue suits and helmet hats, 13″ length	1400.00	1600.00
☐ **Fire Patrol**, Kenton, 1929, three horses, three firemen and driver, painted		
13″ length	1000.00	1200.00
14½″ length	1100.00	1250.00
☐ **Fire Patrol**, Kenton, 1929, two horses, driver, three firemen, gong, painted		
19″ length	700.00	800.00
18″ length with three horses	650.00	700.00
18″ length with two horses	600.00	650.00
☐ **Galloping Horse**, Carpenter, 1880, removable from platform	500.00	600.00
☐ **Hansom Cab**, Kenton, 1952, painted bright blue and yellow with gold bronze trim, driver and lady passenger removable, 15¼″ length	300.00	400.00
☐ **Ice Wagon**, Hubley, 1920, one horse, painted, 9½″ length, other sizes	150.00	200.00
☐ **Ice Wagon**, Kenton, 1929, two horses, painted, 16½″ length	250.00	300.00
☐ **Log Wagon**, Kenton, 1929, Negro driver, painted, 16″ length	600.00	700.00
☐ **Milk Wagon**, Kenton, 1952, removable driver, 12¾″ length	300.00	350.00
☐ **Mule and Coal Cart**, Kenton, 1929, Negro driver, painted, 14″ length	500.00	600.00
☐ **One-Horse Coal Tipping Cart**, Carpenter, 1880	700.00	800.00
☐ **One-Horse Dray**, Gong Bell, 1903, painted 11½″ length	250.00	300.00

Price Range

☐ **One-Horse Dump Cart**, Carpenter, 1880, removable figures, galloping horse and tipping cart 400.00   450.00

☐ **Ox Cart**, Kenton, 1929, Negro driver, ox, 7″ length painted 150.00   200.00
   silver finish 125.00   250.00

☐ **Police Patrol**, Kenton, 1929, gong, lines, and traces, one driver, two policemen and one prisoner, painted, 19″ length 1200.00   1400.00

☐ **Pony Cart**, Carpenter, 1880, removable figures and galloping horses 900.00   1000.00

☐ **Pony Express Wagon**, 1893, 14″ length ..   400.00   450.00

☐ **Road Phaeton**, Kenton, 1929, painted, 10½″ length 250.00   300.00

☐ **Sand and Gravel Wagon**, Kenton, 1952, two horses, 15″ length, also 10″ and 10½″ lengths 200.00   250.00

☐ **Small Horse and Cart**, Carpenter, 1880 ...   800.00   900.00

☐ **Stake Wagon**, Kenton, 1952, two horses, 10½″ length, also 11″ size with single horse 250.00   300.00

☐ **Sulky**, Kenton, 1929, 9¼″ length, also other sizes 150.00   200.00

☐ **Sulky**, Kenton, 1952, 7¼″ length 50.00   75.00

☐ **Surrey**, Kenton, 1929, 12″ length 300.00   350.00

☐ **Surrey**, Kenton, 1929, 14″ length 350.00   400.00

☐ **Transfer Wagon**, Kenton, 1929, two horses, 19″ length 400.00   450.00

☐ **Two-Horse Dump Cart**, Carpenter, 1880, removable figures, galloping horses and tipping cart 400.00   500.00

☐ **Two-Horse Express Wagon**, Carpenter, 1880, removable figure, galloping horses ...   600.00   700.00

Price Range

Painted Tin

☐ **Bow Cart**, Althof Bergmann, 1874, high-wheeled cart drawn by white horse, 8″ length and 11½″ length sizes 600.00   700.00

☐ **Boy Soldier With Gun**, Althof Bergmann, 1874, running figure on four-wheeled platform carries gun over left shoulder, 3½″ and 7″ height sizes 800.00   1000.00

☐ **Boy Soldier on Wheels**, Althof Bergmann, 1874, grim looking young man on four-wheeled platform wields saber in left hand, 3½″ and 7″ height sizes 800.00   1000.00

☐ **Boy on Wheels**, Althof Bergmann, 1874, running boy on four-wheel platform blowing bugle, 3½″ height 1000.00   1200.00

☐ **Bread, Cakes, Pies, Bakery Wagon**, Althof Bergmann, 1874, 10″ and 14″ length sizes ....   2000.00 plus

☐ **Cab**, Althof Bergmann, 1874, tin with cast-iron wheels, drawn by one white horse, 8″ and 10½″ length sizes 500.00   600.00

☐ **Cab With Girl, Sheep-Drawn**, Althof Bergmann, 1874, another bit of whimsey, with girl on small wheeled platform tending sheep as it draws cab, 8″ and 10½″ length sizes 700.00   800.00

☐ **City Car**, Althof Bergmann, 1874, four wheeler, pair of horses, "City Car" stenciled on side, several variations, one features only a single wheel under car, another reads "City R. R. Cars," 12″ to 19″ length sizes ....   1500.00   2000.00 plus

☐ **Dog Cart**, Althof Bergmann, 1874, open two-wheel dray, white dog prances in style, 4½″ length (several variations by A. Bergmann, including pulling cab and several elaborate carriages, all drawn by identical dog, St. Bernard type) 450.00   500.00

Price Range

☐ **Express Wagon**, Althof Bergmann, 1874, Bergmann produced over a dozen variations, from single horse to as many as a team of four cantering steeds, sizes ranged from 6″ to 47″ lengths, the larger rigs fall into the "well nigh unattainable" category ...... 1200.00   2000.00 plus

☐ **Gig With Boy**, Althof Bergmann, 1874, single horse, 10½″ length, boy runs along side of horse on small wheeled platform, approximately 3″ length, also an 8″ length size .. 700.00   800.00

☐ **Girl on Wheels**, Althof Bergmann, 1874, girl skipping rope, 3½″ height 1000.00   1200.00

☐ **Goat Drawn by Bow Cart**, Althof Bergmann, 1874, billy goat pulls two-wheeled open cart, 8″ and 10″ length sizes 550.00   650.00

☐ **Hard-Soft Coal Two-Wheeled Cart With Driver**, Althof Bergmann, 1874, "Coal, Kindling, Wood" stenciled in arc above cast-iron wheels, driver seated low in front of cart with feet dangling just behind horse, 17″ length 1500.00   2000.00

☐ **Horse-Drawn Dump Cart**, Althof Bergmann, 1874, cart on two wheels tilts backward to unload, 13″ length, several versions, including example with driver 500.00   600.00

☐ **Julian Carriage**, Althof Bergmann, 1874, drawn by two horses, four-wheeled open carriage, horses with single wheel under each, 21″ length 1000.00   1200.00

☐ **Milk Wagon**, Althof Bergmann, 1874, pair white horses, four milk cans in front of elaborate open wagon, driver sits primly in rear, painted tin with cast-iron wheels ...... 2000.00 plus

☐ **Milk Wagon With Driver**, Althof Bergmann, 1874, single horse, milk cans in front, "Pure Milk" stenciled on side of wagon, 8¾″, 13½″, 14″ length sizes 1200.00   1400.00

Price Range

☐ **Omnibus**, Althof Bergmann, 1874, driver and pair of horses, "People's Line" appears atop side of four-wheel rig, 9½", 11½", 17", and 21" length sizes, a variation by Bergmann in 14" and 21" sizes featured stenciled words "U. S. Mail Wagon" .... 1500.00 | 2000.00 plus

☐ **Open-Sided Cab**, Althof Bergmann, 1874, two-wheeled cab is no wider than its cast-iron wheels, features passenger, 8" length   500.00   600.00

☐ **Patent Racer**, Althof Bergmann, 1874, boy sits high up on cart drawn by single horse, also available with adult driver 1200.00   1400.00

☐ **Pony Cart With Boy**, Althof Bergmann, 1874, boy again on wheeled platform carries small whip, pony on same platform as boy, 8" and 10½" length sizes 600.00   700.00

☐ **Railroad Omnibus**, Althof Bergmann, 1874, four horses, lad driving, long casketlike shape of omnibus, 40" length ....   2000.00 plus

☐ **Rockaway**, Althof Bergmann, 1874, single horse-drawn four-wheel wagon with canopy, 13" length, also 10" length 800.00   900.00

☐ **Rockaway**, Althof Bergmann, pair of horses with driver, tin with cast-iron wheels, 22" and 15½" length sizes 900.00   1000.00

☐ **Sulky**, Althof Bergmann, 1874, horse drawn, man driver, one of the classic Bergmann examples with intricate web of wire and tin comprising the rig itself 1500.00   1600.00

☐ **Two-Horse Buggy and Driver**, Althof Bergmann, 1870–1890, gold pair horses, red saddles, red cart with gold stenciling, green wheels and trim, clockwork mechanical, 17" length 900.00   1000.00*

*Sold for $2470.00 at Skinner Auction, Bolton, Massachusetts, December 1985.

17-Passenger cross-country bus, Kingsbury, pressed steel, $550–$650.

	Price Range	
☐ **Water Cart,** Althof Bergmann, 1874, horse-drawn flat cart with large barrel on brackets, driver perched atop barrel (water tank), 11½ ″, 13 ″, 17 ″ length sizes	1500.00	2000.00 plus

BUSES

☐ **American Car and Foundry Bus,** 1925, ACF logo, 11½ ″ length	400.00	450.00
☐ **Auto Bus,** Kenton, 1929, painted in assorted colors and trim, 6½ ″ length		
No passengers on top	350.00	450.00
With passengers (8½ ″ length)	450.00	550.00
☐ **Century of Progress Buses,** 1933, cast iron, Greyhound logos on side, 6 ″, 7⅝ ″, 10½ ″ models, all cast as one piece	200.00	250.00
☐ **City Bus,** Kenton, 1927, assorted colors, 10 ″ length	600.00	700.00
☐ **Coast-to-Coast Bus,** Hubley, 1928, 13 ″ length, other sizes	650.00	750.00
☐ **Double-Deck Bus,** 1932, cast iron, red, green, blue with gold trim, nickeled tires, rubber tires optional extra, 11¼ ″ length ...	600.00	700.00
☐ **Double-Deck Bus,** 1938, cast iron, cab over engine model, includes three nickeled passengers, removable, 8 ″ length	750.00	800.00

Price Range

☐ **Double-Deck Bus,** 1936, cast iron, Chicago Motor Coach logo on top deck, may have been marketed exclusively in Midwest, 8¼" length 650.00   750.00

☐ **Double-Deck Yellow Coach Bus,** 1926, cast iron, yellow, logo appears on top deck panel, 13⅓" length 350.00   400.00

☐ **Feagol Safety Coach,** 1925, cast iron, 12" length 200.00   250.00

☐ **Great Lakes Expo Bus,** 1936, cast iron, blue, white, silver, Greyhound logo stenciled on top, 11¼" length 600.00   700.00

☐ **Inter-City Bus Coach,** 1927, Kenton, painted and trimmed in assorted colors, 11" length 350.00   450.00

☐ **Inter-urban Bus,** Dent, 1920, bright assorted colors, bronze trim, black enameled top, nickel-plated disc wheels with red centers, 10¾" length, other sizes (also made in cast aluminum) 250.00   350.00

☐ **New York-Chicago Twin Motor Coach,** Dent, 1920, finished in bright enameled colors, bronze trim, top is black enamel, nickel-plated disc wheels, red centers, 10" length 500.00   600.00

☐ **New York World's Fair Sightseeing Bus,** 1939, orange, 10½" length, also featured several smaller sizes, 7", 8", 8½" length sizes 450.00   500.00

☐ **New York World's Fair Sightseeing Bus, Tractor Version,** pulled trailers, blue body, canopy is blue and orange stripes, orange seats, 4½" length trailer, 3¾" length tractor 500.00   550.00

☐ **Public Service Bus,** Dent, 1920, assorted enamel color finish, gilt trim, black top, nickel-plated disc wheels, red centers, dual-type spare wheel attached to rear, 14¼" length 700.00   800.00

Price Range

☐ **Pullman Railplane,** mid-1930s, cast iron,
5″ length 150.00   200.00

☐ **Short Line Bus,** 1936, cast iron, local-type
Pennsylvania Bus Co., 7¾″ length 200.00   250.00

☐ **Travel Coach,** Hubley, 1932, 4¼″ length   300.00   350.00

☐ **White Bus,** 1932, cast iron, green, red,
blue, nickeled tires, 13¼″ length 500.00   600.00

☐ **Yellow Parlor Coach Bus,** 1925, cast iron,
Pennsylvania Rapid Transit logo (PRT),
iron wheels, 13″ length 400.00   450.00

EMERGENCY VEHICLES

☐ **Aerial Ladder Truck,** Kingsbury, 1930,
ladder raises, 45″ height, 34″ length 1400.00   1600.00

☐ **Ambulance,** Keystone, 1933, white flag
with green cross is attached to radiator,
27½″ length 500.00   550.00

☐ **Auto Chemical Truck,** Hubley, 1928
15″ length 700.00   800.00
12¼″ length 500.00   600.00

☐ **Auto Hook and Ladder,** Hubley, 1933,
gong, 22″ length 400.00   500.00

☐ **Auto Hook and Ladder,** Hubley, 1934, red
with gold striping, rubber tires, gong and
two ladders, electric headlights, 11¾″
length 250.00   350.00

☐ **Auto Hook and Ladder,** Kenton, 1929,
three ladders and gong, 17″ length 500.00   600.00

☐ **Auto Hook and Ladder,** Kenton, 1929,
8½″ length, other sizes 150.00   200.00

☐ **Auto Hose Wagon,** Kenton, 1929, assorted
colors with hose
7″ length 150.00   200.00
9″ length 175.00   200.00

☐ **Chemical Truck,** Kingsbury, 1930, 14″
length 300.00   350.00

Cast-iron fire rig toys. *Top row:* Hose Cart, Hubley, 1906; $800–$1000; *second row:* Patrol Wagon, Hubley, 1906, $900–$1100; *third row:* Ladder Wagon, Hubley, 1906, $900–$1100; *bottom row:* Fire Station, Carpenter, $1600–$1800.

Price Range

☐ **City Ambulance,** 1932, cast iron, white, also available in blue, 8″ and 6″ length sizes (smaller version appears in packaged fire toy set circa 1935) 250.00   300.00

☐ **City Fire Dept.,** Steelcraft, 1933, red double-disc wheels, 29″ length 350.00   400.00

☐ **Fire Engine,** Buddy "L", 1933, equipped with pressure pump and separate hose, 23½″ length 350.00   400.00

☐ **Fire Engine,** 1928, cast iron, red, spoked wheels, 8″ length 400.00   450.00

☐ **Fire Engine,** 1928, cast iron, red with gold trim, rubber disc wheels, driver, 9″ length 350.00   400.00

☐ **Fire Engine,** En-Es, 1932, red and gold with rubber balloon tires, 23⅞″ length 300.00   350.00

☐ **Fire Engine,** Kingsbury, 1930, 14″ length 350.00   400.00

☐ **Fire Engine,** maker unknown, 1904, clockwork motor runs in circle or straight, with driver 250.00   300.00

☐ **Fire Engine,** Schieble, 1932, red and gold hose reel, bell, rubber tires, and friction mechanical, 20″ length 250.00   300.00

☐ **Fire Ladder Truck,** 1928, cast iron, red with gold trim, removable yellow ladders, rubber disc wheels, 12½″ length 300.00   350.00

☐ **Fire Pumper,** 1920, red with gold and aluminum trim, nickel-plated bumper, gong, 13″ length, other sizes 300.00   325.00

☐ **Fire Pumper,** Turner, 1926, red with gold trim, 22″ length 300.00   400.00

☐ **Fire Truck,** Marx, 1949, siren, tower ladder, two 8″ ladders on side of truck, spring motor, 14″ length 75.00   100.00

Price Range

☐ **Ford Wrecker,** Arcade, 1928, red truck with green crane, nickel-plated wheels, crane actually works, 6⅛″ length and 5¼″ length sizes 150.00   200.00

☐ **"Heavy Transport,"** Fernand Martin, circa 1910, covered bed 350.00   400.00

☐ **Hook and Ladder,** Dent, 1920, bright red with ladders attached, nickled wheels, 7″ and 5½″ length sizes 150.00   200.00

☐ **Hook and Ladder,** Dent, 1920, red with bronze trim, three 1½″ wooden ladders painted yellow on red painted racks, 18¼″ length 500.00   600.00

☐ **Hook and Ladder,** Dent, 1920, red with nickeled wheels, ladders attached, 6⅞″ and 7⅛″ length sizes 100.00   125.00

☐ **Hook and Ladder,** Hubley, 1906, with three horses and driver; 14″ length 900.00   1000.00

☐ **Hook and Ladder,** Hubley, 1906, with two horses, driver
    9½″ length 600.00   700.00
    13″ length 700.00   800.00

☐ **Hook and Ladder,** Hubley, 1920, 17½″ length, three horses without gong, also 22″, 23″, 27½″, 28″, 29″, 35″ length sizes, each 1200.00   1400.00

☐ **Hook and Ladder,** Turner, 1926, red with gold trim
    27″ length 500.00   600.00
    16″ length 350.00   400.00

☐ **Hook and Ladder,** Hubley, 1928, came with and without gong, 9¼″ length, other sizes 150.00   200.00

☐ **Hook and Ladder,** Hubley, 1936, red with nickel chassis, radiator and ladders, 13″ length, other sizes 250.00   300.00

☐ **Hook and Ladder,** Kenton, 1928, gong and ladders, 17″ length, other sizes 500.00   600.00

Three horse-drawn fire-fighting rigs from Ideal Toy Catalog, early 1900s. Hook and Ladder, $550–$650; Hose Carriage, $650–$750; Fire Engine, $750–$850.

	Price Range	
☐ **Hook and Ladder,** Kenton, 1929, three galloping horses, with gong, nickel-plated body, 29″ length	1200.00	1400.00
☐ **Hook and Ladder,** Kenton, 1929, three galloping horses, with gong, 32½″ length	1200.00	1400.00
☐ **Hook and Ladder,** 1910, yellow, red stripes, driver and steersman, two 8″ ladders painted blue, 15″ length	350.00	450.00
☐ **Hook and Ladder,** Steelcraft, 1933, red with solid rubber tires, reel, hose, nozzle, brass bell and pull cord, 27¼″ length	400.00	500.00

Price Range

☐ **Hook and Ladder,** Structo, 1933, two 15″ extension ladders, bell, red and green headlights, 22″ length 300.00   400.00

☐ **Hook and Ladder Truck,** Boycraft, 1931, red with gilt trim, two ladders, 18″ length 150.00   200.00

☐ **Hook and Ladder Truck,** Kenton, 1927, gong and 4 ladders, 19½″ and 22″ length sizes 450.00   500.00

☐ **Hook and Ladder Truck,** Republic, 1932, red trimmed in green striped with gold, 18″ length 250.00   300.00

☐ **Hook and Ladder Truck,** Wilkins, 1911, with gong, detachable horses, driver and steersman, 34″ length .... 2000.00 plus

☐ **Hook and Ladder Truck,** with gong, horses with galloping motion, driver and steersman, 34″ length 1500.00   2000.00

☐ **Hose Cart,** Kenton, 1929, three horses, with hose, 13″ length 500.00   600.00

☐ **Hose and Ladder Truck,** Kenton, 1927, assorted colors, 6¼″ length 250.00   300.00

☐ **Hose Reel,** Kenton, 1929, one horse, painted with hose, 14″ length 600.00   700.00

☐ **Hose Truck,** Kenton, 1927, assorted colors
6¼″ length 150.00   200.00
8¼″ length 175.00   225.00

☐ **Hose Truck,** Turner, 1935, hose reel, rubber hose and bell, green, red and gold, 16″ length 200.00   250.00

☐ **Hose Wagon,** Kenton, 1929, two horses, painted, with gong, man and hose, 17″ length 500.00   650.00

☐ **Ladder Truck,** Dayton, 1932, red and gold, 30″ length 400.00   500.00

Price Range

☐ **Ladder Truck,** Dent, 1920, red with gilt trim, nickeled wheels, two 10″ yellow wood ladders on blue racks, with gong bell, 14¼″ length 450.00   500.00

☐ **Ladder Truck,** Hubley, 1933, has gong, 13″ length 250.00   300.00

☐ **Ladder Truck,** Kingsbury, 1930, 11″ length 350.00   400.00

☐ **Ladder Wagon,** En-Es, 1932, red with gold trim, rubber balloon tires, 16¾″ length 300.00   350.00

☐ **Mack Fire Apparatus Truck,** 1928, red with gold ladders, firebell, driver, artificial hose, 21″ length 450.00   500.00

☐ **Mack Motor Fire Truck,** Dent, 1920, red with gilt trim, nickeled wheels with red centers, dual wheels in rear, two 10″ wood ladders, hose reel, nozzle and two suction rubber pipes, 15″ length 450.00   500.00

☐ **Mack Wrecker,** Champion, circa 1930, red with rubber tires, 8½″ length, also 7″ length 125.00   150.00

☐ **Packard Fire Engine,** Turner, 1926, red and gold, rubber tires, 26¼″ length 250.00   300.00

☐ **Pontiac Wrecker,** Arcade, 1937, green, with nickel radiator, bumper, white rubber tires, red hubs, 4¼″ length 100.00   125.00

☐ **Pumper,** Dayton, 1932, red and gold, 22″ length 250.00   300.00

☐ **Pumper,** Dayton, 1932, red, green, and gold, 14½″ length 175.00   200.00

☐ **Pumper,** Hubley, 1928, 8″ length 150.00   200.00

☐ **Pumper,** Hubley, 1928, two horses, gong, 14″ length 250.00   300.00

☐ **Pumper,** Kenton, 1929, three horses, gong, gallop, lines, traces and suction hose, painted with gold trim, 22″ length 1200.00   1400.00

Price Range

☐ **Pumper,** Kenton, 1929, three galloping horses, nickeled boiler, suction hose and gong, 21½″ length 1200.00   1400.00

☐ **Pumper,** Kenton, 1929, three horses, with gong
    14″ length 275.00   300.00
    16″ length 350.00   400.00

☐ **Pumper,** Kenton, 1929, two horses, nickeled boiler, suction hose and gong, 21½″ length 250.00   300.00

☐ **Pumper,** 1937, cast iron, 4½″ length 350.00   400.00

☐ **Pumper,** Turner, 1935, red, green, and gold equipped with hose reel, two lengths of hose and bell, 31″ length 500.00   600.00

☐ **Pumping Fire Engine,** Structo, 1933, large water tank with hose, brass nozzle, two ladders, bell, electric swivel spotlight is movable, red and green headlights with polished brass finish reflector, 22″ length 350.00   400.00

☐ **Red Baby Wrecker,** Arcade, No. 216, 1932, red body, nickeled supports, chain, hook man and crank, red disc wheels, green crane trimmed in gold, gold bronze headlights, nickeled tires or real rubber tires, two-wheeled jack, 12″ length 250.00   300.00

☐ **Red Cross Ambulance,** Kenton, 1929, nickel plated (also came painted in various colors), 16″ length 500.00   600.00

☐ **Service Car,** Hubley, 1932, 5″ length 100.00   125.00

☐ **Turner Fire Department,** 1926, house with red engines, 21″ length 50.00   75.00

☐ **Turner Garage Set,** 1926, 21″ length 50.00   75.00

☐ **Water Tower,** Hubley, 1920, over a dozen sizes, rarest is 26″ length, two horses and gong, or 29″ length, two horses, each 1400.00   1600.00

One of the largest of Wilkins' horse-drawn ladder rigs, on exhibit at "Built to Last—The Toys of Kingsbury," at the New Hampshire Historical Society over Christmas, 1986. $700–$800.

	Price Range	
☐ **Wrecker,** Dent, circa 1920, bright red with gilt trim, black enameled top, yellow wrecking gear mechanically operated, nickeled disc wheels with red centers, 10¼" length ..	300.00	350.00
☐ **Wrecker,** Hubley, 1933, two-color detachable body, rubber-tired wheels, red hubs, 6¼" length, also 5¼" length	150.00	200.00
☐ **Wrecker,** Hubley, 1934, black chassis with light blue, red or orange body, nickel radiator, 6" length	150.00	175.00
☐ **Wrecker,** Hubley, 1934, two-color detachable body, rubber-tired wheels with red hubs and two spare tires, 6¼" length, also 5¼" length	150.00	200.00
☐ **Wrecker,** Kenton, 1929, crank and cable with hook attached will raise "wrecked" toys to be towed, ratchet will hold "wreck" at any position desired, 10¼" length	300.00	350.00

FARM AND CONSTRUCTION VEHICLES

Price Range

☐ **Auto Dump Wagon,** 1920, cast iron, number 675 embossed on driver's side, red and gold, later models green and red (toy was a big seller into the 1930s), sand shovel included, 7″ length 350.00   400.00

☐ **Avery Tractor,** 1929, name embossed below engine, green and red, 4½″ length 100.00   125.00

☐ **Caterpiller Tractor,** 1928, cast iron with operator, pull toy, "Ten" embossed on side of radiator denotes 10 HP, 7½″ length 175.00   200.00

☐ **Contractor's Dump Wagon,** 1915, features logo of Ellis Tiger Co., Gladstone, New Jersey, 14½″ length 250.00   300.00

☐ **Farmall Tractor,** 1928, cast iron, green, red, nickeled farmer, lug wheels, 6″ length 150.00   175.00

☐ **Farmall Tractor,** 1932, cast iron, gray with gold, red wheels, 6″ length 150.00   200.00

☐ **Ford Dump Truck,** 1928, red cast iron, green disc wheels or rubber wheels
   6″ length 125.00   150.00
   7½″ length 150.00   200.00

☐ **Ford Dump Truck,** 1941, 6½″ length (this and the International Pick-Up were the last cast-iron toys produced by Arcade) 350.00   400.00

☐ **Fordson Tractor,** 1924, cast iron, red and gray, cleated rear wheels, nickeled steering wheel and removable driver, 4¾, 5 or 6″ length 125.00   150.00

☐ **Fordson Tractor,** 1928, cast iron, smooth wheels, 6″ length 100.00   125.00

☐ **Hay Rack,** 1930, cast iron, red and green, removable rack, 15″ length 150.00   200.00

☐ **Industrial Caterpillar Derrick,** 1932, cast iron, two models, one with four wheels, one with treads, 4½″ length × 11″ height 1000.00   1200.00

Price Range

☐ **International Dump Truck,** 1930, cast iron, dual wheels, 10¾ length 200.00   250.00

☐ **International Harvester "K" Line Dump Truck,** 1941, cast iron, dual rear wheels and heavy duty coil spring, 11″ length 250.00   275.00

☐ **John Deere Combine,** 1930, cast iron, silver trimmed green with gold lettering, yellow wheels, many revolving parts, operator, 16″ length 400.00   450.00

☐ **John Deere Gas Engine,** 1930, green with gilt lettering, flywheel-silver, front wheels pivot, 5½″ length 75.00   100.00

☐ **John Deere Manure Spreader,** 1930, cast iron, red with gold trim and lettering, yellow wheels, green beaters, hooking tongue for rear attachment to tractor, 16¼″ length 300.00   325.00

☐ **John Deere Tractor,** 1930, cast iron, green with gold lettering, yellow wheels, nickeled flywheel, pulley and driver, silver steering wheel, 6½″ length 150.00   200.00

☐ **John Deere Utility Wagon,** 1930, cast iron, red, green with gold trim, removable wagon box, 15″ length 150.00   200.00

☐ **Mack Dump Truck,** 1925–1930s, cast iron (the best selling Mack that Arcade produced), disc wheels, painted wheels, or at extra charge rubber tires, Mack emblem embossed on door panel, 12″ length 300.00   350.00

☐ **Mack High Dump Truck,** 1930s, cast iron, thumb lever opens truck bed gates, nickeled wheels, "Coal" often appears stenciled on truck bed, 8½″ length 200.00   250.00

☐ **Mack Hoist Truck,** 1928, green and red, revolving cab, solid rubber disc wheels, nickeled chain, crane and driver, 13″ length 750.00   800.00

	Price Range	

☐ **Mack Side Dump Truck,** 1928, red-yellow, nickeled driver, solid rubber or disc wheels, cast iron, 9″ length 275.00 325.00

☐ **McCormick Deering Plow,** 1925–1930, cast iron, red and yellow, silver moldboard, shares and coulters, 7¾″ length 75.00 100.00

☐ **McCormick Deering Thresher,** 1928, cast iron, gray with red trim, cream-colored wheels, 12″ length, 18″ length with stacker and feeder extended 225.00 250.00

☐ **McCormick Deering Thresher,** Arcade, 1929, cast iron, 13½″ length 250.00 300.00

☐ **McCormick Deering Thresher,** 1929, cast iron, red, green or blue, gold trim and logo, movable grain spout and stacker, nickeled wheels, 9½″ length 300.00 325.00

☐ **McCormick Deering Thresher,** 1930, cast iron, aluminum trimmed, green and gold lettering, yellow wheels, nickeled pulley and flywheel, many parts removable, 20½″ length 350.00 400.00

☐ **McCormick Deering Tractor,** Arcade, 1925, cast iron, plows, rakes, etc., can be attached, gray, gold trimmed, red wheels, 7¼″ length 175.00 200.00

☐ **McCormick Deering Weber-Wagon,** Arcade, 1925–1930, horse drawn, cast iron, Deering logo embossed in both wagon thresher and tractor 250.00 300.00

☐ **Oliver Plow,** 1928, cast iron, attaches to Fordson tractor, 5¾″ length 75.00 100.00

☐ **"Red Baby" Dump Body Truck,** 1928, cast iron, red, 10¾″ length 250.00 300.00

☐ **Road Construction Set,** 1930s, 7″ × 11″ box contains 12 components, including tractor and cart, truck, wheelbarrow, road signs, picks, shovels .... 350.00 400.00★

★Set with original box sold for $425.00 at Lloyd Ralston Auction in 1981.

Price Range

☐ **Road Roller and Scraper,** Arcade, 1932, cast iron, 16″ length 350.00 400.00

☐ **Road Scraper,** 1932, cast iron, green with red wheels, swing-over dump box, 8¼″ length 250.00 300.00

☐ **Sandloader,** mid-1920s, cast iron and pressed steel, 8½″ length 350.00 400.00

☐ **Sand Loading Shovel,** 1928, cast iron and pressed steel, rubber disc wheels, nickeled chain and levers, 12½″ length 800.00 850.00

☐ **Side Dump Trailer,** 1932, red chassis, cast iron, green dumper, nickeled wheels, dumps either side, 7″ length 250.00 300.00

☐ **Steam Roller,** 1929, green, red with gilt trim, cast iron, nickeled wheels and roller, plus operator, 7¾″ length 250.00 300.00

☐ **Tractor,** 1937, Arcade, cast iron, green with red hubs, rubber tires 200.00 250.00

☐ **Tractor and Trailer,** 1928, cast iron, lug back wheels, 12½ length 125.00 150.00

☐ **Truck Trailer,** 1928, cast iron, removable sides 125.00 150.00

☐ **White Dump Truck,** 1929, cast iron, green, red or blue, nickel-plated wheels, rubber tire wheels extra, 11½″ length 275.00 300.00

☐ **"Yellow Baby" Dump Truck,** mid-1930s, cast iron, "Yellow Baby" appears on cab door, "International Harvester" on truck bed, possibly a promotional piece, The Red Baby re-christened, yellow, 10¾″ length .. 150.00 200.00

MOTORCYCLES

☐ **Harley,** Hubley, 1933, assorted colors, 5¼″ length 100.00 150.00

☐ **Harley-Davidson Cycle,** Hubley, 1928, with two men, 9″ length 300.00 350.00

Price Range

☐ **Harley-Davidson Hill Climber,** Hubley, 1932, olive, blue or orange demountable rider, 8½" length 350.00   400.00

☐ **Harley-Davidson Motorcycle and Side Car,** Hubley, 1936, cycle painted red, side car light blue with white rubber tires, 5¼" length, also 6½" length 100.00   150.00

☐ **Harley-Davidson Side Car Motorcycle,** Hubley, 1932, painted olive green, 5¼" length, also 6½" length 100.00   125.00

☐ **Harley-Davidson Solo Motorcycle,** Hubley, 1932, olive, blue or orange, rubber tires, demountable rider, motor exhaust, came with either sport rider or cop, 9" length, also 4½" length 450.00   500.00

☐ **Indian Armored Car,** Hubley, 1932, painted red, rubber tires, exhaust sound, two demountable cops and removable armor plate, 8½" length 600.00   650.00

☐ **Indian Crash Car,** Hubley, 1932, painted green cycle with red body, came with hose and reel and gasoline cans, 10" length 500.00   600.00

☐ **Indian Delivery,** 1933, "Say It With Flowers," painted in light blue with black top, rubber tires, separate rider, motor exhaust, rear door, 10¼" length 1500.00   2000.00

☐ **Indian Side Car Motorcycle,** Hubley, 1932, red rubber tires, two demountable riders, imitation exhaust sound, 9" length .. 450.00   500.00
With sports figures instead of cops, 9" length 475.00   525.00

☐ **Indian Solo Motorcycle,** Hubley, 1932, painted red, yellow or green, rubber tires, demountable rider, motor exhaust, came with cop or sport rider, 9" length 450.00   500.00

☐ **Indian Traffic Car,** Hubley, 1932, painted red and blue, 12" length 600.00   650.00

Price Range

☐ **Indian Traffic Car,** Hubley, 1933, assorted colors, 6¼" length, also 3⅜" length 150.00   200.00

☐ **Motorcycle,** Champion, 1930, enameled blue with gold trim, rubber tires, 4¼" length, other sizes 75.00   100.00

☐ **Motorcycle,** Hubley, 1933, painted red with rubber tires, exhaust sound and demountable cop, featured electric headlight, 8½" length 200.00   250.00

☐ **Motorcycle,** Hubley, 1934, painted red, dark blue or orange, electric headlight, 6½" length 150.00   200.00

☐ **Motorcycle Cop,** Hubley, 1928, with two men, 9" length, other sizes 300.00   350.00

☐ **Motorcycle Cop With Side Car,** Champion, 1930, motorcycle and officers enameled blue, side car enameled red, air-cushion rubber tires, 6½" length, also 5" length ... 150.00   200.00

☐ **Motorcycle With Side Car,** Hubley, 1928, 4" length 75.00   100.00

☐ **Parcel Post Harley-Davidson,** Hubley, 1928, 10" length 500.00   600.00

☐ **Side Car Motorcycle,** Hubley, 1933, red with gold striping, rubber tires, exhaust sound and demountable cop, electric headlight, 8½" length 400.00   450.00

☐ **"Speed" Cycle,** Hubley, 1933, came in various colors, 3¼" length, other sizes 50.00   100.00

☐ **Tandem Cycle,** Hubley, 1936, painted assorted colors, 4⅛" length 100.00   150.00

PLEASURE CARS

Arcade

☐ **Buick Sedan,** 1938, aluminum bronze headlights, Buick logo embossed on radiator, 8½" length 1200.00   1400.00

Top row: a selection of horse-drawn, cast-iron rigs from Wilkins Toy Co., Keene, NH, c. 1890s. Acquired by Kingsbury in 1894, Wilkins' name was retained until 1918. $800-$1200 range. *Bottom row, left to right:* Automobile Phaeton, Wilkins, 1905, 9″ length (unusual in that it has lady driver); Kingsbury Cabriolet, 1930, 14″ length, pressed steel and rubber tires; Kingsbury ambulance, 1928, pressed steel, rubber tires; Kingsbury roadster, 1930s, pressed steel, rubber tires, friction mechanical. $800-$1000 range. From Toys of Kingsbury Exhibition, November 23-January 3, 1987, at New Hampshire Historical Society, Concord, NH.

	Price Range	
☐ **Chevrolet Coupe,** 1925–1928, also provided a companion sedan, cowl parking lights, disc wheels, 8¼″ length	900.00	1000.00
☐ **Chevrolet Coupe,** 1928, yellow, blue, red, gray, approximately 12″ length	1000.00	1200.00
☐ **DeSoto Sedan,** 1937–1938, blue with white bumpers, 4″ length (part of Arcade's Miniature series)	250.00	400.00
☐ **Ford Coupe,** 1932, red, green, blue, spoked wheels, 5″ length	250.00	300.00
☐ **Ford Coupe,** 1932, red, green, blue, spoked wheels, 5½″ length	350.00	400.00
☐ **Model A,** 1928, red, green, blue, yellow, featured rumble seat, 6¾″ length	750.00	900.00

Price Range

☐ **Model A Sedan,** 1928, Tudor model, orange, 6¾" length 700.00 900.00

☐ **Model A Sedan,** 1928, 4-door model, red 700.00 900.00

☐ **Model T Ford Fordor Sedan,** 1924, spoke wheels, dubbed the "Tin Lizzie," black, 6½" length
Small size 400.00 450.00
Large size 600.00 700.00

☐ **Pontiac Sedan,** 1937–1938, miniature, 4½" length 350.00 400.00

☐ **Pontiac Sedan,** 1937–1938, 6½" length ... 450.00 500.00

☐ **Runabout Auto,** 1908–1910, wood, pressed steel, cast iron, with nickeled driver, 8¾" length (possibly first auto off Arcade's assembly line) 350.00 400.00

Champion

☐ **Auto Coupe,** 1930, red, green or blue, air cushion-type rubber tires, rear spare tire, 4¼" length 250.00 300.00

☐ **Coupe,** 1930, red, green or blue enamel, air cushion-type rubber tires, rumble seat and spare tire, 7½" length 300.00 350.00

☐ **Sedan,** 1930, red, green or blue enameled finish with air cushion-type rubber tires, spare tire at rear of car, 4½" length 100.00 150.00

Dent

☐ **Coupe,** 1920, finished in bright colors with nickeled disc wheels, 5⅜" length (car also came in cast aluminum) 200.00 250.00

☐ **Coupe,** 1920, 6¼" length × 3¾" height .. 250.00 300.00

☐ **Roadster,** 1920, bright assorted colors, nickel-plated disc wheels, 4⅞" length 100.00 150.00

Price Range

☐ **Sedan,** 1920, bright colors, black enamel top, nickel wheels with red centers and spare wheel, 7½" length, other sizes (4½" size also came in case aluminum) 300.00   350.00

☐ **Sedan,** 1920, finished in bright colors, gilt trim, black enameled top with nickel wheels, 6½" length (also made in cast aluminum) 250.00   300.00

Harris

☐ **Roadster,** 1903, cast iron mechanical, 7½" length 1100.00   1400.00

Hubley

☐ **Airflow DeSoto,** 1934, assorted colors, nickel-plated radiator, bumper and windshield, with electric headlights, 3¼" length 450.00   500.00

☐ **Chrysler,** 1936, 6¼" length 150.00   200.00

☐ **Chrsyler Airflow,** 1936, painted various colors, nickel-plated radiator, bumpers and windshield, came with electric headlights, 8¼" length, also 6¼" length size 450.00   500.00

☐ **Chrysler Roadster,** 1936, assorted colors with electric headlights, 7½" length 200.00   250.00

☐ **Chrysler Sedan,** 1936, assorted colors, electric headlights, aluminum radiator, bumpers, running board, spare tire, 6½" length ..   350.00   400.00

☐ **Chrysler Sedan,** 1936, assorted colors, electric headlights, 7¼" length 400.00   450.00

☐ **Chrysler Town Car,** 1936, assorted colors, electric headlights, 7½" length 400.00   450.00

☐ **Coupe,** 1933, two-color detachable body, rubber-tired wheels with red hubs, 6¼" length 200.00   250.00

Price Range

☐ **Coupe,** 1934, black chassis, light blue, red or yellow body, contrasting color top, 6″ length 150.00   200.00

☐ **Coupe,** 1934, black chassis, light blue, red, yellow or orange body, 3¾″ length 100.00   150.00

☐ **Coupe,** 1934, green chassis, orange body with contrasting color top, aluminum finish on radiator and bumper, black rubber-tired wheels with aluminum hubs, 6½″ length .. 100.00   250.00

☐ **Coupe,** 1936, assorted colors, silver bronze radiator, running boards, bumpers, 4¼″ length 75.00   100.00

☐ **Hill Climber,** 1936, light blue and black trim, 6¼″ length 150.00   200.00

☐ **Limousine,** 1920, gray-striped cast iron, 8¼″ length 300.00   350.00

☐ **Lincoln Zephyr,** 1936, assorted colors with aluminum bronze radiator, 6″ length 250.00   300.00

☐ **Open Roadster,** 1938, cast iron, 4½″ length 100.00   150.00

☐ **Phaeton,** 1934, black chassis, light blue, red or yellow body, contrasting top, 6″ length .. 350.00   400.00

☐ **Phaeton,** 1934, black chassis, light blue, red, yellow or orange body, nickel radiator, 3¼″ length 150.00   200.00

☐ **Roadster,** 1920, cast iron with driver, 8½″ length 500.00   600.00

☐ **Roadster,** 1933, two-color detachable body, rubber-tired wheels with red hubs, 6¼″ length 200.00   250.00

☐ **Roadster,** 1934, black chassis, light blue, red or yellow body with contrasting color seat, nickled radiator, spare tire on rear, 6″ length 150.00   200.00

Price Range

☐ **Roadster,** 1934, painted light blue, light green or red with aluminum radiator and bumper, six black rubber-tired wheels with aluminum hubs, detachable body, 6¹/₂″ length 200.00   250.00

☐ **Roadster,** 1936, assorted colors with aluminum bronze radiator, running boards and bumpers, 6⁵/₈″ length, other sizes 150.00   200.00

☐ **Sedan,** 1933, two-color detachable body, rubber-tired wheels, red hubs, 5″ length, other sizes 150.00   200.00

☐ **Sedan,** 1934, black chassis, light blue, red or yellow body, contrasting color top, nickel radiator, 6″ length 250.00   300.00

☐ **Sedan,** 1934, black chassis, light blue, red, yellow or orange body, nickel radiator, 3¹/₄″ length 125.00   150.00

☐ **Sports Roadster,** 1932, 4³/₄″ length 150.00   200.00

☐ **Station Wagon,** 1933, two-color detachable body, rubber-tired wheels, red hubs, 6¹/₄″ length 350.00   400.00

☐ **Studebaker Sedan,** 1936, painted various colors, with aluminum bronze radiator, running boards and bumpers, spare tire on rear of car, 5″ length 150.00   200.00

☐ **Town Car,** 1936, assorted colors, aluminum bronze radiator, running boards and bumpers, 6⁵/₈″ length, other sizes 350.00   400.00

Kenton

☐ **Auto Cab,** 1929, 8″ length, other sizes 700.00   800.00

☐ **Auto Roadster,** 1929, 7¹/₂″ length, other sizes 250.00   300.00

☐ **Auto Touring Car,** 1929, painted and trimmed in various colors, 9¹/₄″ length 800.00   900.00

Price Range

☐ **Auto Touring Car,** 1929, painted in assorted colors and trim, 9¼" length 800.00 900.00

☐ **Coupe,** 1929, 8½" length 400.00 500.00

☐ **New Model Coupe,** 1929, detachable wheel, 10" length 600.00 700.00

☐ **Roadster,** 1929, painted and trimmed in assorted colors, 8½" length 700.00 800.00

☐ **Sedan,** 1929, assorted colors with extra detachable wheel, 10" length, other sizes 650.00 700.00

☐ **Sedan,** 1929, various colors with extra tire and red and green lights showing in rear of car, 3¼" length, other sizes 400.00 450.00

☐ **Yellow Taxi,** 1929, 6½" length, other sizes 300.00 350.00

Kilgore

☐ **Open Ford Roadster,** 1929, 3½" length .. 200.00 250.00

Williams

☐ **Coupe,** 1934, red, blue, green and tan with rubber tires, nickeled rumble seat, 5¼" length 150.00 200.00

Makers unknown

☐ **Packard,** 1930, hood and front doors open, rubber balloon tires, driver, 11" length 1200.00 1400.00

☐ **Roadster,** 1929, blue, imitation spare tire, nickeled driver and wheels, 9⅛" length 300.00 350.00

☐ **Sedan,** 1910, red striped with gold and silver, 8" length 300.00 350.00

☐ **Sedan,** 1924, red and black with chauffeur, 12" length 250.00 300.00

Straight-eight Packard sedan, Hubley, $2000 plus. (Photo courtesy of Phillips Auctions.)

RACERS

A. C. Williams Co.

Price Range

☐ **Racer,** 1932, cast iron, yellow with red hubs and rubber tires, two passengers, built long and low to the ground, 8½″ length 200.00   250.00

AO (France)

☐ **Racer,** circa 1900s, painted tin clockwork, red with gold trim, this ingenious car speeds along then completely falls apart, 7.9″ length [Blondinat (France) made a similar version] 900.00   1000.00

Arcade Manufacturing Co.

☐ **Bullet Racer,** 1928, cast iron, blue, red, green rubber disc wheels, 7⅝″ length 350.00   400.00

☐ **Bullet Racer,** 1932, cast iron, red, green yellow, with or without rubber tires, nickeled wheels, 8½″ length 275.00   300.00

Price Range

☐ **Racer,** 1932, cast iron, red, green, blue, 3¼″ length 200.00   250.00

☐ **Racer,** 1935–1936, cast iron, red, silver, blue, two drivers, known as the #1440, 8″ length 250.00   300.00

Champion Hardware Co.

☐ **Racer,** 1930, cast iron, front bumper and tail fin, rubber tires, red car with blue driver, 8½″ length 250.00   300.00

Dayton Toy and Speciality Co.

☐ **Racer,** 1932, cast iron, red body with gold trim, 11″ length 200.00   225.00

Georges Carette

☐ **Racing Car #3,** 1920s, lithographed tin clockwork, 12½″ length (rare classic) 2000.00   3000.00

Greppert Kelch (GK), German

☐ **Racing Car,** 1910s, painted tin, red, 5½″ length 650.00   700.00

Hubley Manufacturing Co.

☐ **Golden Arrow Racer,** 1929, tail fin, nickeled wheels (popular for over 7 years), 6¾″ length, made in several other sizes 250.00   300.00

☐ **Racer No. 1,** 1932, cast iron, assorted colors, 8″ length 200.00   250.00

☐ **Racer,** 1933, cast iron, tail fin in 6¾″ length and 8¼″ length 150.00   200.00

☐ **Racer,** 1933, cast iron, without tail fin, 6¾″ length 100.00   150.00

☐ **Racer,** 1934, cast iron, pale blue, red or orange, electric headlights, without tail fin, 6½″ length 250.00   275.00

Price Range

☐ **Racer,** 1934, orange or red with silver radiator, tail fin, rubber tires 150.00   200.00

☐ **Racer,** 1934, assorted colors, with electric headlights, raised hood feature to replace battery, rubber tires 300.00   350.00

☐ **Racer,** 1934, silver with red trim, 5¼" length 150.00   175.00

Kenton Hardware Co. (Jones and Bixler)

☐ **Racer,** 1929, silver finish, 5½", 6½" and 7½" length 250.00   300.00

☐ **Sport Racer,** 1925–1927, cast iron, assorted colors, sizes 7", 9", 10¼" length 200.00   250.00

☐ **Track Racer,** No. 8, 1927, cast iron, sizes 7", 9", 10¼" length, assorted colors, more compact, higher off wheels version with doors and step 250.00   300.00

Kingsbury Manufacturing Co.

☐ **Bluebird Racer,** 1930, pressed steel, disc wheels, rubber tires and bumper, clockwork, 8" length 400.00   450.00

☐ **Golden Arrow Racer,** 1929, pressed steel, bright gold (also red versions), spring motor, rubber tires, 21" length (exact replica of racer driven by Major Seagrave, world's fastest driver in 1929) 450.00   500.00

☐ **Mystery Sunbeam Racer,** 1929, pressed steel, bright red finish, tag that originally came with toy indicates Major H. O. Seagrave is at wheel, 19" length (based on model of actual racing car which set world's land speed record in 1927, futuristic even by today's standards) 400.00   450.00

Louis Marx

Price Range

- ☐ **Giant King,** 1929, lithographed tin wind-up, has No. "11" on radiator, "7-11" on driver's door panel, available in three colors, 12½" length 150.00   200.00

- ☐ **Racer,** 1930, lithographed tin wind-up, has "61" on door panel, 5½" length 50.00   75.00

- ☐ **Sparks Auto Racer,** 1929, lithographed tin wind-up, multi-color, shoots sparks from rear, runs straight or in circles, 8½" length 200.00   250.00

- ☐ **Speed King Racer,** 1929, lithographed tin wind-up, yellow with red trim, rocket-like contour, "Speed King" appears in bold black letters in engine cowling, 16" length 250.00   300.00

- ☐ **Stutz Racer,** 1929, lithographed tin wind-up, available in three colors, 16" length 175.00   225.00

Pinard (France)

- ☐ **Delage Racer,** 1900s, painted tin, 12.2" length 500.00   550.00

- ☐ **Racer,** 1900s, painted tin, blue, battery-powered spot lamp, 11" length 350.00   400.00

- ☐ **Racer,** 1900s, painted tin, deep green with gold trim, 15.7" length 350.00   400.00

- ☐ **Racer,** 1900s, painted tin, light blue, 8.6" length 350.00   400.00

- ☐ **Racer No. 4,** 1900s, painted tin, yellow, electric headlamp, 13" length 450.00   500.00

Note: All the Pinard racers above are long running clockwork models.

Rossignol

- ☐ **Racing Car,** late 1930s, lithographed tin wind-up, modeled on a Peugeot, 15" length   350.00   400.00

S. G. Gunthermann (German)

Price Range

☐ **Gordon Bennett Racing Car,** 1920s, lithographed tin clockwork, tan with gold trim, silver headlamps, rubber-rimmed spoke wheels, small squeeze horn, many deem this the gem of all racing toys, 11.8″ length (this race car also came in 5.9, 6.3, 7.1 and 8.5 sizes; the 6.3 blue version is rated the most uncommon of all) 2000.00   3000.00

☐ **Race Car No. 5,** 1920s, lithographed tin, clockwork runabout, "No. 5" appears on radiator, 8.7″ length 1000.00   1200.00

Structo Manufacturing Co.

☐ **Auto Builder No. 8,** 1915, pressed steel, green with red spoked wheels, 12½″ length 250.00   300.00

☐ **Bearcat Racer,** 1920s, pressed steel and cast iron, clockwork, 12¼″ length 250.00   300.00

Vindix (National Sewing Machine Co.)

☐ **Racer,** 1928, cast iron, red, yellow wheel hubs, "2" embossed on side, 11″ length .. 450.00   500.00

Wilkins Toy Co.

☐ **Racer,** 1911, cast iron and pressed steel, silver finish with red striping, clockwork motor, driver in yellow, rubber tires, 10″ length (the classic among early race cars) .. 1000.00   1200.00

☐ **Racer,** 1912, pressed steel, 9¼″ length (what looked like a casket on wheels sold successfully over five years in the Wilkins line) 650.00   700.00

Miscellaneous

Price Range

☐ **Hiller Comet Racing Car,** 1930s, gas engine, sheet metal, blue body, original decals with "4" and HC logo, 18″ length 300.00   350.00

☐ **Oh Boy Racer,** 1929, pressed steel, red with silver windshield, radiator and hood, No. "110" appears at rear, 19¾″ length 200.00   250.00

☐ **Racer,** 1924, tin mechanical, orange car with red and black disc wheels, gray driver, rubber tires, 6⅜″ length (probably European) 125.00   150.00

☐ **Racer,** 1947, tin mechanical, key wind, 13″ length 100.00   125.00

☐ **Rex Racer,** 1924, tin mechanical, red with black trim, has spare tire, mud guard and running board, blue driver, 8″ length 100.00   125.00

☐ **Rocket Racer,** 1930, strong spring motor, has rubber bumper, tail fins, 16″ length ...   125.00   150.00

TAXI CABS

Note: See also the "Still Banks" listings for Arcade Yellow Cab examples.

☐ **Checker Cab,** 1925, cast iron, green checker design across chassis, gray wheel hubs, 8″ length 350.00   400.00

☐ **Ford Yellow Cab,** 1933, cast iron, four-door sedan, special Chicago World's Fair edition: "Century of Progress" stenciled on roof, 6⅞″ length 450.00   500.00

☐ **Limousine Yellow Cab,** 1930, cast iron, license #3300, 8½″ length 400.00   450.00

☐ **Red Top Cab,** 1924, cast iron, red top, white bottom, gray wheel hubs, Red Top logo on rear door panel, 8″ length 400.00   450.00

☐ **Yellow Cab,** 1925, cast iron, 9″ length (1927 model is 5¼″ length) 350.00   400.00

Price Range

☐ **Yellow Cab,** 1932, cast iron, black top and trim, Goodrich rubber tires, nickeled radiator, cast iron sign over windshield, embossed "Checker" logo, 9¼ length 450.00   500.00

☐ **Yellow Cab,** 1932, cast iron, with black top, 8⅛" length 500.00   550.00

☐ **Yellow Cab,** 1933, cast iron, bronze bumpers, 9¼" length 550.00   600.00

TOOTSIE TOYS (Pre-1941)

The following numbers are taken from the Dowst Catalog.

☐ **23, Racer,** 1927–33, 74 mm. length 35.00   45.00

☐ **170, Interchangeable Truck,** 1925–31, 82 mm. length 25.00   35.00

☐ **185, Fire Department,** 1927–31, 91 mm. length 35.00   40.00

☐ **190, Auto Transport Truck,** 1931–33, 215 mm. length 25.00   35.00

☐ **190x, 4-Car Transport,** 1933–36, 272 mm. length 35.00   50.00

☐ **4258, Limousine,** 1911–28, 47 mm. length 30.00   35.00

☐ **4570 Model T Ford,** 1914–26, 77 mm. length 40.00   50.00

☐ **4610, Truck-Ford,** 1916–32, 77 mm. length 30.00   35.00

☐ **4629, Sedan-Yellow Cab,** 1923–33, 72 mm. length 35.00   40.00

☐ **4630, Delivery Van,** 1924–33, 75 mm. length 35.00   40.00

☐ **4636, Coupe,** 1924–33, 76 mm. length 30.00   35.00

☐ **4638, Mack Stake Truck,** 1925–33, 82 mm. length 35.00   50.00

☐ **4639, Mack Coal Truck,** 1925–33, 82 mm. length 35.00   50.00

Price Range

☐ **4640, Mack Tank Truck,** 1925–33, 82 mm. length 30.00   40.00

☐ **4641, Touring Car,** 1925–33, 78 mm. length 30.00   40.00

☐ **4642, Long Range Cannon,** 1931–41, 95 mm. length 25.00   30.00

☐ **4643, Anti-Aircraft Gun,** 1931–41, 70 mm. length 25.00   30.00

☐ **4644, Searchlight,** 1931–41, 70 mm. length 25.00   30.00

☐ **4645, New Mail Truck—Mack,** 1931–33, 76 mm. length 35.00   50.00

☐ **4646, Caterpillar Tractor,** 1931–39, 77 mm. length 35.00   50.00

☐ **4647, Army Tank,** 1931–41, 79 mm. length 25.00   35.00

☐ **4648, Steam Roller,** 1931–34, 73 mm. length 25.00   35.00

☐ **4651, Fagcol Safety Coach,** 1927–33, 90 mm. length 50.00   60.00

☐ **4652, Hook and Ladder,** 1927–33, 105 mm. length 50.00   75.00

☐ **4653, Water Tower,** 1927–33, 91 mm. length 35.00   40.00

☐ **4654, Tractor,** 1927–32, 76 mm. length ... 45.00   55.00

☐ **4655, Model A Ford Coupe,** 1928–33, 65 mm. length 40.00   50.00

☐ **4656, Buick Coupe in Tin Garage,** 1931–32, 58 mm. length 25.00   35.00

☐ **4657, Sedan in Garage,** 1931–32, 58 mm. length 25.00   35.00

☐ **4658, Insurance Patrol in Garage,** 1931–32, 58 mm. length 30.00   40.00

☐ **4666, Racer—Bluebird Daytons,** 1932–41, 95 mm. length 35.00   45.00

	Price Range	
☐ **4670, Trailer Truck,** 1929–32, 100 mm. length	25.00	35.00
☐ **4680, Overland Bus With Separate Grill,** 1929–33, 95 mm. length	25.00	35.00

General Motors Series

☐ **6001, Buick Roadster,** 1927–33, 79 mm. length	45.00	55.00
☐ **6002, Buick Coupe,** 1927–33, 77 mm. length	45.00	55.00
☐ **6003, Buick Brougham,** 1927–33, 79 mm. length	55.00	60.00
☐ **6004, Buick Sedan,** 1927–33, 79 mm. length	45.00	55.00
☐ **6005, Buick Touring Car,** 1927–33, 79 mm. length	45.00	55.00
☐ **6006, Buick Delivery Truck,** 1927–33, 82 mm. length	45.00	55.00
☐ **6101, Cadillac Roadster,** 1927–33, 79 mm. length	45.00	55.00
☐ **6102, Cadillac Coupe,** 1927–33, 77 mm. length	55.00	65.00
☐ **6103, Cadillac Brougham,** 1927–33, 79 mm. length	55.00	65.00
☐ **6104, Cadillac Sedan,** 1927–33, 79 mm. length	45.00	55.00
☐ **6105, Cadillac Closed Touring Car,** 1927–33, 79 mm. length	45.00	55.00
☐ **6106, Cadillac Delivery Truck,** 1927–33, 82 mm. length	50.00	60.00
☐ **6201, Chevrolet Roadster,** 1927–33, 79 mm. length	35.00	45.00
☐ **6202, Chevrolet Coupe,** 1927–33, 77 mm. length	35.00	45.00

	Price Range	
☐ **6203, Chevrolet Brougham,** 1927–33, 79 mm. length	45.00	55.00
☐ **6204, Chevrolet Sedan,** 1927–33, 79 mm. length	35.00	45.00
☐ **6205, Chevrolet Touring Car,** 1927–33, 79 mm. length	35.00	45.00
☐ **6206, Chevrolet Delivery Truck,** 1927–33, 82 mm. length	50.00	60.00
☐ **6301, Oldsmobile Roadster,** 1927–33, 79 mm. length	50.00	60.00
☐ **6302, Oldsmobile Coupe,** 1927–33, 79 mm. length	50.00	60.00
☐ **6303, Oldsmobile Brougham,** 1927–33, 79 mm. length	55.00	65.00
☐ **6304, Oldsmobile Sedan,** 1927–33, 79 mm. length	50.00	60.00
☐ **6305, Oldsmobile Touring Car,** 1927–33, 79 mm. length	50.00	60.00
☐ **6306, Oldsmobile Panel Delivery Truck,** 1927–33, 82 mm. length	50.00	60.00
☐ **6665, Ford Sedan,** 1929–33, 68 mm. length	35.00	40.00

Miniature Series

☐ **101, Coupe,** 1931–34, 58 mm. length	45.00	55.00
☐ **102, Roadster,** 1932–34, 58 mm. length ...	40.00	50.00
☐ **103, Sedan,** 1931–34, 58 mm. length	40.00	50.00
☐ **104, Insurance Patrol,** 1931–34, 59 mm. length	40.00	50.00
☐ **105, Tank Truck—Mack,** 1932–34, 59 mm. length	40.00	50.00
☐ **108, Caterpillar Tractor,** 1932–34, 52 mm. length	40.00	50.00
☐ **109, Ford Stake Truck,** 1932–34, 57 mm. length	40.00	50.00

	Price Range	
☐ **110, Racer,** 1932–34, 68 mm. length	55.00	65.00

Large Mack and Graham Commercials

☐ **191, Contractor Set,** 1933–41, 311 mm. length	75.00	100.00
☐ **192, Milk Truck Trailers,** 1933–41, 337 mm. length	75.00	100.00
☐ **198, Auto Transport,** 1935–41, 277 mm. length	75.00	100.00
☐ **801, Mack Stake Trailer,** 1933–41, 137 mm. length	75.00	100.00
☐ **802, Mack Oil Trailer,** 1933–39, 138 mm. length	75.00	100.00
☐ **803, Mack Van Trailer,** 1933–36, 139 mm. length	75.00	100.00
☐ **804, Mack Coal Truck,** 1933–38, 100 mm. length	75.00	100.00
☐ **805, Mack Milk Trailer,** 1933–39, 145 mm. length	75.00	100.00
☐ **806, Wrecking Car,** 1933–39, 105 mm. length	75.00	100.00
☐ **807, Delivery Cycle,** 1933–39, 76 mm. length	75.00	100.00
☐ **808, Milk Delivery Car,** 1933–39, 98 mm. length	75.00	100.00
☐ **809, Ambulance,** 1935–41, 98 mm. length	75.00	100.00
☐ **810, Wrigley American Railway Express Truck,** 1935–41, 103 mm. length	100.00	125.00

Graham Series (RM refers to rear-mount spare tire, SM to side-mount spare tire)

☐ **511, Graham RM Roadster,** 5-wheel, 1933–35, 102 mm. length	60.00	70.00

Price Range

☐ **512, Graham RM Coupe,** 1933-35, 102 mm. length 60.00   70.00

☐ **513, Graham RM Sedan,** 1933-35, 102 mm. length 60.00   70.00

☐ **514, Graham RM Convertible Coupe,** 1933-35, 102 mm. length 60.00   70.00

☐ **515, Graham RM Convertible Sedan,** 1933-35, 102 mm. length 60.00   70.00

☐ **516, Graham RM Town Car,** 1933-35, 102 mm. length 60.00   70.00

☐ **611, Graham SM Roadster,** 1933-35, 98 mm. length 60.00   70.00

☐ **612, Graham SM Coupe,** 1933-35, 98 mm. length 60.00   70.00

☐ **613, Graham SM Sedan,** 1933-35, 98 mm. length 60.00   70.00

☐ **614, Graham SM Convertible Coupe,** 1933-35, 98 mm. length 60.00   70.00

☐ **615, Graham SM Convertible Sedan,** 1933-35, 98 mm. length 60.00   70.00

☐ **616, Graham SM Town Car,** 1933-35, 98 mm. length 60.00   70.00

☐ **712, La Salle Coupe,** 1935-39, 108 mm. length 100.00   125.00

☐ **713, La Salle Sedan,** 1935-39, 108 mm. length 100.00   125.00

☐ **714, La Salle Convertible Coupe,** 1935-36, 108 mm. length 100.00   125.00

☐ **715, La Salle Convertible Sedan,** 1935-36, 108 mm. length 100.00   125.00

☐ **716, Doodlebug,** 1935-37, 102 mm. length 65.00   75.00

☐ **6015, Lincoln Zephyr,** 1937-39, 104 mm. length 100.00   125.00

1934-1935 Ford Series

	Price Range	
☐ **111, Ford Sedan,** 1935–41, 76 mm. length ..	60.00	75.00
☐ **112, Ford Coupe,** 1935–41, 76 mm. length ..	60.00	75.00
☐ **113, Ford V-8 Wrecker,** 1935–41, 81 mm. length	75.00	85.00
☐ **114, Ford Convertible Coupe,** 1935–36, 76 mm. length	75.00	85.00
☐ **115, Ford Convertible Sedan,** 1935–36, 76 mm. length	75.00	85.00
☐ **116, Ford Roadster,** 1935–39, 78 mm. length	75.00	85.00
☐ **117, Zephyr Railcar,** 1935–36, 97 mm. length	75.00	85.00
☐ **118, Airflow DeSoto,** 1935–39, 76 mm. length	75.00	85.00
☐ **120, Oil Tank Truck,** 1936–39, 77 mm. length	75.00	85.00
☐ **121, Ford Pick-Up Truck,** 1936–39, 73 mm. length	75.00	85.00
☐ **123, Ford "Special Delivery,"** 1937–39, 77 mm. length	75.00	85.00
☐ **180, Roamer (Car and Trailer),** 1938–39, 215 mm. length	75.00	85.00
☐ **187, Auto Carrier,** 1939–41, 216 mm. length	75.00	85.00
☐ **4634, Supply Truck,** 1939–41, 111 mm. length	65.00	75.00
☐ **4635, Armored Car,** 1938–41, 100 mm. length	65.00	75.00
☐ **1006, Standard Oil Truck,** 1939–41, 149 mm. length	75.00	85.00
☐ **1007, Sinclair Oil Truck,** 1939–41, 149 mm. length	75.00	85.00
☐ **1008, Texaco Oil Truck,** 1939–41, 149 mm. length	75.00	85.00

	Price Range	
☐ **1009, Shell Oil Truck,** 1939–41, 149 mm. length	75.00	85.00
☐ **1040, Hook and Ladder,** 1937–41, 139 mm. length	60.00	70.00
☐ **1041, Hose Car,** 1937–41, 116 mm. length	60.00	70.00
☐ **1042, Insurance Patrol,** 1937–41, 111 mm. length	50.00	60.00
☐ **1043, Camping Trailer,** 1937–41, 139 mm. length	45.00	55.00
☐ **1044, Trailer,** 1937–39, 120 mm. length ...	45.00	50.00
☐ **1045, Greyhound Deluxe Bus,** 1937–41, 150 mm. length	50.00	60.00
☐ **1046, Station Wagon,** 1940–41, 113 mm. length	45.00	50.00

"230" Series (all are small one-piece castings with front fender skirts)

☐ **230, Sedan,** 1940–41, 85 mm. length	25.00	35.00
☐ **231, Coupe,**1940–41, 80 mm. length	20.00	25.00
☐ **232, Touring Car,** 1940–41, 76 mm. length	20.00	25.00
☐ **233, Roadster,** 1940–41, 81 mm. length ...	20.00	25.00
☐ **234, Box Truck,** 1940–41, 79 mm. length ...	20.00	25.00
☐ **235, Oil Truck,** 1940–41, 79 mm. length ..	20.00	25.00
☐ **236, Hook and Ladder,** 1940–41, 77 mm. length	20.00	25.00
☐ **237, Insurance Patrol,** 1940–41, 77 mm. length	20.00	25.00
☐ **238, Hose Car,** 1940–41, 79 mm. length ..	20.00	25.00
☐ **239, Station Wagon,** 1940–41, 77 mm. length	20.00	25.00
☐ **260, Yellow Cab,** 1940–41, 185 mm. length	20.00	25.00

	Price Range	
☐ **261, Checker Cab,** 1940–41, 185 mm. length	20.00	25.00
☐ **262, Fire Engine,** 1940–41, 185 mm. length	20.00	25.00
☐ **263, Hook and Ladder,** 1940–41, 185 mm. length	20.00	25.00

TRUCKS

☐ **Army Truck,** maker unknown, 1929, canvas tarpaulin can be rolled back, 13½" length	150.00	200.00
☐ **Army Truck,** Steelcraft, 1935, body is beige, wheels red, double steel disc wheels, rubber tires, 23¼" length	200.00	250.00
☐ **Army Truck,** Structo, 1933, removable canvas tarpaulin, tailgate, headlights, army green finish, 17" length	150.00	175.00
☐ **Army Truck,** Structo, 1933, has three lights, removable canvas tarpaulin, 21½" length	175.00	200.00
☐ **Baggage Truck,** Buddy "L," 1931, steel running skid, two-wheel hand truck, three service tanks, 16" length	700.00	800.00
☐ **Baggage Truck,** Buddy "L," 1932, 26¼" length	250.00	300.00
☐ **Beer Truck,** maker unknown, 1933, wooden beer kegs, 15½" length	450.00	500.00
☐ **"Big Load Van Company" Truck,** Marx, 1929, spring motor, rear doors open, 13" length	100.00	150.00
☐ **Delivery Truck,** Buddy "L," 1932, canopy top, drop end gate, curved bottom body, 14½" length	250.00	300.00
☐ **Delivery Truck,** Dayton, 1932, gray and red, 14½" length	200.00	250.00

Price Range

☐ **Dump Truck,** maker unknown, 1929, Mack-type truck dumps load, 13⅛" length 200.00   250.00

☐ **Express Truck,** Buddy "L," 1932, black enameled body, drop end gate, silver wheels enameled red, 24" length 450.00   500.00

☐ **Express Truck,** Buddy "L," 1932, open flare board body with cab, stake pockets, end gate, 14½" length 250.00   300.00

☐ **Express Truck,** Oh Boy, 1932, black chassis, dark green body, red disc wheels, 22" length 300.00   350.00

☐ **Grocery Truck,** Kingsbury, 1932, olive green with red wheels, rubber tires, 8" length 250.00   300.00

☐ **Insurance Patrol,** Buddy "L," 1932, bright red with brass handrails and bell, aluminum wheels, 27" length 800.00   900.00

☐ **Mack Tanker,** maker unknown, circa 1927, 9" length 150.00   200.00

☐ **Mail Truck,** Buddy "L," 1932, screen side panel body, closed cab, double-hinged rear doors and end gate, black with red wheels, 14½" length 300.00   350.00

☐ **Model T Flivver Truck,** maker unknown, 1925, spring motor, 8½" length 150.00   200.00

☐ **Railway Express,** Buddy "L," 1931, removable top converts to ordinary truck, rear door with Corbin brass lock, 24¼" length   500.00   600.00

☐ **Tip Top Dump Truck,** Strauss, 1927, body lifts when crank at side of truck is turned, 10¼" length 100.00   150.00

☐ **Toyland Milk Truck,** Marx, 1931, has milk case containing 12 wooden milk bottles, each about 2" tall 100.00   125.00

Utility Trucks Cast Iron

Arcade

Price Range

☐ **Austin Delivery Truck,** 1932, cast iron,
blue, green, red, 3¾" length 450.00   500.00

☐ **Borden's Milk Bottle Truck With Dodge
Chassis,** 1936, all white with classic milk
bottle shape, deep patterned tread tires,
6½" length 300.00   350.00

☐ **Brinks Express Truck,** 1932, cast iron, red
with gold and black trim, rear doors open,
11¾" length 3000.00   3500.00

☐ **Car-Carrier,** 1932, cast iron and sheet steel,
red with green trailer, four cars: one red
coupe, one blue coupe, one red Tudor, one
green Tudor, 24½" length 2000.00   3000.00*

☐ **Car Transport,** 1938, cast iron, double
deck, semi-trailer, with four sedans resem-
bling '38 Chevys, but not as authentically
detailed, 18½" length (atypical of Arcade)   350.00   400.00

☐ **Chevrolet Delivery Truck,** 1937, cast iron,
10¼" length 1000.00   1200.00

☐ **Chevrolet Utility Express Truck,** 1923,
cast iron with driver, 9¼" length 300.00   350.00

☐ **Ford Anthony Dump Truck,** 1926, cast
iron, gray cab, Anthony logo appears on
tailgate, operable hand lever, 8½" length ..   350.00   400.00

☐ **Ford Express Truck,** 1932, cast iron, red,
green, blue, wire wheels, 5", 5⅞" and 7½"
length sizes 450.00   500.00

☐ **International Delivery Truck,** 1937, cast
iron, bronze bumpers, rear door opens,
green with gold trim, driver in blue uniform
.... 450.00   500.00

☐ **International Dump Truck,** 1935, cast iron,
green with red rear chassis, 10½" length ..   200.00   250.00

---

*About 50% less without cars.

Price Range

☐ **International Stake Truck,** 1935, cast iron, green, nickeled radiator, I.H. decal on door panel, 12″ length 200.00   250.00

☐ **Mack Dump Truck,** 1932, cast iron, blue cab, yellow dumper 400.00   450.00

☐ **Mack Dump Truck,** 1937, cast iron, red or green, 6½″ length 250.00   300.00

☐ **Mack Gasoline Truck,** 1925, cast iron, nickel driver, 13¼″ length 350.00   400.00

☐ **Mack Lubrite Tank Truck,** 1925, cast iron, 13¼″ length 450.00   500.00

☐ **White Co. Ice Truck,** 1941, cast iron, White logo on door panel, 6¾″ length 200.00   250.00

☐ **White Dump Truck,** 1932, cast iron, red, blue, green, nickeled driver, dual rear wheels, 13½″ length 650.00   750.00

Miscellaneous

☐ **Car-Carrier,** 1928, cast iron, green and red, rubber disc wheels, carries Austin green coupe, Austin red delivery truck, Austin blue stake truck, 14¼″ length 650.00   700.00

☐ **Carry Car Trailer,** 1933, cast iron, green cab, red trailer, holds two green stake trucks, blue Tudor, red coupe, 20″ length 1500.00   2000.00

☐ **Carry-Car Truck Trailer,** 1928–1931, cast iron, cab is cast iron, trailer-welded steel, nickeled wheels, 24½″ length 300.00   350.00

☐ **Delivery Truck,** 1928, cast iron, yellow paneled 350.00   400.00

☐ **Ford Weaver (Ton Truck) Wrecker,** 1928, cast iron, featured realistic rachet to two other toy vehicles, 13″ length 350.00   400.00

☐ **International Delivery Truck,** 1936, cast iron, red, International decal on door panel, nickeled radiator and headlights, white rubber tires, 9½″ length 200.00   250.00

Price Range

☐ **Mack Tank Truck,** 1929, cast iron, tin tank
for gas, 12¾″ length 200.00   250.00

☐ **Milk Truck,** 1928, cast iron, word "Milk"
embossed on panel, 12″ length 175.00   200.00

☐ **Pontiac Stake Truck,** 1930, cast iron, red,
green, blue, white, rubber wheels, 6¼″
length 175.00   200.00

☐ **White Dump Truck,** 1929, cast iron, red,
green, blue, wheels nickel plated or optional
rubber, 11½″ length 175.00   200.00

☐ **White Moving Van,** 1928, cast iron, comes
with four Model A coupes and sedans or
three Model A cars, 13½″ length 450.00   500.00

☐ **Wrecker and Service Car,** 1929, cast iron,
with walker hoist chain, 12½″ length 250.00   300.00

WAR VEHICLES

☐ **Armored Tank,** Hubley, 1928, 4½″ length
....   100.00   150.00

☐ **Army Tank With Gun,** 1940, cast iron, featured box set of cast iron soldiers, fires steel
balls via spring-activated crank, 8″ length
(scarce toy as it was pulled from market because it proved to be dangerous as a child's
plaything) 1000.00   1200.00

☐ **Midget Tank,** maker unknown, 1932, steel,
5½″ length 75.00   100.00

☐ **Pull Tank,** Structo, 1933, steel wheels, revolving turret with machine gun, no swivel
spotlight, brass reflector, 12½″ length 100.00   150.00

AUCTIONEERS

Noel Barrett Auctions & Appraisals
Carversville, PA 18913
(215) 297-5109
Barrett and Bill Bertoia managed the first Atlanta Toy Museum Auction in October 1986. There will be at least three more ATM auctions through 1987.

Christie's East
219 East 67th Street
New York, NY 10021
(212) 570-4141
Collectibles Specialist: Julie Collier

Hake's Americana & Collectibles
P.O. Box 1444
York, PA 17405
(717) 848-1333

Stephen Leonard
P.O. Box 127
Albertson, L.I., NY 11507
(516) 742-0979

Ted Maurer
1931 N. Charlotte Street
Pottstown, PA 19464
(215) 323-1573

New England Auction Gallery
Box 682
Methuen, MA 01844
(617) 683-6354

Richard Opfer Auctioneering, Inc.
1919 Greenspring Drive
Timonium, MD 21093
(301) 252-5035

Phillips Auctioning & Appraising Phillips Ltd.
406 East 79th Street
New York, NY 10021
(212) 570-4830
Contacts: Harry I. Kurtz or Eric Alberta
Toy Consultant: Jack Herbert

Lloyd W. Ralston Auctions
447 Stratfield Road
Fairfield, CT 06432
(203) 366-3399

Robert W. Skinner, Inc.
Route 117
Bolton, MA 01740
(617) 779-5528
Auctions general line of antiques, but normally has several major toy auctions each year. Skinner also has a Boston gallery.

Sotheby's
1334 York Avenue at 72nd Street
New York, NY 10021
(212) 606-7000
Collectibles Contact: Dana Hawkes (212) 606-7424

Rex Stark
49 Wethersfield Road
Bellingham, MA 02019
(617) 966-0994

Richard W. Withington, Inc.
Auctions & Appraiser
Hillsboro, NH 03244
(603) 464-3232
Holds periodic toy and game auctions but specialty is dolls.

TOY COLLECTOR
PUBLICATIONS

The following publications regularly cover the subject of toy collecting:

Antiques & Collecting HOBBIES
1006 South Michigan Avenue
Chicago, Illinois, 60605
Monthly

Antiques & The Arts Weekly (Newtown Bee)
Newtown, Connecticut 06470
Weekly

Antique Toy World
P.O. Box 34509
Chicago, Illinois 60634
Monthly

Antique Trader Weekly
P.O. Box 1050
Dubuque, Iowa 52001
Weekly

Automobile Miniature
9, rue de Saussure, 75017
Paris, France
11 issues per year

Collector's Gazette
17 Adbolton Lodge, Whimsey Park
Carlton, Nottingham, England
Bi-monthly

Collectors' Showcase
P.O. Box 27948
San Diego, California 92128
Bi-monthly

The Doll Reader
Hobby House Press
Riverdale, Maryland 20840

Doll Talk
Kimport Dolls
P.O. Box 495
Independence, Missouri 64051

The Doll and Toy Collector
International Collectors Publications
The Old Exchange, Pier Street, Swansea SA1 1RY,
United Kingdom

Guide to Buyers, Sellers, and Traders of Black Collectibles
CGL, Box 158472
Nashville, Tennessee 37215
Monthly newsletter

Maine Antique Digest
71 Main Street
P.O. Box 645
Waldoboro, Maine 04572
Monthly, regularly covers toy antique auctions and shows

Miniature Tractor and Implement
R.D. 1, Box 90
East Springfield, Pennsylvania 16411

Model Auto Review
P.O. Box MT1, Leeds LS17 6TA
United Kingdom
Quarterly, for model vehicle collectors

Old Toy Soldier Newsletter
209 North Lombard
Oak Park, Illinois 60302
Bi-monthly

Polichinelle
14 Rue Andre-del-Sarte
75018 Paris, France
Quarterly, covers toys, dolls, games, in French

Sound Investment Toy Trader
P.O. Box 263304
Escondito, California 92026
Monthly, new publication

Toymania Magazine
60190 Avrigny, France
(4) 450-27-88
Quarterly, Paris Toy Show coverage

PUBLIC TOY, TRAIN, DOLL AND GAME COLLECTIONS

Many museums, historical societies, and restoration villages will, on occasion, hold special exhibitions of toys on loan from the hobby's foremost collections.

Regrettably, one of the finest specialty museums in the country, the Toy Museum of Atlanta in Atlanta, Georgia, closed its doors in 1986. A new toy museum, however, in Pittsfield, Massachusetts, is scheduled to open soon, hopefully in 1987.

The following sources mount impressive permanent collections:

New England

Massachusetts—Andover: American Museum of Automotive Miniatures. Salem: Salem Children's Museum, Essex Institute. Sandwich: Sandwich Glass Museum, Yesteryear's Museum. Sturbridge: Old Sturbridge Village. Wenham: Wenham Historical Association and Museum.

New Hampshire—Peterborough: Game Preserve (110 Spring Road).

Vermont—Shelburne: Shelburne Museum.

Mid-Atlantic Region

Delaware—Winterthur: Henry Francis du Pont Winterthur Museum.

New Jersey—Flemington: Raggedy Ann Antique Doll and Toy Museum. Newark: Newark Museum.

New York—New York City: Forbes Museum, Brooklyn Children's Museum, Cooper-Hewitt Museum, the Smithsonian Institution's National Museum of Design, the Metropolitan Museum of Art,

Museum of American Folk Art, Museum of the City of New York, The New-York Historical Society. *Rochester*: The Margaret Woodbury Strong Museum.

Pennsylvania—Douglassville: Mary Merritt Doll and Toy Museum. Philadelphia: Perelman Antique Toy Museum. Strasburg: Toy Train Museum.

Washington, D.C.—National Museum of American History, Smithsonian Institution, Washington Dolls' House and Toy Museum.

South

Kentucky—Bardstown: The Sterling Collection.

Virginia—Williamsburg: Abby Aldrich Rockefeller Folk Art Center; Colonial Williamsburg.

Midwest

Illinois—Chicago: Art Institute of Chicago, The Field Museum of Natural History, Museum of Science and Industry.

Iowa—Dyersville: Scale Model Farm Toy Museum.

Indiana—Auburn: Auburn-Cord-Duesenberg Museum.

Indianapolis—Children's Museum of Indianapolis.

COLLECTING ORGANIZATIONS

A number of the collecting organizations listed on these pages may lack a permanent headquarters address. The mailing address, therefore, could vary from time to time. Check your toy periodicals to stay posted on such changes; listed in italics are titles of various organizational newsletters or bulletins.

Note: Membership in some of these organizations may be contingent on recommendations by at least two members in good standing of that club or society. There also may be restrictions due to size limitations.

American Game Collectors Association
Game Box 1179
Great Neck, New York 11023

American Model Soldier Society
American Military Historical Society
1528 El Camino Real
San Carlos, California 94070

Antique Toy Collectors of America
Rte. 2, Box 5A
Baltimore, Maryland 21120

Maerklin Enthusiasts of American
P.O. Box 189
Beverly, New Jersey 08010

Marble Collectors Society of America
P.O. Box 222
Trumbull, Connecticut 06611
Marble Mania

Matchbox Collectors Club
P.O. Box 119
Wood Ridge, New Jersey 07075

Mechanical Bank Collectors of American
H. E. Mihlheim, Secretary
P.O. Box 128
Allegan, Michigan 49010

Miniature Figure Collectors of America
813 Elliston Drive
Wynmoor, Pennsylvania 19118

Miniature Truck Association
3449 N. Randolph Street
Arlington, Virginia 22207
Miniature Truck News

National Association of Miniature Enthusiasts
P.O. Box 2621
Brookhurst Center
Anaheim, California 92804

National Capital Military Collectors
P.O. Box 166
Rockville, Maryland 20850

Puppeteers of America, Inc.
2311 Connecticut Avenue, N.W. #501
Washington, D.C. 20008

Schoenhut Toy Collectors
Attention: Norman Bowers
1916 Cleveland Street
Evanston, Illinois 60202

Still Bank Collectors Club
62 South Hazelwood
Newark, Ohio 43055

Teddy Bear Club
P.O. Box 8361
Prairie Village, Kansas 66208

Toy Train Operators Society (TTOS)
25 West Walnut Street
Suite 305
Pasadena, California 91103

Train Collectors Association (TCA)
P.O. Box 248
Strasburg, Pennsylvania 17579

REPAIR AND RESTORATION SERVICES

The following listing of Restorers of Antique Toys does not constitute an endorsement of any kind. These people, however, have an established reputation for doing quality work in the hobby.

Marc Olimpio's Antique Toy Restoration Center
Marc Olimpio
Sanbornville, NH 03872
Specialty: Early handpainted German,
French-American tin toys, iron and pressed steel, also cast iron

Phantom Antique Toy Restoration
Buddy George
1038 North Utica
Tulsa, Ok
Specialty: Pressed-steel toys and pedal cars

Russ Harrington's Repair and Restoration Service
Russ Harrington
1805 Wilson Point Road
Baltimore, MD 21220
Speciality: Mechanical and still banks, iron toys

Tin Toy Works
Joe Freeman
1313 N. 15th Street
Allentown, PA 18102
Speciality: Tin toy autos, boats, go-rounds

BIBLIOGRAPHY

GENERAL

Barenholtz, Bernard, and McClintock, Inez: *American Antique Toys, 1830–1900*. Harry Abrams Pub., NY, 1980. (From one of our premier toy collections; captures the essence of what toy collecting is all about.)

Botto, Ken: *Past Joys*. Prism Editions, Chronicle Books, San Francisco, CA, 1978. (A visual treat using toys as part of a mixed-media celebration.)

Cadbury, Betty: *Playthings Past*. Praeger Pub., NY, 1976.

Culff, Robert: *The World of Toys!* Hamelyn, NY, 1969.

Daiken, Leslie: *Children's Toys Through the Ages*. Prager Pub., NY, 1953.

Dictionary of Toys Sold in America, Vols. I & II. Long's Americana Pub., Mokelumne Hill, CA, 1971 and 1978. (Rates toys on scale of 1-20; reproduces cuts from old catalogs.)

Foley, Daniel J.: *Toys Through The Ages*. Chilton Co., Philadelphia, PA, 1962.

Fondin, Jean and Remise, Jac: *The Golden Age of Toys*. New York Graphic Society, Grenwich, CT, 1967.

Fraser, Antonia: *A History of Toys*. Delacorte Press, NY, 1966.

Freeman, Ruth and Larry: *Cavalcade of Toys*. Century House, NY, 1942.

Fritzsch, Karl Ewald, and Bachman, Manfred: *An Illustrated History of Toys*. Translated by Ruth Michaelis-Jena. Abbey Library, London, 1966; reprinted Hastings House, NY, 1978.

Grober, Karl: *Children's Toys of Bygone Days*. Frederick Stokes, NY, 1928.

Hertz, Louis: *Handbook of Old American Toys*. Mark Haber Pub., Wethersfield, CT, 1947.

Hertz, Louis: *The Toy Collector*. Funk & Wagnells, Inc., NY, 1969.

Hillier, Mary: *Pageant of Toys*. Tapplinger Pub. Co., NY, 1966.

Ketchum, William: *Toys and Games*. The Smithsonian Institution, Washington, D.C., 1981.

King, Constance: *The Encyclopedia of Toys*. Crown Pub., NY, 1978.

McClintock, Inez and Marshall: *Toys in America*. Public Affairs Associates Press, Washington, D.C., 1961.

McClinton, Katherine Morrison: *Antiques of American Childhood*. Clarkson N. Potter, Inc., NY, 1970.
Murray, Patrick: *Toys*. Vista/Dutton, London, 1968. (Murray was Curator, Museum of Childhood, Edinburgh, Scotland.)
Perelman, Leon J.: *Perelman Antique Toy Museum*. Wallace-Homestead, Des Moines, IA, 1972.
White, Gwen: *Antique Toys and Their Background*. Arco, NY, 1971.
Whitton, Blair: *Toys*. The Knopf Collector's Guide to American Antiques Series. Alfred A. Knopf, NY, Chanticleer Press Edition, 1984.
The Wonderful World of Toys, Games, Dolls, 1860–1913. Follett, Chicago, IL, 1971.

MECHANICAL AND STILL BANKS

Bellows, Ina Heywood: *Old Mechanical Banks*. Lightner Pub., Chicago, IL, 1940.
Ellinghaus, Bernard: *Other Old Mechanical Banks*. Vol. I. (Booklet) Mechanical Bank Collectors of America, Allegen, MI, 1977.
Ellinghaus, Bernard: *Other Old Mechanical Banks*. Vol. II. (Booklet) Mechanical Bank Collectors of America, Allegen, MI, 1982.
Griffith, F. H.: *Mechanical Banks*. F. H. Griffith, 1972.
Hertz, Louis: *Mechanical Toy Banks*. Mark Haber Pub., Wethersfield, CT, 1947.
Long, Earnest: *Dictionary of Still Banks*. Long's Americana Pub., Mokelumne Hill, CA, 1981.
McCumber, Robert L.: *Toy Bank Reproductions and Fakes*. Self-published, Glastonbury, CT, 1970. (Contains base tracings of original mechanical banks.)
Meyer, John D.: *Handbook of Old Mechanical Banks*. Rudusill & Co. Pub.,* Lancaster, PA, 1952. (Meyer reference numbers are used in the Mechanical Bank section of this book.)
Moore, Andy and Susan: *The Penny Bank Book: Collecting Still Banks*. Self-published, Chicago, IL, 1984.
Norman, Bill: *The Bank Book: The Encyclopedia of Mechanical Bank Collecting*. Accent Studios, San Diego, CA, 1984. (An annual or biannual supplement containing updated prices, trends, etc. is planned for the near future.)

---

*Reissued as *Old Penny Banks*, with Larry Freeman, Century House, Watkins Glen, NY, 1960, 1979 (updated with section on Still Banks by Freeman).

Rogers, Carole: *Penny Banks: A History and a Handbook*. E.P. Dutton, NY, 1977.

Whiting, Hubert B.: *Old Iron Still Banks*. Self-published. Out-of-print. (Whiting reference numbers are used in the Still Bank section of this book.)

COMIC AND CHARACTER TOYS

Harman, Ken: *Comic Strip Toys*. Wallace-Homestead, Des Moines, IA, 1975.

Heide, Robert, and Gilman, John: *Cartoon Collectibles: 50 Years of Dime-Store Memorabilia*. Dolphin Book, Doubleday & Co., Garden City, NY, 1983. (Main focus is on Mickey Mouse and other Disneyana.)

Hillier, Bevis: *Walt Disney's Mickey Mouse Memorabilia*. Harry Abrams, Inc., NY, 1986. (Our nomination for the best coverage of Mickey Mouse and his friends lionized in toys, games, and novelties.)

Lesser, Robert: *A Celebration of Comic Art and Memorabilia*. Hawthorn Books, NY, 1975.

Longest, David: *Character Toys and Collectibles*. Collector Books, Paducah, KY, 1984.

Munsey, Cecil: *Disneyana*. Hawthorn Books, NY, 1980.

Tumbusch, Tom: *Tomart's Illustrated Disneyana Catalog*. Three Vols. Tomart Publications, Dayton, OH, 1985.

LEADING MANUFACTURERS

Brown, George W.: *The George Brown Toy Sketchbook*. Edited by Edith Barenholtz. Pyne Press, Princeton, NJ, 1971.

Buser, Elaine and Dan: *Guide to Schoenhut Dolls, Toys and Circus*. Collector Books, Paducah, KY, 1976.

Cieslik, Jurgen and Marianne: *Lehmann Toys, The History of E.P. Lehmann: 1881–1981*. New Cavendish Books, London. (Now available through Schiffer Pub., West Chester, PA)

Fuller, Roland and Levy, Allen: *The Bassett-Locke Story*. New Cavendish Books, London, 1984. (History of one of England's eminent model and miniature railway model makers; also a producer of exhibition standard ship models.)

Hertz, Louis: *Messrs. Ives of Bridgeport*. Mark Haber Pub., Wethersfield, CT, 1947.

Manos, Susan: *Schoenhut Dolls and Toys, A Loving Legacy*. Collector Books, Paducah, KY, 1976.

McCollough, Albert: *The Complete Book of Buddy "L" Toys.* Greenberg Pub., Sykesville, MD, 1984.

Parry-Crooke, Charlotte, ed.: *Toys, Dolls, Games: Paris 1903–1914.* Hastings House Pub., Inc., NY, 1981. (Catalog cuts from leading French toy makers reproduced.)

The Great Toys of George Carette. New Cavenish Books, London, 1975.

Whitton, Blair: *Bliss Toys and Dollhouses.* Dover Publications, Inc., in association with The Margaret Woodbury Strong Museum, NY, 1979.

MINIATURES

Force, Dr. Edward: *Miniature Emergency Vehicles.* Schiffer Pub., Ltd., Exton, PA, 1984.

Force, Dr. Edward: *Corgi Toys.* Schiffer Pub., Ltd., Exton, PA, 1984.

Gibson, Cecil: *History of British Dinky Toys, 1934–1964.* Mikansue and Modeller's World, London, 1966.

Ramsey, John: *The Swapmeet and Toy Fair Catalog of British Diecast Model Toys.* Swapmeet Toys & Models Ltd., Suffolk, England, 1984. (Well-researched book, but seven pages are required to explain the value rating system!)

Richardson, Mike and Susan: *Dinky Toys and Model Miniatures.* Schiffer Pub., Ltd., Exton, PA, 1981.

Schiffer, Nancy, ed.: *Matchbox Toys.* Schiffer Pub., Ltd., Exton, PA, 1983.

Viemeister, Peter: *Micro Cars.* Hamilton's, Bedford, VA, 1982.

Wieland, James, and Force, Dr. Edward: *Tootsietoys.* Motorbooks International, Osceola, WI, 1980.

Wieland, James, and Force, Dr. Edward: *Detroit in Miniature.* Miniature Auto Sales, Litchfield, CT, 1983.

MILITARIANA

Bard, Bob: *Making and Collecting Military Miniatures.* Robert M. McBride, NY, 1957.

Garrett, John: *The World Encyclopedia of Model Soldiers.* Overlook Press, NY, 1981.

Johnson, Peter: *Toy Armies.* Forbes Museum, NY, 1984. (The Malcolm Forbes Collection, probably the premier collection of militariana in the world, is beautifully presented in this book.)

Opie, James: *Britain's Toy Soldiers, 1893-1932.* Harper & Row, NY, 1986.

Opie, James: *Toy Soldiers.* Shire Publ., England, 1985.

MOTORTOYS (SEE ALSO MINIATURES BIBLIOGRAPHY)

Crilley, Raymond, and Burkholder, Charles: *International Directory of Model Farm Tractors.* Schiffer, West Chester, PA, 1985.

Gottschalk, Lillian: *Toy Cars and Trucks.* Abbeville Press, NY, 1985. (The most beautifully photographed and designed book on American motortoys published to date; unlike most "picture books," this one is painstakingly researched.)

Massucci, Eduardo: *Cars for Kids.* Rizzoli International Pubs., NY, 1982. (Children's sidewalk pedal cars featured.)

Remise, Jac and Frederic: *The World of Antique Toys: Carriages, Cars and Cycles.* Edita S.A. Lausanne, Switzerland, 1984. Distributed by Schiffer Pub. Ltd., Exton, PA. (Beautiful pictorial coverage of European motortoys.)

TOY RAILROADING

Alexander, E.: *The Collector's Book of the Locomotive.* Clarkson N. Potter Pub., NY, 1966.

Carlson, Pierce: *Toy Trains: A History.* Harper & Row, NY, 1986.

Carstens, Harry A.: *The Trains of Lionel Standard Gauge Era.* Railroad Model Craftsmen, 1964.

Fraley, Donald: *Lionel Trains, Standard of the World: 1900-1943.* Train Collectors Association, 1976.

Godel, Howard: *Antique Toy Trains.* Exposition Press Inc., Smithtown, NY, 1976.

Godin, Serge: *The Trains on Avenue de Rumine.* Giansanti Coluzzi Collection. New Cavendish Books/Editions, London, 1982.

Hertz, Louis: *Collecting Model Trains.* Mark Haber Pub., Wethersfield, CT, 1956.

Hertz, Louis: *Riding the Tinplate Rails.* Model Craftsman Pub. Co., 1944.

Jeanmaire, Claude: *Bing, Grandad's Model Railway.* Verlag Eisenbahn, Germany, 1982.

Joyce, J.: *Collector's Guide to Model Railways.* Model & Allied Pub. Co., Argus Books, 1977.

Levy, Allen: *A Century of Modern Trains.* Crescent Books, NY, 1986. Reprint of 1974 edition by New Cavendish.

Reder, Gustav: *Clockwork, Steam and Electric: A History of Model Railways*. Translated by C. Hamilton Ellis. Ian Allan, Shepperton, England, 1972.

Spong, Neldred and Raymond: *Flywheel-Powered Toys*. Antique Toy Collectors of America, Baltimore, MD, 1979.

Williams, Guy R.: *The World of Model Trains*. Andre Deutch Publishing, London, 1970.

TIN MECHANICAL TOYS

Bartholomew, Charles: *Mechanical Toys*. Chartwell Books, Secaucus, NJ, 1979.

Chapius, Droz: *Automata*. Central Book Co., NY, 1958.

Gardiner, Gordon, and Morris, Alistair: *Illustrated Encyclopedia of Metal Toys*. Crown Pub., Harmony Books, Avenel, NJ, 1984.

Hillier, Mary: *Automata and Mechanical Toys*. Jupiter Pub., London, 1976.

Pressland, David: *The Art of the Tin Toy*. Crown Pub., NY, 1976.

Weltens, Arno: *Mechanical Tin Toys in Color*. Sterling Pub., NY, 1979.

Whitten, Blair: *American Clockwork Toys, 1860–1900*. Schiffer Pub., Ltd., Exton, PA, 1979. (The definitive book on pre–1900 clockwork toys.)

Von Boehn, Max: *Puppets and Automata*. Dover Pub., NY, 1972.

Wind-Ups: Tin Toy Dreams. T. Kitahara Collection. Chronicle Books, San Francisco, CA, 1985. (Chronicles Japanese tin toys from 1900s to present.)

Wonderland of Toys. Tin Toys Vol. I. T. Kitahara Collection. Chronicle Books, San Francisco, CA, 1984.

Wonderland of Toys. Tin Robots Vol. II. T. Kitahara Collection. Chronicle Books, San Francisco, CA, 1984. (Covers post-war Japanese tin toys, robots.)

OTHER SPECIALTIES

Avedon, Elliot, and Sutton-Smith, Brian: *The Study of Games*. John Wiley & Sons, NY, 1971.

Bauman, Paul: *Collecting Antique Marbles*. Prarie Winds Press, Wallace-Homestead, Leon, IA, 1970.

Bell, R.C.: *The Board Games Book*. Marshall Cavendish, London, 1979.

Best, Charles W.: *Cast-Iron Toy Pistols-1870–1940*. Rocky Mountain Arms & Antiques Pub., Englewood, CO, 1973.

Coleman, Dorothy S., Elizabeth A., and Evelyn J.: *Collector's Encyclopedia of Dolls.* Crown Pub., NY, 1976.

Conway, Shirley, and Wilson, Jean: *Steiff Teddy Bears, Dolls, and Toys With Prices.* Wallace-Homestead, Des Moines, IA.

Eikelberner, George, and Agadjanian, Serge: *American Glass Candy Containers.* Two volumes. Belle Meade, NJ, 1967.

Gibbs, P.J.: *Black Americana Sold in America.* Collector Books, Paducah, KY, 1987.

Hannas, Linda: *The English Jigsaw Puzzle.* Wayland, London.

Heide, Robert, and Gilman, John: *Cowboy Collectibles.* Harper & Row, NY, 1982.

Hewitt, Karen, and Roomet, Louise: *Educational Toys in America: 1800 to the Present.* The Robert Hull Fleming Museum, University of Vermont, Burlington, VT, 1979.

Kaiser, Von Wolf, and Baecker, Carlernst: *Toy Steam Engines and Accessories* (Blechpielzeug Dampfspielzeug). Berlin, Germany, 1984. (Printed in German only. Well illustrated, definitive work on a vastly underrated area of toy specialization.)

Lavitt, Wendy: *Dolls.* The Knopf Collector's Guides to American Antiques. Chanticleer Press Edition, NY, 1983.

Mandel, Margaret: *Teddy Bears and Steiff Animals.* Collector Books, Paducah, KY, 1984.

Milet, Jacques, and Forbes, Robert: *Toy Boats: 1870–1955.* Charles Scribner's Sons, NY, 1979.

Moran, Brian: *Battery Toys.* Schiffer Pub., Ltd., West Chester, PA, 1984. (Featuring over 150 color plates of battery operated toys from the 1950s to date.)

Murray, H.J.R.: *A History of Board Games Other Than Chess.* Clarendon Press, Oxford, England, 1952.

Schiffer, Margaret: *Holiday Toys and Decorations.* Schiffer Pub., Ltd., West Chester, PA, 1985.

Slocum, Jerry, and Botermans, Jack: *Puzzles Old and New.* Distributed by University of Washington Press, Seattle, WA, 1986.

INDEX

ABOUT THE AUTHOR

Richard Friz has collected toys, folk art, and political memorabilia for over 25 years. He writes reviews of books, toy auctions, and shows as well as other specialty events for *Maine Antiques Digest, Ohio Antiques Review, AB Bookman's Weekly,* and *New England Antiques.* His feature articles on toys, ephemera, and other antiques and collectibles topics have appeared in *Yankee, Collectibles Illustrated,* and *Collectors Showcase.* Friz edits the Ephemera Society of America's quarterly *News* and recently completed their first *Journal.* He has served as consulting editor on a number of toy books, as well as for *Collectibles Illustrated.*

☐ *Please send me the following price guides —*
☐ *I would like the most current edition of the books listed below.*

THE OFFICIAL PRICE GUIDES TO:

☐ 199-3 **American Silver & Silver Plate**
5th Ed.   11.95
☐ 513-1 **Antique Clocks** 3rd Ed.   10.95
☐ 283-3 **Antique & Modern Dolls**
3rd Ed.   10.95
☐ 287-6 **Antique & Modern Firearms**
6th Ed.   11.95
☐ 738-X **Antiques & Collectibles**
8th Ed.   10.95
☐ 289-2 **Antique Jewelry** 5th Ed.   11.95
☐ 539-5 **Beer Cans & Collectibles**
4th Ed.   7.95
☐ 521-2 **Bottles Old & New** 10th Ed.   10.95
☐ 532-8 **Carnival Glass** 2nd Ed.   10.95
☐ 295-7 **Collectible Cameras** 2nd Ed.   10.95
☐ 277-9 **Collectibles of the Third Reich**
2nd Ed.   10.95
☐ 740-1 **Collectible Toys** 4th Ed.   10.95
☐ 531-X **Collector Cars** 7th Ed.   12.95
☐ 538-7 **Collector Handguns** 4th Ed.   14.95
☐ 290-6 **Collector Knives** 8th Ed.   11.95
☐ 518-2 **Collector Plates** 4th Ed.   11.95
☐ 296-5 **Collector Prints** 7th Ed.   12.95
☐ 001-6 **Depression Glass** 2nd Ed.   9.95
☐ 548-4 **'50s & '60s Collectibles** 1st Ed.   9.95
☐ 589-1 **Fine Art** 1st Ed.   19.95
☐ 311-2 **Glassware** 3rd Ed.   10.95
☐ 243-4 **Hummel Figurines & Plates**
6th Ed.   10.95
☐ 523-9 **Kitchen Collectibles** 2nd Ed.   10.95
☐ 291-4 **Military Collectibles**
5th Ed.   11.95
☐ 525-5 **Music Collectibles** 6th Ed.   11.95
☐ 313-9 **Old Books & Autographs**
7th Ed.   11.95
☐ 208-1 **Oriental Collectibles** 3rd Ed.   11.95
☐ 746-0 **Overstreet Comic Book** 17th Ed.   11.95
☐ 522-0 **Paperbacks & Magazines**
1st Ed.   10.95
☐ 297-3 **Paper Collectibles** 5th Ed.   10.95
☐ 529-8 **Pottery & Porcelain** 6th Ed.   11.95
☐ 524-7 **Radio, TV & Movie**
Memorabilia 3rd Ed.   11.05
☐ 288-4 **Records** 7th Ed.   10.95
☐ 247-7 **Royal Doulton** 5th Ed.   11.95
☐ 280-9 **Science Fiction & Fantasy**
Collectibles 2nd Ed.   10.95
☐ 299-X **Star Trek/Star Wars**
Collectibles 1st Ed.   7.95
☐ 248-5 **Wicker** 3rd Ed.   10.95

THE OFFICIAL:

☐ 445-3 **Collector's Journal** 1st Ed.   4.95
☐ 549-2 **Directory to U.S. Flea Markets**
1st Ed.   3.95
☐ 365-1 **Encyclopedia of Antiques**
1st Ed.   9.95
☐ 369-4 **Guide to Buying & Selling**
Antiques 1st Ed.   9.95
☐ 414-3 **Identification Guide to Early**
American Furniture 1st Ed.   9.95
☐ 413-5 **Identification Guide to**
Glassware 1st Ed.   9.95
☐ 448-8 **Identification Guide to**
Gunmarks 2nd Ed.   9.95
☐ 412-7 **Identification Guide to**
Pottery & Porcelain 1st Ed.   9.95
☐ 415-1 **Identification Guide to**
Victorian Furniture 1st Ed.   9.95

THE OFFICIAL (SMALL SIZE) PRICE GUIDES TO:

☐ 309-0 **Antiques & Flea Markets**
4th Ed.   4.95
☐ 269-8 **Antique Jewelry** 3rd Ed.   4.95
☐ 737-1 **Baseball Cards** 7th Ed.   4.95
☐ 488-7 **Bottles** 2nd Ed.   4.95
☐ 544-1 **Cars & Trucks** 3rd Ed.   5.95
☐ 519-0 **Collectible Americana** 2nd Ed.   4.95
☐ 294-9 **Collectible Records** 3rd Ed.   4.95
☐ 545-X **Collector Guns** 3rd Ed.   5.95
☐ 306-6 **Dolls** 4th Ed.   4.95
☐ 520-4 **Football Cards** 6th Ed.   4.95
☐ 540-9 **Glassware** 3rd Ed.   4.95
☐ 526-3 **Hummels** 4th Ed.   4.95
☐ 279-5 **Military Collectibles**
3rd Ed.   4.95
☐ 278-7 **Pocket Knives** 3rd Ed.   4.95
☐ 527-1 **Scouting Collectibles** 4th Ed.   4.95
☐ 439-9 **Sports Collectibles** 2nd Ed.   3.95
☐ 494-1 **Star Trek/Star Wars**
Collectibles 3rd Ed.   3.95
☐ 307-4 **Toys** 4th Ed.   4.95

THE OFFICIAL BLACKBOOK PRICE GUIDES OF:

☐ 743-6 **U.S. Coins** 26th Ed.   3.95
☐ 742-8 **U.S. Paper Money** 20th Ed.   3.95
☐ 741-X **U.S. Postage Stamps** 10th Ed.   3.95

THE OFFICIAL INVESTORS GUIDE TO BUYING & SELLING:

☐ 534-4 **Gold, Silver & Diamonds**
2nd Ed.   12.95
☐ 535-2 **Gold Coins** 2nd Ed.   12.95
☐ 536-0 **Silver Coins** 2nd Ed.   12.95
☐ 537-9 **Silver Dollars** 2nd Ed.   12.95

THE OFFICIAL NUMISMATIC GUIDE SERIES:

☐ 481-X **Coin Collecting** 3rd Ed.   9.95
☐ 254-X **The Official Guide to**
Detecting Counterfeit
Money 2nd Ed.   7.95
☐ 257-4 **The Official Guide to Mint**
Errors 4th Ed.   7.95

SPECIAL INTEREST SERIES:

☐ 506-9 **From Hearth to Cookstove**
3rd Ed.   17.95
☐ 530-1 **Lucky Number Lottery Guide**
1st Ed.   4.95
☐ 504-2 **On Method Acting** 8th Printing   6.95

	TOTAL	

SEE REVERSE SIDE FOR ORDERING INSTRUCTIONS